第三届国际工程教育论坛
The 3rd International Forum on Engineering Education

电子信息技术与可持续创新

Sustainable Innovation in Information Technology

UNESCO 国际工程教育中心　编

图书在版编目（CIP）数据

电子信息技术与可持续创新：第三届国际工程教育论坛 / UNESCO 国际工程教育中心编. -- 北京：中央编译出版社，2025.7
ISBN 978-7-5117-4561-3

Ⅰ. ①电… Ⅱ. ①U… Ⅲ. ①高等教育－工科（教育）－教学研究－国际学术会议－文集 Ⅳ. ①G642.0-53

中国国家版本馆 CIP 数据核字（2024）第 003610 号

电子信息技术与可持续创新：第三届国际工程教育论坛

责任编辑	郑菲菲
责任印制	李　颖
出版发行	中央编译出版社
网　　址	www.cctpcm.com
地　　址	北京市海淀区北四环西路 69 号（100080）
电　　话	（010）55627391（总编室）　（010）55627392（编辑室）
	（010）55627320（发行部）　（010）55627377（新技术部）
经　　销	全国新华书店
印　　刷	廊坊市印艺阁数字科技有限公司
开　　本	889 毫米 × 1194 毫米　1/16
字　　数	438 千字
印　　张	25.25
版　　次	2025 年 7 月第 1 版
印　　次	2025 年 7 月第 1 次印刷
定　　价	286.00 元

新浪微博：@中央编译出版社　　微　信：中央编译出版社（ID：cctphome）
淘宝店铺：中央编译出版社直销店（http://shop108367160.taobao.com）（010）55627331

本社常年法律顾问：北京市吴栾赵阎律师事务所律师　闫军　梁勤
凡有印装质量问题，本社负责调换，电话：（010）55627320

编辑委员会

主 任
李晓红　邱 勇

委 员
王光谦　袁 驷　罗 毅　王孙禺　王亚愚　汪 玉
张 利　黄天荫　康重庆　王建强　薛 澜　王 晶
雷 环　刘 震　陈涛涛　谢喆平

编辑人员
徐立辉　李晶晶　朱 盼　李懋坤　乔伟峰　黄 蓓
罗 菲　方欣然　郝富霖　王雪琪　甘之正　沈一帆
黄 铮　陈伟翔

李晓红
中国工程院院士，中国工程院院长
LI Xiaohong
President of Chinese Academy of Engineering（CAE）；Member of CAE

夏泽翰
联合国教科文组织驻华代表处主任
Shahbaz KHAN
Director of UNESCO Beijing Office

秦昌威
中国联合国教科文组织全国委员会秘书处秘书长
QIN Changwei
Secretary-General of the Chinese National Commission for UNESCO

王希勤
清华大学校长
WANG Xiqin
President of Tsinghua University

王光谦
中国科学院院士，清华大学副校长
WANG Guangqian
Member of CAE; Vice President of Tsinghua University

益一哉
东京工业大学校长
Kazuya MASU
President of Tokyo Institute of Technology

龚克
南开大学教授，南开大学学术委员会主任，中国新一代人工智能发展战略研究院执行院长
GONG Ke
Professor of Nankai University, Director of Academic Committee of Nankai University, Executive Director of Chinese Institute of New Generation Artificial Intelligence Development Strategies

王晓云
中国移动通信集团有限公司技术部总经理
WANG Xiaoyun
General Manager of Technology Department, China Mobile

郝智彪

清华大学电子工程系教授、电子工程系学术委员会主任

HAO Zhibiao

Professor and Chair of Academic Committee of Department of Electronic Engineering, Tsinghua University

王孙禹

清华大学教育研究院教授，国际工程教育中心副主任兼秘书长

WANG Sunyu

Professor of Institute of Education, Tsinghua University; Deputy Director and Secretary-General of ICEE

王大同

柏林工业大学教授，德国科学院院士，美国国家工程院院士，俄罗斯科学院院士

Dieter BIMBERG

Member of German Academy of Science; Member of National Academy of Engineering; Member of Russian Academy of Science; Professor of Technical University of Berlin

詹姆斯·埃文斯

芝加哥大学社会学系和计算机研究所知识实验室主任

James EVANS

Director of the Knowledge Lab in the Department of Sociology and the Institute for Computer Science, University of Chicago

周永祖
普渡大学教授，美国国家工程院院士
Weng Cho CHEW
Professor of Purdue University; Member of National Academy of Engineering, US

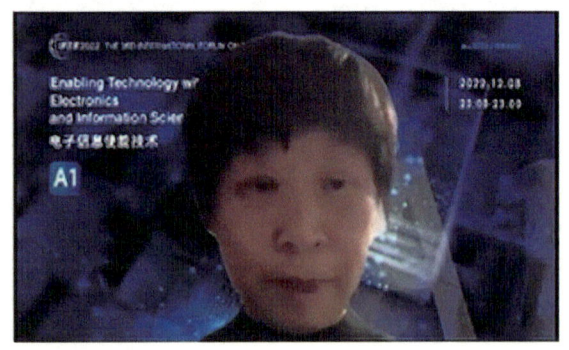

王蕴红
北京航空航天大学教授、计算机学院院长
WANG Yunhong
Professor and Dean of the School of Computer Science and Engineering, Beihang University

张悦
北京航空航天大学教授、集成电路科学与工程学院副院长
ZHANG Yue
Professor and Vice Dean of the School of Integrated Circuit Science and Engineering, Beihang University

马歆
微软亚洲研究院学术合作总监
MA Xin
Outreach Director of Academic Collaboration, Microsoft Research Asia

杨旭东
清华大学建筑学院教授、建筑学院副院长
YANG Xudong
Professor and Vice Dean of the School of Architecture, Tsinghua University

沈渊
清华大学电子工程系教授
SHEN Yuan
Professor of the Department of Electronic Engineering, Tsinghua University

江亿
中国工程院院士，清华大学建筑学院教授
JIANG Yi
Member of CAE; Professor of the School of Architecture, Tsinghua University

庄惟敏
清华大学建筑学院教授，中国工程院院士，全国工程勘察设计大师
ZHUANG Weimin
Professor of the School of Architecture, Tsinghua University; Member of CAE; National Engineering-Survey-and-Design Master

张利
清华大学建筑学院教授、建筑学院院长，
全国工程勘察设计大师
ZHANG Li
Professor and Dean of the School of
Architecture, Tsinghua University;
National Engineering-Survey-and-Design
Master

沈振江
日本金泽大学教授，日本工程院外籍院士
SHEN Zhenjiang
Professor of Kanazawa University;
Foreign Fellow of the Engineering
Academy of Japan (EAJ)

叶青
深圳市建筑科学研究院股份有限公司董事长
YE Qing
Chairman of Shenzhen Building Research
Institute Co., Ltd

康健
英国伦敦大学学院教授，英国皇家工程院
院士
KANG Jian
Professor of University College London;
Fellow of Royal Acaclemy of Engineering

黄天荫

清华大学医学学科带头人，美国国家医学院外籍院士

WONG Tien Yin

Chair Professor and Founding Head of Tsinghua Medicine; Foreign Member of the US National Academy of Medicine

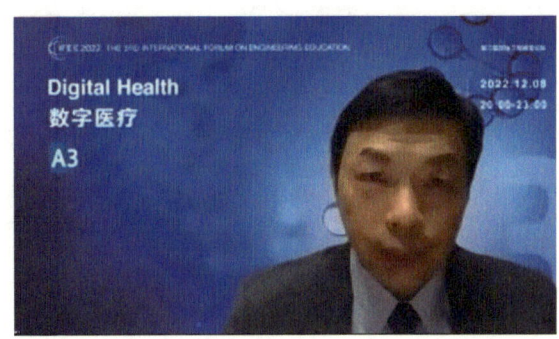

吴及

清华大学电子工程系教授、电子工程系副系主任

WU Ji

Professor and Vice Dean of the Department of Electronic Engineering, Tsinghua University

张亚勤

清华大学智能产业研究院院长，中国工程院外籍院士

ZHANG YaQin

Dean of the Institute for AI Industry, Tsinghua University; Foreign Member of Chinese Academy of Engineering (CAE)

房建成

北京航空航天大学教授，中国科学院院士

FANG Jiancheng

Professor of Beihang University; Member of Chinese Academy of Sciences (CAS)

董家鸿
清华大学临床医学院院长,中国工程院院士
DONG Jiahong
Dean of the Clinical School of Medicine,
Tsinghua University; Member of CAE

黄广斌
南洋理工大学教授,广智微芯创始人
HUANG GuangBin
Mind PointEye Pte Ltd Founder
Professor of Nanyang Technological
University

张大磊
鹰瞳科技创始人
ZHANG Dalei
Founder of Airdoc

柳楠
杜克-新加坡国立大学医学院定量医学和
卫生服务与系统研究中心副教授
LIU Nan
Associate Professor at the Centre for
Quantitative Medicine and Programme in
Health Services and Systems Research,
Duke-NUS Medicine School

林水德
新加坡国立大学生物医学工程学会主席，
健康创新与技术研究所所长
Chwee Teck LIM
NUS Society Chair Professor of Biomedical Engineering; Director of the Institute for Health Innovation and Technology

王广志
清华大学生物医学工程系教授
WANG Guangzhi
Professor, Department of Biomedical Engineering, Tsinghua University

吴文达
腾讯健康副总裁
Alex Ng
Vice President of Tencent Healthcare

李阳
北京航空航天大学教授、自动化科学与电气工程学院副院长
LI Yang
Professor and Vice President of the School of Automation Science and Electrical Engineering, Beihang University

李德彪
加州大学洛杉矶分校医学教授，Cedars-Sinai 生物医学成像研究所所长
LI Debiao
Director of Biomedical Imaging Research Institute, Cedars-Sinai;Professor of Medicine, UCLA

叶哲伟
武汉协和医院数字医学实验室主任
YE Zhewei
Director of Digital Medicine Laboratory of Wuhan Union Medical College Hospital

康重庆
清华大学电机系教授、电机系系主任
KANG Chongqing
Professor and Dean of the Department of Electrical Engineering, Tsinghua University

李冬梅
清华大学电子工程系副教授
LI Dongmei
Associate Professor of the Department of Electronic Engineering, Tsinghua University

王成山
天津大学教授，中国工程院院士
WANG Chengshan
Professor of Tianjin University;
Member of CAE

赛义夫·拉赫曼
弗吉尼亚理工大学教授，IEEE 候任主席
Saifur RAHMAN
Professor at Virginia Tech；
IEEE President-Elect

戈兰·斯奇贝克
帝国理工大学教授、电力能源系统学科主任
Goran STRBAC
Professor and Chair in Electrical Energy
Systems at Imperial College London

王忠东
埃克塞特大学教授，副校长
WANG Zhongdong
Vice President and Professor of University
of Exeter

别朝红
西安交通大学副校长、教授
BIE Zhaohong
Vice President and Professor of Xi'an Jiaotong University

曾祥君
长沙理工大学副校长、教授
ZENG Xiangjun
Vice President and Professor of Changsha University of Science and Technology

曾嵘
清华大学副校长、教授
ZENG Rong
Vice President and Professor of Tsinghua University

毕天姝
华北电力大学副校长、教授
BI Tianshu
Vice President and Professor of North China Electric Power University

孙宏斌

清华大学教授，太原理工大学副校长（主持工作）

SUN Hongbin

Professor of Tsinghua University; Executive President of Taiyuan University of Technology

王淑娟

哈尔滨工业大学教授、电气学院院长

WANG Shujuan

Professor of Harbin Institute of Technology; Dean of School of Electrical Engineering

周青

清华大学车辆与运载学院教授、车辆与运载学院学术委员会主任

ZHOU Qing

Professor and Director of Academic Committee of the School of Vehicle and Mobility, Tsinghua University

周盛

清华大学电子工程系副教授

ZHOU Sheng

Professor of Department of Electronic Engineering, Tsinghua University

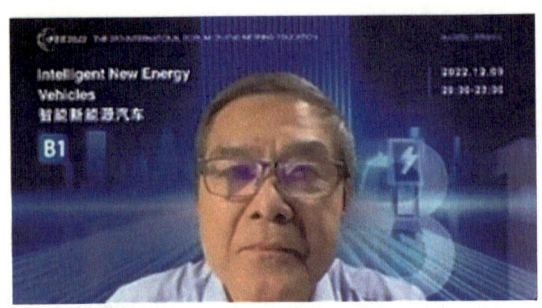

欧阳明高

中国科学院院士,清华大学学术委员会副主任,清华大学车辆与运载学院教授

OUYANG Minggao

Member of Chinese Academy of Sciences; Professor of School of Vehicle and Mobility; Deputy Director of Academic Committee of Tsinghua University

巴特·范·阿雷姆

荷兰代尔夫特理工大学博士、事务副校长,交通建模领域教授

Bart Van AREM

Pro Vice Rector Magnificus for Doctoral Affairs and Professor of Transport Modelling, Delft University of Technology, the Netherlands

胡·威廉姆斯

伯明翰大学工程学院汽车工程领域荣誉教授,英国皇家统计学会研究员

Huw WILLIAMS

Honorary Professor of Automotive Engineering of School of Engineering, University of Birmingham; Fellow of Royal Statistical Society (RRS)

管欣

吉林大学汽车研究院院长,中国汽车工程学会副理事长

GUAN Xin

Dean of Automotive Research Institute, Jilin University; Vice President of the Society of Automotive Engineers of China

埃米尔·卡捷普

加拿大滑铁卢大学机械与机电工程系教授，美国机械工程师协会研究员，加拿大机械工程学会研究员

Amir KHAJEPOUR

Professor of the Department of Mechanical and Electromechanical Engineering, University of Waterloo; Canadian Society of Mechonical Engineers (CSME) Fellow

左磊

密歇根大学讲席教授，美国机械工程师协会会士

ZUO Lei

Endowed Professor of University of Michigan; American Society of Mechanical Engineers (ASME) Fellow

李越

清华大学继续教育学院教授、继续教育学院教学委员会主任委员

LI Yue

Professor and the Chair of Teaching Committee of the School of Continuing Education, Tsinghua University

宋健

清华大学电子工程系教授，ITU-R 中国专家组成员

SONG Jian

Professor of the Department of Electronic Engineering, Tsinghua University; Board Member of ITU-R

韩星
中国联通国际有限公司新加坡运营公司总经理
HAN Xing
General Manager of Singapore Operation Company of China Unicom International Co., LTD. (in charge of ASEAN region)

郭永新
新加坡国立大学电子与计算机工程系教授
GUO Yongxin
Professor of Department of Electronic and Computer Engineering, National University of Singapore

德斯塔·梅布拉图
联合国环境规划署非洲司前副司长，南非斯泰伦博斯大学工程学教授
Desta MEBRATU
Former Deputy Director of the Africa Division, United Nations Environment Programme; Professor of Stellenbosch University, South Africa

萨特里奥·苏曼特里·布罗德乔内戈罗
印度尼西亚科学院院长
Satryo Soemantri BRODJONEGORO
President of Indonesian Academy of Sciences

李晓潮
厦门大学电子科学与技术学院教授、委员会主任
LI Xiaochao
Professor and Director of Professor Committee of School of Electronic Science and Engineering, Xiamen University

罗威妮·西格玛
联合国教科文组织工程规划专家
Rovani SIGMONEY
UNESCO Engineering Planning Expert

弗朗西斯科·马丁内斯
智利大学工程学院院长
Francisco MARTINEZ
Dean of Faculty of Engineering, University of Chile

尹峰
国网浙江省电力有限公司科学研究院能源技术中心主任
YIN Feng
Director of Energy Technology Center of Zhejiang Electric Power Research Institute of State Grid Co., LTD

康立新
苏世民学者
Konstantin TKACHUK
Schwarzman Scholar; Russia

陈兰
清华大学电子工程系本科生
CHEN Lan
Undergraduate student of the Department of Electronic Engineering, Tsinghua University

王婧怡
清华大学电子工程系博士生
WANG Jingyi
Ph.D. Student of the Department of Electronic Engineering, Tsinghua University

陆智泓
清华大学电子工程系硕士研究生
LU Zhihong
Master Student of the Department of Electronic Engineering, Tsinghua University

傅天予
清华大学电子工程系博士生
FU Tianyu
Ph.D. Student of the Department of Electronic Engineering, Tsinghua University; China

司锐雅
苏世民学者
Sreya VANGARA
Schwarzman Scholar, United States of America

德胜纳森
苏世民学者
Jonathan Peter-Oswin DASON
Schwarzman Scholar, Malaysia

袁斯陶
苏世民学者
Si Tou UN
Schwarzman Scholar; Macau S.A.R., China

孟乐笛

苏世民学者

Melody KIRIMA

Schwarzman Scholar, Kenya

吴舒遥

苏世民学者

Kelly WU

Schwarzman Scholar, United States of America

吴启迪

国际工程教育中心副理事长、主任，教育部原副部长

WU Qidi

Director and Vice Chairperson of Governing Board of ICEE, Former Vice Minister of Education, China

伊丽莎白·泰勒

国际工程联盟《华盛顿协议》主席

Elizabeth TAYLOR

Executive Committee Chair of Washington Accord, International Engineering Alliance

周爱军
中国工程教育专业认证协会常务理事、秘书长
ZHOU Aijun
Executive Director and Secretary-General of China Engineering Education Accreditation Association

达米恩·欧文斯
国际工程联盟《国际职业工程师协议》主席
Damien OWENS
Chair of International Professional Engineers Agreement, International Engineering Alliance

孙楠
清华大学电子工程系教授
SUN Nan
Professor of the Department of Electronic Engineering, Tsinghua University

安妮特·科莫斯
丹麦奥尔堡大学工程科学与可持续发展问题基础学习中心（UCPBL）主任
Anette KOLMOS
Director of Aalborg Centre for Problem Based Learning in Engineering Science & Sustainability, Aalborg University

黄翊东
清华大学学术委员会副主任，电子工程系原主任
HUANG Yidong
Deputy Director of Academic Committee, Tsinghua University; Former Dean of Department of Electronic Engineering, Tsinghua University

李曼丽
清华大学教育研究院教授
LI Manli
Professor of Institute of Education, Tsinghua University

罗毅
中国工程院院士，清华大学电子工程系教授
LUO Yi
Member of CAE; Professor of Department of Electronic Engineering, Tsinghua University

袁驷
国际工程教育中心执行主任，清华大学校务委员会副主任
YUAN Si
Executive Director of ICEE; Vice Director of the Council of Tsinghua University

论坛部分场景
Forum Scenes

"电子信息使能技术"分论坛部分参会嘉宾合影

Group Photo of the "Enabling Technology with Electronics and Information Science" sub-forum

"城市韧性"分论坛部分参会嘉宾合影

Group Photo of the "City Resilience" sub-forum

"数字医疗"分论坛部分参会嘉宾合影
Group Photo of the "Digital Health" sub-forum

"新型电力系统"分论坛部分参会嘉宾合影
Group Photo of the "New Power System" sub-forum

"智能新能源汽车"分论坛部分参会嘉宾合影
Group Photo of the "Intelligent New Energy Vehicles" sub-forum

"发展中国家可持续创新"分论坛部分参会嘉宾合影
Group Photo of the "Sustainable Innovation in Developing Countries" sub-forum

"青年学生可持续创新"分论坛部分参会嘉宾合影

Group Photo of the "The Sustainability Generation: Students Talk" sub-forum

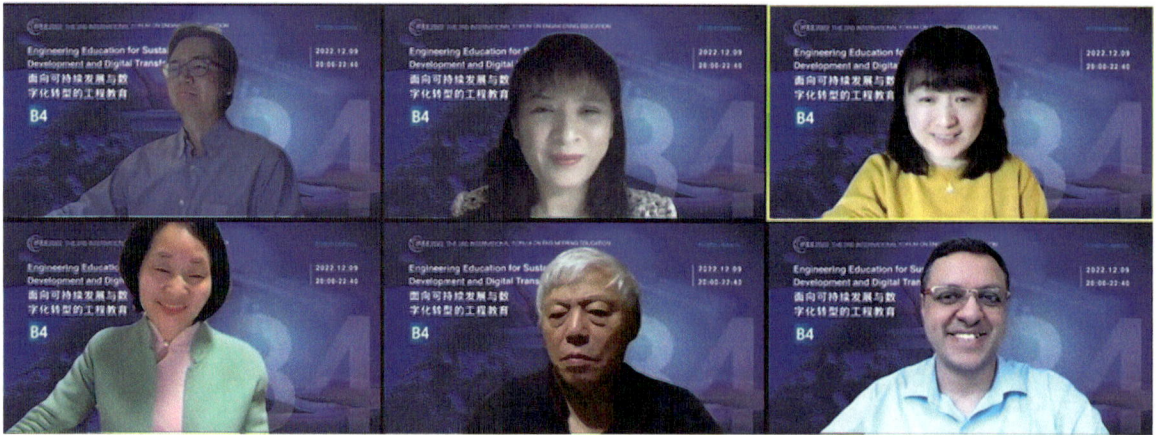

"面向可持续发展与数字化转型的工程教育"分论坛部分参会嘉宾合影

Group Photo of the "Engineering Education for Sustainable Development and Digital Transformation" sub-forum

前　言

"岁月不居，时节如流。"世界之变、时代之变、历史之变在加速演进。随着新一轮科技革命和产业变革的快速发展，工程教育的发展面临着前所未有的新机遇和新挑战，第三届国际工程教育论坛召开，适逢其时。全球工程教育、工程科技和工程管理领域的知名学者与杰出领袖，共同期待研讨工程教育的创新发展，促进世界工程科技和社会的进步，应对全球性大挑战。

2022年12月7日至9日，清华大学、中国工程院和联合国教育、科学及文化组织（以下简称联合国教科文组织，UNESCO）在清华大学共同举办以"电子信息技术与可持续创新"为主题的第三届国际工程教育论坛。来自世界各地的专家学者围绕与联合国可持续发展目标（SDGs）相关的"电子信息使能技术""城市韧性""数字医疗""新型电力系统""智能新能源汽车""发展中国家可持续创新""青年学生可持续创新""面向可持续发展与数字化转型的工程教育"等主题，展开了为期三天的学术探讨。本书汇集了这些学者的思想精华，展现了可持续发展、电子信息技术以及工程教育领域的新思想与新理念，反映了工程教育发展的新形势。

本书包括了来自联合国教科文组织、国际工程联盟等国际组织，中国工程教育专业认证协会、电气与电子工程师学会、印尼科学院等专业机构，东京工业大学、南开大学、柏林大学、清华大学、芝加哥大学、普渡大学、埃朗根–纽伦堡大学、北京航空航天大学、日本金泽大学、英国伦敦大学、杜克–新加坡国立大学、新加坡国立大学、加利福尼亚大学、天津大学、弗吉尼亚理工大学、帝国理工学院、埃克塞特大学、西安交通大学、长沙理工大学、华北电力大学、太原理工大学、哈尔滨工业大学、荷兰代尔夫特理工大学、伯明翰大学、吉林大学、滑铁卢大学、南非斯泰伦博斯大学、厦门大学、智利大学、丹麦奥尔堡大学等国内外知名大学的校长、工学院院长、专家学者、研究机构，以及中国移动通信集团、微软亚洲研究院、深圳市建筑科学研究院、广智微芯、鹰瞳科技、腾讯健康、华中科技大学同济医学院附属协和医院、中国联合网络通信集团、国家电网等国内外知名企业代表近 60 位专家学者的主题报告。论文集的出版对于推动我国工程教育发展、电子信息技术领域创新等，具有重要的学术和实践参考价值。

  国际工程教育论坛是国内外工程和工程教育领域的一场盛会，希望充分发挥论坛的国际影响力，让论坛成为一个由来自世界范围内的国际组织、科研机构、高校及行业等的专家、学者、领袖及同行们积极参与、共谋发展的协同合作的平台。

吴启迪

联合国教科文组织国际工程教育中心副理事长、主任

2023 年 10 月

目　　录

开幕式 ··· 1

    开幕式主持 ·· 3

    聚焦可持续创新：探讨电子信息技术在工程教育中的前景 ··············· 4

    欢迎致辞 ··· 5

    工程教育与可持续创新 ··· 6

    电子信息技术与可持续创新 ··· 9

    工程教育的变革 ··· 12

    主旨演讲 ··· 14

    为可持续的未来培养创新者 ·· 15

    工程教育：推动可持续发展和数字化智能化转型 ·························· 19

    特邀报告 ··· 26

    双重转型下的工程教育 ··· 27

A1 电子信息使能技术 ··· 31

    承办单位简介 ··· 33

    分论坛主持 ·· 35

    绿色数据通信：智能物理和工程技术支持可持续社会 ··················· 38

    高速光电子器件是信息技术的使能技术 ···································· 43

    互补型人工智能可以改进人类技术的发展 ································· 49

    培养下一代工程师 ·· 53

    合成分子通信：原理、进展和挑战 ·· 57

    探索 AI 时代的工程教育 ··· 61

A2 城市韧性 ·· 65

    承办单位简介 ··· 67

    分论坛主持 ·· 69

人居环境的群智能控制技术 ································· 73
　　以科学方法论为导向的建筑设计创新研究 ··················· 79
　　基于人因分析技术的建成空间体验预测与实证 ··············· 84
　　日本地方都市的城市设计 ································· 88
　　回到原来，一起创未来 ··································· 92

A3 数字医疗 ·· 95

　　承办单位简介 ··· 97
　　分论坛主持 ··· 98
　　AI+ 生命科学 ··· 101
　　医工交叉的北航实践 ····································· 105
　　精准肝胆外科范式与技术体系 ····························· 109
　　人工智能驱动的医疗保健新时代 ··························· 113
　　数字医疗的挑战与创新 ··································· 117
　　人工智能在健康领域的挑战与机遇 ························· 121
　　工程学在推进医学和医疗保健中的重要作用 ················· 125

A4 新型电力系统 ·· 129

　　承办单位简介 ··· 131
　　分论坛主持 ··· 133
　　关于智能配电系统几个问题的思考 ························· 137
　　工程教育和智能电网以及不断演进的电力系统的研究 ········· 141
　　数据科学及其对智能电网教育的影响 ······················· 145
　　面向新型电力系统的"电气 +"人才培养探索 ················ 149
　　为实现"双碳"目标，地方院校应如何为能源电力领域培养相关人才 ······· 153

B1 智能新能源汽车 ·· 155

　　承办单位简介 ··· 157
　　分论坛主持 ··· 158
　　新能源、新动力和新工科 ································· 161
　　迈向负责任的自动驾驶 ··································· 165
　　可持续车辆的最优系统 ··································· 169

数字汽车时代产品开发学科高等教育的几点思考 ········· 172
　　体验式学习与工程专业的研究生教育 ················· 175
　　能源采集：汽车节能和智能化的途径 ················· 179

B2 发展中国家可持续创新 ····················· 183

　　承办单位简介 ································· 185
　　分论坛主持 ··································· 187
　　东盟区域数字经济——发展状况与产业互联网实践机会 ···· 190
　　新加坡国立大学苏州研究院在人才培养、技术创新与交流方面的实践分享 ··· 194
　　工程教育和非洲的优先事项 ························ 198
　　创新印度尼西亚 ································ 202
　　全球化可持续性对厦门大学马来西亚分校电气和电子工程教育的影响 ······ 206
　　发展中国家的可持续创新 ·························· 210
　　更多样化、更好的工程技术实现可持续发展——来自南半球的创新 ······· 214
　　自动化领域的国际合作与需求 ······················ 218

B3 青年学生可持续创新 ······················· 221

　　承办单位简介 ································· 223
　　分论坛主持 ··································· 225
　　校园垃圾管理 ································· 228
　　智能碳足迹记录和共享平台 ························ 231
　　基于图神经网络的慈善资源匹配 ····················· 234
　　发展可持续的人道主义技术 ························ 238
　　利用数字平台开展由青年领导的可持续发展目标运动 ······· 242
　　为什么包容性数字化转型很重要？ ··················· 246
　　可持续发展的汽车设计 ··························· 250
　　理解能源、气候和可持续性领域的方法 ················ 253

B4 面向可持续发展与数字化转型的工程教育 ·········· 255

　　分论坛介绍 ··································· 257
　　承办单位简介 ································· 259
　　分论坛主持 ··································· 261

可持续发展的工程教育认证 ································ 264

可持续发展与数字化转型下的中国工程教育质量保障 ············ 267

将可持续性纳入认证和能力标准 ···························· 270

面向可持续工程教育转型 ·································· 273

面向可持续创新人才培养的电子信息课程体系 ················ 276

面向创造的学习：数智时代的工程教育 ······················ 281

闭幕式 ··· 285

闭幕式主持 ·· 287

第三届国际工程教育论坛总结和闭幕词 ······················ 289

附录：英文演讲稿（节选） ································· 292

后记 ··· 365

第三届国际工程教育论坛
The 3rd International Forum On Engineering Education

开幕式
Opening Ceremony

2022 年 12 月 7 日 20:00–22:30

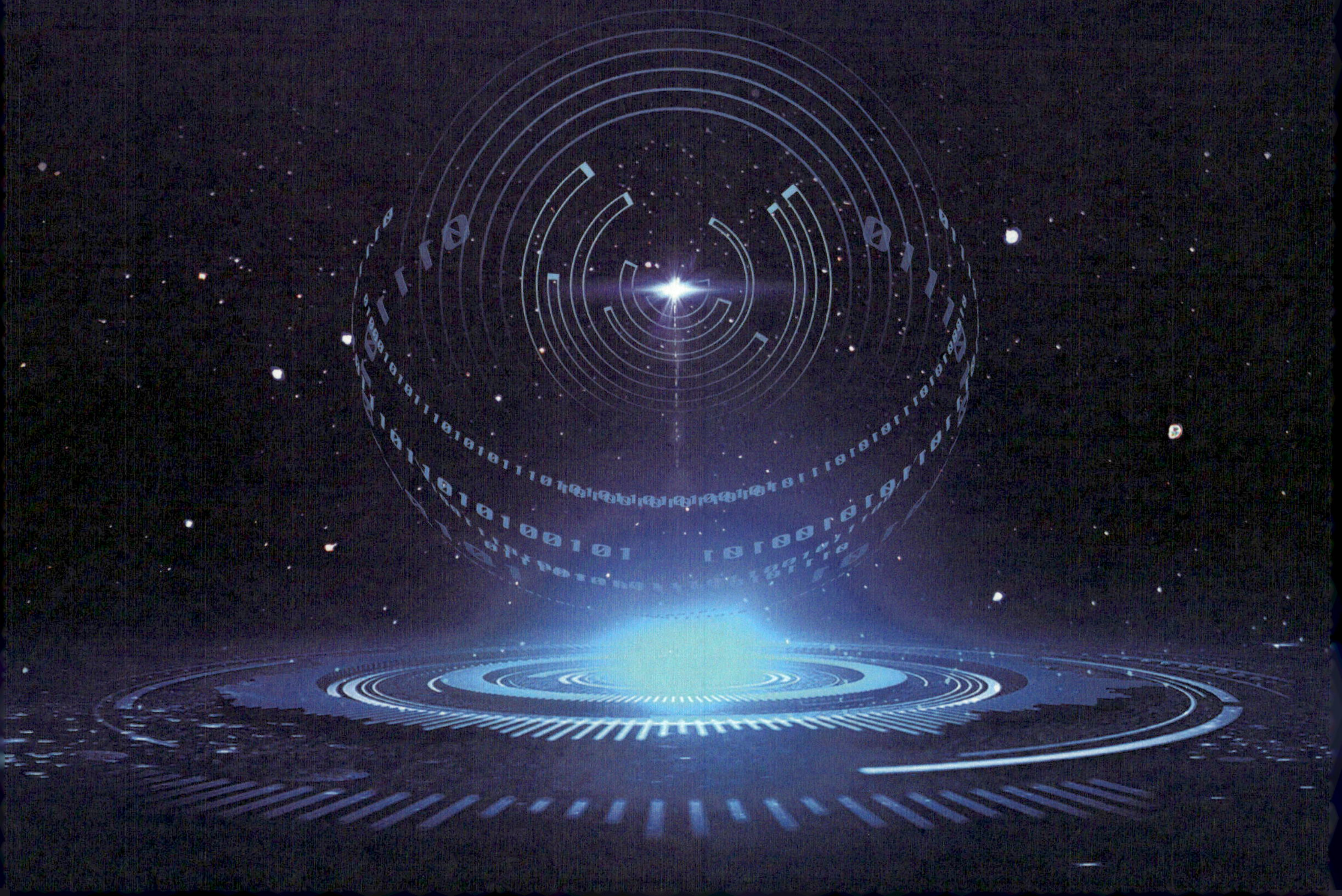

开幕式主持

主持人

王光谦
中国科学院院士，清华大学副校长
WANG Guangqian
Member of CAE; Vice President, Tsinghua University

清华大学水利系教授，中国科学院院士。现任清华大学副校长。第十三届全国政协常委，人口资源环境委员会委员，中国民主同盟第十二届中央委员会常务副主席。主要从事水沙科学与江河治理的研究工作，1995年获国家杰出青年科学基金资助，2000年获聘教育部"长江学者"特聘教授，2009年当选中国科学院院士。

Wang Guangqian is the Vice President of Tsinghua University. He is a member of the Standing Committee of the 13th CPPCC National Committee, and Vice Chairman of the 12th Central Committee of the China Democratic League. He became a member of the Chinese Academy of Sciences in 2009, and his research fields focus on hydroscience, sediment and river dynamics.

聚焦可持续创新：探讨电子信息技术在工程教育中的前景

王光谦

尊敬的各位领导，各位来宾：

大家好！由清华大学、中国工程院、联合国教科文组织共同举办的第三届国际工程教育论坛现在开始。本次论坛的主题是"电子信息技术与可持续创新"，很高兴我们用这样特别的方式齐聚一堂，共商工程教育发展的新机遇与新挑战。

本次论坛的来宾中既有全球工程教育、工程科技、科技管理领域的著名学者，也有很多来自各界的领军人物。请允许我介绍一下参会的各位领导和嘉宾，他们是：中国工程院院长李晓红，联合国教科文组织驻华代表处主任夏泽翰，中国联合国教科文组织全国委员会秘书处秘书长秦昌威。参会的国内外大学代表有：东京工业大学校长益一哉教授，清华大学校长王希勤教授，南开大学学术委员会主任、中国新一代人工智能发展战略研究院执行院长龚克教授。本次论坛还邀请到知名企业代表，中国移动通信集团有限公司技术部总经理王晓云参会。欢迎大家的到来！

欢迎致辞

李晓红
中国工程院院士，中国工程院院长
LI Xiaohong
Member of Chinese Academy of Engineering, President of Chinese Academy of Engineering

中国工程院院士，矿山安全技术专家。第十九届、二十届中央委员，第十一届全国政协委员，第十二届全国人大代表。现任中国工程院党组书记、院长。长期致力于水射流技术及其在煤矿安全工程中的应用研究，在煤层气开采及复杂煤矿瓦斯灾害防治方面取得了多项重要研究成果。曾获多项国家级、省部级科学技术进步奖和国际学术奖励，出版著作6部，发表论文200余篇。

Li Xiaohong, member of Chinese Academy of Engineering, a technical expert in mine safety, a member of the 19th and 20th Central Committees of the Communist Party of China, a member of the 11th National Committee of the CPPCC, and a deputy of the 12th NPC. Currently, he is the Secretary of the Leading Party Group and the President of the Chinese Academy of Engineering (CAE). Long been committed to the research of water jet technology and its application in coal mine safety engineering, he has made numerous significant research achievements in coalbed methane exploitation and gas disaster prevention in complex coal mines. Among these, the gas disaster prevention technology, listed as a national major-scientific-and-technological-achievements-transformation project, has been widely promoted and applied throughout the country and has generated remarkable economic and social benefits. Besides, he has won multiple science and technology progress awards at national and provincial levels as well as international academic awards, and published 6 works and more than 200 papers.

工程教育与可持续创新

李晓红

各位来宾，各位朋友，女士们，先生们：

大家好！

值此第三届国际工程教育论坛召开之际，我谨代表中国工程院，向参加此次论坛活动的海内外嘉宾和朋友们表示热烈欢迎！感谢联合国教科文组织对论坛的大力支持，感谢清华大学的精心筹办。

此时，正值北半球的初冬与南半球的初夏。正是数字技术和无数工程师的努力，让全球工程教育界的同仁不受时空限制，在云端相聚，"天涯若比邻"，这体现了工程的魅力，也正契合我们这次盛会的主题——电子信息技术与可持续创新。

"科技是第一生产力，人才是第一资源，创新是第一动力"。工程科技、工程教育、工程人才的高质量发展在今天显得尤为重要。借此机会并结合大会的主题，我有三点思考和建议与大家分享。

第一，电子信息技术推动与可持续创新，工程人才是关键。世界新一轮科技革命加速演进，产业数字化和数字产业化进程持续加快。这对工程人才的知识结构和能力素质提出了新要求，更加强调人才的技术创新能力、解决复杂工程问题的能力、计算思维和数据分析能力、终身学习能力、工程伦理责任，等等。工程教育需要应时而变，主动创新，源源不断地培养出能引领和服务产业发展的各种类型的人才。

第二，应对全球可持续发展重大挑战，工程科技和工程教育是关键。当前，国际形势风云变幻，气候变化、能源危机等全球性问题交织叠加。2021年3月，"世界工程日"，我和联合国教科文组织总干事阿祖莱女士共同发布了联合国教科文组织第二份工程报告——《工程——支持可持续发展》。这份报告全面阐述了工程和工程师在实现联合国17项可持续发展目标中产生的关键作用，提出了一系列重要建议。近年来的国际实践也表明，要应对经济、社会、环境的可持续发展，工程科技、工程教育至关重要。

第三，工程教育高质量发展，国际交流互鉴是关键。人类是命运共同体，全球工程界也是共同体。各国工业化发展进程不同，工程教育体系有别，传统和模式各具特色，本土挑战不尽相同。本次论坛的报告人来自国际社会的各个方面：既有教育专家，也有企业专家；既有大学教授，也有青年学生。期待大家的真知灼见和思想碰撞，共享成功经验，共商发展大计，共建全球伙伴关系。

女士们、先生们、朋友们，工程增进全人类福祉。我相信，在我们的共同努力下，工程科技、工程教育和工程人才一定能为更可持续、更加美好的世界做出更大贡献。

谢谢！

夏泽翰
联合国教科文组织驻华代表处主任
Shahbaz KHAN
Director of UNESCO Beijing Office

联合国教科文组织驻华代表处代表，2008年加入联合国教科文组织，在总部担任水资源和可持续发展处主任，曾在澳大利亚、法国、印度尼西亚和巴基斯坦从事与水文和可持续发展有关的各种研究、咨询和政策工作。荣获2017年北京市长城友谊奖、2019年中国政府友谊奖等。

Shahbaz Khan is the Director of the UNESCO Office in Beijing. He joined UNESCO in 2008 at its Headquarters as the Chief of the Water and Sustainable Development Section. He has worked in Australia, France, Indonesia and Pakistan in various research, consultancy and policy positions around hydrology and sustainable development. He has been widely recognized for his work, receiving the 2017 Beijing Great Wall Friendship Award and the 2019 China Friendship Award, etc.. He holds a Hon Doctorate Environment and Development from the National University of Malaysia (2016) and a Hon DSc from the University of Birmingham (2018).

电子信息技术与可持续创新

夏泽翰

尊敬的各位来宾，女士们、先生们，同事们，大家晚上好！

很高兴今天能够与大家相聚在此，共同庆祝第三届国际工程教育论坛的召开，这是由清华大学、中国工程院和联合国教科文组织共同主办的盛会。2015年，联合国教科文组织在清华大学设立了国际工程教育中心（ICEE）。多年来，我们一直致力于促进工程教育领域的交流和沟通，并积极参与各项合作项目。我们深知，推动工程教育的发展，需要各方的积极参与和共同努力。本次论坛的举办，为全球工程教育领域的专家学者提供了一个交流互动的平台，在此我们可以共同分享经验，探讨问题，寻求解决之道，实现合作共赢。

女士们、先生们，科学家们研究的是世界本来的面目，而工程师则创造了前所未有的世界。伟大的匈牙利裔美国数学家、航空航天工程师和物理学家西奥多·冯·卡门曾这样说过，工程学是关于解决问题的知识和实践，作为一种职业，工程师在满足人类基本需求、消除贫困、促进安全和可持续发展、应对紧急情况、重建基础设施、弥合知识鸿沟，以及促进跨文化合作等方面扮演着至关重要的角色。

我们将社会需求与适当的技术创新和商业应用联系起来，工程在社会经济可持续发展中是主要的驱动力，有助于我们应对灾害和公共卫生方面的挑战，提供食品、水、通信和交通等基础服务，更重要的是创造新的产品和服务。工程学一直是联合国教科文组织重要的组成部分。早在1945年11月，联合国教科文组织的创始人就致力于推进科学和技术的发展。实际上，联合国教科文组织是在伦敦的土木工程学院基础上建立起来的，该学院是世界上最古老的工程学院之一。本次论坛的主题"电子信息技术与可持续创新"非常符合联合国在2015年发起的《变革我们的世界：2030年可持续发展议程》，在这个议程下，工程师一直站在最前沿，利用他们的科学知识和经验实现可持续发展目标，将创新理念转化为可持续发展项目，最终造福全人类。因此，本次论坛为我们提供了一个宝贵的机会，让我们了解工程在社会经济可持续发展中所发挥的关键作用，并交流关于工程教育的见解。我们正处于人类历史上一个独特的转折点，危机与机遇交织。第四次工业革命的曙光被紧迫的全球挑战的阴影笼罩，例如气候变化、不平等、暴力和不安全，同时，颠覆性新兴技术如生物技术和人工智能也带来了复杂的伦理问题。

在当前的背景下，工程创新正成为影响和改变社会发展格局的关键要素，并对未来的工程师和工程教育的实践者和研究者提出了更高的要求。我很荣幸能够作为一名工程师与大家一起参加这次论坛。通过这个平台，我们可以利用可用的信息技术突破物理界限和学科障碍，促进跨学科合作，推动以可持续发展为导向的研究、创新和持续的人才培养。同时，我也要感谢组委会为这次全球范围的对话做出的努力。

尽管面临各种挑战，本次会议依然彰显了工程学为社会带来益处的能力，让我们共同努力推动可持续创新。我相信在发展中国家，尤其是那些致力于可持续发展的国家，通过不断升级工程、发展教育，将来能够成为数字化转型的领跑者，实现人与人之间的共享和交流，为早日实现可持续发展目标提供解决方案。这将创造一个创新型和绿色的社会，并减少类似新冠疫情带来的影响。

最后，再次感谢大家参与本次论坛，并期待在未来的讨论中，我们能够共同探讨更多关于工程创新和可持续发展的话题，为社会的进步贡献自己的力量。谢谢！

秦昌威
中国联合国教科文组织全国委员会秘书处秘书长
QIN Changwei
Secretary-General of the Chinese National Commission for UNESCO

中国联合国教科文组织全国委员会秘书处秘书长。长期从事重要国家教育规划与监测工作，牵头起草了《全国教育事业发展"十三五"规划》。2015年至2018年，担任2030教育目标国家协调员，参与制订了中国实施2030目标教育方案。曾任教育部发展规划司规划处副处长、处长，中国联合国教科文组织全国委员会副秘书长，发展规划司副司长。

Qin Changwei is a senior expert in the planning and monitoring of China's educational development. He led the drafting of the 13th Five-Year Plan for Educational Development of China. Between 2015 and 2018, he served as China's National Coordinator for SDG4-Education 2030 and one of the key drafters of China's national document for the implementation of Education 2030 agenda-China's National Plan for Education Modernization. He once worked as the Deputy Director, Director of Division, and the Deputy Secretary-General of the Chinese National Commission for UNESCO, as well as Deputy Director-General of the Department of Development Planning in the Ministry of Education.

工程教育的变革

秦昌威

大家好，很高兴参加第三届国际工程教育论坛，我谨代表中国联合国教科文组织全国委员会向本次论坛的召开表示热烈祝贺，向论坛主办方表示衷心的感谢，并向长期投身于工程教育事业的各位专家学者致以崇高敬意。

工程科技是改变世界的重要力量，工程科技的每一次重大突破都会推动社会生产力的深刻变革，都会推动人类文明迈向新的更高的台阶。当前，新一轮科技革命不断加速，电子信息技术作为当代最活跃、渗透力最强的科学技术，能够有效打通学科壁垒，助推多学科交叉融合发展，在新一轮科技革命中起着至关重要的推动作用，而加快电子信息技术的工程科技人才培养，对于电子信息技术的可持续创新至关重要。电子信息科技技术类工程教育担负着支撑科技革命，促进人类更可持续发展的历史作用。

2022年9月，联合国召开教育变革峰会，发布了联合国秘书长关于全球教育变革的愿景声明，提出要从根本上重新审视教育目的和课程体系，支持学习者学会学习，学会共处，学会做事，学会做人，获得数字技能和科学技能，提高发展自我和促进社会发展的能力，激发创造和创新潜能。

当前，全球正在共同推动教育变革，面对当前工程科技日益加快的迭代升级，工程教育同样面临着加速变革的任务和要求，这迫切需要我们加强工程教育的交流合作，共同推动工程教育的变革，特别是电子信息技术这一前沿领域需要培养出更多全球都需要的高质量电子信息领域工程科技人才。因此，本次论坛意义重大。作为联合国系统负责推动教育领域和科技领域研究与国际合作的专门机构，联合国教科文组织高度重视工程教育，在2021年还通过了《开放科学建议书》等国际准则性文件，倡导科学和教育资源共享，通过合作共享，推动各国特别是发展中国家可持续创新发展。

国际工程教育中心是中国与联合国教科文组织合作建设的二类中心，自成立以来，在中国工程院和清华大学的共同指导与支持下，围绕促进世界工程科技和社会进步的问题，应对全球性重大挑战，汇聚全球工程教育、工程科技和工程管理领域知名专家，开展教科文组织工程报告编写，面向发展中国家开展教育培训，为国际工程教育交流合作做了大量工作。特别是举办国际工程教育论坛，为世界工程教育交流搭建了重要合作平台。

衷心希望并且相信本届论坛能够秉持教科文组织的开放科学理念，基于全球教育变革的共同愿景，围绕电子信息技术的工程教育，深入探讨解决当前工程教育面临的重大问题的有效途径，分享培养更多更高质量电子信息技术人才的最佳经验，提出推动工程教育变革的方向与策略，汇聚推动电子信息领域工程教育合作的新共识，为全球教育变革和世界工程教育的发展做出新贡献。

中国联合国教科文组织全国委员会将继续发挥协调和联络职能，全力支持国际工程教育中心充分利用相关组织的合作网络，持续办好国际工程教育论坛，并建立、发展国际工程教育伙伴关系。我们将不断汇聚推动工程教育变革与可持续发展的强大力量，为实现2030年可持续发展目标，建设一个更加美好的世界而努力。

最后，预祝本次论坛取得圆满成功！谢谢大家！

主旨演讲

益一哉
东京工业大学校长
Kazuya MASU
President of Tokyo Institute of Technology

自2018年4月1日，担任东京工业大学第22任校长。领导东京工业大学的转型，将东京工业大学的不同研究中心、实验室和单位整合为一个综合中心。他是电子设备、集成电路和无线传感器网络方面的专家，分别于1977年、1979年和1982年在东京工业大学获得工程学士、硕士和博士学位。

Kazuya Masu has served as the 22nd president of Tokyo Tech since April 1, 2018. His flexible, dialogue-based leadership has guided the Institute during a time of important transformation, uniting Tokyo Tech's diverse research centers, laboratories, and units into one integrated hub. Together with his profound understanding of Tokyo Tech, Masu's ability to inspire and manage changes through collaborative teamwork continues to propel the Institute toward the achievement of a shared vision. A specialist in electronic devices, integrated circuits, and wireless sensor networks, Masu earned his bachelor's, master's, and doctoral degrees in engineering from Tokyo Tech in 1977, 1979, and 1982, respectively. In April 1982, he took an assistant professor position at the Research Institute of Electrical Communication at Tohoku University, where he became an associate professor in 1993. In June 2000, Masu returned to Tokyo Tech as a professor at the Precision and Intelligence Laboratory. He subsequently held professorial positions at the Integrated Research Institute from 2005 to 2010, the Solutions Research Laboratory from 2010 to 2014, and the Frontier Research Center from 2014 to 2016. During the two years prior to his inauguration, Masu served as the first director of the Institute of Innovative Research.

为可持续的未来培养创新者

益一哉

本次论坛的目的是促进以可持续发展为导向的创新研究，培养工程人才，因此，我想向大家介绍东京工业大学的工程教育，并分享我对培养未来社会需要的创新领导者的看法。

当前，世界正进入一个把应对气候变化作为进一步发展经济的巨大机遇的时代——可以说，这是一个"绿色增长"的时代。2020年10月，日本宣布到2050年实现碳中和。而为了做到这一点，日本政府在2021年6月制定了"绿色增长战略"，该战略规定了14个有望增长的领域。这意味着要实现碳中和，各行业的创新都势在必行。毋庸置疑，在信息技术领域进行创新是必要的，这也是本次论坛的主题。"绿色增长"离不开强大的数字基础设施支撑，因为"绿色"和"数字"是一个车的两个轮子。然而，仅凭信息技术领域的创新还不足以实现碳中和，更不能应对气候变化，以及实现可持续发展目标和社会发展。日本有着通过提高各个领域的技术能力推动社会发展的历史，并且由于缺乏自然资源而建立了多样化的工业基础。可以说，多元化产业的创新基础已经具备。

简单介绍一下东京工业大学的历史。它成立于1881年，是日本第一所科学和技术教育机构。其中一位创始人曾说，建立这所学校不是为了满足现有工厂和工业的需要，而是为了培养创造新工业的人才。今天，新产业的创造可以用一个词概括：创新。因此，东京工业大学的创始理念强调通过培养创新者为社会做出贡献，这一使命一直延续到今天。

现在，我想谈谈东京工业大学的两项培养不同行业年轻创新者的很重要的举措。

第一个举措是文科教育。作为日本领先的国家科学和技术大学的校长，我认为我们的责任不仅要培养具备高度专业技能的人才，而且要培养具备更广泛的社会科学和人文知识背景的人才，并在此基础上深刻理解社会如何运行、人们如何思考。为此，东京工业大学以相互关联的方式呈现文科教育和专业教育，并实行楔形教育，旨在实现知识和能力的螺旋式上升。这是东京工业大学的传统教育方法，受到了师生们的广泛欢迎。2016年，我们对东京工业大学的教育体系进行了大规模的改革，成立了文科研究所（Liberal Arts Education，简称ILA），以进一步加强文科教育。除了一年级学生的各种必修课程外，ILA还提供了一个更注重学生主动学习的课程，这就是"东京科技愿景项目"，它是东方工业大学所有1100名本科生的必修课程之一。通过小组讨论、项目和演讲，使学生能够相互激励，提高他们对紧迫问题的认识，并提高其沟通技巧。

另一个举措是我们于2018年9月成立了大学与社会联系的平台——全球网络社会创新设计实验室（Laboratory for Design of Social Innovation in Global Networks，简称DLab）。我们的学生可以在这里与研究所以外的人交流他们的想法和观点。DLab举办了许多主题是"我们想要的未来"的研讨会。这些活动旨在将东京工业大学社区——学生、教职员工和校友——与来自工业界、政府和学术界的参与者以及高中生聚集在一起。研讨会的开放和友好氛围引发了关于我们真正想要创造的未来的互动和活跃的讨论。

在与社会沟通方面，大学通常会听取并回应其利益相关者的需求。另外，DLab旨在促进东京工业大学与公众之间更具有包容性和互动性的对话。此外，DLab的愿景是分享一个"我们想要的未来"，而不是一个"大学认为应该有的未来"。下面我将详细说明这一概念。

DLab设计未来的方法是通过从未来看现在来实现的。这种方法不同于仅仅预测技术趋势或者寻找解决社会可能面临的挑战的方式。相反，DLab设计从设想一个我们都想要的更好的未来开始，就在考虑当前的问题，以及现有的、新兴的科学与技术。然后，他们逆向思考，从目标向后推导出必要的步骤，并确定实现这些目标的优先次序。通过这个过程，他们能够在科技、社会科学和人文科学领域提出新的研究方向。这个方法被称为"逆向预测"，并已经被DLab设计成功地运用了。

在过去的研讨会上，与会者试图避免简单地扩展线性思维，预测一个已经可以预见的未来。相反，他们寻求"我们想要的未来"与新研究和商业概念的可能性之间的交集。利用"逆向预测"方法产生的讨论和想法，在这些研讨会上被完善和概念化为24个未来的情景，这些情景构成了"东京科技未来年表"。

每个未来情景都描述了在我们的日常生活中"我们想要的未来"。这个视觉工具帮助研讨会参会者查看现有的组成部分，同时鼓励讨论如何进一步发展这些情景或创造新的情景。

联合国的可持续发展目标定义了我们"应该采取的行动",力争在2030年实现这些目标。相比之下,DLab 从一个更自由、更广泛的角度,利用大学的优势,提出"我们可以为我们想要的未来做些什么"。"东京科技未来年表"目前囊括了2030—2200年的时间跨度,它将根据需要进行修改。每个未来情景包括四个主要元素:标题和描述,现在和未来之间的主要变化,技术和社会挑战,大学在该情景中的预期作用。

通过例子,让我们看一下如下情景。该情景描述了未来个人健康能够自动维护,在这种情况下,每个人在睡觉时都会被监测身体状况,这些数据会被发送到相关的医疗机构。因此,他们可能会收到有关建议,例如,他们的下一餐应包含他们所需的所有特定营养物质。

这里的关键变化是,我们可以摆脱定期体检的不便,个人健康将不费吹灰之力就得到维护。推进或发展 CMOS-MEMS 惯性传感器的新研究可以为实现这一未来提供途径。这一设想表明,大学需要与医疗机构深入合作。事实上,东京工业大学的研究人员已经与医生合作使用高灵敏度惯性传感器用于诊断早期帕金森病。这种合作可以加强并应用于实现这一未来情景。

因此,描述的每个未来情景都揭示了研究如何与理想的未来相联系,并强调为实现该未来可能需要做什么。实际上,这些未来情景中的一些已经部分实现。东京工业大学的 DLab 是一个各研究领域和社会各界之间的交流平台,旨在促进学术界、学生和更广泛的社区之间的公开对话。换句话说,DLab 不仅作为大学和社会之间的对话场所,而且作为博士研究生教育的场所,具有极其重要的地位。

我们认为工程教育不仅需要培养专业领域内的专家工程师,更需要培养具有广阔视野并能将其专业知识应用于社会的人才。通过履行我们作为一个培养创新者而不仅是工人的教育机构的使命,我们将在各个工程领域为更美好的未来做出贡献。

最后,让我们一起创造一个光明的、可持续的未来。谢谢大家!

王希勤
清华大学校长
WANG Xiqin
President of Tsinghua University

电子工程系教授，博士。清华大学党委副书记、校长。兼任中国高等教育学会副会长、中国电子学会副监事长、清华大学校友总会会长。主要研究方向为信号与信息处理（雷达信号与数据处理、雷达成像等）。曾获北京市科学技术进步二等奖、中国船舶工业总公司科技进步二等奖、国家教委科技进步三等奖等奖励。作为项目负责人，完成了国家高技术研究发展计划（863计划）、"十一五"预研专项、国家重点基础研究发展计划（973计划）等国家级科研项目。

Wang Xiqin is a professor in the Department of Electronic Engineering and the President of Tsinghua University. He is also the Vice President of China Association of Higher Education, Vice Chairman of the Board of Supervisors of Chinese Institute of Electronics, and President of Tsinghua Alumni Association. Wang's research interests focus on signal and information processing (radar signal and data processing, radar imaging, etc.). He has won the Second Prize of Beijing Municipal Science and Technology Progress Award, the Second Prize of China State Shipbuilding Corporation Science and Technology Progress Award, and the Third Prize of State Education Commission's Science and Technology Progress Award of China. As the project leader, he has completed a series of national-level scientific research projects, including the project of the National High-Tech R&D Program, the pre-research project of the "Eleventh Five-Year" Plan, and the project of the National Key Fundamental R&D Program.

工程教育：推动可持续发展和数字化智能化转型

王希勤

全球工程教育界、学术界和产业界的朋友们相聚云端，共同见证第三届国际工程教育论坛开幕。首先，我谨代表清华大学向与会嘉宾表示热烈的欢迎！向参加论坛演讲与讨论的各位专家学者表示衷心的感谢！

随着新一轮科技革命和产业变革的快速演进，工程教育面临前所未有的机遇和挑战。在这一背景下，国际工程教育论坛应运而生。2018年，我们在清华大学举行了首届国际工程教育论坛，围绕"工程教育创新发展"的主题展开了精彩演讲与热烈讨论。2020年，我们克服新冠疫情带来的困难，以线上的方式举行了第二届国际工程教育论坛，围绕"生态环境与可持续发展"的主题，共同研讨工程教育的创新发展。两届论坛的成功举办，体现了专家学者和社会各界对工程教育的高度重视和持续关心，凸显了工程技术创新和工程人才培养在全球发展中发挥的重要作用。

在本次论坛上，可持续创新是基于可持续发展理念和视角的技术创新模式。在当前的全球局势和时代背景下，工程教育将在推动可持续发展和数字化智能化转型中发挥不可替代的作用。

第一，工程教育最能体现高等教育发展的时代特征。当前，世界之变、时代之变、历史之变正以前所未有的方式展开。世界百年未有之大变局的加速演进深刻影响着全球高等教育进程，高等教育正进入一个新的发展阶段。在新的发展阶段，高等教育呈现出一系列新的时代特征。

一是学科分化与问题综合的矛盾日益突出。我们处在一个知识爆炸的时代，知识总量极速增长，知识领域不断分化、细化，知识为越来越多的个体掌握。但是，我们面临的问题却越来越综合、复杂，单靠单个学者、单一学科无法有效解决，团体合作已成为科学研究的主要方式，多学科、交叉学科、跨学科现象日益普遍。学科和知识的分化与解决重大问题需要的学科和知识整合之间的问题日益凸显。

二是知识的正统性与知识的原创性之间的相互作用日益增强。传统大学强调知识的正统性，现代大学强调知识的原创性，通过科学研究打破既定范式、创造新的知识，从而产生新兴学科。当前，大学的新兴学科与传统学科互利共生：新兴学科正从传统学科中汲取智慧、蓬勃发展，而传统学科也正以新理论、新技术与新方法为载体探寻新方向，正统性知识与原创性知识之间的良性互动日益显著。

三是自然科学与人文科学的方法论日益融通。传统上，自然科学与人文科学泾渭分明。自然科学以客观性理念研究物质现象，人文科学以主观性理念研究精神现象，研究者与研究现象直接联系。如今，新兴技术的应用使针对研究现象的数据的收集与共享成为可能，数据成为连通研究者与研究现象之间的桥梁。科学家与人文学者能够通过共同的数据，以相似的方式分析不同的物质或精神现象，二者在研究方法上的鸿沟正逐步被填平。

四是大学教育与经济社会发展的结合日益紧密。传统的大学教育强调知识，追求研究的"纯净"，远离社会现实，因而造成了教育与生产之间、大学与社会之间的分离，教育的异化现象显著。当前，大学越来越回归社会，大学培养的人才兼具知识分子与劳动者双重属性，大学不仅为了学术而学术，同样也要服务社会，大学不仅能够为人类社会提供丰富的知识与文化基础，也日益成为经济发展与社会进步的动力站，大学与社会的关系日益密切。

作为高等教育的子领域，高等工程教育也受到了这一系列新趋势的影响，其教育模式与教育形态正悄然发生变化。

一是工程教育更具融合性，人才培养呈现跨学科特性。过去的工程人才培养往往囿于单一学科，侧重对学科内知识、专业内技能的学习，培养口径较窄，培养的毕业生缺乏解决日益复杂的工程问题方面的能力。为应对这一问题，全球工程教育正在打破专业壁垒，增进学科融合，向跨学科人才培养模式转型，一批高校通过设置跨学科的整合性课程、组建跨学科的师生团队、成立跨学科工程研究中心等方式，为工科学生打造有利于学习、合作与交流的跨学科平台，培养具备广博的知识、丰富技能的跨学科人才。

二是工程教育更有创新性，新兴工程学科打破传统教育模式。传统工科建立在既有的经典理论体系与专业技术之上，呈现"课堂讲授—课后学习（研究）—实习实践"的教育模式。新兴工程学科根植于科学研究的前沿交叉地带，知识的内容与形态不断更新，新理论、新方法、新技术层出不穷。面对知识的快速发展，新兴工程学科转向以学生为中心的教育模式，通过采用翻转课堂、基于项目的学习、探究式学习等多种模式，激发学生自主学习潜能，使学生以更主动、更快速、更灵活、更具研究性的方式快速汲取新知，获得更好的学习成效。以学生为中心的学习模式正快速渗透到传统工科领域。

三是工程教育更为全面，培养环节融入人文社会科学元素。传统上的工程教育只包含工程的科学与技术要素。然而，随着现代工程的外延迅速向经济系统、生态系统和社会系统延伸，工程师需要具备更全面的能力。工程教育除了培养工程师的科学与技术能力，还需使学生兼备社会情怀、人文素养和企业家精神。一批高校正在开展面向可持续发展的工程教育，在培养项目中加入与环境保护、经济发展、社会包容、工程伦理相关的课程与环节，提升工科学生的反思能力、社会责任与职业精神，促进工程人才的全面发展。

四是工程教育更为有效，直面真实场景中的真实问题。一段时期内，工程教育过于注重对理论知识的学习，忽视了对学生实践能力的培养，工程教育与工程实践脱节。20世纪90年代，随着工程教育"回归工程"，迈入"工程范式"阶段，一批工程学院和工程专业回归工程实践、回归工作场景，通过开设实践类课程、开展创新创业教育、进行校企联合培养、组织学生参与真实工程研发项目等方式，促进学生在真实的工程环境中了解社会的实际需求，培养学生从真实场景中发现真问题、解决真问题的能力。

第二，工程教育最有推动实现可持续发展目标的潜能。近代以来，工业化进程创造了前所未有的物质财富，也导致了日益严重的生态创伤。大自然屡屡向人类发出警示，提醒我们只有尊重规律、敬畏自然，人类才能与地球家园和谐共生，才能拥有安全而美好的未来。2015年9月，在联合国成立70周年之际，193个成员国一致通过了《变革我们的世界：2030年可持续发展议程》（以下简称《可持续发展议程》）。该议程提出的17项可持续发展目标（Sustainable Development Goals，SDGs），是人类基于历史经验和未来愿景提出的系统的发展框架和共同的行动计划。

教育传承过去、造就现在、开创未来，是推动人类文明进步的重要力量。2022年5月召开的第三届世界高等教育大会指出，高等教育在建设更可持续、更具韧性、更和平的社会的过程中发挥着战略性的、不可替代的作用。当前，人类正面临气候变化、粮食和能源安全等诸多问题带来的共同挑战，人类发展指数30年来首次下降。在此关头，全球的大学应当勇担时代责任，以更加积极的姿态推动人类朝着可持续发展的目标迈进。

科学、技术和工程对如期实现《可持续发展议程》至关重要。作为学术和创新机构，大学应及时关注关系到可持续发展的关键问题，努力为可持续发展目标的实现提供新知和解决方案。我们要把握新一轮科技革命和产业变革新机遇，坚持问题导向，推动学科交叉，促进全球合作，努力通过学术突破、技术变革和工程创新，探寻实现可持续发展的创新路径，在促进经济社会发展的同时实现人与自然和谐共生。

青年是创新动力的重要来源，也是可持续发展的重要推动者。作为教育和文化机构，大学应在各类课程和培养环节中有机融入可持续发展的理念，努力为可持续发展目标的实现培养高层次人才。我们要教育引导青年勇于承担，超越当下、超越本地本国、超越人类自身的责任，树立民族共同体意识，传承本民族的优秀传统文化；树立人类命运共同体意识，成为促进世界团结的一股力量；树立人与自然生命共同体意识，让良好的生态环境成为人类可持续发展的不竭源头。

发展是人类社会的永恒主题。改革开放后，我国创造了经济快速发展的奇迹，但由于一些地方和部门存在片面追求速度和规模、发展方式粗放等问题，发展不平衡、不协调、不可持续的问题十分突出。党的十八大以来，中国经济已经由高速增长阶段转向高质量发展阶段。习近平总书记在党的二十大报告中指出："高质量发展是全面建设社会主义现代化国家的首要任务。"高质量发展是体现新发展理念的发展，是全面的发展、充分的发展、着眼于长远的发展。从本质上讲，创新、协调、绿色、开放、共享的新发展理念，与可持续发展的理念是一致的。我们坚持把联合国《可持续发展议程》同本国发展战略和国情有机结合，明确创新是引领发展的第一动力，协调是持续健康发展的内在要求，绿色是永续发展的必要条件和人民对美好生活追求的重要体现，开放是国家繁荣发展的必由之路，共享是中国特色社会主义的本质要求，努力实现更高质量、更有效率、更加公平、更可持续的发展。

随着人类全面进入知识经济时代，全球发展越来越依靠知识和创新，而驱动知识和创新的"三架马车"就是教育、科技和人才。中国把教育、科技、人才作为全面建设社会主义现代化国家的基础性、战略性支撑，通过教育优先发展夯实人力资源深度开发基础，通过科技自立自强不断开拓创新，通过人才引领驱动巩固发展优势，赢得竞争主动。工程教育是教育、科技、人才三个关键要素的集合体，对于实现高质量发展具有基础性、战略性支撑意义，对于达成可持续发展目标也同样具有基础性、战略性的支撑意义。联合国提出的17项可持续发展目标都与工程有关，每个目标都需要工程来实现。无论是加强基础设施建设以支撑现代经济发展、消除贫困，还是推动农业和粮食生产机械化以消除饥饿、实现全球粮食安全；无论是发展生物医学工程先进技术以改善全球健康状况、提高人民生活质量，还是创造在线学习工具以支撑教育发展、推动优质教育资源共享，工程不断为人类生存与发展问题提供解决方案，使可持续发展成为可能。工程教育承载着培养未来工程师的重要使命。要培养出能够应对未来挑战、实现可持续发展目标的卓越工程师，就必须将跨学科知识整合、工程技术创新、可持续发展价值观等有机融合在工程教育之中。因此可以说，工程教育最具有推动落实联合国2030年《可持续发展议程》的潜能。

第三，工程教育的数字化智能化转型需要电子信息赋能。当前，数字技术正以新理念、新业态、新模式全面融入人类经济、政治、文化、社会、生态文明建设各领域和全过程，给人类生产生活带来广泛而深刻的影响。数据对提高生产效率的乘数作用不断凸显，成为最具时代特征的生产要素。数据的爆发增长、海量集聚蕴藏了巨大的价值，为智能化发展带来了新的机遇。在全球数字化转型、智能化加速的大背景下，数字经济日益成为推动经济高质量发展的重要引擎和影响世界经济格局的重要因素。世界主要国家都高度重视发展数字经济，努力挖掘经济增长新动能，打造国家竞争新优势。党的十八大以来，我国数字经济发展呈现强劲态势，数字经济规模连续多年稳居世界第二位，从2012年的11万亿元增至2021年的45.5万亿元，占GDP的比重由21.6%提升到39.8%，成为推动经济增长的主要引擎之一。

在数字化智能化转型的时代背景下，产业数字化与数字产业化深入推进，新技术、新产品、新业态不断涌现，这对工程创新人才培养提出了更高要求，工程教育同样要拥抱数字化智能化创新。当前，欧洲、美国、印度等已提出了一系列数字化转型背景下工程教育未来发展的战略构想与政策建议，我国也把"实施教育数字化战略行动""加快推进教育数字转型和智能升级"写入了2022年的《教育部工作要点》，数字化智能化转型深刻改变工程教育未来走向的大趋势不可阻挡。

可持续发展和数字化智能化转型都是世界经济增长的新动力，两者能够相互促进。可持续发展为数字化智能化转型指明了基本原则和应用方向，数字化智能化转型是实现可持续发展目标的有效途径，有助于在全球范围内加快落实2030年可持续发展议程。可以说，数字化智能化转型能够推动每一项可持续发展目标的实现，包括清洁饮水和卫生设施、廉价和清洁能源、体面工作和经济增长、可持续城市和社区、负责任的消费和生产、气候行动等。举例而言，未来能源系统将以新能源为主体，以电力、热能等多种能源形式为载体，以能源技术与信息技术深度融合为特征，实现能源的互济互补和安全高效使用。数字化智能化技术在新型电力系统中的应用，将帮助我们更好地应对气候变化，实现可持续发展。研究表明，到2030年，智能电网和综合能源管理系统等能效技术的应用，将帮助减少高达1.8吉吨（Gt）的二氧化碳排放当量，占全球二氧化碳排放量的20%。

在数字化智能化转型的时代，电子信息学科是基石，电子科学与技术追求更精准的操控电荷与电磁场，实现精密传感与测量。在此基础上，通信与信息系统实现海量信息的高速获取、传输、存储与智能化处理，使数字世界与物理世界更加紧密地融合在一起。这样的特质使得电子信息学科成为赋能型学科，通过与产业需求结合和多学科交叉融合，构建"共生型组织"，营造完整的产业生态，更好地赋能产业发展。当前，自动驾驶技术、新型通信网络、空间技术、智能芯片、量子技术等电子信息领域的前沿代表性技术在数字医疗、智能交通、智慧城市、新型能源系统等领域的创新应用，已经为经济社会发展提供了新动力新引擎。例如，在医疗行业，云计算、大数据、人工智能等新兴技术在提升诊断效率、提高准确度、制订有效治疗方案、推动个性化治疗等方面发挥了巨大作用。在政策推动、技术迭代、市场演变等因素的共同作用下，数字医疗正在与医疗保健深度结合，精准医学、移动医疗、远程保健等在5G、大数据、区块链和人工智能等技术的保障下，促进了数字医疗保健行业的发展。

电子信息赋能数字化智能化转型，是高等工程教育的发展方向。首先，工程教育需主动对接产业数字化智能化发展需求，将电子信息技术纳入各工程领域的人才培养方案，实现工程人才培养供给侧与产业数字化智能化发展需求侧的有效匹配。全球很多大学的电子信息类课程已被纳入各工科院系的培养方案，电路、编程、数据分析正在成为每位工程专业学生的必修课。其次，需加快数字化智能化技术在工程教育领域的深度应用，借助电子信息技术变革传统的工科教学、学习方式，提升工程教育效果。计算机辅助设计、虚拟现实、3D打印等技术的应用，可以使抽象的概念具象化，更易于学生理解和掌握。此外，将电子信息技术与学习科学相融合，可以获得真实教育情境下学生的学习行为、师生互动、学习兴趣等数据，并以此为基础改进教师的教学方式和学生的学习方法，提升工程教育质量。最后，电子信息技术强化了人与人、人和组织之间的联系，使得工程教育能够与行业密切互动，促进产教融合、协同育人。越来越多的企业专家可以通过前沿讲座、工程实践、课程讲授等方式参与到人才培养中。2022年，清华大学成立了国家卓越工程师学院，并与业界紧密结合，推进工程硕博生培养体系重构和流程再造，探索工程人才培养新格局。

世界正在变化，教育也必须改变。作为教育改革中跑得最快、需求最多、动静最大、影响最深远的领域，工程教育正在迈向更具融合性、更有创新性、更全面、更有效的发展方向，充分彰显了当前高等教育发展的时代特征，描绘了高等教育可能的未来图景。在全球积极落实2030年《可持续发展议程》，我国将高质量发展与《可持续发展议程》有机结合的时代背景下，工程教育对全球的可持续发展具有基础性、战略性支撑意义，将为人类社会实现可持续发展目标提供巨大潜能。当前，数字化智能化转型如火如荼，高等工程教育要充分回应数字化智能化转型引起的产业变革新需求，渗透性、交叉性极强的电子信息技术将为面向数字化智能化时代的工程教育改革创新提供有力抓手、赋予不竭动力。

最后，让我们以更先进的、更人性化的电子信息技术，携手步入一个全新的数字化智能化时代；让我们充分发挥电子信息技术的赋能优势，为工程教育的发展绘就美好的明天，为人类社会的可持续发展创造光明的未来！

谢谢大家！

特邀报告

龚克

南开大学教授，南开大学学术委员会主任，中国新一代人工智能发展战略研究院执行院长

GONG Ke

Professor of Nankai University, Director of Academic Committee of Nankai University, Executive Director of Chinese Institute of New Generation Artificial Intelligence Development Strategies

    教授，南开大学学术委员会主任，中国新一代人工智能发展战略研究院执行院长，曾担任世界工程组织联合会（WFEO）主席（2019—2021），联合国秘书长科学顾问委员会成员（2014—2017），清华大学副校长（1999—2006），天津大学校长（2006—2011），南开大学校长（2011—2018），第七、八届中国科学技术协会常务委员会委员等。在主持中国数字电视无线传输标准和微型技术试验卫星的研发等工作中获国家技术发明奖和国防科学技术进步奖等荣誉。

    Professor, Chairperson of the Academic Committee of Nankai University, Executive Director of Chinese Institute of New Generation Artificial Intelligence Development Strategies. He had served as President of World Federation of Engineering Organization (2019–2021), member of the Science Advisory Board of UN Secretary General (2014–2017), Vice President of Tsinghua University (1999–2006), President of Tianjin University (2006–2011), President of Nankai University (2011–2018), and a member of the 7th and 8th Standing Committee of China Association for Science and Technology. He obtained the National Technological Invention Award and National Defense Science and Technology Award for his achievements in directing the research and development of China's digital television wireless transmission standard and micro-technical test satellite.

双重转型下的工程教育

龚 克

很高兴听到益一哉校长和王希勤校长的主旨发言,特别是对工程教育在可持续发展和数字化转型两个方面的基础性及战略性作用的讨论。

工程是运用科学技术解决人类生产生活问题的实践,也是经济社会发展的主要驱动力。在当前的数字化转型和可持续发展的双重转型时代,工程技术需要具备绿色低碳、高效安全和公平包容等特点,而工程教育的任务就是培养能够负责任地运用和创新科学技术的工程人才。为了适应这一新时代,工程教育需要进行改革转型。

为什么需要转型呢?因为实现可持续发展是当前人类最迫切的需求。17个可持续发展目标涵盖了经济、社会、环境三个维度,而工程技术和工程师在其中发挥着至关重要的作用。因此,为了适应可持续发展的要求,工程教育需要调整教学内容和方法,强化可持续发展的理念,并将数字化技术与绿色技术相结合,培养具有创新能力和责任心的工程人才。

怎么转型呢?需要从三个方面入手:一是调整课程体系和教学方法,把可持续发展的理念和知识,融入通识的和专业的课程,特别是将数字化技术与绿色技术相结合;二是建立产学研合作机制,让学生在实践中学习,并将科研成果应用到工程实践中;三是加强跨学科、跨国界的交流合作,培养与不同学科、不同文化的团队合作的能力,吸收先进经验,拓宽视野,提高人才解决复杂问题的全球竞争力。

总之,工程教育需要适应双重转型的时代需求,加强与可持续发展和数字化转型的结合,培养具备创新能力和责任心的工程人才。

工程对可持续发展至关重要,工程师作为工程的实践者,肩负实现可持续发展的重要责任。可持续发展目标是一个目标体系,这个目标体系围绕的核心问题是人类福祉与保护自然环境之间的矛盾,解决这个矛盾就要在自然可承受的前提下实现人类的福祉,这就需要协调连接目标,如清洁能源、产业创新、消除不平等等。气候变化是人类共同面临的严峻挑战,控制温度必须实现零碳排放。自工业革命以来,可以说人类一直在以碳排放发展生产和组织生活，所以说，实现碳中和是一个革命性的转型，工程技术、工程教育都要适应这个转型。不仅是降碳，其他全球问题包括饮用水、卫生设施和数字连接等，都与工程息息相关。可以说，联合国《可持续发展议程》确定的17个目标，每一个都关系到工程科学技术，工程教育必须适应这个需求。

再拿减碳来说，它的关键在于能源变革。《可持续发展议程》中的目标7，要求提高全球可再生能源比例和能效改善率。中国煤炭资源相对丰富，目前是世界上最大的能源消费国和燃煤国，我们需改变以煤炭为主的能源结构才能达到碳中和目标，这是一个严峻挑战。同时，控制化石能源消费、推动能源革命和建设新型能源体系都需要工程技术创新和实施。电子信息技术应成为这些使能者，在光伏、风力、水力和地热等方面，电子信息技术大有可为。能源革命涉及工程的各个方面，现代工程依托化石能源发展起来，现在要转向低碳发展，这是一个非常深刻的变革和转型。

第四次工业革命是数字化革命，是以数字技术为革命性通用技术的产业革命。为适应这场工业革命的要求，工程教育也需要进行转型，即要适应可持续发展和数字化双重转型。

此外，还必须认识到，可持续发展是经济、社会、环境三个维度的全面发展，不仅仅是环境保护。它特别强调要确保包容和公平的优质教育，让全民拥有终身学习的机会。其中，一个具体目标是确保所有参与学习的人都掌握可持续发展所需的知识和技能。因此，工程教育必须确保实现这个目标，确保所有参与工程教育学习的人都具备这些知识和技能。

可持续发展所需的知识和技能包括认知能力与实践能力。认知能力需要结合自身的专业和行业，认知可持续发展的指标，并超越自身的专业和行业，从经济、社会、生态三个维度更深入地了解和认识可持续发展问题。实践能力需要在规划、设计、制造、检测、使用、维护管理的所有工程环节中，结合各自专业领域工作，通过创新技术来破解可持续发展的问题。

另外，工程教育还需进一步打牢科学基础，增强数字化创新能力。新兴的数字技术已经不再是一项专门的技术，而是推动经济社会发展的一个通用使能技术，必须成为现代工程教育中的重要角色。未来的工程师必须适应在普遍互联的、数据驱动的、人工智能（AI）赋能的、开源开放的数字化的工程环境中，来从事自身专业领域的数字化的创新。

工程教育的目标是提升工程师的职业胜任力。为了做到这一点，工程教育需要加强对可持续发展的认知和实践能力的培养，夯实宽广的科学基础知识，提升数字化创新能力、动手实践的能力，以及跨专业、跨行业、跨国界、跨文化的协同工作能力，等等，并且提升履行工程伦理的操守，从而担起当代工程师推动数字化和绿色化双重转型的历史使命。

2021年，习近平总书记在中央人才工作会议上强调了培养卓越工程师的重要性。总书记指出，制造业需要大量高质量的工程师，当前我们面临的问题是工程师数量不足、质量不高。因此，在深化改革的过程中，我们需要实现产教融合，打破学科框架限制，探索建立中国特色世界水平的工程师培养体系。

深化改革实现产教融合，要调动好高校和企业的积极性。高校要深化工程教育改革，加大理工科人才培养的分量，探索实施高校和企业联合培养高素质复合型工程人才的有效机制。而企业则需要加大对工程教育的支持力度，同时也需要与高校紧密合作，共同推动工程教育的发展。

总的来说，工科教育在培养卓越工程师方面担负巨大责任。我们需要适应可持续发展和数字化双重转型的要求，实现产教融合，跳出学科框架限制，只有这样，我们才能确保工程教育能够为推动社会进步作出更大的贡献。

IFEE 2022

第三届国际工程教育论坛
The 3rd International Forum On Engineering Education

分组论坛 A1
Panel A1

电子信息使能技术
Enabling Technology With Electronics And Information Science

2022 年 12 月 8 日 20:00–22:30

承办单位简介

清华大学电子工程系

清华大学电子工程系于1952年建系，已发展成为清华大学规模最大的院系之一，构建起了"电子科学与技术""信息与通信工程"两个一级学科，参与共建"集成电路科学与工程"一级学科。下设6个研究所，涵盖物理电子学与光电子学、电路与系统、电磁场与微波技术、通信与信息系统、智能信号与信息处理、复杂系统与网络等研究领域，学科齐全、综合性强；建成了工学学士，工学硕士、工程硕士，工学博士、工程博士的完整培养体系，构建起了世界领先的覆盖两个一级学科核心概念的新课程体系，向社会输送了大批优秀人才；形成了"亦工亦理、教研并重"的办学理念、"严谨、勤奋、求实、创新"的学术风格，以及"团结务实、学术自由、追求卓越"的文化传统。学科的专业排名近年来居国际前十。

About the Organizer

The Department of Electronic Engineering, Tsinghua University

The Department of Electronic Engineering of Tsinghua University, formally established in 1952, has been developed to be one of the largest departments at Tsinghua University. The Department has two national first-level disciplines, namely Electronic Sciences and Technology and Information and Communication Engineering, which encompass the research areas of Physical Electronics and Optoelectronics, Circuits and Systems, Electromagnetic Field and Microwave Technology, Communication and Information Systems, Signal and Information Processing, and Complex Systems and Network. The Department composes the most complete and comprehensive disciplines in Electronic Engineering in China. Complete programs of Bachelor of Science, Master of Science, Master of Engineering, Doctor of Science, and Doctor of Engineering have been set up, and a new world-class curriculum system covering the core concepts of both first-level disciplines has been constructed accordingly. More than ten thousand students have graduated and contributed to the development of China and the world in relevant fields. It established a culture that integrates both science and engineering, teaching and research, promoting diligence, pracmatism, solidarity, academitic liberty and creativity. The Department has been ranked around tenth in the recent worldwide university ranking of electronic engineering.

分论坛主持

主持人 Chair

郝智彪
清华大学电子工程系教授，电子工程系学术委员会主任
HAO Zhibiao
Professor and Chair of Academic Committee of Department of Electronic Engineering, Tsinghua University

分别于1996年7月和2002年1月获清华大学电子工程系学士学位和工学博士学位，后留校从事教学科研工作。2006—2007年在美国加州大学洛杉矶分校进行访问研究。主要研究方向是低维半导体材料的外延生长、新型光电子器件及应用技术。发表科学引文索引（SCI）论文230余篇，授权国家发明专利15项，获得省部级科技一等奖3项。

Hao Zhibiao received his B.S. and Ph.D. Degrees from the Department of Electronic Engineering at Tsinghua University in 1996 and 2001, respectively. He worked at the University of California Los Angeles as a visiting scholar from 2006 to 2007. His research interests include the epitaxial growth of low-dimensional III–V semiconductor materials and novel optoelectronic devices based on low-dimensional semiconductors. He has published more than 230 peer-reviewed SCI papers.

王孙禺
清华大学教育研究院教授，国际工程教育中心副主任兼秘书长
WANG Sunyu
Professor of Institute of Education, Tsinghua University; Deputy Director and Secretary-General of ICEE

清华大学教育研究院教授。现任联合国教科文组织国际工程教育中心副主任兼秘书长。曾任清华大学教育研究所所长，人文社科学院副院长、党委书记，《清华大学教育研究》杂志主编，中国工程教育专业认证协会学术委员会主任等。曾获国家级教学成果奖，多次获哲学社会科学优秀成果奖、教育科学研究优秀成果奖。2019年11月，获世界工程组织联合会（WFEO）主席特别致谢奖章。主持和参与中国工程院、国家自然科学基金委员会、教育部重大研究课题多项，包括我国加入国际工程教育认证组织《华盛顿协议》等。

Wang Sunyu once served as the Director of the Institute of Education as well as the Vice President and the Party Secretary of the School of Humanities and Social Sciences at Tsinghua University, Editor-in-Chief of *Tsinghua Journal of Education*, and Director of the Academic Committee of China Engineering Education Accreditation Association (CEEAA), etc. He is a winner of the National Teaching Achievement Award, and also a repeat winner of the Award for Outstanding Achievements in Philosophy and Social Sciences and the Award for Outstanding Achievements in Educational Scientific Research in China and Beijing for many times. In November 2019, he was awarded a Special Acknowledgement Medal by the President of World Federation of Engineering Organizations (WFEO). He has presided at and participated in multiple major research projects of the Chinese Academy of Engineering, the National Natural Science Foundation of China and the Ministry of Education, including China's accession to the Washington Accord, the most influential agreement of international recognition of engineering education programs.

王大同

柏林工业大学教授，德国科学院院士，美国国家工程院院士，俄罗斯科学院院士

Dieter BIMBERG

Member of GAS; Member of NAE; Member of RAS; Professor of Technical University of Berlin

德国法兰克福大学博士。2018年4月，任中国科学院长春光学精密机械与物理研究所"Bimberg中德绿色光子学研究中心"主任。德国科学院、欧洲科学院的成员，俄罗斯科学院、美国国家工程院和美国国家发明家科学院院士，美国物理学会和电气与电子工程师协会（IEEE）的终身会员，获得英国兰卡斯特大学和俄罗斯科学院圣彼得堡大学的名誉博士学位。获得多个国际奖项，发表1500余篇论文，获得61项专利，出版6本专著。总引用量超过65000次，H因子高达111。研究领域包括纳米结构的物理和技术，纳米结构的光电器件以及节能数据通信等。

Dieter Bimberg received his Ph.D. from Goethe University. In 2018, he assumed the directorship of the "Bimberg Chinese German Center for Green Photonics" of the Chinese Academy of Sciences at CIOMP, Changchun. Bimberg is a member of the German Academy of Sciences Leopoldina, the EU Academy of Sciences, a foreign member of the Russian Academy of Sciences, the US Academies of Engineering and of Inventors, a life fellow of the American Physical Society and the Institute of Electrical and Electronics Engineers, IEEE. He is recipient of multiple international awards, He received honorary doctorates of the University of Lancaster, UK, and the St. Petersburg University of the Russian Academy of Sciences. He has published more than 1500 papers, 61 patents, and six books. His research works has been cited for over 65,000 times and his Hirsch factor reaches 111. His research interests include the physics and technology of nanostructures, nanostructured hotonic and electronic devices, and energy-efficient data communication, etc.

绿色数据通信：智能物理和工程技术支持可持续社会

王大同

大家好，我今天的演讲主要包括三个方面。首先介绍当前互联网技术遇到的主要问题，其次探讨我们对未来互联网的预测，最后简单聊一聊与技术相关的问题。

对于互联网技术而言，当前一个很严重的问题就是能耗。我们需要开发一些新型的技术，包括光子的技术、光子的设备、电子的技术、电子的设备，从而降低能量的使用。现在我们的数据中心对能源的消耗十分巨大，每一个基于数据中心的应用必须通过量身制做的设计才能提升本身的能效。为了提升能效，我们认为有效的途径主要包括如下三种：一是几何的变化；二是改变光子的寿命；三是改变设备的使用方式。

首先介绍当前应用消耗能量的现状。目前，我们的数据中心的使用频率以每年60%的速度在增长，这个速度比前几年斯科公司预测的要快得多。那么，是哪些应用在使用数据中心呢？我们发现很多都是最近几年兴起的技术，如区块链、流媒体、车联网等。相关数据显示，区块链在全球的耗电量达到了70.3TWH，相应会导致34Mtons的二氧化碳排放；流媒体耗电量达到了350 TWH，相应会导致1.7Mtons的二氧化碳排放。此外，像谷歌这样的搜索引擎也需要消耗大量的能量。我们再看一看最近几年出现的车联网技术，当前，与车联网相关的数据流动大概有3~5Gbit/s，如果按天计算的话，每天就会有10 Tbit的数据，如果再考虑端口数的话就更多了。我们再从以太网标准的角度看一看，2020年的标准是200Gbit/s，2030年则会达到1.6Tbit/s。按此计算，每条车道的速率需要达到25~28Gbit/s或50~100Gbit/s，甚至还会更多。

2022年，数据中心使用的电量达到了新的高峰，大数据方面的耗电量已经占到全球总量的10%，预计到2030年，数据中心的用电量还会在此基础上增长4倍，这些电量的主要用途是降温。当然，增长4倍是最糟糕的情况，而最理想的情况是增长2倍。那么，为此我们应该做些什么呢？目前，数据会在服务器内部以及服务器之间流动，不同数据之间、数据连接之间都会有很多能耗。比如，当服务器内部流动1Kbit数据时，这1Kbit数据除了在传输和处理时需要能量，还需要额外的能量为服务器降温。降温的成本会比购买硬件的成本还要高，如果考虑能耗成本，设备采购成本都可以忽略不计。因为相比之下，采购成本是太小的一部分了。根据统计的数据，美国耗电量的8%~10%用于计算中心。而在未来，我们希望能够以更大速率传输数据，达到100~400Gbit/s。因此，传输每一个比特的能耗需要很低才行，目前我们期望这个数值低于100fJ/bit（要求传输2km以上）。虽然单纯提升数据传输速率并不是特别难，但是同时兼顾低能耗的要求则是一个很大的挑战。因为，按照目前的技术，比特率是与电流的平方根成正比的，在这样的情况下，上述速率和能耗的要求之间是相互矛盾的。因此，我们需要找寻新的解决途径。在数据传输的过程中，能量与比特速率比值（EDR）按以下公式计算：

$$比特速率（BR）= \frac{传输的比特数}{时间} \quad 能量与比特速率比值（EDR）= \frac{(I \cdot V)}{BR}$$

首先，我们考虑在电缆的传输过程中降低EDR。电缆的结构非常复杂，共有50层。每一层的材料都需要精心地选择。在柏林的研发中心，我们研制电缆的寿命能够达到20年，每秒传输20~25Gbit数据，中央处理器处理1~3Tbit数据。其次，保持恒定的温度是非常重要的，但是在这方面，我们还没有开展具体的实验，在下一步实验中，我们会重点关注温度的因素。

进一步地，我们看一看单模速率的方程等式，该等式如下：

$$H(f) = \frac{f_R^2}{\left(f_R^2 - f^2 + i\frac{\gamma}{2\pi}f\right)} \frac{1}{1 + i\frac{f}{f_p}}$$

大家可以看到γ是一个因子，它代表阻尼效应。除此之外，存在着以下公式：

$$\gamma = 4\pi^2 \cdot \tau_p\left(1 + \frac{\Gamma_\epsilon}{g'}\right)f_R^2 + FSS$$

对于镍化硅这样的材质，在蚀刻（etching）和涂层（coating）二者的作用下，功率反射会有不同的值以及不同的变化趋势，我们会使用这些性质进行一个综合的设计。举一个简单的例子，当我们改变光子的寿命时，镍化硅的厚度就从87nm变到了188nm。

其次，对于大数据中心来讲非常重要的一点是光子的寿命必须有适应性，必须与数据传输速率保持一致。从图1可以看出，如果不断地提高比特率，每秒达50Gbit时（左图中标记五角星的位置），选择小会是更好的选择；而当数据率为25Gbit/s时（右图中标记五角星的位置），能耗更小。因此，我们可以对功率反射率做一个优化，将能够减少75%的能量。

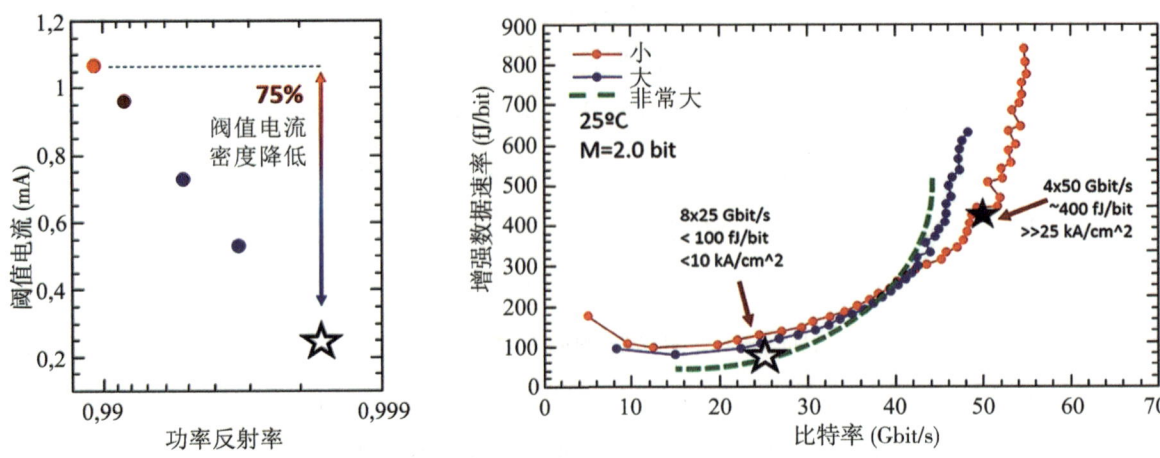

图1 能量与数据率比值关于数据率的曲线

接下来，我们自然会问，数据中心应该以什么样的数据率运行呢？是20Gbit/s、25Gbit/s，还是50Gbit/s？这在很大程度上决定了耗能。通过光纤并行传输能够提升速率，但需要考虑最优的并行光纤数量，以降低建设成本。我们通过实验发现4个信道是比8个信道更好一些的选择。然而，采用多维复用的技术时，一些部件会产生热量，这使得整体线路的性能受到影响，需要进一步限制散热造成的影响。为此，我们提出采用单模单孔或者是单模多孔结构的垂直腔面发射激光器（VCSEL），并对里面的小孔进行布局优化。在图2左上角的子图中，一共有6个小孔围绕着中间的激光点，相当于它的接收面积增加了6倍。我们又尝试一些其他的分布状况，右下角的子图是我们最新的研究成果，它可以实现非常低的功率。

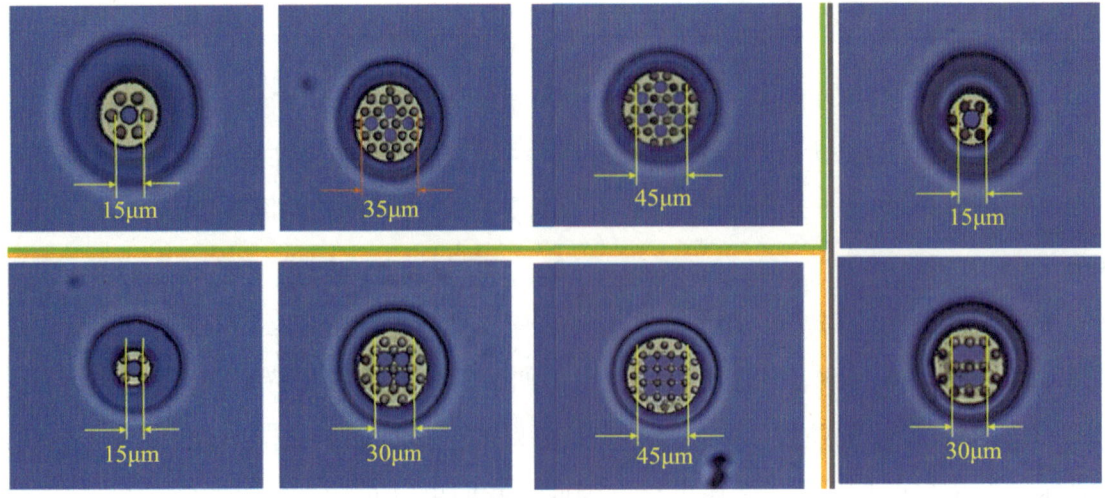

图2 垂直腔面发射激光器孔径设计

除此之外，我们对于光缆之间连接的耗电损耗也有一定的要求，希望小于1pJ/bit；进一步地，我们测试了我们研发的垂直腔面发射激光器，它的功耗为100fJ/bit，其中一个65nm的互补金属氧化物半导体（CMOS）能耗为0.56pJ/bit，而一个硅锗双极晶体管（BiCMOS）的能耗可以达到3.2pJ/bit。然而，目前几乎没有大型电路的开发商关注高速互补金属氧化物半导体的能效问题。一些研究表明，电压型互补金属氧化物半导体对功耗的要求更低，22nm的全耗尽型绝缘体上硅（COMS FDSOI）的能耗可以在0.5pJ/bit。在实验中，我们成功实现了数据率为60Gbit/s时，将EDR控制在500fJ/bit以下。

最后我想说，我们看到的这些技术，在过去20年，有很多的成果来自中国，中国有非常优秀的专家，他们非常值得骄傲。最后，我引用中国一位哲学家的话结束今天的演讲，那就是"学以致用"。谢谢！

罗毅
中国工程院院士，清华大学电子工程系教授
LUO Yi
Member of CAE; Professor, Department of Electronic Engineering, Tsinghua University

1995年，获国家杰出青年科学基金资助，1999年，获聘教育部"长江学者奖励计划"特聘教授。1997—2012年，连续三届担任集成光电子学国家重点联合实验室主任，现任北京信息科学与技术国家研究中心副主任。2021年，当选为中国工程院院士。主要研究化合物半导体光电子器件及其集成应用技术，包括激光器、发光二极管（LED）、光调制器、光探测器，以及其在光纤通信、宽带信息感知、半导体照明等领域的应用。发表学术论文367篇，授权发明专利34项。获得国家技术发明奖二等奖3项，国家科学技术进步奖二等奖1项。

Luo Yi is a professor of the Department of Electronic Engineering at Tsinghua University, an academician of Chinese Academy of Engineering, the deputy director of Beijing National Research Center for Information Science and Technology. He received his B.S. degree from Tsinghua University in 1983, and his M.S. and Ph.D. degrees from the University of Tokyo, Japan, in 1987 and 1990, respectively. He has been a professor in the Department of Electronic Engineering at Tsinghua University since 1992. His research focuses on compound semiconductor optoelectronic devices and their integrated application technologies (including DFB lasers, LEDs, light modulators, and photodetectors), as well as their applications in optical fiber communication, broadband information sensing, and semiconductor lighting.

高速光电子器件是信息技术的使能技术

罗 毅

我想跟大家探讨的是高速光电子器件。首先，我想问一个问题，为什么高速光电子器件是信息技术的驱动力呢？我觉得主要有以下三个方面的原因：一是光波具有非常高的带宽；二是光波可以传递能量或者信息；三是光的波动性。

基于光波的这三种性质，我们可以知道高速的光纤网络是非常重要的，它是我们信息技术的骨干之一。一根光纤在理论上每秒能够传输100Tbit的数据，不难想象，要实现这样超高速的传输，这个过程是非常复杂的，不是一台简单的设备能够实现的，它是一项系统性工程，需要几百台设备集合在一起，才能把数据以每秒100Tbit的速度传输出去。

中国国土面积很大，建设全国范围的光纤网络是一项大工程。据了解，目前中国几乎所有的乡村都已经覆盖了光纤。我们曾去过新疆的边远地区，那里的光纤网络已经非常发达。现在的光纤网络已经成为我国通信网络的骨干，我国有10亿的手机用户，他们需要使用无线网络（Wi-Fi）、5G，而在无线接入的背后，就是发达的有线光纤网络。因此，光通信技术已经给我们带来了很多便利。

光纤网络当然不能缺乏核心的通信设备，如高速单模激光器、调制器，单模的激光器加调制器、单片集成光源以及高速探测器等。对于高速的设备，我们重点关注的是如何实现高速率的目标，速率对于数字光纤通信、数据中心和无线通信来说，都是一项重要的指标。

在光通信中，数据传输是一项非常重要的环节。我想简单介绍一下模拟传输和数字传输的优缺点。对于数字传输而言，最简单的通信模式叫作通断键控调制（OOK），这种技术的速率与带宽成正比，如果我们想要很高的数据率传输数据，就需要很大的带宽，同时需要很大的功率。但是如果我们想发送相同的数据量，却没有充足的带宽资源，模拟系统和先进调制方式的结合是一个更好的选择。然而，模拟系统对噪声和扰动更为敏感，因此对数据传输的管理也更加严格。

接下来介绍一下我们团队在光电子器件领域取得的一些科研成果。如图1所示的模型是我们设计的一种激光调制器，这里面集成了四个并行的调制器。图2则给出了该激光器件在预置电流下的输出功率以及四个光源调制响应的光谱。

图1　团队研发的激光调制器

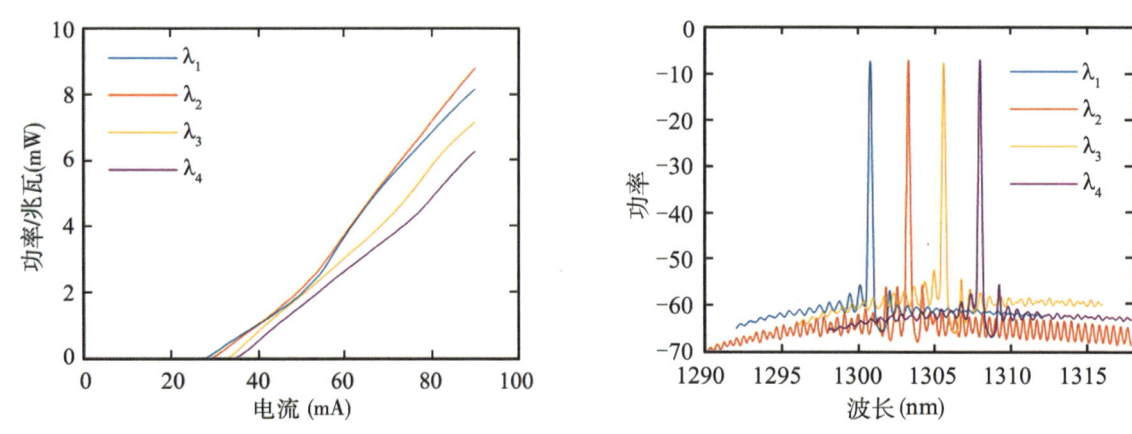

图2　预制电流与输出功率关系曲线（左）和调制器光谱图（右）

图3展示了大信号调制下的性能，我们的实验是在采用28Gbits/s非归零编码（Non-Return-to-Zero coding，NRZ）和通断键控调制情况下得到的。可以看到，信号在传输22km之后，接收的眼图还是很清晰的开眼。

除此之外，我们还设计了一个类似的设备，图4给出了比特率为56Gbits/s时，传输10km之后的接收眼图。

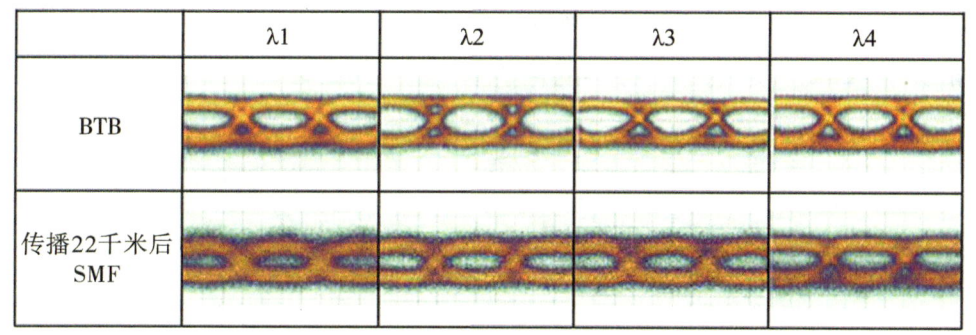

图3　28bits/s 大信号调制下传输前与传输22km 后的眼图

图4　56Gbits/s 大信号调制下传输前与传输10km 后的眼图

接下来，我想向大家介绍一下高速设备对模拟信号的传输情况。对于调制器而言，模拟信号要求很低的半波的电压，很低的插入损耗，以及更高的带宽，这些要求是模拟传输有别于数字传输的方面。我们与麻省理工学院合作，设计了如图5所示的薄膜铌酸锂调制器。通过将电子和光学的整合，该器件改进了光学的约束（optical confinement）以及速度匹配（velocity matching)的情况。

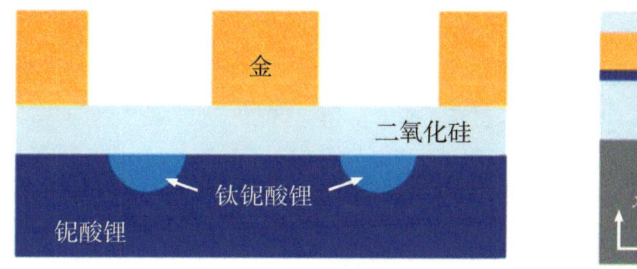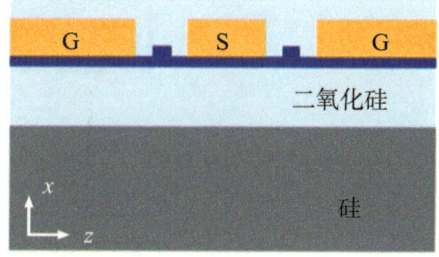

图5　传统的铌酸锂调制器（左）和合作中提出的薄膜铌酸锂调制器（右）

图6给出了我们提出的薄膜铌酸锂调制器半波电压,可以看到,我们的半波电压为 $V_\pi L=1.7V\ cm$,这是一个很棒的性能。

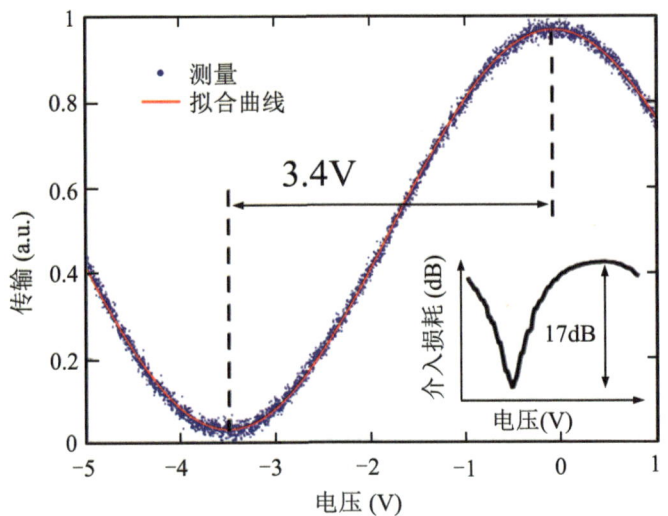

图6 薄膜铌酸锂调制器的低频调制性能(调制波长 =5mm)

但是,这个器件有一个缺点,从图7我们可以看到,在饱和功率点附近,如果稍微增加功率,电场将会降到零。

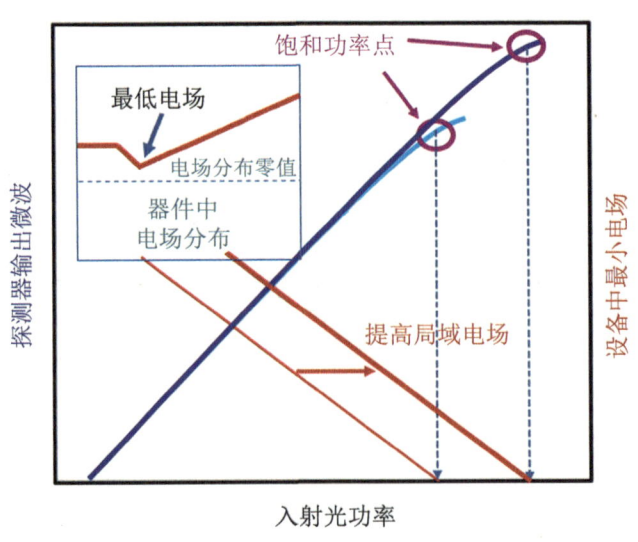

图7 饱和功率点附近电场变化

为此,我们改进了设备的结构,让响应率可以达到0.165A/W,响应情况见图8。可以看到,这是一个很棒的性能。

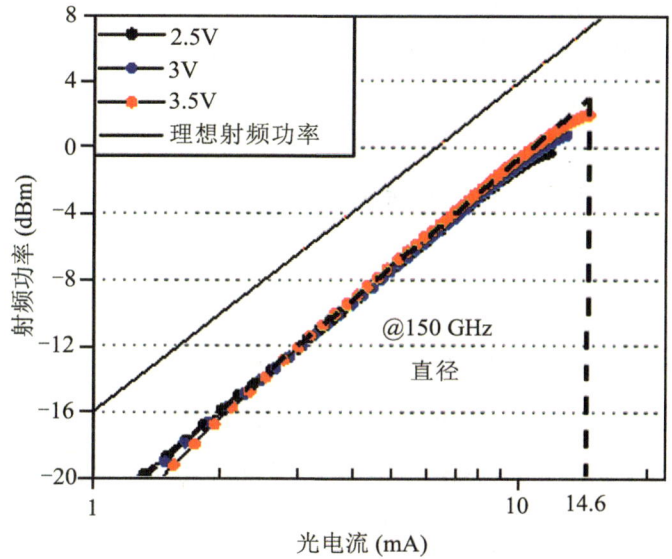

图8 光电流与射频功率响应

由于时间关系，我就介绍到这里。最后，非常高兴能够与来自不同国家的专家们分享我们的一些研究成果。超宽带通信是数字经济的基础，高速光电子器件是光信通信的基石，希望我们的工作能够推动高速光电子器件的发展，让我们离超宽带通信更近一步。谢谢！

詹姆斯·埃文斯
芝加哥大学社会学系和计算机研究所知识实验室主任
James EVANS
Director of the Knowledge Lab in the Department of Sociology and the Institute for Computer Science, University of Chicago

芝加哥大学马克斯·帕列夫斯基教授、知识实验室和计算社会科学项目主任，圣达菲研究所客座教授。重点研究对象是思考和认识的集体系统，研究范围包括人类注意力和直觉的分布、想法的起源和共同的逻辑推理习惯。致力于通过众包、文本处理和图像识别以及使用分布式传感器，创建用于理解人类行动的新型观测方法。使用机器学习、生成建模、社会和语义网络表示探索知识的产生过程，并创建了当前科学发现机制的替代方案。他在《科学》《自然》《美国科学院院刊》，以及顶级社会和计算机科学媒体上发表了多篇文章，并被媒体广泛报道。

James Evans is a Max Palevsky Professor of Sociology, Director of the Knowledge Lab and the Computational Social Science program at the University of Chicago and the Santa Fe Institute. His research focuses on the collective system of thinking and knowing, ranging from the distribution of human attention and intuition, the origin of ideas and shared habits of logical reasoning. He is devoted to create a new observatory approach to understand human behavior through crowd-sourcing, information extraction from text and images, and the use of distributed sensors. He employs machine learning, generative modeling, social and semantic network representations to explore knowledge-producing processes, to scale up interpretive and field-methods, and to create alternatives to current discovery regimes. He has been published in *Science, Nature, PNAS*, and top social and computer science outlets. His work has been exposed widely in mass media.

互补型人工智能可以改进人类技术的发展

詹姆斯·埃文斯

我们讲一下与人类互补的技术——AI技术，以及它的一些优越性。我现在主管一个实验室，主要负责一些大数据和机器学习的业务以及智能的一些技术，我们的基本愿望是要建构一个系统，通过创新优化，影响和改变社会。

我们的第一个问题是：我们想要什么样的AI技术。AI技术是在1945年由图灵（Alan Turing）提出的。当时是在一款电脑游戏中提出了这样的概念，这款游戏叫作模拟游戏（imitation game）。游戏主要通过模拟人类，如模仿人类下棋等，和人类一样完成任务。但是，当时的想法还比较初步，许多步骤还需要人的参与，机器只能承载其中的一小部分任务，尤其是一些具体细节的操作。现在我们谈到AI技术，去谷歌上搜索AI的词条，出现的很多图片都是与人脑相关的图片，因此，现在的AI技术更多是对人类大脑的模拟。但是，这里面存在着一些伦理的问题。目前，全球有70多亿人口，以人为研究对象得到的智能可能并不是最符合道德规范的，也不是最有效的计算智能投资。因此，我今天想要分享一个新概念，叫作外星人智能（alien intelligence），它与人工智能相互补充，通过理解科学本质，增强自然与科学的互补关系，也能够让我们了解科学，以科学的角度去了解自然。

我的教育背景是社会学，从我的角度出发，我想要了解的是社会是怎样思考的，以及我们（作为社会成员）是怎样思考的？通过研究AI与社会的互补关系，我们有以下三点发现。一是多样性、彼此断联的群体能够在科学与社会领域产生更为有力的见解；二是多种彼此不关联的探索能够产生新颖的集体推理；三是AI设计的多样性超越人类的极限。

首先，我们谈一谈中心式群体（centralized communities），在这种群体中产生的科学结论很少有可复制性。在这些方面我们做了很多研究，也发表了很多论文。我们利用AI工具可以对现有科学结论的可靠性和正确性做检测。同时，我们也可以用AI工具对现有科学研究进行关联与分类。因此，对于中心式群体，我们也可以利用AI技术分析其内部存在的关联性和互动性，通过一种可再生的方式，以系统的视角进行观察。我们发现，相较于去中心式群体（decentralized communities），中心式群体中学科之间的关联性更弱，一些结论的复制性也更低。我们在每一个地方都做了这样的观察，希望在这个基础上做一些设计，让 AI 系统和社会之间是可以相互促进的，而不是相互为敌。

我们还做了一些预测地研究，在详细的数据和研究的基础上，依赖 AI 的预测制定相关的政策。我们还会在不同的集群之间做验证性的研究，思考怎样把科学在社会中的作用进行表征，主要用到了推断、演绎和归纳的方法，这些方法都是非常重要的工具。我们用到最多的是归纳方法，用归纳的方法构建一些理论，找寻数据中的规律。在技术方面的研究，我们常常使用演绎的方法，看一看在目前的基础上未来会是什么样子，并做出预判。目前有许多人在和我们做相同的事情，相关方面的研究受到了广泛关注。

我们可以通过不断引入新的思想，验证新的思想，完善我们的模型。对于工程师、科学家来说，当他们进入一个自己不熟悉的领域时，往往能够给这一领域带来一些全新的见解。这些见解中有我们需要挖掘的东西，但是我们如何将这种外化的见解转化为实际模型的提升呢？也就是说，我们如何设计和利用这样的多样性呢？

举个例子，2019年，《自然》杂志刊登了一篇伯克利实验室发表的论文，这篇论文是与物质材料相关的。文章提出，材料有各种物理化学的特性，目前预测这些物理、化学的特性大概有 40% 的准确率，也就是说我们有 40% 的概率发现新的现象与新的技术。因此，我们需要了解如何构建一个假设的世界，通过验证我们的假设，把它慢慢地变成现实。现在大家都会写论文，但是这些理念不应该只是停留在我们的论文中，而是应该转变成实际的东西。以预测人口数量为例，很多文章在预测人口数量什么时候能够达到一个顶峰，我们根据大家预测的结果，可以预测谁会做出最准确的判断。通过收集这些文献的结论，我们可以通过预测，对现有的结论加以干预。

反过来说，我们如何在毫无连接的群体中建立连接呢？如何真正地判断实现这些技术的可能性呢？我们考虑的外星人智能，其实跟现有的系统科学有相悖的地方，有时我们对系统本身越不熟悉，最终发现的结果或是技术反而是越好的。这种相关性或者对准确性的需求，是我们技术进步的重要动力。

在设计的过程中，我们需要考虑什么是最重要的因素。例如库伯基金会，他们做了一些关于药学的研究，放在社会背景之下，有其他的一些论文会探索相关研究多样化的可能性，或者考虑进一步的优化，让机器能够处理更多不同的任务。因为，不同的任务建立在不同的社会基础上，我们需要通过不断地假设和验证改善我们的模型，适应具体的情况。无论是人工智能还是增强现实，都是遵循假设—验证—提升这个循环的，这是我们解决各种挑战的一种基本方式，当然，这需要大量的协作、设计、协调等工作。以上就是我介绍的所有内容，谢谢大家！

周永祖
普渡大学教授，美国国家工程院院士
Weng Cho CHEW
Professor of Purdue University; Member of NAE, US

普渡大学教授，美国国家工程院院士，PIER 期刊的联席主编，IEEE 天线与传播协会平等促进委员会主席。清华大学、香港大学和台湾大学杰出的客座教授。获麻省理工学院的学士、硕士及博士学位。着眼于研究散射成像和计算电磁学的快速算法。最近的研究兴趣是将量子理论和微分几何与电磁学相结合。合著了三本书，发表了 450 多篇期刊论文和 600 多篇会议论文。2000 年获得了 IEEE 研究生教学奖。2008 年获得了 IEEE 天线与传播协会戴振铎杰出教育家奖。2013 年当选为美国国家工程院院士。2015 年获得美国文化交流协会（ACES）计算电磁学奖。2017 年获得 IEEE 电磁学奖。

W.C. Chew is a professor of Purdue University, a member of National Academy of Engineering, the co-Editor-in-chief of PIER Journals and also the chair of the committee on Promoting Equality at IEEE AP society, a distinguished visiting professor at Tsinghua University, HKU, and Taiwan University. He received all his degrees from MIT. His research specialize in fast algorithms for multiple scattering imaging and computational electromagnetics in the last 30 years. His recent research interest is combining quantum theory with electromagnetics, and differential geometry with computational electromagnetics. He has co-authored three books, lecture notes, over 450 journal papers, and over 600 conference papers. In 2000, he received the IEEE Graduate Teaching Award in 2008, he received the IEEE AP-S CT Tai Distinguished Educator Award in 2013, elected the National Academy of Engineering, and in 2015 received the ACES Computational Electromagnetics Award the 2017 IEEE Electromagnetics Award.

培养下一代工程师

周永祖

谢谢主办方邀请我参加这样一个非常有意义的论坛，我汇报的主题是《培养下一代工程师》。首先，我们都在做教育，是教育界的工程师，我们需要方法论，需要科学，因此，我们也必须基于科学去做工程。打个比方，知识就像一棵树，基于科学的工程就是应用我们的知识，等知识长到树顶的时候就会分出很多树杈，这些树杈就相当于我们在真实世界中具体的技术应用了。

相较于简约的知识原理，真正的技术应用往往是非常复杂的。之前在微电子纳米课上，我举过一个例子：一个很小的芯片就有60亿个晶体管，几年后，我们可能会用到万亿级晶体管的芯片，这就像树一样越来越高、越来越大、越来越复杂，但是带来的助力也会越来越大。因此，我想我们是不是可以讲一些非常简约和基本的原理，这对于我们的教育来讲是最为重要的。

如果把一个人比喻成一棵大树，那么我们身体的每一个零件都像树上的一片树叶，任何一个零件出现了问题，身体就工作不了了。所以，我们要确保知识的大树能够成长，任何一个知识细节都不可以漏掉，不可以被忽视。那么，未来的工程师会是什么样子呢？从知识大树的角度分析，首先，他们是跨学科的人才，他们必须有能力融合来自不同学科的知识并且把它应用到工程中；其次，他们需要有团队精神，必须有能力把不同学科的知识融入工程实践，如果缺乏团队精神，也就不可能融合多领域的知识，做出更复杂的系统。

当下，我们面临着越来越严峻的问题：地球变暖、气候变化、日益频繁的战争、日益不平等的社会问题。不平等问题，从殖民时代葡萄牙亨利开始到非洲使用奴隶再到现在，一直都存在。世界上有很多地方生活着比我们贫困得多的人，拥有良好生活条件的我们，更要做好地球的"管家"，保护好我们的地球，尽可能减少碳排放，这也是未来工程师要承担的社会责任。此外，我们要意识到跨学科是十分重要的。知识不会仅在一棵树上生长，而是在很多大树上一起生长。我们需要跟不同的工程师沟通、互动，让教育实现知识的传播与共享。

我的研究方向是电磁学，涉足该领域已经有几十年了。在研究过程中，我也采用了"知识树"这个模型解决问题：看看我们需要什么，找到一些发展的驱动力，跟应用领域的人交流，知道什么是重要的，什么是值得我们关注的，进而获得灵感。

那么，我们如何实现团队的合作呢？爱因斯坦说过一句名言："如果做不到，说明你不懂这个话题。"类比来说，如果我们在上课的时候不能用简单的话语解释它，说明我们本身没有很好地理解要讲解的知识。因此，在跨学科的交流上，我们需要思考如何通俗易懂地表达我们的观点，如果我们讲得深奥难懂，其他行业的工程师就很难理解我们，也无法实现跨学科交流与团队合作。跨学科的培养，给我们开辟了一条道路，可以让我们实现更广泛地交流，让全世界不同地区的人都可以参与。

作为一名老师，我们要教给学生很多的知识，要把知识加以简化，教给学生其中的精华，让学生容易理解。詹姆斯·克拉克·麦克斯韦写的《电磁论》在当时很少有人能读懂，但是随着知识的传播，如今《电磁论》已经是电子领域的基础课程，现在我们已经能够以简单易懂的方式将其中的核心内容讲明白了。另外，就是要避免"填鸭式"教学，不能把知识硬塞到学生的脑子里。学生的大脑不仅是来记忆的，还需要进行逻辑上的锻炼，就如同电脑一般，要使用相关的逻辑运行内存中存储的程序，才能得到各种各样的数据和结果。如何让学生具备吸收更多知识的能力呢？我认为需要延伸他们的思想，只要思想延伸了，很多知识就容易理解，也可以灵活掌握了。除此之外，知识的交流和融合也特别重要，新的知识往往在不同的知识"孤岛"的连接中被发现。我们不能觉得不同的专业需要在不同的田地、农场里深耕。以解决全球变暖问题为例，我们可以联合生物医学、量子力学、化学等领域的同事一起，共同解决温室气体排放的问题，而不是狭隘地认为这件事情仅是由环境领域的工程师负责。

近年来，我一直在推动STEM教育的理念，STEM代表科学（Science）、技术（Technology）、工程（Engineering）、数学（Mathematics）四门学科。从统计数据来看，中国每年的毕业生大概500万，是美国的4~5倍，但是中国培养的STEM教育毕业生却是美国的10倍。为什么会有这样明显的优势？我觉得这与孔子的教育思想有关，孔子很早就提出过"有教无类"，这样的思想让历代中国学子有了更多学习和实践的机会。这些优秀的思想也传播到了新加坡、马来西亚等东南亚国家，他们学习这样的教育方式，并且非常重视对基础技能的培养。反过来，我们也应该注重对基础技能的培养，因为拥有基本技能的毕业生更容易找到工作。

另外，我们应该在交流中学会取长补短。世界上有很多合资企业，中国的工程师们也许一开始做得不是很好，但他们可以通过与其他国家的工程师交流合作，学习其他国家的工程知识，促进中国技术的进步，创造更多就业机会，推动中国经济的发展。这就是我认为我们应该成长的一些地方，我们可以做一些很低成本的事情，这些低成本的事情可以慢慢地帮我们衍生出一些其他的事情。

我在香港大学教过工程科学技术方面的课程，我认为科技是上天赐给我们的礼物，我们必须做好地球的"管家"，照顾好地球，管理好地球。我们要通过绿色的技术改善我们的环境，我们一定要朝着这个方向走，一起实现将全球温度上升范围控制在1.5℃内的目标。在此，我也呼吁所有的科学家、工程师联合起来，通过知识的分享，保护环境甚至创造更好的环境。同时，企业应该承担更多的社会责任，意识到环境的重要性，意识到减少不平等的重要性，意识到技术改善人类社会的重要性。最主要的是，我们需要注重培养未来工程师的职业道德，让他们明确自己承担的社会责任，如果他们拥有这样的意识，我们的社会就会在技术的推动下变得更加绿色、更加团结、更加公平。谢谢！

罗伯特·肖伯
埃朗根 – 纽伦堡大学教授，加拿大工程院院士
Robert SCHOBER
Professor of University of Erlangen-Nuremberg; Canadian Academy of Engineering Fellow

加拿大工程院院士、加拿大工程学院院士、德国国家科学与工程院院士。研究方向涵盖通信理论、无线通信、分子通信以及统计信号处理等领域。目前，他担任 Proceedings of the IEEE 期刊编委、IEEE 无线通信技术协会董事会成员、IEEE 无线通信技术协会财务主管。

Robert Schober a Fellow of the Canadian Academy of Engineering, the Engineering Institute of Canada, and the German National Academy of Science and Engineering, received his Bachelor's and Ph.D. degrees in electrical engineering from Friedrich-Alexander University of Erlangen-Nuremberg (FAU), Germany, in 1997 and 2000, respectively. From 2002 to 2011, he was a professor and Chief Scientist at the University of British Columbia (UBC), Vancouver, Canada. Since January 2012, he has been an Alexander von Humboldt Professor and the Chair for Digital Communication at FAU. His research interests fall into the broad areas of Communication Theory, Wireless and Molecular Communications, and Statistical Signal Processing.

He served as the Editor-in-Chief of IEEE *Transactions on Communications* from 2012 to 2015 and as VP Publications of the IEEE Communication Society (ComSoc) from 2020 to 2021. Currently, he serves as Member of the Editorial Board of the *Proceedings of the IEEE*, the Member at Large of the ComSoc Board of Governors, and the ComSoc Treasurer. He is the ComSoc President-candidate for 2023.

合成分子通信：原理、进展和挑战

罗伯特·肖伯

非常高兴能够参加这次的国际论坛，我分享的内容是我和多个合作伙伴共同工作的成果。我要分析的是一个跨学科的研究项目，有医学、化学、药学、生物学的同事一起参与。首先我会介绍什么是分子通信（molecular communications），然后讲一讲分子通信的策略，接着分享分子通信的相关应用，最后进行总结。

我想大家对于传统的通信系统还是比较熟悉的。传统通信通常为远距离通信，通信节点的大小大概是厘米到米数量级；鉴于这样的节点尺寸，天线的大小是毫米到米数量级，它们用于电磁波的传输与接收；进一步地，根据天线尺寸，我们可以用以下公式估算载波的频率：$f_c \approx \dfrac{c}{s} = \dfrac{3 \times 10^8 m/s}{mm/m}$，载波的频率在0.3~3GHz。

后来，随着技术的进步，研究者研发了纳米通信系统。纳米通信系统节点的尺寸为纳米（nm）到微米（μm）数量级，主要应用于医学、生物学及纳米技术领域。这些节点也被称为纳米机器人，如果同样采用金属天线，根据上述公式估计，载波频率为300~30000THz，这样高的载波频率非常不利于传输，因此，传统的基于电磁波的通信方式并不适用于纳米通信网络，必须找到新的通信方式。

其中一个选择就是分子通信，它在自然系统中被大量地使用，尤其是在生物系统中，如两个神经元突触信号之间的信息传递、细菌网络的群体感应、细胞间的通信以及细胞内部的通信等。在这些通信过程中，信息被编码成分子的浓度、类型和释放的时间等。我们就是在自然中汲取了灵感，萌发了利用分子通信设计、合成纳米级通信系统的想法。

那么，什么样的物体大概是纳米尺寸呢？我来举一些例子：人类头发的直径大概是40~220μm；生物细胞的尺寸为1~100μm；细胞的亚单位，即细胞的器官，尺寸为25nm~1μm；只有单个原子的直径在1nm以下，一些小的分子直径也大约为1nm；除此之外，蛋白质分子直径在5~10nm，病毒则在100nm这个数量级。通过这些例子，大家对纳米有了一个更加直观的认识，总结来说，纳米的确是一个很小的单位。

那么，自然界分子的通信策略是什么呢？一种常见的方法就是扩散：细胞释放信号分子，通过布朗运动在环境中扩散，扩散至能够接受它们的受体细胞，完成细胞之间的交流，神经元中突触之间的交流就是这样实现的。还有一种方法叫作间隙连接。在这种通信方式下，相邻的细胞之间有间隙连接通道（gap function channel），这些通道只允许特定类型的分子穿过。以钙离子为例，开始的细胞首先产生钙离子信号分子，这些信号分子通过间隙连接通道进入邻近的细胞，邻近的细胞同样产生钙离子放大信号，产生传递效应，进而再传给下一个细胞。另一个例子是分子马达（molecular motor），这种情况下，细胞之间的细胞器通过微管状轨道相互连接，分子马达沿着这些轨道从发射机传输到接收机。最后一个例子是细菌马达，细菌可以当作从发射机到接收机的信号分子，在食物梯度（food gradient）的推动下，从发送端到达接收端。

这些分子通信策略中，扩散是最常见的。因此，我们接下来介绍基于扩散的分子通信系统。最基本的通信系统包括发射机、信道、接收机。考虑最基本的调制方式——二进制调制，分子通信系统的基本工作流程为：在发端释放 N 个 A 类型分子，这 N 个分子在环境中自由地传播，会有一部分能够到达接收端；接收端计算接收分子的数目，进行阈值判断，如果大于阈值，则判定发送的信号为 1，否则就判定为 0。

接下来，我介绍一些关于合成分子系统的应用。相关的应用可以划分成微观应用和宏观应用两大类。第一类微观应用，主要包含靶向给药、健康监控、生物纳米物联网，以及在环境领域的一些应用，如监测和降解一些污染物。除此之外，还有质量控制，判别一些产品的缺陷。当然了，我认为最令人兴奋的应用是在医疗保健中药物的靶向传递。第二类是宏观应用，比如检测石油和天然气管道的情况、在工业应用中检测爆炸性气体、飞行器涡轮机之间的通信以及控制化学过程等。

然而，到目前为止，这些应用都没有完全成熟，那么实现这些应用需要什么呢？我认为需要以下三个方面的努力。第一是要发展高效的理论模型，首先是发射机的模型，这些分子怎么通过发射机释放到信道之中；其次是信道模型，分子在信道中会经历怎样的传输过程，以血管为例，血管中分子的流动和扩散模型需要被刻画；最后是接收机模型，这些分子要怎样转换成可测量的信号。第二是设计通信系统所需的所有功能，包含调制、编码、检测、信道估计及干扰抑制。在传统的通信系统中遇到的一些问题，如干扰，同样会发生在分子通信系统中：第一个释放的信号分子会因为传输的延迟，在第二个分子脉冲传输阶段到达接收端，干扰第二个分子脉冲的接收。在传统的通信系统中，我们采用均衡的手段消除符号间的干扰，而在合成分子通信系统中，通常采用化学降解的方式，比如说使用一种酶做诱导化解这种干扰。第三就是要开发实验平台进行验证，首先确定需要的组件，其次搭建平台，最后进行实验验证。

最后向大家简单介绍一下我和同事们一起开发的实验平台：我们使用转基因的细菌，通过光学信号调节化学信号，这些细菌会在不同光照下产生不同的酸碱度（pH值）变化。在此基础上，我们采用pH传感器检测信号。我们还模拟了血管的通道，用来检查磁性纳米粒子，这些磁性纳米粒子扮演着信号粒子的角色，而模拟血管的通道就发挥了接收器的作用，我们在这里面进行测量。我们开发的平台是一个二进制的平台，如果想要传输信息，就注入粒子，反之就不注入。

接下来，我对所讲的内容做一个小结。首先，分子通信是一个发展非常快且非常重要的跨学科领域。大家从我们的实验可以看出，相关研究需要不同领域的学者参与，需要不同领域的知识，这使其非常具有挑战性，当然也有非凡的价值。在学术界，近几年创办了许多关于分子通信的IEEE期刊，召开了一些会议。可以说这是一个非常年轻的研究领域，有很多问题没有解决，不管是通信领域还是其他相关的生物、流体、医学领域等。我们必须在这些领域上加强合作，才能有一些有效且具有挑战性的新设计。为了推动这一点，我们要培养学生们的合作意识，在未来的教育中加入更多的跨学科元素。再次感谢主办方对我的邀请！

马歆
微软亚洲研究院学术合作总监
MA Xin
Outreach Director of Academic Collaboration, Microsoft Research Asia

现任微软亚洲研究院学术合作总监，负责制定和开展微软亚洲研究院与亚洲地区高校、学术机构在科研合作、人才培养、学术交流等方面的战略规划，包括微软—教育部联合实验室、微软学者奖学金项目、"明日之星"实习生项目、联合培养博士生项目等。曾负责微软亚洲研究院亚太区文化遗产数字化保护研究计划。兼任中国计算机学会常务理事，中国计算机学会女性工作者委员会主任，以及微软亚洲研究院院友会常务副秘书长。

Ma Xin is the Outreach Director of Academic Collaboration, Microsoft Research Asia, in charge of the strategic planning of collaboration between universities and academic institutions in Asia and Microsoft Asia Research. Her work includes research cooperation, talent cultivation, academic exchanges, etc., with Microsoft-Ministry of Education Joint Lab program, Microsoft Fellowship program, Internship program, Joint Ph.D. program as representative programs. Xin Ma was also responsible for the e-Heritage program, which preserved cultural heritage through the application of advanced computing research. Xin Ma is also currently a board member of China Computer Federation (CCF), the director of CCF Women in Technology Committee, as well as the Deputy Secretary-General of Microsoft Research Asia Alumni Association.

探索 AI 时代的工程教育

马 歆

大家好,非常高兴参加第三届国际工程教育论坛,我作为一名企业界代表出现在这里,体现了企业在国际工程教育中的重要性;整个工程教育最后的出口就是企业,企业是人才最大的需求方。各位分享的报告都提到了培养学生的综合能力,这让我们非常欣慰和喜悦,从企业的角度来讲,这意味着今后有更多的复合型人才可以成为企业的中流砥柱。我的报告围绕着企业在工程教育方面的探索展开,和大家讲讲过去这些年企业所做的一些探索。

众所周知,现在技术的革新日新月异,尤其是最近几年,技术的发展更是进入了快车道。快速的技术变革对工程教育、工程人才提出了许多要求,我们的学生需要用很短的时间掌握新的技术,如云计算、大数据、人工智能等,在未来走向工作岗位尤其是进入企业时,还必须具备实践的经验。几年前,教育部提出一个新名词,叫作"新工科概念",它对工程人才提出了具有创新能力以及国际化的竞争力的要求,对我们培养全面的、面向未来的国际工程人才提出了全方位、多维度的要求。

微软研究院于1998年在中国成立。微软研究院能够在中国成为一个非常成功的研究机构,与在中国有非常好的人才培养体系,与技术的不断迭代、不断创新是密不可分的。通过对人才培养的重视,我们受益于越来越多的中国本土人才。作为企业,我们并不是简单地接收人才,而是从教育参与和人才建设的角度出发,从企业的角度配合学校、配合学院进行人才培养。

相信大家对于计算思维这个概念并不陌生。那么,微软为什么要参与计算思维的教育呢?这源于2012年,中国的大学中有一门基础的课程叫作计算机基础教育。当时的大学存在一个普遍的现象:很多学生对这门课没有很大兴趣,尤其是非计算机专业的学生,他们认为对这门课程的内容已经掌握得很好了,无须再学习一门课程。教育部基础教育教学指导委员会的老师们也在思考,如何大刀阔斧地进行改革,为学生们提供计算思维,让大一的学生在进入学校后就知道如何思考,培养通过计算科学获得学习其他学科的一些兴趣，因此，计算思维变成一种尝试。

提出计算思维想法的是周以真教授，他时任微软研究院院长，我们组织召开一些国际研讨会。我们团结了对计算教学感兴趣的老师，举办了一系列活动。除此之外，我们还和国内的顶级高校合作，围绕计算思维的概念进行了设计，通过慕课的形式进行分享。2014—2017年，我们搜集到第一手的教学资料，对课程以及教授的内容进行了多次修改、迭代，并对老师们进行培训。通过在慕课上发布课程，还吸引了更多高校参与进来。目前，我们已有126门课程在慕课上线，这些课程从不同的角度出发讲授计算机思维，在这个过程中，我们也培训了非常多的老师。从2017年开始，这门课程慢慢交给了计算机科学与技术教学指导委员会，从大学渗透到中小学教育中。如清华大学、中国科学技术大学等许多大学，他们在进行通识教育改革时，都把计算机思维教育放在了非常重要的位置上。

除此之外，微软亚洲研究院一些有专长的同事也跟学校合作，开设了一些有特色的课程。其中有一门是与北京大学合作开设的软件实践基础课程，这还要追溯到20年前，那时中国成立了第一批软件学院，北京大学找到了微软研究院，希望跟我们一起开设一门软件实践基础课程，双方一拍即合。作为技术公司，我们有两个出发点：一是中学，学生如果不会写程序，不可能从软件学校毕业；二是我们尽量让所有的实验环节融合学校和企业的特色。因此，所有环节都是双方一起设计并且共同授课。学校老师设计关于软件工程基础方面的知识，我们从微软的角度带来实战经验。在过去20年中，微软先后有30名工程师参与这门课程，不断用最新的技术迭代更新课程内容，包含基础知识及学生参与的实际项目。

在应用云计算后，我们为学生提供了许多云计算的资源，包括一些真实数据，学生可以使用我们提供的服务，在云计算环境下编程和设计相应的软件及应用程序。最近几年，尤其是在人工智能不断普及，变成学生硬核技能以后，软件工程这门课程变得越来越基础与重要。我们与北京大学一起开设这门课程近20年，微软本身也有非常多的收获，每年从软件学院毕业的学生有很多都进入了微软公司工作。这是因为这门课程需要实打实的工程实践，学过这门课程的学生在应聘的时候具有很大的优势。

以这门课程为起点，我们陆续与高校合作开设了许多有特色的课程，比如在2014年，我们跟清华大学合作开设了一门课程，并且迅速在慕课上线，吸引了5万多名学生注册与学习。当人工智能开始在各个学科兴盛起来的时候，我们与北京大学合作开设了人工智能和信息社会这门课程，把人工智能里最热门的一些话题，包括伦理方面的一些思考融入这门课程，这门课程也被评选为教育部的精品课程，每年都有非常多的学生选修。在机器学习越来越普及、越来越热的时候，我们收到了清华大学电子系的邀请，开设了一门面向全校的高等机器学习课程，介绍机器学习与其他学科的交叉研究。我们不仅讲授前沿知识，还提供了一些在研的项目，要求学生们在学习这门课程的过程中动手实操，积累实践经验。选修这门课程的学生不仅来自电子系，有的还来自化学系、精密仪器系等，大家的学习热情高涨。

不管是计算思维还是跟学校老师共同开设课程，我们感受很深的一点是，学生应该具备终身学习的能力。我们也在思考能否借助社区平台的力量，让我们在课程案例、人工智能方面积累的经验，可以更多地传播到有兴趣学习的学生手里。所以我们在 Github 上做了一个 AI Edu 的项目，在上面放了很多我们在人工智能领域的一些经验案例以及理论课程。现在这个项目受到很多关注，积累了很多人气。在这个平台，我们会不断地分享一些真实、开源的项目，欢迎学生们在上面实践，并把这些实践的成果反馈给社区平台，不断丰富社区的教学内容。当前，我们的工程师、研究员将神经网络的学习归纳成了九步学习法，相关的课程、案例、演示文稿也都放在了这个社区里面，其中有很多有意思的小模块，老师和学生可以自主学习，像搭乐高一样，自己搭建学习模块，积累知识经验。

在未来的国际工程教育中，我们相信一定是学校、学生、企业三方共同合力的，只有这种合力才能让我们做可持续的国际工程教育，让学生具备可持续的创新能力，让我们企业能够吸收更多具有创新能力的学生，所以这是学生、学校、企业共同受益的事情。在国际工程教育领域中，未来会有更多的构建模式，国际工程会变得无处不在，在所有的学科中贡献更大的力量。这就是我的分享，谢谢大家！

承办单位简介

清华大学建筑学院

　　清华大学建筑学院的前身是清华大学建筑系，由著名建筑学家梁思成先生创办于1946年10月；1988年，成立建筑学院，设建筑系和城市规划系；2001年4月，原暖通空调专业从热能系并入建筑学院，组建建筑技术科学系；2003年，成立景观学系。目前，建筑学院设有4个系，即建筑系、城市规划系、景观学系和建筑技术科学系。

　　自1946年创建以来，清华大学建筑学院的学科发展大致可划分为三个阶段。前30年以建筑学院的创办者梁思成先生提倡的建筑"体形环境论"为基础，构建建筑学科核心体系；后30年以中国科学院和中国工程院两院院士吴良镛先生提出的"广义建筑学"和"人居环境科学"为指导，学科领域不断拓展；最近10年立足"一个基础、两点关注、三项结合"的办学思想，积极引领学科发展，努力实现"立足中国特色、培养建筑帅才、跻身世界一流"的发展目标。

About the Organizer

The school of Architecture of Tsinghua University

　　As one of Tsinghua University's 15 schools, the School of Architecture (referred to as Tsinghua SA or the School hereafter) was transformed in 1988 from the former Department of Architecture established by Prof. LIANG Sicheng in October 1946. Currently, it is composed of four departments, nine research institutes, three professional practical sites, and three ministerial laboratories. In addition, the Institute of Architectural & Urban Studies, the Center for Human Settlements, and the Research Center of Building Energy-Saving affiliated to Tsinghua University are also located at School of Architecture.

　　Since its establishment in 1946, Tsinghua SA has insisted on the goal of cultivating professional leaders of architecture and gradually confirmed its development strategy based on the Sciences of Human Settlements, paying due attention to the requirements of China's construction and development and the challenges of academic frontiers, and combining education with research and practice. In the past decades, the School has finished over a hundred research projects of various levels commissioned by the government, as well as international collaborative research projects. These projects cover regional study, urban and rural study, urban planning and design, housing, architectural design and theory, architectural history and historic preservation, landscape planning & design, tourism planning and natural preservation, ecological planning and green architecture, built environment simulation and building energy-saving, computer aided design GIS and remote sensing, and so on.

分论坛主持

主持人 Chair

杨旭东
清华大学建筑学院教授，建筑学院副院长
YANG Xudong
Professor and Vice Dean of the School of Architecture, Tsinghua University

清华大学建筑学院副院长，教育部"长江学者奖励计划"特聘教授，国际期刊《建筑与环境》（*Building and Environment*）主编，美国供热、制冷和空调工程师协会会士（ASHRAE fellow）和国际室内空气质量与气候协会会士（ISIAQ fellow），国际能源署—建筑与社区节能技术合作委员会（IEA-EBC）执行委员和中国代表。长期致力于建筑节能及室内环境控制研究，是该领域国际知名学者，提出以可再生能源清洁利用为主的"无煤村镇"发展理念及技术措施、北方农村地区清洁取暖可持续发展"四一"模式，牵头开发了低温空气源热泵热风机、生物质清洁取暖炉、太阳能热风取暖等多项关键技术并被大规模应用。入选爱思唯尔（Elsevier）建设和建造领域中国高被引学者、斯坦福大学全球前2%顶尖科学家终身榜单，获得多个国家奖项。

Yang Xudong is the Vice Dean of the School of Architecture of Tsinghua University, and the guest professor of the "Changjiang Scholar Program" sponsored by Ministry of Education of China.

Yang Xudong is a fellow of the American Society of Heating, Ventilating & Air-conditioning Engineers (ASHRAE), and of the Research Management Committee of International Society of Indoor Air Quality and Climate (ISIAQ). He is also the founder of the *SCI source journal Building Simulation*, as well as the Editor-in-Chief of the SCI source journal Building and Environment. Xudong Yang also serves as a member of the Executive Committee and the China representative of International Energy Agency-Energy Business

Council (IEA-EBC), and of the international expert group of UN environment Programme-Sustainable Builings and Climate Initiative (UNEP-SBCI). In addition, he is a member of the academic committee of State Key Laboratory of Building Safety and Built Environment, and the chair of Clean Heating in Rural Area Working Committee.

主持人 Chair

沈渊
清华大学电子工程系教授
SHEN Yuan
Professor of the Department of Electronic Engineering, Tsinghua University

清华大学长聘教授，入选国家青年海外高层次人才引进计划。主要研究方向包括定位感知、协同系统和生物信息等。在IEEE和Nature等期刊发表论文80余篇，并获中国和美国发明专利授权20项。论文曾多次荣获IEEE期刊和会议最佳论文奖。曾荣获美国马可尼协会青年学者奖、IEEE通信协会亚太地区杰出青年学者奖、中国电子学会科技进步一等奖、北京市教育教学成果一等奖等荣誉。

Shen Yuan is a Professor with the Electronic Engineering Department at Tsinghua University. His research interest includes localization and sensing, multi-agent systems, and bioinformatics. He has published over 80 papers in IEEE and Nature research journals and authorized 20 invention patents. His papers have received several best paper awards in IEEE journals and conferences. He is a recipient of the Marconi Society Paul Baran Young Scholar Award and IEEE ComSoc Asia-Pacific Board Outstanding Young Researcher Award, and a co-recipient of the First-Class Prize of Science and Technology Progress Award of Chinese Institute of Electronics and the First-Class Prize of Beijing Municipal Education and Teaching Achievement Award.

江亿
中国工程院院士，清华大学建筑学院教授
JIANG Yi
Member of CAE; Professor of the School of Architecture, Tsinghua University

清华大学建筑学院教授、教育部建筑节能工程研究中心主任、中国工程院院士。从事建筑节能领域的研究工作，主持出版《中国建筑节能年度发展研究报告》。参与国家碳达峰碳中和技术和政策机制的研究，系统地提出我国实现碳中和的路径和相关政策机制。曾获两项国家科技发明二等奖，两项国家科学技术进步奖二等奖，多项省市部级科学技术奖。

With his B.S. and Ph.D. from Tsinghua University, Jiang Yi serves as a professor of the School of Architecture at Tsinghua University, the Director of Engineering Research Center for Building Energy Efficiency of the Ministry of Education, and an academician of the Chinese Academy of Engineering. He has been exploring in research fields of building energy efficiency and has presided over the annual publication of *China Building Energy Efficiency Annual Research Report* and the annual Building Energy Efficiency Academic Week, which has a great impact on the China's building energy efficiency. He participated in the research on the national carbon neutral technology and policy mechanism of carbon peak, and systematically proposed the path to achieve carbon neutrality in China with relavant policy mechanism. He has won two National Science and Technology Invention Second Class Awards, two National Science and Technology Progress Second Class Awards, and multiple provincial, municipal, and ministerial science and technology awards.

人居环境的群智能控制技术

江 亿

我要介绍一套围绕城市韧性，包括建筑韧性的群智能技术。这一套新技术服务于建筑和城市的生命线保障系统。就像人有两套神经系统，一套系统主导我们的意识、思考与创作，还有一套迷走神经系统主导整个身体运行，这部分是人的基本生命保障，这一套系统非常重要但又不参与大脑主导人的工作。

建筑物也是如此。建筑物的生命保障系统的作用就是为了保障建筑物正常运行。同时，它的特点很像分散在人体各个部位的迷走神经系统，它也分散在建筑物内的各个部位，而且符合扩散方程，相邻的空间影响大，相远的彼此影响小。城市更是这样，人们在这里进行各种社会活动。但是为了保障城市正常运行，它必须有分布在城市各个角落的生命线系统，并且确保其正常运行。对于这些系统的管理和运行，现在还有很多问题。

现在的主要问题是各个系统都是单独设置，彼此之间缺少连接和位置信息，而人的各个器官是以位置为中心组合起来的，有任何问题都自动协调，实在不行才传达给大脑。这种体系问题就导致了现在的建筑和城市其实没有真正的智能化。

40年来，建筑和市政系统的技术水平大幅提高，而在互联互通、即插即用、管理系统自匹配自适应方面，跟40年前没有本质变化。

城市和建筑的共同特点是：一是多——设备种类多，系统种类多；二是散——分布在建筑和城市的各个地方；三是变——建筑和城市不断地扩张和新建，也不断地演变和成长；四是各异——没有两个相同的建筑和城市，其中空间位置和拓扑关系是关键信息。

为什么40年都没有进步？问题出在体系架构上，而不是没有足够的技术支撑。

第一，异。每个工程项目都需要单独定制，如何最大限度地找到可重复的单元？什么是建筑或者城市里性能不变且可以重复的最大基本单元？第二，变。如果是基本单元拼起来的，面对系统组态的变化，能否实现自适应？第三，多。分析软件能否像智能手机似的即插即用？第四，散。建筑和城市是否也应该发展类似于人体的就地处理和集中协调相融合的体系结构？第五，调试过程。现在控制管理系统需要先把参数调好，正常运行后再上智能化。但是，如果这个系统永远无法正常运行、永远处在变动中呢？第六，终端机电设备都要变成智能化，但现在终端智能化与系统智能化之间无法兼容，好像变成了解不开的难题。

这些问题的突破必须有新的认识，即构成新的模型——由有限的基本模块拼成各种各样的城市和建筑，或者用这种模型在最大基本单元不变的前提下去适应、描述各种形态的城市和建筑。这是核心思想。一个要点是支持分布式计算，无中心扁平化，各个末端、各个模块都有自己的计算功能，各个节点是等同的，然后互相协同、互相计算。另一个要点是整个计算像智能手机的通用应用软件，实现即下载即运行。

目前已经有了很多基础，包括50年前伯努瓦·曼德尔布罗提出的分形体系，以及塔马斯·维克塞克最早提出的群智能的理论，解决了很多分形问题。首先，建筑和城市可以在这些基础上形成新的体系架构——所有的单元是平等的、分散的、互相联系的；其次，用标准的空间单元，每个空间单元有清晰严格的定义，这些空间单元拼起一个建筑或者城市，只要知道空间拓扑关系，就可以了解建筑或城市的全部信息。最后，这些都符合扩散过程，可以建立起共性模式。

在群智能建筑架构中（如图1所示），它是一层一层搭出来的，每一点对应一个建筑空间，连线代表空间拓扑关系。通过计算节点（Computing Processing Node，CPN）承担每个基本单元的信息采集，以及与其他各单元之间的分布式平等无中心计算。为了支撑这套东西，我们又做出分布式计算机操作系统（Thing's Operating System，TOS），这套东西的关键点是支撑海量并行分布式计算。根据每个单元的内容，建筑信息输入后，与房间里的终端自动组态，具有自识别、自建模、自组织，即插即用，软件下载即能运行的功能。

无中心扁平化计算怎么运行？比如说，一层楼的每一个房间都有一个节点和计算节点，以前想要知道这些房间的最高或者最低温度是多少，需要把各个房间的温度都通过传感器采集回来，再集中分析。而扁平化、无中心计算方式不同，这些点都连成了一片，所以从任何一个节点都可以发出信息，传到邻近节点。作为发起者的节点将自己的温度传到邻近节点，邻近节点将其与自己的温度比较后，再把这里的高温传到下一个节点。这样，当这个活动传遍所有节点后，最后返回发起者得到的就是所有节点中温度最高者的温度数值。通过这种分布式计算和信息传递，就可以很快进行类似的很多分步的分析和计算功能。

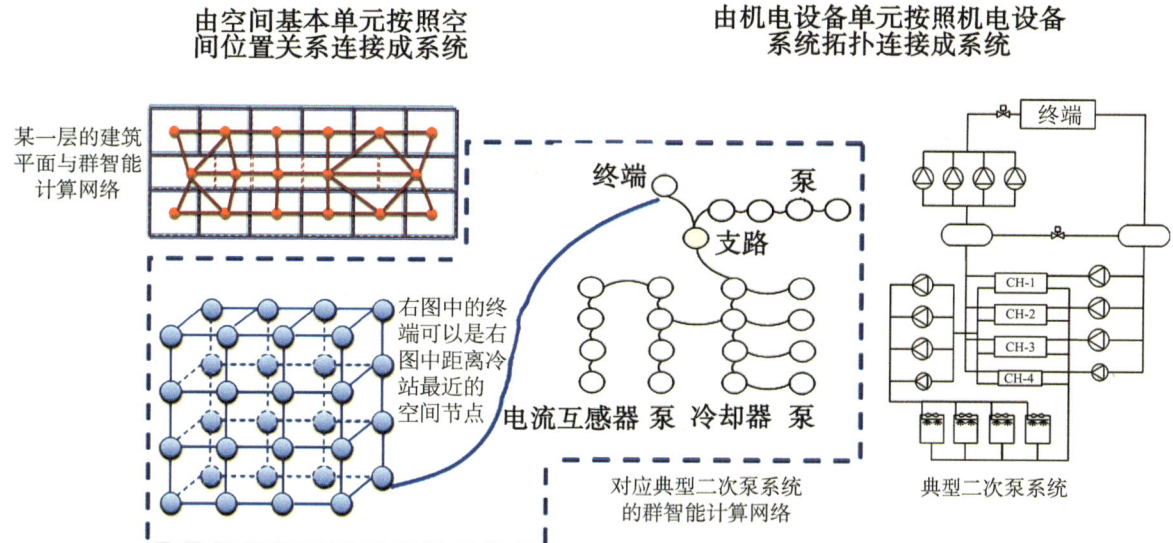

图1 群智能建筑系统

类似地，例如，我所在的办公楼的一层平面图（图2），这栋楼有两个火灾逃生口，分别在一层和四层，一般使用者都不知道四层逃生口，利用群智能就给出引导信息。每个计算节点不断测量各房间人数，并将这些群智能计算节点连接在一起，理解整个建筑拓扑关系。当某一个点发生火灾报警，需要找到逃生口信息时，就从这个点周围的计算节点自动搜索逃生口，再反过来计算疏散人流的时间。

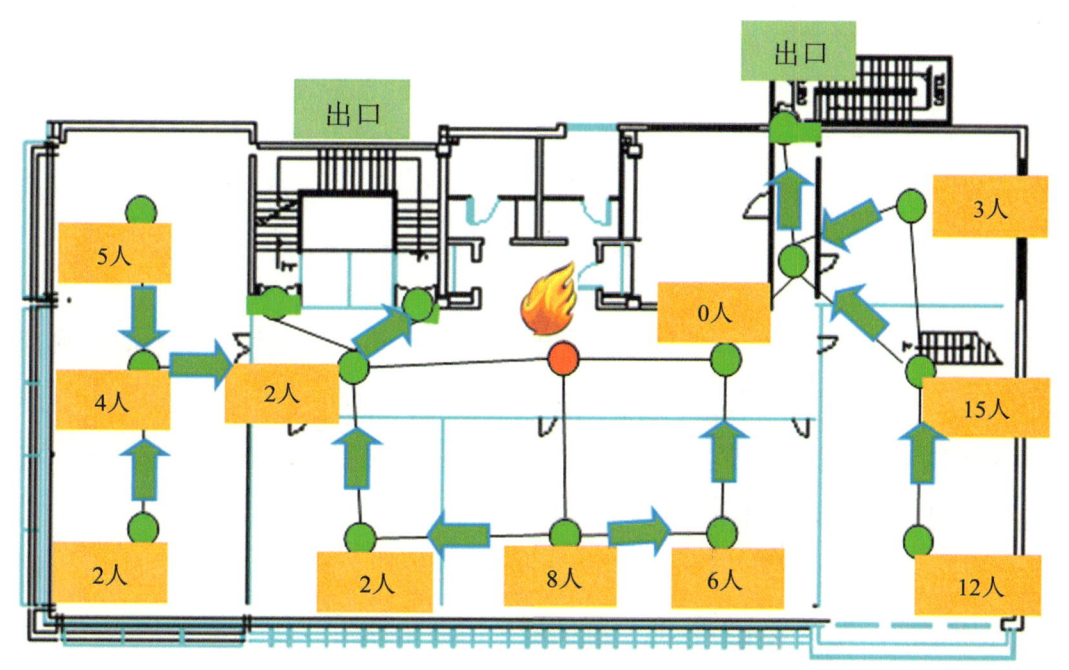

图2 一层平面图

2014年，这个系统就做成并演习过一次。第一次发出警报时没有群智能导引，绝大多数人跑到一楼逃生口，少数人从四楼逃生口逃跑，用时1分46秒全部疏散完毕。第二次由群智能指导逃生，人们被自动疏散到两个逃生口，用时降到1分10秒。这套算法也可以实现无论哪里出现火灾，都能够自动寻找最佳逃生路线，同时动态监测人数，避免拥挤等情况的发生。

随着系统规模增大，计算效率也提高。图3是计算步骤随系统规模和拓扑结构的变化。群智能计算，无论多少节点，时间几乎无增长；而集中计算，随着节点数目增加，计算时间也会增加。

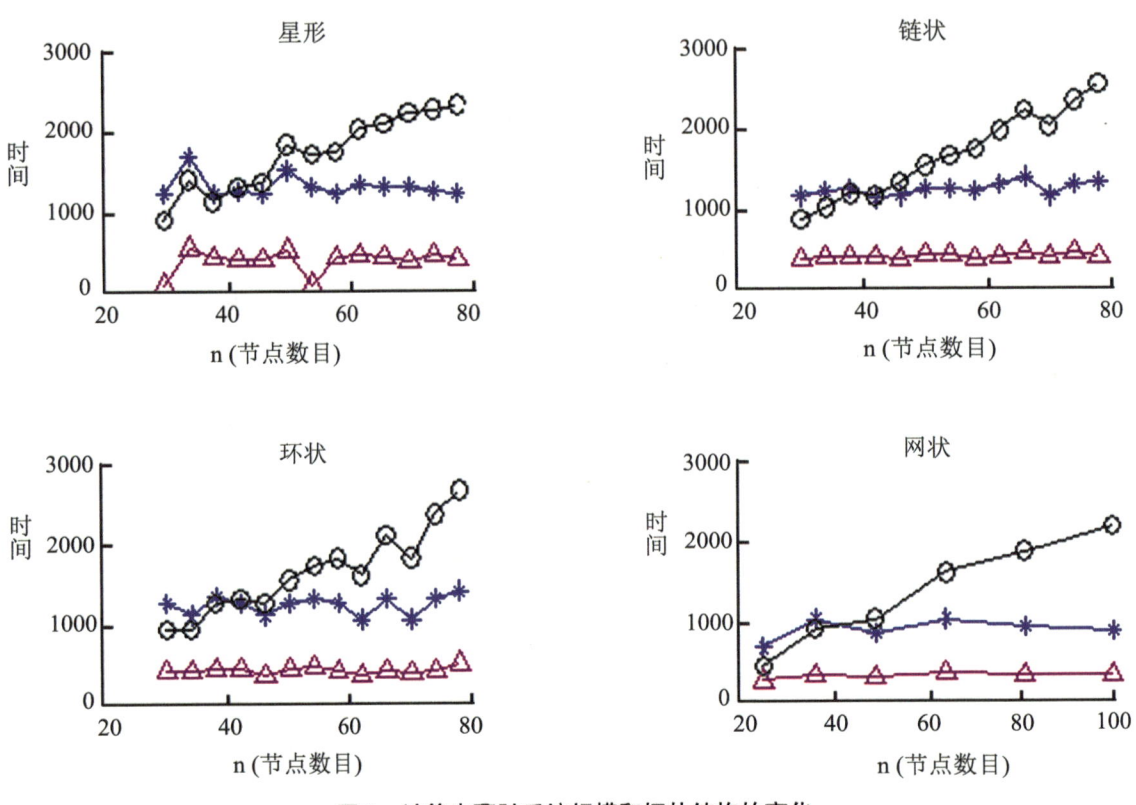

图3　计算步骤随系统规模和拓扑结构的变化

分布式计算跟人的思维不同，为此，我们开发出一个专门用于群智能的编程语言Swarm，按照人的逻辑思维，用串行方法对整个楼或城市要做的计算分析进行描述，按照语法规则可以翻译成用在计算节点上的程序，解决了编程者的开发问题，按照这个思路已经开发了很多软件。

与一般的方式相比，最显著的特点是这种系统在现场调试时间很短，而且能在机电系统完成之前，先调试完群智能，再反过来检查安装是否有误。

未来，机电设备智能化是非常重要的发展趋势，在各种机电设备装上计算节点，使得它既能满足智能化要求，又能组网对外联系，只要楼里有计算节点网络和符合群智能的装置，就能自动连接并控制管理。再就是群智能系统实现了各种软件的共享，从而可以动员各个行业的开发小组，分别开发用在建筑和城市基础设施管理中的各种软件，它们都可以"即插即用"。

作为关键节点的计算节点目前还是一个散件，成本稍高。将来把它集成为专用芯片，这个领域就不再需要通用控制器，而且系统成本会大幅降低。

总的来说，群智能系统不论是解决建筑还是解决城市，都在模仿人。人有大脑，互联网解决的也是人和人之间的联系，通过互联网使人的思维互相碰撞，解决问题。而迷走神经是支持人体功能正常实施的无中心分布式系统，群智能不管对建筑还是对城市，也是模仿这套系统。人需要大脑系统做事，需要迷走神经系统支撑；建筑和城市也是一样，需要互联网做建筑与城市要干的大事，也需要群智能作基础设施系统的支撑。我们要好好学习人的结构，让我们的建筑、城市真正实现智能化。

庄惟敏
清华大学建筑学院教授，中国工程院院士，全国工程勘察设计大师
ZHUANG Weimin
Professor of the School of Architecture, Tsinghua University;
Member of CAE; National Engineering-Survey-and-Design Master

梁思成建筑奖获得者，国家一级注册建筑师。现任清华大学建筑设计研究院院长、总建筑师，清华大学建筑学院教授、博士生导师。曾获教育部科学技术进步奖一等奖（2018年），中国建筑学会科技进步奖一等奖（2017—2018）和中国建筑学会建筑教育奖（2012年）。长期从事建筑设计及其理论研究，20世纪90年代初创建中国建筑策划理论，研发设计决策平台，率先实践全过程工程咨询，最早在我国践行"前策划—后评估"的设计全体观，主持"十二五"国家科技支撑计划、"十三五"国家重点研发计划项目，以及国家自然科学基金和住房和城乡部课题。有《建筑策划导论》等专著12部，发表学术论文200余篇。曾主持国家会展中心、2008年奥运会国家射击馆、国家冬季两项中心、九寨沟景区沟口立体式游客服务设施等重大工程的设计工作。设计作品多次获国家金、银奖及国际奖项。

Zhuang Weimin is a recipient of Liang Sicheng Architecture Award, national first-class registered architect, the Dean and Chief Architect of the Institute of Architectural Design and Research at Tsinghua University, and a professor and doctoral supervisor of School of Architecture at Tsinghua University. He has won the First Prize for Science and Technology Progress from the Ministry of Education (2018), the First Prize for Science and Technology Progress from the Chinese Architecture Society (2017–2018), and the Architecture Education Award from the Chinese Architecture Society (2012). His work focuses on Architecture design and method theory. In the early 1990s, he established a Chinese architectural planning theory and developed a design decision-making platform, took the lead in practicing the entire process of engineering consulting, and was the first to practice the "pre planning-post evaluation" design concept in China. He also led the National Science and Technology Support Plan for the 12th Five-Year Plan, the key research and development projects for the 13th Five-Year Plan, as well as the projects from the National Natural Science Foundation of China and the Ministry of Housing and Urban Rural Development. He has authored 12 monographs such as *Architectural Programming and Design* and published over 200 academic papers.

以科学方法论为导向的建筑设计创新研究

庄惟敏

谢谢各位邀请我参加论坛，我想跟大家分享一下最近的研究成果，这个研究也是基于我们"十四五"项目的一些思考。

首先是研究背景。大家一直认为建筑是一门创意工科，所谓创意就是通过人的大脑进行一种创造性的研究和呈现。脑科学发展到今天，仍无法将人脑的创新机制完美呈现出来。而我要探讨另外一个问题：科学方法引领或影响的一种创新机制，它以认识论为基础、以科学研究为过程，人为提出的一套科学研究方法。

建筑是一个复杂的系统，如果我们仅仅依靠人脑本身的创新机制，就会出现问题。改革开放以来，我国城市建设成就巨大，但大量的建筑呈现出一定程度上短命的状态。所以能否借助某些方式，展开一定的科学性、逻辑性、系统性的思考，作为一种补充，改变人脑在某些层面上的不足呢？

要进行科学的设计决策研究，需要利用智能化技术。随着科学信息技术的发展，机器学习能力变得越来越强。2016年前后，大规模的机器学习呈现出新的趋势，需求越来越多，速度越来越快，量级越来越大，涵盖面也越来越广。

不同学者的关注点并不完全一样，美国对于数据形式的问题研究更多，而中国学者在人工智能方面研究更多，从图像识别过渡到关系挖掘，这种转变使得在建筑设计层面的决策问题中，或者在建筑策划和建筑设计中使应用人工智能变成了可能。

建成环境的复杂性需要将数据形式和变量间的关系，通过机器学习构成一种对位关系。建成环境具有数据形式多元、变量空间复杂的特征，可以通过图表示学习将其转变成图论计算。图表示学习有很多优势，比如多源异构的数据都可以用图的方式表达出来，而读图变成了一个更喜闻乐见的事情，所以将问题的求解转变为图的计算变成了一种可能。

在最近的十几年里，很多西方国家都有大量的研究，通过探索智能化路径不确定性问题，关注建筑全寿期策划流程，指向了设计科学的决策研究。而我们聚焦于建筑的"前策划—后评估"方式，解决建筑设计的决策问题。随着《中华人民共和国国民经济和社会发展第十四个五年规划和2035年远景目标纲要》的发布，智慧韧性变成了最重要的核心命题。2019年，中共中央办公厅、国务院办公厅提出，明确"前策划—后评估"制度，完善建筑设计审查机制，提高建筑设计水平和设计方案决策水平。采用国外的全流程模式对于我国来说仍存在许多风险，直接影响我们的建筑缺乏自己的智能化特征，城市缺乏韧性，所以智慧运维应提上议事日程。

回顾传统的基建流程，从规划、设计、施工到运营，缺乏一个保证设计决策过程中的科学性、合理性、逻辑性的环节，即全寿期"前策划—后评估"的技术，强调与当今人工智能技术的结合。所以我们要研发一套这样的技术，强调智能策划、智能后评估，以及前策划和后评估之间推演及映射的技术，实现大型复杂工程的全过程智能管控。如图1所示，针对若干个问题点和科学问题，不能仅仅依靠人脑的创造力，需要结合科学方法论。而后研发一个贯穿全寿期的前馈和推演技术的平台，最终从理论建构、数据耦合、设计整合到系统闭环，形成一个集成示范模型。

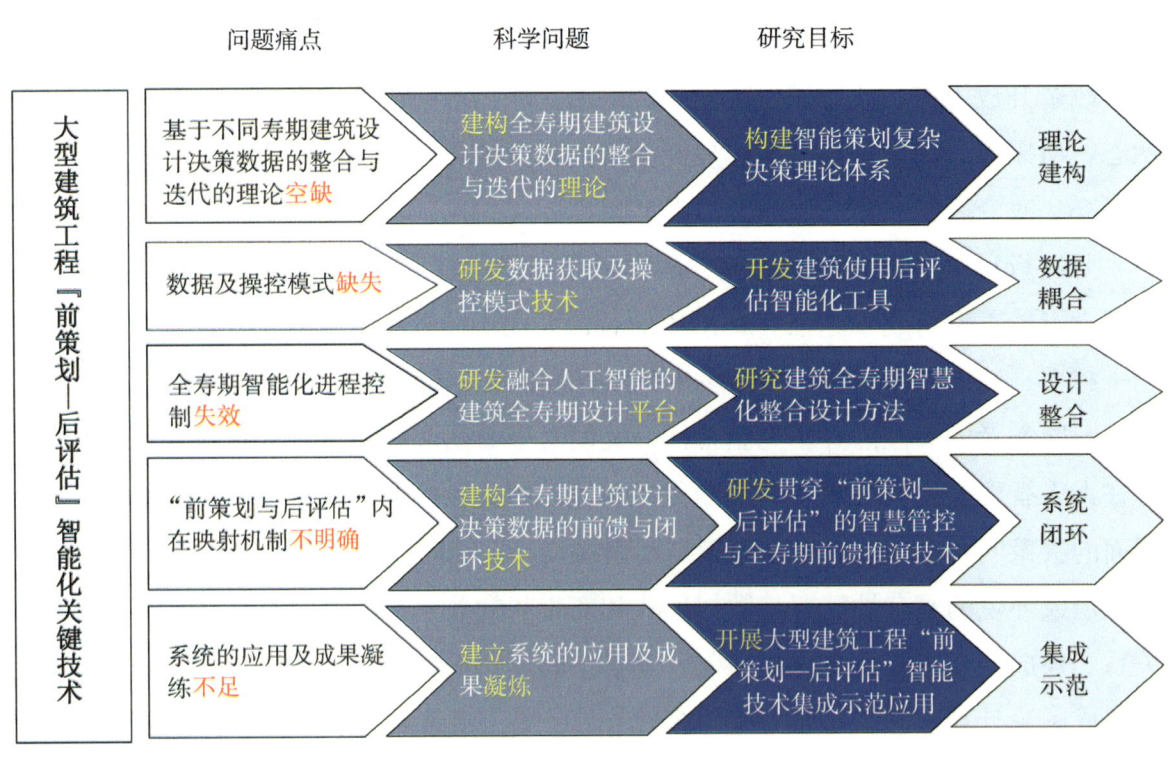

图1 智能管控数据链

智能建设策划就是要解决不确定、模糊复杂决策问题，即建筑后评估的感知问题。如今客观评价系统很成熟，而人体的主观感受是很重要的一部分，也是最欠缺的。这里包括泛在感知的数据耦合问题，以及算法和模型相互对位耦合问题。在这个基础上，通过全要素机器学习、系统整合、自适应的一套混合多目标系统，建立整合设计，最终通过因果逻辑的建构，实现推演。

其中有若干目标点：一是提出智能策划复杂决策模型，提出图拓扑智能生成逻辑和模糊评价算法，开发可量化决策的智能推荐工具；二是研发大型建筑环境内非传感器人体感知技术，基于移动机器人的环境场感知技术，进行泛在人体感知的数据提取，耦合感知空间和信息；三是研发针对全寿期品质和性能提升的多专业智能设计方法技术，开发优化算法及应用平台；四是解决前策划多维度定量化指标体系与使用后评估指标回馈的对位映射关系，推演实现"前策划—后评估"的循环。

技术路线是多学科交叉融合的，包括建筑学、计算机科学、数学、信息技术和系统科学。抓住突破性的关键技术，需要融合理论、模拟预测、数据分析。第一个目标是将建筑学、计算机科学、数学结合起来，通过多元智能识别、语义识别、机器学习的方式研发智能代理模拟。第二个目标基于泛在信号的室内定位感知技术，加上信息技术的环境场特征认知和空间评价参数量化算法。第三个目标包括形式生成、空间生成、场地生成和自适应优化算法，将建筑学、计算机科学和系统科学融合起来，最终实现贯穿"前策划—后评估"智能管控的前馈推演技术，并进行技术集成示范。

第一个目标主要应用图拓扑技术。主要研发图机器学习技术，通过图算法和图表示学习图表征；通过行为预测模拟流线和空间偏好；图分类辅助生成气泡图等；组合优化、评估多方案比选，并进行智能推荐，最终实现智能决策。第二个目标主要基于泛在信号的室内人体感知技术。泛在感知为泛在计算提供感知能力，包括建构物理空间中人、机器、物、环境、信息相互映射，交互协同。通过感知系统耦合物理空间信息，进行数据读取与挖掘。第三个目标主要将策划性能数据用在建筑形式、空间和场地设计，以此实现多目标优化整合。第四个目标是融合课题一、二、三的全链条过程，实现前馈和推演技术，将后评估和前策划的内容形成映射对位。

显然，这里有大量的跨学科研究。第一个目标需要融合建筑学、计算机科学和数学。第二个目标基于泛在信号，首先使用移动感知机理研究移动感知系统，通过计算机科学，实现移动与固定感知环境场特征认知和环境问题快速回溯与评估诊断。第三个目标是建筑学、计算机科学和系统科学之间的融合，它是一个单向低维决策向双向高维决策的精细化算法的过程。第四个目标是实现前后回馈之间的对位关系。通过建立指标体系，在前策划阶段和后评估阶段对指标的反馈、修正，形成一种对位映射，而后通过数据和指标的因果关系的推理，实现因果信息的补全，通过交互式推演关系形成全流程控制。

综上所述，以基础研究为最基本的内核，实现理论建构。而后研发若干项关键技术，得出相应的产品，最终落实到示范应用项目中。

我们希望这一项研究能够向未来拓展，未来研究的趋势是从建筑向城市全空间，而后从数据导向变成数据驱动，从助力低维决策向破解高维复杂难题进发，最终实现用人工智能技术、信息技术补足人脑的空间创意，实现我们的科学决策。

张利
清华大学建筑学院院长、教授，全国工程勘察设计大师
ZHANG Li
Professor and Dean of the School of Architecture, Tsinghua University;
National Engineering-Survey-and-Design Master

清华大学建筑学院院长、教授，全国工程勘察设计大师，清华大学建筑设计研究院副总建筑师，《世界建筑》主编。国际建筑师协会理事、中国建筑学会常务理事、中国城市科学研究会总师专业委员会副主任委员。

其学术方向聚焦于设计科学的"城市人因工程学"领域。曾率先将人因分析与设计干预方法用于冬奥场馆的可持续设计，主持了"雪如意""雪飞天"等体现中国元素、服务赛后长期利用的冬奥项目。其在玉树地震灾后重建、上海世界博览会中也承担重要任务，曾主持玉树嘉那玛尼访客中心、上海世界博览会中国馆地区馆及屋顶花园等项目。

Zhang Li is the Dean and Professor of the School of Architecture and the Vice Principal THADI at Tsinghua University. He founds the award-winning design laboratory TeamMinus in THADI. In late 2021, he has been elected to the Hall of National Masters in Survey, Engineering and Design. He is currently a Council Member [Region IV] of UIA, a standing board member of the Architectural Society of China, and the Editor-in-Chief of the leading Chinese magazine *World Architecture*. Zhang Li is the founder and a main advocate of Urban Ergonomics, an interdisciplinary domain focusing on human body and space, and the design of active urban spaces.

Zhang Li's design works span overa wide range of scales, from urban designs, buildings to microcosm interventions. He and TeamMinus have won thirty national and international awards in the past decade. He is currently the Architect-in-Chief of Zhangjiakou Zone, and Shougang Big Air, both for Beijing 2022 Olympic Winter Games and. He is also the curator of China Pavilion in Venice Architecture Biennale 2020.

基于人因分析技术的建成空间体验预测与实证

张 利

我分享的题目是《基于人因分析技术的建成空间体验预测与实证》，包括：技术背景、冬奥应用、其他应用及小结。

首先是技术背景。人的空间体验来自人对建成空间的主观感受，这种感受既有普适性规律，又有个体化差异。公共建筑在建成效果上经常不如预期，甚至造成资源浪费，原因是对空间体验的不准确预测，误导设计决策。

空间体验预测是通过设计媒介联系设计者、未来使用者和决策者，在设计过程中发挥重要作用，为设计的发展迭代提供判断依据。预测包括物端和人端两个方面，物端是设计媒介对空间的仿真，人端是对使用者主观感受的衡量。六个多世纪以来，物端的空间仿真准确度快速提升，而人端的主观感受衡量准确度相对滞后，且滞后程度比较大，时至今日，经验判断和主观评价仍是空间体验预测的主流方法。

如今在新技术的支持下，已经到了缩短物端和人端差距的最佳时机。有两个主要原因：第一个是沉浸式环境的成熟，人在沉浸式环境中得到的反馈和真实建筑的相似度能够达到90%；第二个是人因测度技术能提供更可靠、多维的客观数据，用来测量和分析主观的空间体验。

我们据此建立一个技术路径，通过对感官、神经、肌体和时空这四种活动的分析，获得客观数据，链接四项空间体验任务判断主观空间感受，形成新的空间体验预测。这四项空间体验任务包括识别、漫游、共享和体感，分别对应不同空间尺度。

识别任务是城市标志物对人的注意力的吸引强度以及与人的关联度，决定了对城市空间的归属感和自豪感。漫游任务是街区或者园区尺度决定游历城市空间的愉悦感。共享任务是在单体建筑尺度之下，同时发生的组群活动的多样性和互动性，决定使用空间的自由度。体感任务是在近体尺度之下，人体动态的多样性以及与空间界面接触的强度，决定对周遭空间的身体记忆和满意度。

其次是冬奥应用。将此技术路径应用到设计实践中，比如冬奥场馆。在初期，我们要应对因冬奥竞赛远离普通百姓生活，导致冬奥场馆难以可持续利用的问题。我们把赛前超人需求和赛后常人需求相结合，在传统设计流程之外增加人因分析环节，进行空间体验预测，引导设计迭代，提升赛后使用体验。

以北京冬奥会两个标志性跳台场馆为例，人因分析发挥了重要的作用。第一个例子是首钢大跳台"雪飞天"，它的识别性来自赛道曲线和我国敦煌壁画飞天飘带的相似性。在设计过程中基于人因分析，从识别和漫游两个方面提升常人的空间体验和超人的竞赛感受。在识别任务里，跳台的方位是一个关乎成败的设计决策问题，如何放置跳台才能让新的"天际线"被大多数人接受，是传统主观评价难以决策的问题。我们在竞赛工艺允许的情况下，以出发区为圆心每旋转5度，列举一个可能的方案。再把这些方案带入虚拟环境，让观众在沉浸式环境中体验这些场景，用眼动和皮垫的数据进行衡量。我们希望跳台的注视时长和现有冷却塔周边厂房的注视时长相对均衡，也希望跳台引起皮垫反应的唤醒度比较高。实验结果明显区别于传统的选择，我们按照实验结果建造跳台，公众反馈对这条新天际线基本是认可的。我们还在比赛期间收集和分析了运动员在出发区颈部的转向，基本能够判定其视线明确聚集在水平视线上下15度范围内，不同于上届冬奥会的平昌大跳台上运动员视线的随机分布。

首钢跳台的另一个挑战性任务是漫游。跳台周边是原有的工业冷却池——群明湖，借助冬奥的契机，尝试将它改造成可供人环湖漫游的公园。在中国传统的环湖空间里都有作为视觉重心的建筑物，我们希望大跳台能够起到类似的作用。为此，我们需要对人的环湖视觉注意力进行预测，通过360度沉浸式视频，收集人群在各类城市空间漫游时的视觉感知数据，在确定视觉注意力分布存在共性的基础上，用深度神经网络学习潜在规律，实现预测。在群明湖的设计中，首先用颐和园作为参照，通过拓扑同构转译建立一个基础漫游路径，再把漫游路径带入模型，计算路径不同位置上跳台对人的视域偏向度，最后选取两个比较重要的路径作为重要的景观节点进行优化设计。然后采集实际游历数据，将群明湖和昆明湖进行对比，看到标志物大跳台或者佛香阁的占有时长和分布模式有很大相似性。

另一个例子是国家跳台滑雪中心"雪如意"，它的识别性来自跳台的S形曲线，与吉祥器物"如意"相似，其柄身是赛道，柄首是顶层俱乐部，柄尾是多功能体育场。同样通过人因分析技术，对"雪如意"实行共享任务和漫游任务，提升空间体验。共享任务主要针对柄首设计，往届冬奥会跳台没有比较大的室内停留空间，导致普通人很难在赛后使用跳台。在国际滑雪和单板滑雪联合会认可下，我们结合如意的造型，设计了一个直径接近80米的共享停留空间，服务大众日常生活。把它设计成空心圆环的形状，结构更合理，采光和观览的效果也会更好，但是中间的圆应该怎么定位？方法至少有三类：同心圆、内圆前移10米或内圆前移16米。对比这三类形成了一个圆环内前后两个空间相互约束的共享优化问题。我们利用人因分析预测停留时长，将结果导入人因图，发现前部空间过小时，仅被感知为过道，价值下降。后部空间大到一定程度时，它对人的活动增进效益不再增加。因而最后选择前移10米的方案，兼顾前部环视景观和后部多功能集会的功能。

在漫游任务方面，为了让普通人体验跳台，我们在赛道两侧设计了能够攀登的通长台阶。基于面部表情分析锁定了登高过程中可以给人留下深刻记忆的场景节点，进行重点优化。但是在实际建成跳台中发现了一个遗憾的地方，实验模拟人从下往上攀登，但实际上有很多人是先到顶部再往下走，走到飞行曲线顶点处有一些人会恐高，如果实验模拟时发现这个问题，这是可以解决的。

最后，从整体来看，人因分析技术使两个冬奥跳台设计的过程和结果明显区别于传统。客观的实验信息给设计工作带来明显增益，在赛时和赛后反馈中也得到了验证。

人因分析技术已经是近年所有重要设计项目的必要工作流程，对基于人因分析技术的建成空间体验预测和实证有这样的心得，首先是人因分析不是取代传统的设计创意，而是增进它的落地实现，保障其切实为人服务。其次，我们切身体会到在我国特有的数据优势支持下，人因分析可能对我国新型城镇化建成空间的提质和人民美好生活的创造发挥重要的作用，助力我国对幸福生活的国际话语权提升，这一领域将大有可为。

希望大家多多指正，谢谢！

沈振江
日本金泽大学教授，日本工程院外籍院士
SHEN Zhenjiang
Professor of Kanazawa University, Foreign Fellow of The Engineering Academy of Japan

　　日本金泽大学环境设计系教授，日本工程院外籍院士，空间规划与可持续发展国际协会理事长，历任日本建筑学会信息技术委员会委员、日本城市规划研究院学术委员等。长期从事区域规划、城乡规划与设计领域的研究，涉及智慧城市规划与政策模拟平台、空间设计虚拟现实技术可视化、人居环境中的智慧营造与装配式建筑等。出版学术专著6部，发表学术论文300余篇，主持日本文部省与日本学术振兴会的研究项目16项，多项大型国际化教育研究项目，曾获国际建筑师协会建筑遗产保护奖、日本住宅综合研究奖、日本虚拟设计世界杯最优秀奖。

　　SHEN Zhenjiang is a professor at the Division of Environmental Design of Kanazawa University, Japan. He is a fellow of the Engineering Academy of Japan, the President of the International Community for Spatial Planning and Sustainable Development (SPSD), a member of the Information Technology Committee of the Architectural Institute of Japan (AIJ), and a member of the Academic Committee of the City Planning Institute of Japan (CPIJ). His research covers regional planning, urban and rural planning, and design research, involving smart city planning, planning support system, VR for space design, and smart construction and prefabricated buildings in human settlements. He has published 6 academic monographs and over 300 academic papers. He also presided over 16 scientific research projects from the Japanese Minister of Education and the Japan Association for Academic Promotion (JSPS), several large-scale international education projects, and won the 4th Regional Architectural Heritage Conservation Award of the International Union of Architects (2010), Japan Comprehensive Housing Research Award (2014), Japan Virtual Design World Cup Best Award (2015).

日本地方都市的城市设计

沈振江

非常荣幸有这样的机会跟大家汇报。我分享的内容是《日本地方都市的城市设计》，介绍关于加强城市韧性的一些工作。从某些方面来讲，城市的法规和政策的牵引是城市可持续发展的强有力手段。在规划和设计中如何利用专业技术，再现可持续建设的形态是很重要的。

联合国最近提出的可持续发展目标中，第11个目标提到可持续发展的城市和社区，特别强调了自然灾害韧性、城市韧性、城市资源利用有效性。我们的研究针对城市环境、城市灾害、城市资源利用，探讨可持续发展的城市政策，利用计算机技术模拟可视化。我们的工作内容主要包括：政策研究、城市模拟、城市设计的控制、智慧建筑工程。

日本的国土空间规划分为国家规划、省际规划和地方城市规划，把国土分为城市地区、农业地区、森林地区、自然保护地区等，这几个地区是政策法规规定的规划和边界，它对整个城市的可持续发展形态和平衡起到非常重要的作用。

城市规划要运用制度法规对空间形态进行约束，再看如何在边界里发展经济和农业生产、保护自然环境、利用海洋等各种土地保持均衡形态，具体的工作主要是边界管理、边界政策、相应法规、开发许可等一些细节内容。

都市政策规划实施前需要进行城市规划模拟，主要是模拟政策的作用。日本的城市规划有一个整体框架，从经济分配到土地利用再开发、交通，最后考虑对环境的影响。

金泽是日本的一个综合城市，在第二次世界大战后对郊外进行了大面积开发。年轻人追求廉价土地，所以都搬到郊外，这导致周边商业区大面积开发，对城市中心区造成很大影响。一方面，中心区衰退，另一方面，开发占用大面积的郊外用地，对生态环境产生很大影响。同时，整个城市更加老龄化，中心区的土地空地化严重，在城市中心如何使城市再生，如何运用紧凑城市的政策成为地方城市非常重要的课题。我们在地方城市做各种专题研究，比如中心区如何进行老人护理中心建设、大型商业建设，以及灾害、生态环境破坏如何抑制，都与城市韧性相关。

城市化的过程经历了城市扩张、城市衰退，再到都市中心区再生。在这个过程中，每个阶段都有不同的课题需要解决，当地政府也出台了相应条例和政策，这些条例和政策在规划阶段需要对其今后几十年的影响进行分析和预测。

接下来介绍其中两个专题研究：一个是如何促进中心区紧凑都市再生，另一个是灾害分析。第一个是中心区再生政策对居民居住地选择的影响。金泽市是很典型的中心城市，除了城市规划规定的建城区和城市控制区，金泽市还确定了一个中心区位。因为老龄化和年轻人外流，中心区商业萎缩。如何促进中心区的商业繁荣，使财政保持一定收入，是日本城市发展面临的重要课题。因此，金泽市政府出台了中心区居住促进政策，促进年轻人口往中心区回流。这个政策的具体内容是在中心区购买住宅或公寓时，政府提供一定补助，希望促使年轻人回到中心区居住，以加快形成紧凑城市形态。一方面，减少财政压力，因为城市外溢扩大带来财政负担；另一方面，促进中心区的人口增加和商业发展，使中心区能够得到更多财政收入。

居住人口回流的预测方法是居民的生命周期，需考虑这个政策执行30年后中心区人口的增加效果。居民的生命周期是指从出生到读大学，然后到结婚、独立之后，有4个需要购买房屋或者搬家的时期，这几个阶段都有不同的住房需求，我们针对这些人群做规划，看他们是否能接受这个政策。

我们模拟了典型的日本假想都市，把金泽市所有参数导入模拟系统，把促进中心区回流政策也导入系统，分析城市主要中心区、控制区、建城区、郊外人口的变化，分析政策对于人口回流的作用。分析结果是因为老年人的收入比较高，在郊外居住的人进入老龄化阶段之后，愿意回中心区居住，这与促进年轻人回流的初衷有所不同，但也能促进中心区人口增加。

第二个是金泽市的防灾规划和避难设施规划。日本发生了一次大地震之后，各个城市会对地震的危险度进行重新评估。在中部地区的民房规划中，金泽市的地震危险度从原来的5级提高到7级，金泽市约有50万人口，整个城市有近500个避难点，其中主要避难场所是学校。我们除了研究理论模型，也将其应用到实际城市的防震规划中，判断这些避难场所是否足够。我们分析避难所和倒塌房屋之间的关系，模拟房屋倒塌会不会造成道路堵塞、每个避难所大概有多少人、可收容避难人数是否足够等。模拟房屋倒塌和道路堵塞的基本思维是根据建设年度、结构特性和材质模拟房屋倒塌，道路堵塞是对倒塌方向进行模拟。我们分析了各种建筑倒塌的可能性，判别被堵塞的道路能否形成避难路，并分离堵塞道路和避难道路。模拟结果能够显示房屋倒塌的主人可以沿着哪些避难路来到就近的避难所，测算这些避难所能容纳多少人，比对能否容纳那么多人，从而评价防灾能力。模拟结果显示，金泽市对7级地震的防灾能力不够，特别是很多避难所还需要增加可容纳人数。

另外，可持续发展的城市设计也非常重要。从整个城市到街区，再到具体建筑，我们也积累了一些想法。比如在教育过程中，应用现实的网络技术让学生自己设计城市；在城市设计方面，模拟交通和步行道的设计，观察此类设计是否对人车混合的交通起到舒缓作用；促进居民参与工作，把实际的法规放在将来想进行改建或重建的地段上，让居民自己根据地块和法规判断到底可以建多大面积的房子；我们还开发了城市设计相关的网络游戏，利用市民参与的方式支持大多数人能接受的城市设计形态。

最后是建筑节能。要考虑城市韧性，需要多大空间，比如从防灾和紧凑城市的形态到每个建筑，都达到智慧城市的目标——节能。比如在建筑设备方面，计算每个建筑能安放多少太阳能光板、能发多少电，再模拟它的效率。又或者在城市空间做城市智能传导物体，日本除了主动设计和被动设计，还很注重生活方式和工作方式。一方面，安放智能传感设备，通过数字孪生城市，把所有的方式放在虚拟城市中，让所有人在这里活动，然后再测算建筑的实际能耗到底有多少。另一方面，对空调温湿度的控制进行了节能尝试，将空调智能控制温湿度和每个人自己控制温湿度的整体节能效果进行对比。

以上是我们对地方城市从政策制定、政策模拟、具体的城市设计，再到具体的建筑，希望能为城市韧性做贡献，非常感谢！

叶青

深圳市建筑科学研究院股份有限公司董事长

YE Qing

Chairman of Shenzhen Building Research Institude Co., Ltd.

一级注册建筑师、教授级高级工程师，住房和城乡建设部科学技术委员会建筑节能与绿色建筑专业委员会副秘书长、中国城市科学研究会绿色建筑与节能专业委员会副主任、深圳市第七届人民代表大会常务委员会委员。参与编制《民用建筑绿色设计规范》等多项国家行业标准，主持及参与国家重点研发计划等20余项课题，主导设计建科大楼、未来大厦、雄安商服中心等200余万平方米建筑工程项目。曾获全球华人青年建筑师、世界绿色建筑委员会亚太联盟绿色建筑先锋奖之绿色建筑女性领袖、当代中国百名建筑师、全国优秀科技工作者、雄安新区规划评议专家、深圳经济特区建立40周年先进表彰"杰出创新人才"等称号。

Ye Qing is a National First-Class Registered Architect, a Professor-Level Senior Engineer, the Deputy Secretary General of the Building Energy Efficiency and Green Building Committee of Science and Technology Commission of Ministry of Housing and Urban-Rural Development, the Deputy Director of Green Building and Energy Efficiency Committee of Chinese Society for Urban Studies, and a member of the Standing Committee of the Seventh Shenzhen Municipal People's Congress and other social positions. She has been a key contributor to the edition of *Green Design Code of Civil Buildings* and she has presided over more than 20 research projects including the National Key Research and Development Program. She led the design of construction projects of more than 2 million square meters, including the Shenzhen IBR Headquarters, IBR Future Complex, and Xiong'an Commercial Service Center. She is awarded as one of the "Outstanding Innovative Talents" (40 people) for the 40th anniversary of the establishment of the Shenzhen Special Economic Zone. In addition, she is among the Global Young Chinese Architects, a Green Building Female Leader in the Asia-Pacifc region of the World Green Building Council, and she is one of the Top 100 Chinese Contemporary Architects, a National Outstanding Scientific and Technological Worker, and the expert in planning evaluation of Xiong'an New Area.

回到原来，一起创未来

叶 青

我想谈谈近30年来我们做的一些城市实践，我始终认为技术本身没有好坏，只有适用性。我们身边有很多建筑20年就拆了，整个亚洲的建筑平均寿命在30余年，而深圳的历史才40余年，现在已经开始大规模旧城改造，这深刻地阐述了工业化背后的一个商业逻辑——人为设计寿命。我们希望更多地促进消费，更多地建设，向自然索取，促进经济发展。建筑成为最大的工业品，破坏了自然界的平衡，它造成的结果是产生了高额的碳排放。繁荣的经济发展是以每小时灭绝3个物种、每天灭绝75个物种作为代价的，所以我们未来会走向何方变成一个深层次的问题。

绿色转型首先是转念，如果我们不断从自然界索取，不断以资源消耗为代价谋求发展之路，那么无论采用哪一种技术路径，都是无效的。城市发展最终在生态文明时期要回归幸福本源。没有房子和金钱是不幸的，但是为此而牺牲健康快乐也是不幸的，所以城市的发展本质上要回归本源，要有青山绿水，与文化共生。

绿色建筑是城市里最重要的细胞单元，我们在工业文明时期对绿色建筑聚焦于围护结构和设备，从供给侧实现以"物"为主的技术进步，这是必要的，但是还远远不够。到生态文明时期，"以人为本"的动态调节适应更加重要。

重新定义建筑，就是重新定义建筑结果。建筑是城市的"山"，高层建筑林立形成群落的时候，很少想到气候变化，更多关注的是建筑本身，城市的繁荣破坏了自然的平衡，使得它更为脆弱。韧性城市得回归到生命体，绿色建筑是城市的青山，要把建筑看成生命，在全生命周期中节约资源、保护环境、减少污染，在这个前提下高效健康使用空间、与自然和谐共生，成为天人合一的空间载体。

我们国家的绿色建筑设计标准中，对安全耐久、健康舒适、生活便利、资源节约、环境宜居和创新技术建立了一套评价体系，把建筑分成四个等级，等级越高，对人越有利。2010年，世界卫生组织发布报告指出，人在建筑内度过的时间超过87%，与一幢大楼相关的成本里有90%是员工的薪水，因此，提高员工的表现可以成为绿色建筑的重要推动力。也有专家在研究人的疾病时发现有超过62.5%的数量是和建筑有关，因为建筑用了大量的装饰品、工业品，产生的污染会诱发各种疾病。所以，提升人的生命效率和幸福指数会成为绿色建筑的核心价值，从节约理念走向重塑人居价值观。

我们20多年来一直在努力研究以人为核心，从使用者角度出发，把绿色科技跟建筑科技融为一体的"五感六性"，从人的感知角度，让建筑富有生命。它的安全适用、舒适健康、环境经济性是可计量的，这意味着可交易、可复制、可推广，就会有"点绿成金"的可能性。技术不仅要前瞻，我们更希望它能推广，被人所用，所以实践是王道。

接下来，我会通过两个建筑案例阐述我的一些思考。深圳有40余年的历史，我们的总部大楼有20年的历史，这里有幼儿园、食堂、公寓和办公区域，是一个共享的空间。设计是共享权开放的过程，设计使用者要参与设计，还要留给大自然和其他的生命参加设计的可能性，让建筑成为人与人、人与自然、物质与精神的共享平台。这栋建筑大量利用自然通风，减少30%的空调覆盖面积和63%的空调能耗；使用自然采光，较同类照明能耗低71%；建筑上留出空隙，不阻挡左邻右舍的通风道和步行道；做了大量的绿化，还给大自然一个家。此外，雨水收集和人工湿地也减少了43%的污水排放，自然水的使用量是同等办公楼的50%。

当年的42项技术中，除了微风发电，其余的都还在使用中，这42项技术最重要的是提供了一个绿色的生活方式，比如室外开会，骑自行车上下班，等等。大自然是最好的设计师，自然的风、光、影和花草，带来一年四季不同的变化，让钢筋混凝土筑成的冷冰冰的大楼变得越来越像一棵树。如果每一个建筑都是一棵树，城市将是一片可生长的森林。

如果说绿色建筑贵，那是因为开发的理念和投资的理念不一致。如果装饰再加上绿色技术，成本就会叠加，这个过程考验每个人绿色的"心"，还包括运行过程中付出的智慧和坚守。

7年前我们开始研发第二代绿色技术，建造一栋可生长的楼，在2022年拿到了房产证，代表着它在传统建设领域中获得了法律认可，这是非常难得的创新。这栋建筑在深圳的东北部，它的共享变成了空间与规则、资源与时间、人与时间、人与人的全面共享。首次用社会学工作坊跟周围村民一起做设计，整个过程还用区块链建造平台，记录了整个透明建造的全过程。运营阶段引进很多实验室共建，更多使用者入驻后还会改变这栋建筑，但这种改变不是以资源消耗、重复产生废弃物为代价的，而是可生长的。

从功能定位开始解读重构。比如内胆和表皮分离，使所有的门窗和外立面有60厘米的空间，这是城市公共空间、公共属性、公众利益和内空间私权利之间的平衡，同时它也是通风廊道和室外机通道。管线与墙体的分离也是这样，群智能技术会在这个楼里进行实践和使用。

在使用过程中，同一个场景可以有宴会、论坛、农场等多种模式，这都是一个空间的韧性，它可以减少废弃物，更有成长性和价值。它可以自主发电，与储能和电动汽车设备结合，同时又是直流低压配电，是可友好互动的、功率可调的柔性建筑。

在生态环境中，它的海绵韧性能够让年净雨水控制率达到77%。雨水源头、雨水水系、多元海绵的景观、立体海绵的社区在钢筋混凝土中组成了一个体系，种的也都是可视景观，比如垂直森林和生长绿墙。所有的外墙也会慢慢生长，日日换新装，年年有新意。同样它也是全邻友好社区，这里有幼儿园、老人院、青年创意公寓等，围绕着城市韧性和绿色城市的各学科、各专业跨界融合试验，让生命更加高效。

有机生活，让身体健康；有趣生活，让心灵充实；有爱生活，让灵魂升华。生态的韧性社区，也有利于社会的共建，生产、生活、生态三合一，城市边界、空间动态、场景三合一。希望这些案例能够创造超越预期的空间活力，我们也希望在混沌的乌卡时代里，给大家一点点希望的可能性，思想碰撞、技术进步，都是为了未来会有更幸福的人生，能够为更美好的社会贡献我们的力量，所以我说，回到过去，一起去创造未来。我们的国家和地球会更有希望，我们每个人才会生活得更加美好。谢谢大家！

承办单位简介

清华医学院

Tsinghua Medicine（TM）是一个新的学术医学中心，旨在协调清华大学所有与医学相关的发展。TM 成立于2022年初，由来自新加坡的世界著名医学科学家黄天荫教授担任创始领导。TM 统筹规划清华大学的4个学院和3个附属医院的战略方向。

TM 核心要素可以概括为三个部分：一是在医学教育领域为国家培养卓越医师科学家；二是在疾病和医学科学的新疗法和科学知识方面取得突破；三是在临床创新方面通过开拓创新医院管理模式，改善临床结果及促进医学成果的转化。

About the Organizer

Tsinghua Medicine (TM) is a new Academic Medical Centre established to coordinate all the medical-related developments in Tsinghua University. It was formed in early 2022 under the leadership of Founding Head Professor Wong Tien Yin, a world-renowned Physician-Scientist from Singapore. TM oversees and coordinates strategic direction and vision of the 4 constituent Schools and 3 affiliated hospitals of Tsinghua University.

The 3 core elements of TM are as the following.

i) Medical Education-by cultivating the next generation of physician-scientists, leaders and innovators for the future of medical development in China;

ii) Research-by making breakthroughs in new therapeutics and scientific knowledge in diseases and medical sciences;

iii) Clinical Innovation-by pioneering new and innovative hospital management models for improving clinical outcomes and translational medicine development.

分论坛主持

主持人 Chair

黄天荫
清华大学医学学科带头人，美国国家医学院外籍院士
WONG Tien Yin
Chair Professor and Founding Head of Tsinghua Medicine;
Foreign member of the US National Academy of Medicine

教授，眼科医生、医师科学家。毕业于新加坡国立大学医学院，并于美国约翰斯·霍普金斯大学获得博士学位。于2022年出任清华大学医学学科带头人并受聘为清华大学讲席教授。作为视网膜专家，致力于视网膜疾病和眼部成像（含人工智能）的研究和创新。发表论文1400多篇（H因子为184），并在2018年、2020年及2021年入选高被引学者。因在眼科研究领域的卓越贡献，屡获国际奖项与殊荣。2020年，当选美国国家医学院外籍院士。

Wong Tien Yin is a professor, an ophthalmologist and a physician-scientist, graduated from the Medical School at the National University of Singapore (NUS) and he got a Ph.D. from the Johns Hopkins University, USA. In 2022, he took up a new position as the Chair Professor and Founding Head of Tsinghua Medicine at Tsinghua University. He has also served as the Chair of the Department of Ophthalmology at NUS and University of Melbourne, Australia. He is a retinal specialist, with a research portfolio on retinal diseases and ocular imaging, including AI. He has published over 1,400 peer-reviewed papers (h-index 184)。 He was elected as an international (foreign) member of the US National Academy of Medicine in 2020.

主持人 Chair

吴及
清华大学电子工程系教授、电子工程系副系主任
WU Ji
Professor and Vice Dean of the Department of Electronic Engineering, Tsinghua University

1996年和2001年先后在清华大学电子工程系获得工学学士和博士学位，2013—2015年，在美国佐治亚理工学院担任访问学者。主要从事人工智能、机器学习、自然语言处理、模式识别、数据挖掘等领域的研究工作。2006年起，担任"清华–讯飞医疗语言处理技术联合研究中心"主任。入选中共中央组织部"万人计划"科技创新领军人才，IEEE高级会员。参加的项目"智能语音交互关键技术及应用开发平台"于2011年获国家科学技术进步奖二等奖。负责的项目"面向海量语音数据的识别、检索和内容分析技术及其应用"获2014年度北京市科学技术奖一等奖。在重要学术期刊和学术会议上发表论文160余篇。

Wu Ji is a professor, the Deputy Chair of the Department of Electronic Engineering, a co-director of the Center of Big Data and Clinical Research at the Institute for Precision Medicine, and the Deputy Head of the Smart Medical Research Institute at Tsinghua University. In 1996 and 2001, He obtained a bachelor's degree and a Ph.D. degree in engineering from the Department of Electronic Engineering at Tsinghua University. From 2013 to 2015, he was a visiting scholar at Georgia Institute of Technology in the United States.

He is mainly engaged in research work in artificial intelligence, machine learning, natural language processing, pattern recognition, data mining and other fields. Since 2006, he has been the director of Tsinghua-iFLYTEK Joint Research Center. He is now a senior member of IEEE. The project "Key Technologies and Application Development Platform for Intelligent Voice Interaction" that he participated in won the second prize of National Science and Technology Progress Award in 2011. The project "Recognition, Retrieval and Content Analysis Technology and Application for Massive Speech Data" of which he was in charge won the first prize of 2014 Beijing Science and Technology Award. Prof Wu has published more than 160 papers in important academic journals and conferences.

主持人 Chair

张亚勤
清华大学人工智能科学讲席教授，清华大学智能产业研究院（AIR）院长
ZHANG Yaqin
Foreign Member of CAE; Dean of the Institute for AI Industry, Tsinghua University

2019年当选美国艺术与科学院院士，2017年荣膺澳大利亚技术科学与工程院（ATSE）院士，也是该年度当选的唯一一位外籍院士。数字视频和多媒体领域的顶尖科学家之一，发表了558篇论文，获得62项美国专利，有11部著作。联合国开发计划署（UNDP）产业委员会成员，并于2016年获得联合国可持续发展特别奖。担任全球最大的开放式自动驾驶平台Apollo联盟主席，全球合作伙伴超过160家。

He was inducted to the American Academy of Arts and Sciences in 2019. He joined the Australian Academy of Technology and Engineering (ATSE) as the only foreign fellow in 2017. He is one of the top scientists in digital video and multimedia, with 558 papers in leading international conferences and journals, 62 granted US patents, and 11 books. He has received many prestigious academic, technological, and industrial awards, including the IEEE Centennial Medal, IEEE Industrial Pioneer Award, IEEE Richard Merwin Medal, over a dozen best paper awards of various IEEE transactions and journals. He was listed by IT TIMES, BUSINESS WEEK, CNBC, Global Business and *Vision* magazine as one of the top 10 CEOs in Asia, 50 Global innovators, CEO of the Year, and IT Innovator Leader. He had worked for the Board of Directors for five public listed companies in total. He is on the industry board of United Nation Development Program (UNDP), and received UN's special award for sustainable development in 2016. He is the Chairman of world's largest open autonomous driving platform "Apollo" alliance with over 160 global partners. He has been an active speaker in global forums including APEC, Davos World Economic Forum, United Nations, and Bo'Ao Asia Forum.

AI+ 生命科学

张亚勤

大家好,我分享的题目是《AI+ 生命科学》。人工智能已经成为产业和社会变革的重要引擎,我想围绕"AI+ 生命科学"这一主题,介绍生物世界正在发生的数字化和智能化的新变革,并分享清华大学智能产业研究院(AIR)在这些方面的科研进展。

AIR 是 2020 年底成立的、面向第四次工业革命的国际化、智能化和产业化的研究机构,它的使命是用人工智能的技术创新赋能产业,从而推动社会进步。其实要做这件事情,最重要的还是打造学术和产业创新的新引擎。特别幸运在 AIR 成立不长的时间里,在全球范围吸引了一批拥有很深的学术造诣,同时在人工智能领域有丰富产业背景的领军人物,与产业建立深度合作。

我们选择了三个研究方向,这三个方向也是我认为对于产业会有深刻影响的方向,比如自动驾驶、绿色计算,还有 AI+ 生物科学。

在生命科学领域,我们正快速步入数字化 3.0 的时代,基因测序、高通量的生物实验、脑机接口,使得我们的大脑数字化、身体器官数字化,以及细胞蛋白质数字化,这就产生了海量的天文级的数据,这样的数据加上新的 AI 算法和极大的算力,正在形成一种新的智能科学计算范式,我们把它称为第四范式。

第四范式也正在推动生命科学和生物、医疗领域朝着更快速、更精准、更安全、更经济、更普惠的方向发展,人工智能在蛋白质、结构预测、基因编辑、T 细胞抗原受体和个性化的疫苗研发、精准医疗、药物设计等方面的研究已经成为国际前沿的研究热点。从产业角度来看,2015 年之后全球的头部制药企业加速了和 AI 技术公司研发合作的脚步,特别是最近五年,AI 在生物科技方面的投资大幅增加,已经涌现出一大批"独角兽"企业。此外,中国医疗行业也面临着从仿制药到创新药的转型,AI 在转型过程中也会发挥重要的作用。

AIR 也建立了一支第四范式团队,我们选择了三个方向,包括数字治疗 DTx,AI 驱动药物设计——数字药,以及精准治疗——基因疗法或基因药,它们都用了大量的

AI算法及数据。

先介绍我们开发的脑机接口相关的数字疗法。脑机接口是由杭州brainCO公司研发的非侵入式的脑机接口，用于精准检测微弱的大脑皮层的信号，大约50微伏。取得大脑皮层信号之后，人工智能算法包括深度学习和大规模的预训练模型就有用武之地了。脑疾病的研究中脑电数据是一种模态，在不同的疾病中，大脑的自发性电位如果出现异常的波动，就可以得出疾病和脑电之间的关系，除了脑电数据，还可以将不同模态数据比如机电信号结合在一起，利用AI的算法进行关联分析，形成训练的软件，也就是数字钥，再加上智能仿生手段就可以用到很多的场合。

妊娠期糖尿病（gestational diabetes mellitus，GDM）数字疗法，是AIR、智源和北大妇产儿童医院共同研发的。我们知道妊娠期糖尿病的发病率高达17%，如何通过个性化的膳食推荐、精准的营养管理以及健康管理，在孕早期监测以及预防这些问题非常重要。另外，我们和清华大学长庚医院丰田的项目，以高血压、冠心病、心房颤动，以及心力衰竭、慢性的心血管疾病为例，聚焦心血管疾病早期的预防和主动干预，使用的方法都很像，我们要收集用物联网获取的大量数据，构建疾病的健康、营养知识图谱，有了数据就用各种各样的AI算法驱动个性化的健康推荐引擎，实现对健康和习惯的监测、管理和预防。

AlphaFold2人工智能程序是AI应用的典型案例，也是AI应用最成功的案例之一。首先是特殊性，蛋白质的结构预测可以看作一个一维的映射，这本身是科学问题。其次是模型本身的优越性，先有了大量的数据，AlphaFold2的模型架构充分利用了数字驱动端到端的深度学习模型，包括Full都是端到端，是科学性范式的一个典型的应用场景。

同时，AI也被用到抗体构建中，经多方合作，把AI的算法首次应用于抗体方面的设计。这里面用到了深度图网络，用到了计算和实验的抗体设计融合，设计了这样一个平台，来了一个抗体之后其实是可以用各种不同的算法，可以开发更有亲和力的、更广泛普便的抗体，这个工作目前很快进入临床阶段。除了抗体生成，我们还在小分子药物生成，以及分子构象、预测方面做了大量的工作。

AlphaFold2仅仅是一个开始，它的成功正在开启一个新的时代。一方面，蛋白的精确预测为生命科学提供了高效的计算工具，为基于AI的重大生命科学发现提供了可能，未来在抗体、抗原的表位预测，肿瘤的精准疗法，T细胞受体个性化疫苗的设计和优化等方向都会成为研究的热点，并在驱动新的计算模式之下取得更多的进展。我认为AI+大分子制药的黄金时代正在到来，当然也会产生一些新的科学挑战，也预示着会有一些新的方法，比如干湿融合的闭环式的计算框架。另外，AI的模型可以通过高通量、多轮的湿实验的闭环验证和数据补充变得更加智能。最后，通过主动学习或强化学习等方式，AI将主动规划这个湿实验的自动化运行，形成干湿闭环验证，迭代加速生命科学与产业的应用。我们可以预见，通过打通干湿闭环，生命科学的研究和生物医疗产业将产生新的科研产业模式。

总结而言，我们认为生物世界正处于数字化、自动化和智能化进程中，科学计算新的变革、人工智能、数据驱动第四研究范式辅助人们探索并解决生命健康的问题将会成为一个重要的方向，未来需要学术界和产业界共同推动生命科学、生物医学、基因工程和个人健康，各个领域从孤立开环向协同闭环发展，实现更快速、更精准、更安全、更经济、更普惠的生命科学和生物医学创新的模式，这里面还有很多的挑战，比如算法的透明性、可解释性、隐私安全和伦理。整体来讲，未来将会有众多机会，新的科学的发现，新的产业的创新，我也希望能有更多的人才和资源投入这个领域，感谢大家！

房建成
中国科学院院士，北京航空航天大学教授
FANG Jiancheng
Member of CAS；Former Executive Vice President of Beihang University

中国科学院院士，导航、制导与控制专家。"国家杰出青年科学基金"获得者，教育部"长江学者特聘教授"。现任北京航空航天大学常务副校长、党委常委，北京航空航天大学学术委员会主任。长期从事航天器姿态控制磁悬浮惯性执行机构和先进惯性仪表与系统技术研究，主持国家（国防）重大和重点项目20余项，取得了一批重要创新成果。获国家技术发明奖一等奖和二等奖各1项（均排名第一），国家科学技术进步奖二等奖1项（排名第一），中国专利奖金奖1项（排名第一）。带领的科研团队于2008年获批"新型惯性仪表与系统技术"教育部长江学者创新团队，2011年获批"先进惯性仪表与系统技术"国家自然科学基金委员会创新研究群体，并获得两次延续资助。

Fang Jiancheng is a fellow of the Chinese Academy of Sciences, and a specialist in guidance, navigation, and control. He is the winner of "National Science Fund for Distinguished Young Scholars" and "Cheung Kong Scholar" by the Ministry of Education. He is currently the executive vice president and a member of the Standing Committee of the Party Committee of Beihang University (Beijing University of Aeronautics and Astronautics), and the director of the Academic Committee there. Professor Fang Jiancheng has long been engaged in the research of spacecraft attitude control using magnetic inertial actuators and inertial navigation technology. He has presided over more than 20 national (defense) major and key projects and has achieved a number of important innovations. He has won a First Prize and a Second Prize of State Technological Invention Award, a Second Prize of State Scientific and Technological Progress Award, and a gold award of China Patent Gold Award. For all the listed awards, he ranked first. The scientific research team led by him was approved as the "New Inertial Instrument and System Technology" Innovation Team of Changjiang Scholars by the Ministry of Education in 2008, and was approved as the "Advanced inertial Instrument and System Technology" National Natural Science Foundation of China Innovation Research Group in 2011, and he was entitled to a renewl of funding twice.

医工交叉的北航实践

房建成

尊敬的各位专家，非常荣幸受邀参加第三届国际工程教育论坛。我以《医工交叉的北航实践》为主题，分享我和我的团队最近在医工交叉方面做的一些探索。报告内容包括：我对医工交叉的看法和认识；我带领科研团队研究的新技术方向。

极弱磁场的测量如何能够在医学领域得到好的应用，为疾病的诊断提供新的手段呢？现代医疗离不开高端医疗装备，电子计算机断层扫描（CT）、核磁共振成像、医学超声检查这些成像技术的发展越来越快、性能越来越好，外科手术机器人的使用也使外科发展到很高的水平。总而言之，高端医疗装备基本上决定了现代医疗的水平。医疗装备的产生和发展离不开科学家和工程师的合作，比如，伦琴发现X射线获得诺贝尔奖，物理学家和工程家合作发明了断层扫描成像，化学家和物理工程师合作发现核磁共振。因此，医工交叉是发展高端医疗装备的必由之路。

新的物理学发现、新的技术产生和医学的应用产生了新的医疗装备，比如CT的快速发展，归功于伦琴在1895年发现了X射线，1971年，出现了第一台的CT扫描装置，1975年，CT与正电子发射型计算机断层显像（PET）结合，打开了超声的大门，A超、B超、无线超开启了人体动态成像之路。1978年，0.15T核磁被应用，2001年，第一款国产3.0T的核磁被研发出来，后续包括西门子的7T，将人体结构成像分辨率提升到新的高度，这些为人类医疗健康做出了很大的贡献。

然而，中国高端医疗装备做的贡献还不太够。一方面，这与我们国家人才培养的模式有关，中国高等教育人才的培养从大学开始就分类了，高中毕业生考入大学就分医科和工科，学西医的学生很少学工科的知识，学工科的学生对于生命医学意义几乎不学习，这导致医科生与工科生走上了不同的道路，学医不懂工，学工不懂医。国外的人才培养和我们不一样，高中毕业后本科阶段不分医工科，他们的医学博士都有很好的理工科素养，因此他们不仅可以提出问题，而且可以掌握解决问题的基本手段，医学和工科结合就很容易发展以及创新医疗设备，因此我们说医工交叉是中国要补上医疗技术差距的必由之路。

现在中国非常重视人类健康，工科要发挥作用，与医学专家们结合，以问题为导向在医疗装备技术这些方面做出贡献，这也是我的团队这些年来发展医工交叉的原因。具体讲讲我自己带的团队做的一些工作，目前高端的医疗设备无论是X射线、CT，还是B超、结构核磁，都是针对人体的结构性疾病进行结构成像。还有一类疾病叫作功能性疾病，尽管有功能核磁，人体功能测试还是不能满足功能性疾病诊断的需求，需要新的人体功能信息测量或者是成像的新手段。比如细胞，其实细胞里面有非常微弱的电信息，只不过现在没有手段很好地测量它，我们知道人体细胞里面有线粒体，线粒体有电位，有了电位就有电位差，但这个信息以前缺乏检测手段，因为它的信号太弱了，但是现在有了极弱磁场的技术，再弱的电流都会产生磁场，用这个信号就可以反映人体很多的功能信息。

我的团队2018年开始就研究极弱磁场技术，在国家自然科学基金委员会的重大科研专项支持之下，我们与中国科学院的三个所，还有三所大学取得了非常好的结果。我们最初研发的极弱磁成像装置，具有反映极弱磁场的能力，但要想实现医学应用必须做成传感器，而且要很小。因此北京航空航天大学带领一个团队专门做小型化，原来一间大屋子做成仪器，现在做成了很小的传感器，这个为医学应用带来了可能。

此外，心脏的疾病专家将心脏病分为两大类：一类叫作结构性疾病，比如瓣膜是不是狭窄，是不是有反流，是不是心肌梗死，等等；另一类是功能性疾病。结构性的心脏病会引起电生理信息变化，反映功能信息。相比常规心电图的皮层电位测量，极弱磁技术能够提供更多的信息，用磁场反映整个动态的、完整的网络。极弱心磁成像设备灵敏度很高，能够非接触地直接测量非常丰富的信息，完全可以反映心电的信息，还能反映更多心电图反映不出来的信息。另外，极弱心磁成像设备也可以提前发现心脏的电生理功能异常，在心脏病早期及时发出预警。

另外，大脑疾病大多是结构性脑疾病，大脑主要是神经系统发挥作用，结构性脑疾病对于人的影响主要是影响神经系统，脑磁图能发挥巨大作用，为癫痫定位、老年退行性疾病以及儿童发育疾病诊断提供好的手段。更重要的是在中医领域，中医的专家来我们实验室进行了研究，他们用针刺激足部的太冲穴，心磁和脑磁在针灸之后发生很大变化，给专家带来了很大的惊喜。未来，整个电生理信息传输的过程都可以用传感器测出来，可以给针灸的疗效评估以及机理研究提供帮助。另外，我们说细胞是有磁性的，正常的细胞和肿瘤细胞因为代谢功能不一样了，磁性也会发生变化。最近中南大学湘雅医学院团队带来皮肤的肌肉组织，包括黑色素瘤和正常组织，我们发现黑色素肿瘤磁场明显要强很多，是正常磁场的4倍，脂肪组织也大，这是初步的研究，还没有发表。

零磁医学是在极弱的环境下，屏蔽噪声磁场，研究人体的组织、器官、神经离子通道微弱的信息变化。有电就会有磁，反过来磁会干预电，磁场还干预电生理信息，关于这对人体功能疾病是否有帮助这一点，我们正在开展一些技术研究，培育新的学科方向。山东大学成立了第一个省级重点实验室，杭州浙江大学医学院附属第二医院及广东省中医院都大力支持推动零磁医学的研究。此外，我们和四川大学华西医院、同济医院等进行了很多的交流，医学专家都认为这是一个很好的方向。我们国家为这项研究投入巨大，做高端的装备，做仪器，做传感器，我们为什么不研发一个新的功能成像仪器设备让医学专家使用呢？尤其是国家医学中心、培育国家医学中心的研究型医院，他们更需要从共建实验室的平台、共同培养博士研究生着手发展这些方向。我们现在和一批医院已经签约开始建设省级重点实验室，同时帮助他们建立综合类的国家医学中心，将来通过产业创新中心变成产品，给医院提供医学研究和临床应用，这是从科学到技术再到产业的过程。

总而言之，科技创新和人才培养需要双轮驱动，在创新实践中培养拔尖医工交叉的人才。我希望医学专家和工科的专家紧密结合，通过医工交叉对人民健康事业的发展做出应有的贡献。

董家鸿
中国工程院院士，清华大学临床医学院院长
DONG Jiahong
Member of CAE;Dean of the Clinical School of Medicine, Tsinghua University

清华大学教授，中国工程院院士，清华大学临床医学院院长，北京清华长庚医院院长，清华大学精准医学研究院院长，中国医师协会常务副会长。国际著名肝胆外科专家和肝脏移植专家，在国际上首次提出"精准外科"新理念，创立了精准肝胆外科范式。发表SCI论文160余篇，主持制定15部行业指南。主编出版专著6部。主持国家科技支撑计划等项目20余项；以第一完成人获国家科学技术进步奖二等奖1项和省部级一等奖3项，以合作完成人获国家科学技术进步奖一等奖1项。

His research interests include theories and technologies in modern hepatobiliary surgery, liver transplantation and the management of complex biliary diseases. He was the first in the world to propose the concept of "Precision Surgery", and has been endeavoring to establish the surgical paradigm and technological system of hepatobiliary surgery ever since. He has published more than 160 SCI papers either as the first author or as corresponding author, presided over the formulation of 15 guidelines and published 6 books. He also presided over more than 20 projects such as the National Sci-Tech Support Plan, and won a Second Prize of State Scientific and Technological Progress Award and three provincial and ministerial First Prizes as the first finisher, and a First Prize of the State Scientific and Technological Progress Award as the co-winner.

精准肝胆外科范式与技术体系

董家鸿

各位专家同道、与会嘉宾，我从四个方面和大家分享《精准肝胆外科范式与技术体系》的内容。

第一，精准外科理念的源起和迭代。随着科技的发展，科学的不同领域都经历了范式的演变和转变，外科学也不例外。外科学是一门历久弥新的科学和艺术，每一次医学的革新都带来外科学范式的转变。21世纪以来，生物医学取得巨大进步，循证医学日渐兴起，以信息科技为核心的现代科技，它的渗透和融合显著提升了外科实践的确定性，使得外科实践向着基于确定性的精准外科发生范式转变。现代外科的核心价值观就是病患最大化的健康获益，要实现这一目标，需要统筹兼顾安全、高效、微创三个目标要素，这就是我们定义的安全、高效、微创（SEM）宗旨。

肝胆外科在高科技的加持下迅猛发展，然而，临床上的复杂病情常有不确定性因素带来的挑战，经验主义之下复杂肝胆疾病治疗难题难以突破。近20年来，我和团队持续改进复杂肝胆病外科治疗的临床实践，整合现代科技与传统外科精髓，探索肝胆外科学新理念、新技术、新范式，以突破传统肝胆外科学发展的困境，破解复杂肝胆病外科治疗难题。早在21世纪初，我和团队提出了精准肝切除的原创理念，并且建立和推广了肝切除的精准技术规范。2010年，我们提出外科临床全流程、全维度和全要素系统性优化的精准肝脏外科新概念，使病情评估、临床决策、手术规划、外科作业和手术期管理的外科治疗全流程形成闭环，以实现终局的最优化。2015年，随着精准肝胆外科理念得到同行的广泛认可和跨学科的渗透，我们明确定义了精准外科的科学内涵。所谓精准外科，是针对特定疾病的个体或群体准确决策和精确应用，采取最恰当的手术干预方法，达到病灶清除、器官保护和损伤控制三个核心外科要素的精确平衡，实现外科治疗的安全、高效、微创的多目标优化，以及患者健康上获益最大化的最佳临床实践。

精准外科理念的提出和被认可引领了现代肝脏外科理念与技术革新，这是21世纪外科的新理念，精准外科和经验外科两种外科学方式在医学模式、技术特征和实践基础、干预策略、终局目标和科技平台等多个层面存在显著差异。

第二，精准肝脏外科的核心技术。根据精准肝脏外科核心技术的新概念，可归纳为可视化、可量化、可控化三类核心技术，推进精准肝脏外科核心技术的系统化探索与实践，成为支撑确定性外科实践的基石。可视化的技术就是采用影像与显示技术，以及数字医学手段透视和窥视靶器官与病灶的形态与结构。2020年，我们团队打造了首套人工智能肝脏精准手术规划系统，实现了肝脏患者的精确术前评估和精准手术规划。

影像特征与病例特征存在映射关系，影像组学使影像学从定性走向定量。采用影像组学评估肿瘤的异质性，可以精确定位最具恶性特征的肿瘤侵袭前沿区域，定量化预测肿瘤的微转移，从而精准地指导手术规划。我们采用影像组学的技术，定量评估肿瘤降期治疗的效果，基于机器学习与深度学习的技术，对胆管扩张症进行定性定量的诊断分析。为了定义肝切除量，我们提出了必需功能性肝体积，确立了安全肝切除的量化标准，为安全肝切除提供了一把精准的标尺。

此外，利用数字影像技术可以对肝脏体积和脉管结构进行立体几何测量，包括病灶体积以及脉管结构的空间关系、脉管受累的范围长度以及可切除的修复性。我们研发了肝脏多模态影像融合技术，将分子影像和解剖影像融合，从而确定不同区段肝脏的功能体积，这是对于肝脏不均值损坏状态下精确测量肝脏功能体积的唯一可靠的手段，这能够用于临床。

第三，精准肝脏外科的主导术式。针对不同肝胆疾病临床病例特征，我们应用精准肝脏外科的理念和核心技术，形成了系列精准肝脏外科的主导术式。精准外科主导术式包括定位切除术、定量切除术和定构切除术，其中定位切除术是基于病灶病变，精准定位切除的肝脏切除术，我们进行了解剖型肝脏切除治疗肝细胞癌的双盲前瞻性ICT研究。研究证实，规则性肝脏切除术能够减少患者术后3年肿瘤的局部复发率。

该项技术还解决了传统技术病灶定位和结石残留的难题。我们在萎缩增生符合症导致肝脏畸形的病理状态下，精确定位并切除了病变的肝段，这一技术使得肝胆管远期疗效优良率从60.7%提高到90.4%。此外，基于胆管癌的明确特点以及3D精准定位术，我们首创了通过围肝门切除加选择性肝段切除术治疗肝门胆管癌，这些新的理念以及术式，较传统上广泛沿用的大范围肝切除来说，实现了保守根治，降低了术后肝衰竭的发生率。

定量肝切除是针对弥漫性的肝脏病变、基于剩余肝脏功能体积的量化进行的切除技术。基于肝脏储备功能的量化评估和个体必需功能性肝体积的预测，我们制定并在国内推广了定量肝切除决策系统，为个体化设计和安全肝切除的实施提供了一把精准的标尺。同时，我们研发了全定量人工智能肝脏手术规划系统，术前影像精确测量预留肝脏功能体积，并与必需功能性肝体积相比对从而做出安全肝切除的临床决策和手术设计。634例的临床应用证明，该决策系统能够准确降低肝切除后肝功能不全的风险。

第四，精准肝脏外科范式。学术范式的现代概念是指一个学术共同体共享的信仰、价值、法则、规约、方法、技术、工具和范例的集合，是指常规科学赖以运作的理论基础和实践规范，是从事特定科学的学者群体共同遵从的世界观和行为方式，这一概念与中国经典哲学的概念道法术器不谋而合。范式也就是道法术器的集成，核心价值观为道，基本理论定力为法，而核心技术方法实践行为规范和可模仿的范例则为术，工具和手段视为器。精准肝脏外科的理念和原理以及赖以支撑的创新技术体系，得到了数年丰富的临床实践的检验，我们集成的精准肝脏外科的先进技术和理论知识，是以医学准则、外科法则和技术体系为核心的内容，构建了精准肝脏外科范式，为现代肝胆外科的规范化实践和技术创新发展提供学术指引，得到了国内外学界同行的广泛认同。

总的来说，精准肝脏外科范式这一现代外科技术和知识体系的构建与实践，既是我和团队的创新理念和技术元素的集成，也是海内外众多同行专家的学识和经验及智慧的汇集。这一范式破解了肝胆外科领域系列技术难题，提升了复杂肝胆病的外科治疗效果，引领了现代肝胆外科理念和范式的革新与转变。谢谢大家！

黄广斌
广智微芯有限公司创始人，南洋理工大学教授
HUANG Guangbin
Mind PointEye Pte Ltd Founder, Professor of Nanyang Technological University

新加坡南洋理工大学电气与电子工程学院的全职教授，广智微芯有限公司创始人。2016—2018年，新加坡总统科学奖提名人，2014—2018年，连续被汤森路透评为"高被引科学家"（工程和计算机科学两个领域）。他在极限学习机（ELM）领域的两部著作，在2017年谷歌学术搜索的"经典论文"人工智能领域前10名中分列第二名和第七名。

Huang Guangbin is a full-time professor in School of Electrical and Electronic Engineering at Nanyang Technological University, Singapore, and the Founder of Mind PointEye, Singapore. He was a Nominee of the year of 2016, 2017, 2018 Singapore President Science Award, and he was awarded as Thomson Reuters's "Highly Cited Researcher" (in two fields: Engineering and Computer Science) consecutively for the year of 2014, 2015, 2016, 2017 and 2018. His two works on Extreme Learning Machines (ELM) have been listed by Google Scholar in 2017 as the Top 2 and the Top 7, respectively, in its "Classic Papers: Articles That Have Stood The Test of Time" -Top 10 in Artificial Intelligence.

人工智能驱动的医疗保健新时代

黄广斌

谢谢大会的邀请。利用这个机会,我从 AI 的角度跟大家分享我的一些观点。

人工智能经历了比较火爆的10年,但我们还处于人工智能的初级阶段,从某种程度上说还属于"黎明前",曙光就在眼前。50年甚至100年后来看,我认为这是一场智能革命的开始,实际上是解放了另外一种生产力,即数据驱动。这种智能能力的释放,总体来说应该是第三次产业革命的开始。既然是第三次产业革命的开始,就会影响到各行各业,当然也会照亮健康医疗,为健康医疗创造很大的机遇。

为什么说人工智能时代已经到来?2010年是一个重要的分水岭,在这之前人工智能经过几起几落,包括两次人工智能的"冬天",直到2010年,人工智能才真正进入黄金时代。因为在这一年,苹果手机的出现把电话、人、通信和网络全面联结在一起。从此,我们每个人就变成了整个世界物联网的超级传感器,我们每天上网,每天跟人交流,每天产生很多数据,从此就建立了很多的连接,诞生了很多互联网公司,也产生了极多的数据,这些数据的产生带来了很多效益,这使得互联网的应用成为不可逆转的趋势。2010年后,人工智能两个必要的条件同时具备:一是我们通常所说的大数据;二是高效的技术环境和高效的学习算法。我们迎来了黄金时代。

从人工智能角度来说,为什么人工智能可以解决我们的问题?实际应用中大部分都分为两个基础的应用:一个是回归,另一个是分类。我们现在用的人工智能大部分都是神经网络,神经网络早期是被用来模拟人的一层一层相联的神经元,它实际上具备两个能力,即万能逼近能力和万能分裂能力,只要这个函数是连续的,神经网络都可以逼近它;反之,任何可以分类的区域都可以用神经网络分开,二者的组合可以解决很多的问题。

我们思考这样一个问题,人工智能和人脑哪个强?其实这个问题很难有统一的答案,但我们可以说,人脑和人工智能是属于两个不同的函数,所以在不同的应用中有时人会超过机器,有时机器会超过人,那么我们在很多的应用中,如果充分利用好人工智能的特点，它就会超过我们，帮助我们做很多事情，这就是人工智能的用处。

当我们把医疗作为一个特定的应用或者作为一个特定体系，应该怎么应用人工智能、怎么利用人工智能的优势克服人作为医生时面对的局限，这是一个重要的问题。医疗工作人员的能量是有限的，时间也是有限的，像司机开车一样也会疲劳。假设一个医生一天看20个患者，一年大约看7000多个，一辈子就是30多万个，30多万个已经很多了，但如果是机器，如果是人工智能，它可以看几千万、几亿、几十亿，并且可以看上成百上千年，从这个角度来说，医生相对于人工智能，在时间和精力上都是有限的，那么人工智能相对医生来说，有可能是一个"超级医生"。人工智能优于医生的首先是庞大的数据，上下几千年的数据、同一时间全球共享的数据等，医生很难具备相似的数据存储能力。此外，不仅是数据，其他的硬件包括各种传感器、设备、技术都可以与人工智能联动。因此，我们谈人工智能的时候一定是超出数据本身，是人工智能＋各种各样的技术。

是人的脑袋聪明还是人工智能聪明，我认为各有千秋。举个例子，我们在2018年发表了有关睡眠状况的分析报告，调研了2000个患者的睡眠状况，如果是医生、教授去分析，很花时间，但用深度学习的技术分析后，可以看到AI的分析结果和医生的结果类似，但它能够减少大量时间，减少工作量，使得分类工作的效率提高几百倍。此外，随着数据不断增多，人工智能模型会越来越优化，因此，我们预期在某一个特定的行业、某一个特定的方向，人工智能会帮助我们甚至会超过我们，我们应该把人工智能作为有效助手帮助我们解决问题。再举一个例子，黄天一教授借助深度学习进行图像处理然后分析白内障。眼科医生能达到96%~97%的诊断率，但AI的结果可以超过眼科医生，达到99%。图像处理只是一个例子，利用医疗保健的多模数据，未来我们完全有可能将人工智能打造为超级医生。举例来说，中国在医学数据方面有宝贵的财富资源，我们有《皇帝内经》，有扁鹊的《皇帝经》，也有李时珍的《本草纲目》等医学名著，如果我们发明的人工智能把这些都学会之后，它就比我们掌握了更多的信息，可以通过自然语言处理、各种联想等将信息结合起来，帮助医生快速确定治疗方案。

此外，人工智能在脑科学领域的发展潜力也非常巨大，比如马斯克提出把芯片放在脑袋中可以治百病，我认为不是不可能。马斯克最初生产的芯片可以控制猴子的意念，让猴子手指活动的准确率达到了99.3%。换句话说，如果是脑袋当中某一部分出现了问题，我们是否就可以把芯片放进去并且可以做得越来越小，能耗越来越低，如果脑子当中某个神经原出了问题，我们只要把这个结构搞清楚就可以修复它。换句话说，我们认为很多脑部疾病最终都可以通过人工智能类似仿真等方法加以解决，我认为脑部疾病患者的神经元本身不需要调整，要调整的仅仅是神经元和神经元之间的连接。

提出这个理论后，在2013年，我们在老鼠的嗅觉系统、人的嗅觉系统以及猴子的视觉系统中都发现了同样的规律，多所国际知名高校发表的文章也认同我们的观点。后来我们在果蝇身上也发现了同样的神经元机制，即神经元不需要被调整，神经元的连接主导着大脑功能。总的来说，我相信人工智能可以帮助脑科学发展，也能够帮助我们治愈很多脑疾病，同时，脑机制又可以反过来推进人工智能，通过大量的数据学习优化人工智能的模型，实现互利共赢。

简单来讲，医疗健康和人工智能是一个很好的结合点。未来人工智能的发展趋势一定是能力越来越强，能耗越来越低，放在云端的速度越来越快。云端可能把新加坡所有的门诊数据连接起来，中国可以把所有大医院的数据连接起来，进行快速分析。此外，数据共享与分析离不开网络，5G、6G的重要性就会日益凸显。简单来讲，如果所有的医疗健康行业都运用人工智能——当然不是人工智能取代一切，而是人工智能帮助人类——这个时候的医生会感到很愉快，医生变成科学家，患者更加愉快，在家就可以沉浸式看病，这将带动整个行业的变革。

张大磊
鹰瞳科技创始人
ZHANG Dalei
Founder of Airdoc

鹰瞳（Airdoc）科技创始人，现任中国人工智能学会智慧医疗专业委员会秘书长、中国视光产业联盟副理事长。曾任微软总部 Excel 产品经理、PPTV 副总裁、新浪副总裁。

Zhang Dalei is the founder of Airdoc, the secretary-general of Professional Committee of Smart Medical of Chinese Association for Artificial Intelligence, and the vice director-general of Eye Health Industry Alliance of Chinese Health Information and Big Data Association. He once served as a program manager of Microsoft, and a vice president of PPTV and Sina.

数字医疗的挑战与创新

张大磊

此前大家从基础科学的角度分享了数字医疗的应用场景，接下来，我作为一名行业内从业者，将通过几个案例跟大家分享我如何看待数字医疗产业，数字医疗领域将如何被应用，以及在应用和创新过程中可能会碰到哪些问题。

鹰瞳成立之初旨在解决慢性疾病的早期检测和长期管理需求未被满足的问题，从数据可以看出，由于医疗资源供给不足，中国的糖尿病、高血压、心梗、中风等疾病在较多未检出的群体中存在。因此，我们想到借助人工智能将疾病诊断从传统的三甲医院普惠到基层，然而，这并不是一个简单的人工智能算法就能解决的问题。从算法的角度来看，通过对眼底视网膜血管、神经的分类和判读，可以发现正常人与糖尿病、青光眼、白内障或其他缺血性疾病患者的差异，但在真实应用中，即使把分类和判读做好了，大多数场景下也应用不起来。因为传统的视网膜眼底相机的拍摄过程需要在一个相对比较暗的环境中，并且要由专业的操作人员操作，这势必面临着单位经济成本高、用户支付不起的问题。因此，我们要想办法研发用户能够自助拍摄、检查、编写的设备，并且让这个设备不依赖于周围的操作环境和个人经济水平，推动普及慢性病检测。

为什么这个事情如此重要呢？大家可以发现，我国医患比例问题是极其突出的，以眼科为例，我国现在眼科医生仅有4.48万名，很多乡镇卫生院、社区卫生服务中心、二级医疗机构到现在为止没有眼科，全部归为五官科，大部分五官科医生在看眼耳鼻喉齿相关的疾病，供给端没有充足、专业的医生服务患者。再说需求端，现在各种各样的系统，包括远程医疗系统，都没有覆盖眼科疾病患者的需求。举一个简单的例子——近视，公司目前运营着全世界最大的眼健康筛查系统，目前临床端服务86万人次，从我们的数据来看，很多眼科疾病的发病人群越来越年轻化，并且发病率越来越高，随着很多电子产品不断走入千家万户，整个眼健康需求的程度和用户人群增长速度，将远远超出大家的设想。

如何解决这些问题呢？人工智能和机器学习可以做一些辅助工作。例如，我们可以通过图像识别、自然语言处理，构建基于人工智能的决策模型。基层医疗机构的全科医生、校医、普通人在人工智能工具的辅助下，完成初步的筛查工作，第一时间筛选出问题，把可能有问题的患者转去上级医院相对专业的眼科医生那里。随后，由专业的眼科医生把关，对存在常见疾病的患者进行治疗，将有疑难杂症的患者再转诊到眼科专家，以此通过人工智能建立一个真实的专家网络。在整个过程中，我们仅将一部分工作交给医生来做，另外一部分工作由机器、算法完成，以降低单位经济成本，服务更多患者。

但是，仅有单位经济模型并不代表所有的问题都可以解决得好，为把问题解决好，我们需要在技术上做更多的工作。技术方面大家过去比较关注的是"感知"方面的工作，比如如何实现对图像上存在的病变、病灶的识别。以青光眼为例，我们四五年前就通过图像识别和附加算法进行图像感知，告知用户是否患有青光眼、患青光眼的风险、治疗的过程中神经纤维层是否发生了变化等。目前，技术发展主要集中在"认知"领域，比如我们近期尝试在系统中引入医生自动问诊和分诊环节，优化用户和医生的体验。此外，我们开始研究疾病的量化，比如出血、渗血、玻璃膜疣的量化，从而提供更多的参数，从不同维度帮助医生更好地理解疾病。具体来说，过去医生只能看到动脉堵塞、静脉堵塞，现在当我们把血管精细分割出来之后，可以看到不同区域的血管发展变化，这对心梗、中风以及判断用户发生血管改变的部位意义重大。

以上和大家介绍的是我们公司的研究现状，随着样本越来越多，我们已经可以让算法模拟出用户随后的发展变化。我们使用算法对200多万个样本进行持续的学习和训练，使得预期网络在真实世界使用时可以清楚地让每个人知道他在接下来1~5年中眼底分别可能发生什么变化，同时也让用户知道"我"在哪一年会碰到什么问题，"我"需要采取什么干预手段，这对于提高疾病的治愈率会有一定的效果，正如大家认知的那样，我们需要对疾病进行前期预防、干预或早期诊断和治疗，否则疾病可能会越来越严重。

除了对传统眼科疾病的研究和诊断，我们也在尝试把眼底图像的改变和心血管疾病进行联系。我们和北京大学医学部、同仁医院合作多年，持续跟踪了3.9万人在3~5年身体的发展变化，单纯通过眼底的照片来判断一个人患脑梗、中风的风险。我们的模型使轻度改变的识别准确性超0.95，重度识别准确性超0.98，这个模型与传统技术相比，不仅可以捕捉眼科医生能够看到的动脉硬化，而且可以看到心血管医生通过

CT血管造影（CTA）、造影等更多的手段才可以判断出的缺血性的脑血管病和动脉粥样硬化等疾病。因此，我们认为这些工作在普通用户生活中非常重要，它可以通过无创的方式让每个人知道自己身体的发展变化。在这些基础之上，我们也在源源不断地研发产品，希望产品在更多人群中应用起来。

除了检测，我们也可以看到非常多的人在近视治疗上的需求，以及市面上各种各样的治疗方案存在的安全性问题。因此，我们提供了一个可以让医生远程控制指令的安全性平台，在治疗过程中确保既有效又安全。举例来说，我们的系统不像手电筒单纯把激光打过去，但不知道激光被打到哪儿，以及未来会有什么损伤。我们希望通过持续、完整的诊断，提供不断调整的治疗方案，达到最佳治疗效果。我们刚刚提到单位经济成本的降低，因为我们并不相信人工智能是一个独立工作的动作，我们认为人工智能实际上还是人类使用的辅助手段，它可以大幅增加医生服务人群的数量，同时大幅降低整个社会的经济成本。

总的来说，我们可以看到数字医疗这个领域里还有非常多的工作值得向前推进，我们在近视、心脑血管疾病和神经系统性疾病等领域中也仍有大量正在研究的工作，希望未来能够和更多的同仁一起将其发展壮大，把最好的产品呈现给大家。谢谢大家！

柳楠

杜克-新加坡国立大学医学院定量医学和卫生服务与系统研究中心副教授

LIU Nan

Associate Professor at the Centre for Quantitative Medicine and Programme in Health Services and Systems Research, Duke-NUS Medicine School

新加坡国立大学医学院定量医学和卫生服务与系统研究中心的副教授。重点研究人工智能和机器学习，并将其应用于医学信息学、卫生服务研究、急救和重症监护、心脏病学和健康创新。获得了国家医学研究委员会、国家卫生创新中心和国家研究基金会的研究资助。2022年被斯坦福大学和爱思唯尔评为世界前2%顶尖科学家。此外，是80多本国际期刊的审稿人，如《柳叶刀》和《自然医学》。

Liu Nan is an associate professor at the Centre for Quantitative Medicine and Programme in Health Services and Systems Research at Duke-NUS Medicine School. His research focuses on artificial intelligence and machine learning with applications to medical informatics, health services research, emergency and critical care, cardiology, and health innovation. He has been awarded research grants from the National Medical Research Council, National Health Innovation Centre, and National Research Foundation. He was recognized as one of the World's Top 2% Scientists by Stanford University and Elsevier in 2022. Additionally, he is a regular reviewer for more than 80 international journals, including *The Lancet* and *Nature Medicine*.

人工智能在健康领域的挑战与机遇

柳　楠

大家好，我要分享的是从医学的角度探讨人工智能在医疗中的应用。

每次讲到人工智能，我们都会问这样的问题：为什么要将人工智能用在医疗领域呢？这其实也是我在思考的一个问题。由于数据的储存能力提高，数据的分析和分类能力更强，真实世界的数据，比如疾病等级、电子健康记录管理、医疗索赔数据库、可穿戴设备等数据，都可以轻而易举地获得，同时可以支持多种类型的实验设计，不仅有随机实验，也有大型的观察性研究，或者是实用临床实验。分析真实的数据，就能得到数据背后存在的潜在风险和利益。

如果我们仅用临床实验研究的话，数据的收集范围就比较小，同时我们也发现这些数据都是在一些优化的条件之下生成的，但在收集真实数据的过程中，当大量药物和医疗器械进入市场时，我们就可以针对人口规模重新分析数据，比如通过大型医疗机构获得新的数据。然而，如果数据的规模变得非常巨大，且数据是在没有控制和优化的条件下收集的，目前的数据处理能力无法分析大量的异质性的数据，因此，我认为人工智能可能是一个潜在的解决方案。

人工智能并不是一个新兴事物，早在20世纪50年代我们就有人工智能的概念了，那时人们就在考虑是不是能够使用机器模仿人类的行为。直到20世纪80年代，电脑成为个人广为流行的设备，科学家才开始分析和深度学习。深度学习是指一种能够让机器学习数据的方式，在过去10年中由于计算机计算能力的不断增强和云端服务的不断巩固，人工智能和深度学习才逐渐成为广受欢迎的术语。

人工智能和机器学习进一步探索了算法的界限，通过计算机学科分支，人工智能和机器学习能够与数据分析和数据优化相关联，提供预测性的分析和预测性的模型。人工智能有悠久的历史，可以被应用在很多不同的领域，比如搜索引擎，当然，人工智能也能够被应用在其他领域。总体而言，人工智能可以分析一些概念上的数据，我们可以使用人工智能学习选择不同的变量，进一步了解不同的维度。到目前为止，我们发现使用人工智能分析数据都是非常重要的，我给大家举一个例子——自然语言处理。自然语言处理是进一步处理语言和音频的过程，是计算机视觉技术在图像和视频分析中的应用，包含了图像加工，图像分化以及2D、3D图像分析等。将这些技术应用在医疗健康的体系中，对于智能医疗的实现更加重要，因为对于医院而言，近乎一半以上的数据是没有被统一的，是没有被优化的数据，即使是在现代医疗体系中，50%的数据仍旧是在不受控的条件之下得到的。

此外，我觉得人工智能对于信息融合也至关重要。因为数据不只是来自一个数据库，我们希望能够对不同来源的医疗数据进行分析，分析整个数据的整合性和融合性，这就是为什么人工智能和机器学习在数字医疗、医疗物联网以及大规模数据分析中起着至关重要的作用。举个例子，最近我们做了一个比较简单的数据分析，在网站上分析大量的医学论文，如果我们观察一些相关的搜索关键词的话，就可以找出相关的数据，因此数据的数量也在过去几年迅速生长，我们觉得借此可以使用人工智能帮助我们发掘新的研究方向。

其他的嘉宾提到了人工智能在眼科学的应用，能够给我们的眼科学家带来一些标志性的改变，比如可能使用基础性的眼科图像识别预测患者是否具有视网膜病变等。阿尔法狗是一种预测蛋白质结构的机器，这是我们医院医疗科学的一大转折点，并且我觉得蛋白质折叠解析一直是科学家面临且急切想要解决的问题。阿尔法狗可以成为蛋白质结构解析的解决方案，不久的将来会有更多技术帮助我们了解蛋白质。语言分析和图像分析是人工智能的两大支柱，它将在我们传统的数据处理中起到至关重要的作用。同时，我们也可以使用人工智能对人们进行互建。比如有人可能会受到脑卒中的影响，我们可以分析他们的心电图或一些基于视觉的成像图形；此外，我觉得心脑血管可能是人工智能广泛应用的另一个领域，我们开发的 AI in cardiology 人工智能，可以对有胸部疼痛的患者进行实时监控，以防止患者出现心肌梗死或急性心源性猝死等潜在疾病。

另外一种人工智能的应用领域是急诊。这里有一个很好的例子，急诊上需要陪诊，人工智能已经准备好了，并且能够参与医疗决策的过程，且人工智能产品比较简单易于使用，医生和患者都容易掌握。同时，在救护车的服务过程中，人工智能也是能够被广泛应用的，比如，哥本哈根紧急疗服务使用了人工智能助手帮助派遣不同的救护车。现在我们也开发了一种人工智能的体系，它了解患者的具体情况，实时分析患者的情况和体质，现在我们的设备正在进行随机性临床实验三期，我们相信这个设备很快就会进入临床应用。

还有一个例子是人工智能在心理健康方面的应用。心理健康在一些病情中是非常严重的问题，我们设计了一个软件，使其用自然语言处理的方式将手机的数据分析聚集在一起，并基于之前拥有的知识库对未来进行预测。此外，还有人工智能膳食管理的应用。它并不是人工智能在诊疗过程中的使用，而是人工智能在日常保健中的应用。系统将会根据手机的数据，根据你的生活方式、活动方式，检测你平时吃什么，从而更好地管理你的饮食。总而言之，人工智能已经应用在很多不同的医学领域，同时我们相信更多的研究很快就会出现，只有把人工智能和具体的医疗实践结合在一起，才能产生真实的影响。

当然人工智能也面临一些挑战。到目前为止，人工智能和医学领域的挑战就是数据的不明确性。数据质量本身存在一定的问题，数据具有独特性，可能会导致在人工智能领域的数据不平衡。此外，隐私和监控在人工智能里也是一个热点，数据分享的基础是隐私保护和法规的批准。那么机遇和危机总是并存的，这是大家的共识。

毫无疑问，全球都在从一个独立的数据督导进入全球数据网络共享，云计算还有云服务可以实现万物共联，可以将这种医疗服务通过国际化的网络推广开。谢谢！

林水德
新加坡国立大学生物医学工程学会主席，健康创新与技术研究所所长
Chwee Teck LIM
NUS Society Chair Professor of Biomedical Engineering; Director of the Institute for Health Innovation and Technology

新加坡国立大学生物医学工程学会主席，健康创新与技术研究所所长，新加坡卫生技术联盟董事。研究方向是人类疾病机械生物学以及用于疾病诊断和治疗的创新生物医学技术的开发。发表期刊论文450多篇，并发表了420多场全体会议、主题演讲、受邀演讲。

Chwee Teck LIM is the NUS Society Chair Professor of Biomedical Engineering and Director of the Institute for Health Innovation and Technology at the National University of Singapore. He is also the Director of Singapore Health Technologies Consortium. His research interests are human disease mechanobiology as well as the development of innovative biomedical technologies for disease diagnosis and therapy. He is a prolific researcher, having co-authored over 450 journal publications in related journals such as *Nature* and *Science,* and having given more than 420 plenary, keynote, invited lectures.

工程学在推进医学和医疗保健中的重要作用

林水德

大家好，我是来自新加坡国立大学的林水德，我想分享工程学在推进医学和医疗保健中的重要作用。

有数据和研究表明，我们正处于一个快速老龄化的时代，到2050年，每5个人中就有1个人超过65岁，而随着年龄增长会产生一系列的慢性疾病，比如高血压、关节炎、心脏病、糖尿病、抑郁症、阿尔茨海默病或癌症，事实上我们从大流行病中吸取的教训就是我们不仅要快速诊断病情，也要有效治疗患者，如此才能阻止病情的进一步传播。因此，要解决健康问题的第一个重大挑战是疾病的预防，第二个是早发现、早治疗。解决卫生和医学的问题需要多方和跨学科的努力，这就包括科学家、工程师和患者之间的合作。

工程技术正在不断改变医疗保健。新加坡国立大学设立了医疗创新和教育技术机构，旨在提高健康水平和技术创新的能力。那我们如何做到这一点呢？首先，要了解临床面临的挑战，找到合作伙伴进行创新并提出解决方案，其次，更为重要的一点是孵化技术层开发出来的新技术对患者、医生和社会产生积极的影响。这就需要三方的合作，大学不仅要跟医院密切合作，而且要与全球的行业合作。那如何将我们的医疗技术商业化？无论是获得许可还是从大学技术开发中衍生而来，我们都希望进行临床实验并得到反馈，研究如何进一步改善医疗技术。这里展示了我们在自己的实验室开发的技术，包括即时检验（POCT）诊断到可穿戴传感器以及器官芯片，我想谈的第一个问题就是癌症诊断，我们的目标是打破目前癌症的诊断瓶颈。

目前，癌症的标准检查是将一个非常锋利的仪器刺入人体，对肿瘤及癌细胞进行采样，再带到实验室进一步分析。我们知道肿瘤细胞具有高度侵袭性，且这些癌症的细胞首先会去侵袭淋巴系统，其次是整个新陈代谢系统，我们希望能够识别并从血液当中分离循环肿瘤或者癌细胞，将其用于进一步的分析，这就是我们所说的液体活检。我们发现，如果可以从血液当中获得癌细胞，这样就可以减少侵入性测试，患者不用那么痛苦，而且可以经常通过血检检测癌细胞。

这样，我们可以每两周或者每个月通过不同的细胞技术，观察某些特定突变的癌细胞是否被破坏或被杀死，进而判断癌症的疗法对特定的患者是否奏效。我们开发并且最终商业化的芯片，非常简单，是由一个螺旋通道构成，我们所做的是让细胞通过螺旋通道，当它流向曲线通道时开始初始聚焦，较大和较硬的癌细胞和血细胞分离。我们最终将这样的一种微芯片商业化，因为临床对于使用这种特殊芯片从患者血液当中分离癌细胞保持高度的兴趣。这是非常简单的芯片，我们要做的事情就是把设备的顶部打开，放入盒子收集样本，用户将样本拿出来，按一个按钮就可以实现细胞分选。现在我们主张使用技术从血液当中分离癌细胞，再把细胞送去做进一步的分析，不管是基因分析还是分子分析，根据分析的信息将重要的信息放在最终的医疗报告当中。医生看报告的时候不仅可以看到细胞数，还可以看到血液中细胞通过药物治疗后出现的一些变化，从而为患者提供正确的给药途径，提供基于个性化的治疗方案，有效治疗患者。因此，我们开发的技术不仅可以帮助医生更好的进行诊断，而且可以帮助医生进行治疗。

大家都说，将人工智能应用于医疗卫生方面意义重大。我想补充的是，没有技术就没有数据，人工智能需要数据才能有效地运作，因此，我们需要技术收集高质量的数据。患者本身就是健康数据的来源，我们获得健康数据的其中一个途径是医生的真实检查，医生可以在患者来看病的时候收集患者的数据，这是在基于预约的时间点上完成的，或者我们可以获得实验室的真实结果，这也是在时间表上可以获得的。这是一个更加有规律的时间点的收集，不像此前的非常离散的时间收集点。实际上，要获得患者生成的健康数据，我们可以利用一些可穿戴设备。可穿戴设备是研究的热门话题，实际上很多人都会戴手表，从我们的身体中不断收集数据。如果我们使用可穿戴设备，那收集的数据不仅是准确可依赖的，而且是完整的、实时的，能够使数据达到高质量、高标准的要求。同时，我们可以使用可穿戴设备进一步精准监管个人健康，从而帮助我们预防、发现疾病，并带领我们走向精准诊疗的道路。

可穿戴医疗设备在医疗市场占据的规模很大，不仅包括诊疗性设备，还包括可穿戴设备。例如糖尿病截肢的问题，我们发现每两个人中有一个人有未确诊的糖尿病，同时我们发现在成年人中每11个人就会有1人确诊糖尿病。在新加坡，糖尿病的确诊机制是一种比较长期性的机制，而糖尿病会带来眼盲、肾衰竭、心脏疾病、脑卒中、截肢等，所以我们希望能够采取一种方式针对糖尿病进行相关的诊疗。我们希望实时地追踪糖尿病患者足部表面的压力数据以追踪溃疡的发生。最开始的时候我们提供了一个智能解决方案,在智能鞋垫上加入各种不同的传感器,它模拟了相关的电子原件和电子模型,希望探究高压具体在什么位置,模拟实时的糖尿病溃疡生成界面。人们可能感受不到疼痛,但如果我们对异常压力有比较清晰的认知,就能够了解哪些人有潜在的患糖尿病的风险。最后我想总结的是,对于这样一些实时的数据而言,如果想要让人工智能有所作为,健康的人和患者的数据必须准确、完整、实时,我觉得可穿戴设备能够确保这些数据的质量,通过每天收集一些数据,人工智能可以建立一个基线,同时如果患者有任何偏离日常的情况,也能够尽早地提醒患者,尽快就医。

总体而言,我相信医疗可穿戴设备能够帮助我们发掘更好的医疗健康管理体系,当我们考虑到为医疗健康设计工程的时候,要考虑我们的最终目标不仅是进一步提高临床结果、减少医疗健康的花销,而且能够进一步提高我们的寿命预期。医生一次只能诊疗一个患者,但是一项医疗技术能够通过工程师之手影响数千名患者,在任何地方、任何时间都不受限制。

IFEE 2022

第三届国际工程教育论坛
The 3rd International Forum On Engineering Education

分组论坛 A4
Panel A4

新型电力系统
New Power System

2022 年 12 月 8 日 20:00–23:00

承办单位简介

清华大学电机工程与应用电子技术系

清华大学电机工程与应用电子技术系（以下简称电机系）创立于1932年，是清华大学最早成立的三个工程系之一，也是全国首批设立国家一级重点学科和一级学科博士点的院系。在历次学科评估中均获全国第一或被评为A+。

电机系秉承"为学在严，为人要正"的系训，坚持"教书育人"的优良传统，以"培养基础扎实、创新能力突出、国际视野开阔的电气工程领域领军人才"为目标，共培养毕业生19000多名，涌现出以国家最高科学技术奖获得者金怡濂院士、"八一勋章"获得者马伟明院士、国家电网有限公司首任总经理赵希正、国务院总理朱镕基为杰出代表的一大批学术大师、兴业英才和治国栋梁。

电机系以建设世界领先的电气工程为愿景，以推动中国电力电工行业进步为使命，守正根基，创新思路，在长期发展中形成鲜明特色与优势。

About the Organizer

The Department of Electrical Engineering of Tsinghua University

Department of Electrical Engineering, founded in 1932, is one of the three earliest engineering departments established by Tsinghua University, and also one of the first departments in China to set up national first level key disciplines and first level discipline doctoral programs. It always ranked first or A+ in all previous national discipline evaluations.

Department of Electrical Engineering has trained more than 19,000 graduates, under the motto of "Conscientious academics and honest behavior", and the good tradition on Teaching and learning aiming at "Cultivating leading talents in the field of electrical engineering with solid foundation, outstanding innovation ability and broad international vision". A large number of outstanding academic masters, business talents and backbones governing the country are among the graduates.

With the vision of building a world-leading electrical engineering faculty and the mission of promoting the progress of China power and electrical industry, the Department of Electrical Engineering always adheres to its foundation, innovates its thinking, and has created distinctive features and advantages in its long-term development.

分论坛主持

主持人 Chair

康重庆
清华大学电机系教授、电机系系主任
KANG Chongqing
Professor and Dean of the Department of Electrical Engineering, Tsinghua University

清华大学电机系主任，清华大学能源互联网创新研究院院长，清华四川能源互联网研究院院长，中国电机工程学会副理事长。电气电子工程师学会会士，中国电机工程学会会士，北京市教学名师。国家杰出青年科学基金获得者，国家"万人计划"科技创新领军人才。被聘为英国帝国理工学院访问教授、韩国延世大学兼职教授。主要研究方向为电力系统规划、电力系统优化运行、能源互联网、可再生能源、低碳电力技术、负荷预测、电力市场。作为项目负责人，承担国家重点研发计划项目2项，发表论文400余篇，其中 *IEEE Transactions* 文章100余篇，2017年以来连续入选爱思唯尔（Elsevier）中国高被引学者（Chinese most cited researchers）榜单。获国家级教学成果奖二等奖（第一完成人）、2018年度中国电力科学技术杰出贡献奖、2021年电气电子工程学会电力与能源协会电力系统可靠性奖、2021年 IET 成就奖章。

Kang Chongqing is the Dean of the Department of Electrical Engineering and the President of Energy Internet Innovation Research Institute at Tsinghua University, and the President of Tsinghua Sichuan Energy Internet Research Institute. He serves as the Vice Chairman of Beijing Society of Electrical Engineering.

He has been selected as an IEEE Fellow and a CSEE Fellow. He is the recipient of the National Science Fund for Distinguished Young Scholars. He has been selected in the National "Ten Thousand Talents Program". He is appointed as a Visiting Professor at Imperial College London and an Adjunct Professor at Yonsei University in South Korea. His research interests mainly include power system planning, power system dispatch and operation, energy Internet, renewable energy, low-carbon power technology, load forecasting, and power market. He has been the Chief Scientist of 2 projects under National Key R&D Program of China. He has published more than 400 papers, including more than 100 papers published in IEEE Transaction journals. He was continuously selected as the Chinese Most Cited Researchers since 2017 by Elsevier. He has been honored with the Second Prize for National Teaching Achievement, Famous Teacher of Beijing, 2018 Award of Outstanding Contribution to China Electric Power Science and Technology, 2021 IEEE PES Roy Billinton Power System Reliability Award, and 2021 IET Achievement Medal.

主持人 Chair

李冬梅
清华大学电子工程系副教授
LI Dongmei
Associate Professor of the Department of Electronic Engineering, Tsinghua University

清华大学电子工程系副教授。分别于1990年、1994年和2007年在清华大学电子工程系获半导体物理与器件工学学士、电子科学与技术工学硕士和博士学位，于2002—2003年在美国加利福尼亚大学圣地亚哥分校（UCSD）访问进修。主要研究方向为模拟与数模混合集成电路、语音图像信号采集电路及预处理算法与应用系统等。

Li Dongmei is an associate professor of the Department of the Department of Electronic Engineering of Tsinghua University. She received her Bachelor, Master and Doctor degrees from the Department of Electronic Engineering of Tsinghua University in 1990, 1994 and 2007, respectively. From 2002 to 2003, she studied at the University of California, San Diego (UCSD), as a visiting scholar. She mainly researches about the Anolog and Mixed-Signal Integrated Circuits design, the key technology of Speech Enhancement SoC design and applications, and she also works on the circuits suitable in CMOS image sensor.

王成山
中国工程院院士，天津大学教授
WANG Chengshan
Member of CAE, Professor of Tianjin University

中国工程院院士，现任智能电网教育部重点实验室主任，微网与智能配电系统开发与应用国家地方联合工程研究中心主任；国家级人才称号获得者。长期从事智能配电网与微电网研究工作。出版中英文著作6部，发表论文200余篇，文章被引用3万余次，连续七年入选爱思唯尔中国高被引学者；获国家技术发明奖二等奖1项（排名第一）、国家科学技术进步奖二等奖3项（2项排名一，1项排名二），获何梁何利基金科学与技术进步奖、全国创新争先奖、全国五一劳动奖，领导的团队入选教育部创新团队和科学技术部重点领域创新团队。

He is an academician of CAE, and currently the Director of the Key Laborator of Smar Grid of the Ministry of Education, and the Director of the National and Local Joint Engineering Research Center for Microgrids and Intelligent Power Distribution Systems. He has been long engaged in the research on smart distribution network and microgrids, and has published 6 Chinese or English books and more than 200 papers, which were cited for more than 30,000 times. He has been selected as a Highly Cited Chinese Researcher by Elsevier for 7 consecutive years. He has won the Second Prize of the National Award for Technical Invention (ranked first), 3 Second Prizes of the National Science and Technology Progress Award (2 items ranked first and 1 item ranked second), the Science and Technology Progress Award of Ho Leung Ho Lee Foundation, the National Award for Innovation Pioneering and the National Labor Medal. His team was selected as the innovation team of both the Ministry of Education and the Ministry of Science and Technology in key fields.

关于智能配电系统几个问题的思考

王成山

我谨代表天津大学，感谢大家参加今天的论坛。我主要分享我们在新型电力系统背景下，对工程教育的一些思考。报告分为三个部分：储能产业的需求分析，卓越工程师培养策略，以及储能专业工程教育与人才培养。

首先，储能技术是未来新型电力系统的核心支撑技术，其在新能源并网、负荷波动调节及可再生能源消纳等方面发挥着重要作用。对于推动新型电力系统发展，储能技术具有极大潜力。然而，储能产业在储能材料、相关技术、应用安全及运行维护等方面仍存在诸多技术难题，亟须全链条攻关。

另外，随着新型储能产业的快速发展，亟须高层次人才的支持。在这一背景下，我们与华北电力大学、西安交通大学共同获批首批国家储能技术产教融合创新平台。我们将依托这一平台，积极开展技术攻关与人才培养。

为推动储能领域人才培养和科技创新，产教融合创新平台将重点关注以下方面：电化学储能技术中心、燃料储能及应用、储能安全与运维技术及储能经济与政策研究。最终，我们将以推动储能领域人才培养和科技创新为目标，培养推动储能技术产业进步与产业发展的卓越工程师和科学家。

天津大学将通过高水平学科的相互融合，以及在科技创新方面的努力，为储能专业的人才培养提供坚实基础。目前，储能专业已成为天津大学一级学科博士点和硕士学位授权点，我们计划打造一流的储能学科，并在此基础上培养各层次的储能专业人才。

接下来，我们将探讨一些工程师培养的模式。作为此次论坛的主题，工程教育在天津大学一直备受关注和重视。早在2010年，我们就已加入教育部的卓越工程师教育培养计划。2017年，我们又参与了新工科建设，实施了"复旦共识""天大行动"和"北京指南"等重要举措，共同推动新工科发展。2019年，我们又启动了卓越工程师教育培养计划的2.0版本，开启了新的工程教育模式。

在探索新的工程教育模式时，我们始终关注三个重要方向：从学科导向转向产业需求导向，从专业分割转向跨界交叉融合，以及从适应服务转向支撑引领。新工科、卓越工程师教育等计划旨在实现这些转变，以便更好地满足产业需求。

我们认为，在实现这些转变时，应关注以下几点。第一，以产业需求为导向。学科应紧密围绕产业需求，以确保培养的工程师能更好地为社会和产业服务。第二，跨界交叉融合。通过整合不同专业，实现工程教育的全面发展，培养出具有创新思维和跨学科理解能力的卓越工程师。第三，发挥支撑引领作用。在课程体系、实践教学等方面进行创新，提升教育质量，发挥对产业的支撑和引领作用。

我们结合储能专业做了一系列具体工作。我们计划整合机械学院、化工学院、材料学院、自动化学院以及经管学部等多个学院的优势资源，共同建设储能科学与工程专业，培养具有家国情怀、全球视野、前瞻性判断力以及跨学科理解能力的卓越工程师和科学家。

为实现这一目标，天津大学集合了相关学院的优秀师资力量，全方位参与课程设计和人才培养工作。此外，我们还重点关注选拔、培养、评价和保障等多个方面，力求在全过程中实现卓越工程师的培养体系。

随着储能专业的招生工作逐步展开，为确保选拔出最适合储能专业的学生，我们在新生入校后组织了第二次选拔，最终选出22名优秀学生。

在课程体系建设方面，我们重视基础知识，强调学科交叉融合。储能化学基础课程就是一个典型例子，我们将不同学科的知识点有机融合，以满足后续专业课程的需求。同时，我们采用授课、实验、作业和自学等多种考核方式，选拔具备化学化工和储能化学背景且熟悉该领域的教师参与课程建设。

在课程建设中，我们力求构建以实践能力为导向的项目式课程体系。课程以项目为核心，引导学生将所学知识与课程内容相结合。学校老师将与企业共同指导学生完成项目，培养学生的动手能力和实践经验。

将企业的工程问题引入课程是提高学生兴趣和实践能力的关键。我们已在电气工程等专业进行了相关探索，取得了良好效果。然而，这对学生的要求较高，部分学生可能难以适应。尽管如此，我们认为这是未来人才培养的趋势，因此在储能专业课程设计中，我们从大一至大四都设置了相关课程和项目。

为了加强实践能力培养，我们采用了校企双导师制，并建立了储能领域高层次人才的培养体系。此外，我们安排了三次实习，包括基础知识学习后的企业实习、专业课程学习后的企业实习以及大四的综合素养工程实习，全面培养学生的实践能力。

我们还与企业和科研院所建立了实训基地，共享实验设备和数据，共同开展人才培养和科研项目。这种产教融合模式和校企合作模式有利于实现人才培养与企业需求的紧密结合，提高人才培养质量。

在储能专业的培养模式方面，我们强调多种学位结合和多种人才"出口"，毕业生可到储能电池制造企业、燃料电池企业等领域工作，也可从事储能系统集成、电网应用等方面的工作。同时，我们还鼓励学生在其他领域深造，为他们提供更多选择。到大四时，我们会根据学生的兴趣和发展需求进行分流。学生可以选择不同的方向，如直接攻读硕士学位，或在本科毕业后攻读博士学位。我们致力于打通本硕博之间的体制壁垒，将培养节奏和课程体系一起来。

另外，在我们设计的基础课程中，储能专业涉及许多学科。为了更好地教授这些课程，我们将共同的教师组成课题小组，共同设计这一基础课程。同时，我们降低了专业课的总学分要求，并增加了丰富的专业选修课程。

此外，我们强调了四年一贯制的项目制课程。在每个学期，我们都会设置一些项目课程，引导学生学习。我们还为学生提供了储能微专业培训，这对于非储能专业的学生和对储能感兴趣的其他专业学生来说尤为有益。我们开设了几门课程，如果这些学生选择了这些课程，他们将获得相应的证书。这种培训课程旨在引导学生转向储能领域，例如，鼓励我们化工学院的学生从化学和应用化学转向储能方向。此外，电气工程专业的学生也可以学习储能在电力系统中的应用。

另外，我们还在开展高端培训，即非学历的高层次人才储能培训项目。发展改革委员会要求我们为社会培养储能人才，这项培训的参与人数众多。我们通过微专业的形式，鼓励学生选修我们的课程，以便进行人才培养。这些做法旨在培养具有实际工程能力、创新能力和跨学科理解能力的储能专业人才。我们将继续努力，为社会输送更多优秀的储能专业人才。谢谢大家！

赛义夫·拉赫曼
弗吉尼亚理工大学教授，IEEE 候任主席
Saifur RAHMAN
Professor at Virginia Tech; IEEE President-Elect

　　IEEE 候任主席，弗吉尼亚理工大学高级研究所的创始主任。曾担任美国国家科学基金会国际科学与工程咨询委员会主席。长期从事替代能源、智能电网、关键基础设施、评估与建模、不确定性评价和环境影响等方面的研究。2000年因对 IEEE 的杰出成就和贡献被授予 IEEE 千禧年奖章。2013年获得 PES 颁发的杰出动力工程教育家奖，2012年获得先进服务奖，2011年获得 IEEE-USA 专业成就奖。

　　Saifur RAHMAN, IEEE President-elect, the Founding Director of the Advanced Research Institute at Virginia Tech. He has served as the Chair of the US National Science Foundation Advisory Committee for International Science and Engineering. He has been long engaged in the research of Alternate energy, Smart grid, Critical infrastructure, assessment and modeling, Uncertainty evaluation and Environmental impacts. He was awarded the IEEE Millennium Medal in 2000 for outstanding achievements and contributions to IEEE. He received the Outstanding Power Engineering Educator Award from PES in 2013, the Meritorious Service Award in 2012, and the IEEE-USA Professional Achievement Award in 2011.

工程教育和智能电网以及不断演进的电力系统的研究

赛义夫·拉赫曼

大家好。我分享的主题是《工程教育和智能电网以及不断演进的电力系统的研究》。现在智能的电网正在不断发生变化，我们如何培养合适的人才应对当前的变革？以下介绍我的一些研究。

首先，智能电网是什么，大家可能有所了解。我在这里给大家做个简要的背景介绍。智能电网是由多个部分组成的，包括火电厂、核电厂、水电站、太阳能光伏电站、电动汽车、工厂、智能建筑和智能城市等。实际上，在未来几十年的发展过程中，仍有大量电能需要引入智能电网。智能电网涵盖了发电、输电、配电和终端使用的各个环节，可以实现更高效的电力传输。

接下来，我们分析一下智能电网的使用动机。我们为什么需要智能电网？根据图1所示的能源管理三角形，智能电网在这个过程中起到了关键作用。在三角形的一角，

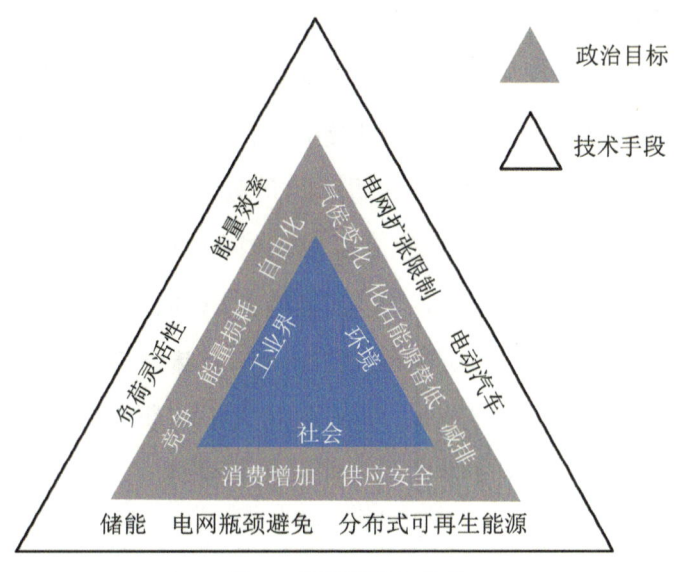

图1　能源管理三角形

政府、政策制定者和行业参与者共同参与，以确保能源供应的稳定和可持续；另一角则涉及终端用户和决策者之间的互动。智能电网在这个过程中起到了一个中心作用，它可以让我们更好地理解不同行业、环境和社会之间的相互作用。

智能电网的目标是提高电网的可靠性、安全性和成本效益。为了实现这一目标，我们需要采用先进的传感器、通信技术和分布式计算技术。这意味着，智能电网不仅需要电力工程师，还需要计算机工程师和传感器工程师等多领域专业人士共同参与。

智能电网与传统电网的区别在于，智能电网不仅可以传输电力，还可以进行实时监控、控制和调度。智能电网的出现让我们不仅可以提高电力传输的便利性，还能实现更多的功能。例如，通过电压控制、电量优化和不同电压等级之间的转换，提高智能电网的运行效率。

电网的演进过程也在智能电网的出现中发生了变化。在智能电网出现之前，电网主要由电站和配电站组成，从高压到低压，再到中压，然后进行长途传输。通过变电站进行电压转换，为不同社区提供电力。然而，随着智能电网的出现，电网的通信技术逐渐成为重要组成部分，实现了信息流与电流的融合。这意味着在电缆线中，我们还需要通信技术，实现从端到端的传输。

综上所述，智能电网的出现使得电网更加智能、安全和可靠，同时实现了更高的单位成本效益。这种技术的普及和发展将对未来能源产业产生深远的影响，有助于实现全球能源转型和减少碳排放。

举一个实际案例，我们常见的电力基础设施包括电站、变压器和配电站等，每个配电站都连接到不同的公用建筑、家庭和商业建筑。然而，随着新技术的出现，我们需要在电力基础设施上增加一个信息基础设施架构。这将带来新的发展，例如，智能网关可以位于家庭中，以使用电网中的智能电量表。这就是我们将要看到的未来发展趋势。对于风能、太阳能与储能技术，以及电动汽车等可再生能源的结合，这是一种变革。在这种情况下，我们需要关注电动车的负载容量，例如，100千瓦的电动汽车负载，如何在分布式发电的情况下为家庭提供足够的功率容量。

分布式发电意味着能源无处不在，但其具有间歇性，无法持续提供电力。当我们讨论智能电网时，它的关键在于实现无缝供电。这意味着在研究过程中，我们需要考虑如何适应分布式发电的变化。例如，美国西北大学的研究数据展示了风能输入与负载需求之间的错配问题，在不同季节，风能和负载需求的变化使得在需求高峰时期，风能输出可能无法满足需求。

在夏季，主要的挑战是空调负荷以及公共和工业领域在早上8点到晚上8点的高峰需求。此外，风能产出在下午5点达到峰值，这意味着在夏季，风能发电在某些时段可能无法满足需求。在秋天，仍有两个需求峰值，因为供热需求开始显现，这在早上的负荷高峰期尤为明显；另一个峰值出现在晚上8点，此时风能输出已经不再强劲。这些事实表明，太阳能和风能的间歇性可能与我们的需求并不完全匹配。

另外，在寒冷的冬季，即使阳光充足，也仍可能出现太阳能电板被积雪覆盖的情况。这意味着即使阳光明媚，太阳能电池板的性能仍会受到一定的影响。例如在弗吉尼亚州冬季会遇到的大雪问题，中东地区虽然通常不会下雪，但是阿布扎比的大型太阳能电厂也可能受到雾霾的影响，导致太阳能发电量降低。另外，沙特阿拉伯的太阳能光伏发电系统也存在问题。尽管屋顶安装了2兆瓦的太阳能光伏板，但在冬季，由于沙漠中的大量沙尘，发电量损失了30%。要解决这个问题，需要采取清洗措施，但这会产生供电间歇性问题，因为当地水资源有限，且需要派人到屋顶进行清洗。综上所述，我们面临着多种挑战，来解决风能、太阳能的不稳定性和需求侧的变化。

在能源供应发生变化时，智能存储系统可以有效地解决问题。通过智能控制，改变负荷以适应波动情况，实现智能建筑和智能存储系统之间的协调。当前，许多智能城市例如北京，在这个方面已经取得了良好的成果。

对于未来的电能系统，我认为应包含一系列智能互联设施和微电网。例如，通过太阳能屋顶光伏、电动车储能和大型建筑连接风力发电等方式，实现多个微电网之间的互联。同时，大型发电站为微电网提供电力，当微电网无法满足需求时，可以从整个系统的角度平衡各个系统的电力需求。

全球变暖和现代化带来的气候挑战也需要我们采取措施。首先，我们需要为学生、教师和工程师提供相关教育。其次，我们需要为学生提供解决全球问题的相关内容，从而激发他们的创新精神。最后，学术机构、产业界和国家实验室需要共同参与研究，确保最新研究成果得到普及。在信息传递方面，我们应确保每个人都能获得最先进的研究成果。

为了让更多人受益于这些研究成果，我们提出了一个名为"列车工程"的在线项目。该项目涵盖了课程教育和针对教师的非科学教育。我们鼓励中学阶段的学生通过这个项目了解未来的知识，使他们在进入高校之前就能进入这个行业。

王忠东
埃克塞特大学教授，副校长
WANG Zhongdong
Vice President and Professor of University of Exeter

埃克塞特大学副校长，电力工程教授。英国工程技术学会（IET）和IEEE的会员。1991年获清华大学学士学位，1993年获清华大学硕士学位，1999年获得曼彻斯特理工大学电气工程专业博士学位。2000—2020年担任曼彻斯特大学电气与电子工程学院电力能源和电力系统组的高电压工程教授。研究方向包括智能电网和低碳电力能源网络，状态监测技术，电力系统网络的热、电瞬态和磁建模技术，介质绝缘老化机制，替代环境友好液体绝缘材料和变压器资产管理。

Wang Zhongdong is the Vice President of University of Exeter, and a professor of Electrical Power Engineering. She is a fellow of IET and IEEE. She received the bEng degree and MSc degree from Tsinghua University in 1991 and 1993, respectively, and her PhD degree in Electrical Engineering from UMIST in 1999. She was a Professor of High Voltage Engineering at the Electrical Energy and Power Systems Group of the School of Electrical and Electronic Engineering at The University of Manchester from 2000 to 2020. Her research interests lie in Smart Grids and Low Carbon Electrical Energy Networks, in particular condition monitoring techniques, thermal, electrical transient and magnetic modeling techniques for power system networks, dielectric insulation ageing mechanisms, alternative environmentally friendly liquid insulating materials, and transformer asset management.

数据科学及其对智能电网教育的影响

王忠东

在这个报告中，我将讨论国际工程教育，特别是数据科学和智能电网教育产生的影响。首先我简要介绍下埃克塞特大学。这是一所致力于能源电力研究和教育的机构。我们在2020年成立了智能电网中心，它关注智能电网和可再生能源。我们还关注地理、社会科学、法学和商学方面的研究，以促进多学科和学科交叉的协同创新。

关于这次的主题——国际工程教育，我主要讨论电力工程教育以及数据科学在能源行业的应用。我通过介绍如何在埃克塞特大学开发一个智能电网融合数据科学的硕士项目展示当前的趋势。此外，还会讨论如何教育下一代电气工程师，以便他们能够适应未来的需求。

英国是电气化的早期实践者，当前的电力系统正在发展成为英国和欧洲电力系统工程教育和研究的基础。我们需要不同类型的电力系统，包括智能电网，以满足当前社会经济环境的需求。

为了实现排放近零目标，英国需要停止排放处在地下的碳。这意味着我们需要依赖绿色能源，如风能、光能、潮汐能、生物质能和水力能，但它们具有间歇性。因此，智能电网在未来至关重要，我们需要在发电者和消费者之间实现实时信息交换。在智能电网中，供需平衡至关重要，进而不再依赖化石燃料。

另外，数据科学对于实现近零排放目标至关重要，因为它可以帮助我们实时追踪和控制能源生产及消费。我们将采用分布计算体系，利用人工智能使电网更加智能化。此外，我们还将把绿色能源纳入网络，确保全社会参与。

对于数据科学如何为近零目标作出贡献，我认为以下几个方面至关重要。第一，让消费者同时成为生产者和消费者，给他们更多的透明度和可获取的数据。第二，更多依赖于数据和技术，以确保电力网络的高效运行。第三，考虑网络安全问题，以抵御网络攻击。

因此，对于工程教育，从智能电网的角度来看，我们需要思考如何教育电气工程师，使他们能够满足近零目标的要求，并实现智能电网的运营需求。

在这一部分，我将继续探讨数字化数据科学和人工智能对整个能源产业的影响，以及它们如何在未来5~10年对能源产业产生影响。

我在前面提到了物联网（IoT）在能源领域的广泛应用，包括发电、定价、输配电市场和电力需求侧分析等方面。为了实现实时反应和自动运行，我们需要利用物联网技术。例如，在2021年发表的一篇文章《人工智能在可持续能源产业中的应用：现状、挑战与机遇》，强调了能源和公用事业部门可以充分利用人工智能（AI）的力量。然而，在这一过程中，我们仍然需要进行投资，将资金引入AI行业并和整个行业相结合。

在未来，AI将在能源系统中发挥哪些作用？这包括AI对市场管理、可再生能源管理以及基础设施数字化、需求规划和未来购买需求预测等方面产生影响，通过AI，我们可以使整个流程更加高效。那么，在过去10年中，能源领域对数据的使用情况如何？我们可以看到，在市场就业方面，来自区块链、大数据、物联网、云计算、机器人和人工智能领域的人员数量相对较少，且在能源行业的就业中，这些具有数据背景的人员比例仍然较低。这说明能源行业通常被认为是资本密集型行业，需要长期投资，而电力行业亦是如此，它需要无时无刻地提供持续服务，不能承受系统运行中断带来的损失。这使得整个行业在采用新技术和最新数据技术方面步伐较慢。

然而，随着电网面临重大调整，特别是在未来20年各国实现近零排放目标的过程中，许多创新型企业希望通过技术创新将AI技术和新兴数据技术引入电力行业，以实现整个行业的进步和创新。在能源领域，我们可能会看到重大变革，越来越多的小企业将成为最新AI技术和应用的推动者。

接下来，我简要介绍埃克塞特大学在这方面的工作，以及我们如何建立一个智能电网中心。我们希望通过这种方式加强未来电气工程师教育，提高整个行业对数据科学的应用，并为智能电网的未来规划提供帮助。

在教育方面，我们设立了多个硕士项目，如保护控制和脉冲控制系统专业等。同时，我们还教授高阶建模科学，如传统建模技术之外的模拟技术。通过这些方法，我们加强了电气工程师对新技术的理解和应用。我们还与数学学院、环境科学学院和计算机科学学院合作，开发了一门关于智能电网和电力系统的课程。在硕士项目中，硕士学生在完成本科教育后，将学习电力电子等课程。此外，他们还考虑如何让电力系统变得更智能。我们开设了一门名为"智能电网与可持续能源系统"的课程，学生在学习大数据分析和数据科学导论基础课程后可选修。

接下来通过一个例子说说我们如何开发电力系统设备和数字孪生项目。我们知道，未来电力网络的基础设施将主要依赖于初级和次级设备，而未来的负载可能会变得更加不可预测，电网变化将更加频繁。对于电力设备来说，它们不应该是黑匣子，因此，在未来的运行过程中，我们需要采用电力系统和数字孪生技术，利用最先进的模型建模和人工智能机器学习算法进行实时决策，以提高资产管理效率。

我们的电力系统设备和数字孪生项目旨在让未来的电气工程师能够利用数据和人工智能，真正智能地管理电力系统基础设施，并通过这些方式增强未来电力系统的实时可预测性和智能管理的有效性。因此在课程设计时，我们主要考虑了以下框架：电力系统分析的重要模块和技术，人工智能技术，以及实时数字技术的教授。

下面我简要总结一下。能源领域是实现"近零排放"未来的前沿领域，正在不断改革与发展。人工智能有助于构建复杂的全新数据能源体系，如能源需求预测、能源建模和能源价格预测等，因此，需要利用人工智能技术及其相关应用，以增强电力系统韧性。能源系统还需要人工智能、大数据、物联网、云计算等技术支持，通过这些方式，电力系统将更具韧性。因此，我们需要出台相关政策推动行业发展，并开发AI技术以帮助人类做出更好的决策。总体来说，我们需要考虑如何改变教育体系，确保未来的电气工程师能够使用数据，实现能源领域的"近零排放"。谢谢大家！

别朝红
西安交通大学副校长、教授
BIE Zhaohong
Vice President and Professor of Xi'an Jiaotong University

西安交通大学教授、博士生导师，国家级人才称号获得者，IEEE 会士，现任西安交通大学副校长、党委常委。长期从事电力系统规划与可靠性的基础理论研究及关键技术开发，在复杂电力系统可靠性评估理论及高效算法、电力系统多随机因素建模和概率性分析等方面取得一系列研究成果，形成新能源电力系统综合规划的关键技术，在多家电网和全国870余家新能源场站推广应用。在国内外权威学术期刊发表学术论文60余篇，入选爱思唯尔"中国高被引学者"；授权发明专利30余项；主持制定国际标准2项、行业标准1项；主持国家重点研发计划项目、国家自然科学基金重点项目等10余项国家级科研项目；获省部级科技奖励5项。

Bie Zhaohong is a professor Ph.D. superior of Xi'an Jiaotong University, a winner of the national talent title, an IEEE Fellow, and the Vice President/member of the Standing Committee of the Pary of Xi'an Jiaotong University. She has been engaged in the fundamental theory and key technology of power system planning and reliability over decades, and has made a series of research achievements regarding the theory and efficient algorithm of reliability evaluation for complex power systems, as well as the multi random factor modeling and probabilistic analysis of power systems. The achievements constitute the key technology of comprehensive planning of the power systems with renewables, which has been promoted and applied in many power grids and over 870 renewable energy stations across the country. In the past five years, she has published more than 60 academic papers in authoritative academic journals, and has been selected as "China's highly cited scholar" by Elsevier. She has more than 30 authorized invention patents, presided over the formulation of 2 international standards and 1 industrial standard, acted as the principal investigators for over 10 national scientific research projects, including the national key R&D projects and the key projects of the National Natural Science Foundation of China. She is also the winner of 5 provincial and ministerial science and technology awards.

面向新型电力系统的"电气+"人才培养探索

别朝红

我分享的主题是《面向新型电力系统的"电气+"人才培养探索》。

第一,"双碳"与新型电力系统。在"双碳"战略和新型电力系统建设的背景下,西安交通大学的电气学科进行了"电气+"人才培养的探索。这一探索主要涉及学科交叉、产教融合、科教融合和全球汇聚四个方面。探索"电气+"人才培养,还需要回应四个关切。首先,为了回应世界关切,我们需要积极应对新一轮科技和产业革命的挑战。其次,为了回应国家关切,我们需要推动国家创新发展,坚持四个面向。再次,为了回应社会关切,我们需要与经济社会深度融合,为区域地方经济发展贡献力量。最后,为了回应人民关切,我们需要落实立德树人的根本任务,提升人才培养质量。

第二,学科交叉,大力推进"电气+"教学改革。在大力推进"电气+"教学改革的探索过程中,我们首先关注学科交叉。为了适应这一变化,西安交通大学的整体学科布局以"三中心、两高地"为目标,面向国家重大需求和国民经济主战场,发展传统优势学科,同时开辟新兴方向,如储能和等离子体医学。我们还与材料、信息、生命等进行学科交叉,以探索聚变能源。

基于这一背景,我们将五个研究方向作为"电气+"人才培养的学科布局。反应到人才培养上,我们需要在以下方面进行改革:奉献精神和电气大能源观、跨学科知识和综合能力分析、工程师素养和实践创新,以及学术志趣和重大攻关能力、国际视野和全球胜任力。

为了实现这些改革,我们在人才培养方面采取了一系列措施。例如,2019年,我们在全国率先创建了储能专业。我们设置了储能硕士点和博士点,储能专业涵盖了热能工程、储能、电磁储能和储能系统的六大学科,三位院士参与了这一交叉融合项目。这是我们在储能专业方面的探索。

此外，我们还在其他领域进行人才培养的改革，如新增能源互联网专业。能源互联网、微电网和多能互补。通过项目制、跨学科课程和实践教学等方式，培养学生的综合能力和创新能力。与企业合作，建立实践教学基地，让学生在实践中提升技能。鼓励教师参与国际合作与交流，培养具备全球胜任力的人才。

针对新的要求，我们建立了"电气+"教学育人体系。这个体系分为三大板块。第一是学科基础板块，也就是传统电气工程的基础。第二是前沿交叉板块，这是电气与其他学科的交叉。在课程方面，我们有20门课程，还有一系列新教材来支持这一板块。第三是校企协同板块，重点关注实践教学、产教融合和科教融合能力。配套的新课程和教材使三大板块共同组成了"电气+"教学育人体系。

第三，产教融合，围绕新型电力系统，深度推进校企协同。产教融合在为新型电力系统建设培养卓越工程师方面也非常重要。2019年，西安交通大学搬到了中国西部科技创新港，在这个广阔的空间里，我们建设了校企联合研究院和校内实践育人项目，将大型企业引进校园。我们与国家电网共同成立了先进的电力能源科学技术研究院，还与华能集团共建了能源安全技术研究院。目前，我们一共有26个研究院，这为学生提供了更多实践机会。将企业引入校园后，我们还建立了校企协同精英班，全方位进行产教融合建设。目前，电气学院一共有将近10个精英班。我们还邀请了一线专家授课。这些工程专家开设的实践类课程共有16门。此外，我们还牵头成立了中国新型电力系统技术创新联盟，为学生的创新创业能力提供实践平台。通过多措并举，我们将产教融合落到实处。

第四，科教融汇，新型电力系统在创新攻关中培养拔尖人才。科教融汇，重点关注如何将科研优势反馈到人才培养中。在创新港，我们新建了六个平台。目前，智慧输变电装备多工况模拟和宽禁带半导体平台已经建成，其他四个平台已经投入使用。我们希望将科研优势反哺到教学中，在大平台上培养学生的创新能力。

已使用的第一个平台是国家大设施平台，已列入"十四五"规划。大设施平台主要用于强脉冲辐射物理和极端条件材料科学等领域的研究。已使用的第二个大平台是电磁脉冲环境模拟平台，这是军民融合重大示范平台。第三是储能技术产教融合创新平台。我们的储能专业涵盖本科和研究生教育，在创新港我们已经开始建设这一平台。第四是与国家电网共建了能源互联网创新实验平台。国家电网依托我们牵头的能源互联网国家重点研发计划项目，以及目前正在建设的能源互联网工程专业，开展人才培养。这意味着我们不仅要注重产教融合，还要关注科教融汇，将科研优势反馈到人才培养中。

第五，全球人才汇聚，高水平国际交流与合作。在全球范围内汇聚优质资源，培养具有国际竞争力的高水平人才。我们的做法包括：从2012年开始，与米兰理工大学和法国高等电力学院开展对等交换、共同组班的双学位培养项目，累计有300多名意大利和法国的学生参与了这一项目。这种人才培养模式受到了各方好评。

我们依托两个全国引智基地，聘请了32名海外院士和教授担任研究生导师，并承担研究生课程。目前，我们已经开设了一套全英文的本科生和研究生课程体系。此外，还加入了欧洲的TIME联盟，以便共享全球优质课程资源，目标是让学生享受到全球最优质的电气工程教育资源。

同时，我们也依赖西安作为电气和能源领域国际合作的重要起点，广泛开展国际交流与合作。如今，我们在CSC的创新型人才国际合作培养项目中拥有三项合作项目，该项目每年输送的学生数量达40多人。依托这个平台，我们已经培养了来自15个国家的1200多名电气工程技术人才，创办了高等电力电子技术亚洲博士生学校，学员超过200人，每年暑期我们会邀请10名教授来给博士生授课，通过这些措施，提升学生的全球胜任力。

曾祥君
长沙理工大学副校长、教授
ZENG Xiangjun
Vice President and Professor of Changsha University of Science and Technology

博士、长江学者特聘教授、国家杰出青年科学基金获得者，现任长沙理工大学副校长，《电力科学与技术学报》主编。主要研究配电系统接地故障处置技术与电网故障行波定位技术及装备，发明了配电网中性点经可控电压源柔性接地的新型接地方式，获国家技术发明奖二等奖、中国电机工程杰出青年工程师奖、日内瓦国际发明展金奖等。

Zeng Xiangjun an appointed Changjiang Distinguished Professor, and a winner of National Science Fund for Distinguished Young Scholars. He is currently the Vice President of Changsha University of Science & Technology, and the Editor-in-Chief of *Journal of Electric Power Science & Technology*. His research focuses on the technology & equipment of grounding fault processing and traveling wave based fault location for distribution systems. He invented a novel neutral point fexible grounding method with controllable voltage source for distribution networks. He won the Second Prize of the State Technological Innovation Award, the Outstanding Young Engineer Award of China Electrical Engineering, and the Gold Prize of Geneva International Invention Exhibition.

为实现"双碳"目标，地方院校应如何为能源电力领域培养相关人才

曾祥君

我国自制定一系列节能经济政策以来，2006年的节能减排战略，2013年掀起全国低碳热潮，2020年，提出"双碳"目标，2021年，发布《2030年前碳达峰行动方案》，2022年5月，教育部出台了《加强碳达峰碳中和高等教育人才培养体系建设工作方案》。实现"双碳"目标的关键在于人才培养。在"双碳"领域，电力作为先行者，电力电网在减碳方面扮演着重要角色，电网建设中的"十四五"规划目标明显高于"十二五"和"十三五"规划。到2030年，能量总消耗控制在60亿吨标准煤，非化石能源占比达20%左右；到2050年，非化石能源占比将超过一半，建成绿色低碳的能源系统。

教育部提出要注重通专结合、加强绿色低碳交易、促进传统专业转型升级、打造高水平科研攻关平台，以及深化产教融合。"双碳"人才培养要求具备扎实基础、产业意志、学科交叉和国际视野等特质。

地方院校在能源电力人才培养方面存在很多挑战。新能源专业人才严重短缺与需求激增之间的矛盾日益严重。高校在新能源产业人才培养方面落后于产业发展，迫切需要培养满足产业发展的高素质复合型人才。

在教育部发布的关于加强碳达峰碳中和人才培养的方案中，强调实行通专结合、加强绿色低碳交易、促进传统专业转型升级、打造高水平的科研攻关平台以及深化产教融合、协同创新育人。对"双碳"人才培养提出了一些要求，包括培养基础扎实、具备产业意志、具备学科交叉能力和国际视野的高水平碳中和复合型人才。

传统电力行业、能源电力行业每年的人才总需求人数约为5.85万人，2020年风力发电总需求人数为18.5万人，2022年新能源人才需求同比增长66.4%。

长沙理工大学成立于1956年，是以电力行业为特色的地方院校，学校主要培养

工作在一线的靠得住、下得去、干得好的人才，为电力行业的一线岗位批量培养满足"双碳"目标需求的人才。

另外，地方高校在"双碳"人才培养方面面临以下两个困境。第一是地方高校对"双碳"人才培养具体要求和实现目标不明确。第二是"双碳"多元复合人才需求广泛，各个分散性地方高校培养的人才存在如传统专业面较窄、交叉难、人才培养模式单一等问题。

针对这些问题，长沙理工大学采取了一系列创新和实践举措，以培养复合型"双碳"人才。首先，通过新建、提升和交叉专业，实现跨学科的专业设置，如新能源工程、新能源材料与器械、新能源科学与智能电网信息系统等，以满足现场需求。其次，我们设置了"电力＋经济"双学位班，实现复合型人才的培养。覆盖从发电到储能、充电以及电力系统管理的全过程，满足现场运行需求。最后，我们还开展了课程体系改革。结合通用课程和专业课程，开设与企业相关的实践类课程，实现电气信息和经济的多学科交叉。依托智慧电力现代产业学院和校企联合基地，与企业联动发展，实现产教融合。

同时，针对"双碳"人才培养，长沙理工大学还采取了以下具体举措。一是创建校企协同的教育教学中心，满足企业发展需求，依托企业资源培养竞争性人才。设置联合课程，进行师资培训以及新教材编写，以满足企业对实际人才的需求。二是重视实践能力培养，包括提升工程意志、现场实训和解决实际问题的能力。拥有国家级实验室和工程实验实训中心，与企业共建平台培养老师和学生的实践能力。创建专业实习与社会实践相结合的模式，将学生派到电力公司进行一对一培养，解决本科生实习压力大的问题。

在创新创业能力培养方面，针对地方院校提出了五阶递进式人才培养模式。从熟悉元器件、专业课程、实践实习到创新创业，形成阶梯式"学中做""做中学"的创新训练方式。创建科研平台，培养实践创新能力。另外，鼓励学生参加比赛、撰写专利和成果转化，提高创新创业能力。在国际合作方面，与海外企业和高校接洽，培训实用化工程人才。创新实践成效显著，培养的"双碳"人才数量多、就业质量高，培养的学生创新实践能力强，多次获得国家级奖项。

在社会影响方面，我们在社会实践和暑期实践使用的工程实践模式入选创新人才模式，被收录《中国工程教育质量报告》。

综上所述，长沙理工大学的"双碳"人才培养模式在实践、创新和就业等方面取得了显著成效，为地方高校提供了可借鉴的经验。

IFEE 2022

第三届国际工程教育论坛
The 3rd International Forum On Engineering Education

分组论坛 B1
Panel B1

智能新能源汽车
Intelligent new Energy Vehicles

2022 年 12 月 9 日 20:00–23:00

承办单位简介

清华大学车辆与运载学院

清华大学车辆与运载学院成立于2019年，前身为1980年成立的汽车工程系，是国内最早开展车辆工程人才培养的院系之一。车辆与运载学院同时拥有车辆工程和动力机械及工程两个国家重点学科，下设四个研究所，涵盖了车辆动力与智慧能源、车辆工程与智能安全、智能车辆与智慧出行、特种车辆与动力工程等研究领域，学科全、交叉性强；瞄准国际前沿、面向国家需求，成为车辆低碳化、电动化、智能化、网联化等科技变革的重要力量。学院秉持"研究型、开放式、国际化"的人才培养理念，向行业输送了在国际学术界具有较强竞争力、在国民经济和社会发展中能发挥核心作用的高水平技术人才与管理人才。

About the Organizer

School of Vehicle and Mobility (SVM), Tsinghua University

Established in 2019, the School of Vehicle and Mobility (SVM) at Tsinghua University is derived from the Department of Automotive Engineering founded in 1980. SVM is one of China's earliest academic departments for training talents in automotive engineering feild. It has two national key disciplines: Vehicle Engineering and Power Machinery and Engineering. The four research institutes of the school conduct interdisciplinary and specialized research in different fields of automobile engineering, such as vehicle power and smart mobility, vehicle engineering and intelligent safety, intelligent vehicles and smart mobility, and special vehicles and power engineering, bringing cutting-edge research from around the world into China and playing a pivotal role in the low-carbon, electrification, intelligence, and shared mobility of vehicles. SVM stays research-oriented and open-and global-minded when training its students and aims to cultivate high-level and high-quality science, technology and management talents with competence in international academic feild and taking leading roles in national economy and social development.

分论坛主持

主持人 Chair

周青
清华大学车辆与运载学院教授、车辆与运载学院学术委员会主任
ZHOU Qing
Professor and Director of Academic Committee of the School of Vehicle and Mobility, Tsinghua University

清华大学车辆与运载学院教授，中国汽车工程学会汽车安全技术分会主任委员，《国际冲击工程学报》（*International Journal of Impact Engineering*）副主编，国际损伤生物力学学会（International Research Council on Biomechanics of Injury）理事。1985年本科毕业于北京大学，1994年获得美国麻省理工学院（MIT）博士学位，1994—2003年分别在美国通用汽车公司研发中心和美国联邦政府交通部Volpe研究中心工作，2003年到清华大学任教。研究领域为汽车安全、人体碰撞保护、材料和结构在碰撞载荷下的大变形失效、电池碰撞安全等。

Zhou Qing is a professor at the School of Vehicle and Mobility at Tsinghua University. Zhou Qing serves as the Director of Vehicle Safety Committee of the Chinese Society of Automotive Engineers, an Associate Editor of the *International Journal of Impact Engineering*, and a Council Member of the International Research Council on Biomechanics of Injury (IRCOBI). Zhou Qing received his B.Sc. degree (1985) in mechanics from Peking University, China, and Ph.D. degree (1994) in applied mechanics from Massachusetts Institute of Technology, USA. As a vehicle safety researcher, Zhou Qing worked at the US Department of Transportation (1999–2003) and at General Motors (1994–1999), respectively. His research interests include vehicle safety, human body impact protection, material and structural failures under impact loads, and crash safety of batteries.

主持人 Chair

汪玉
清华大学电子工程系教授，电子工程系主任
WANG Yu
Professor and Dean of the Department of Electronic Engineering, Tsinghua University

长期从事智能芯片、高能效电路与系统研究，计算机协会设计自动化特别兴趣小组执行委员会成员，计算机协会可编程逻辑器件技术委员会亚太地区唯一成员。发表论文300余篇，电气电子工程师协会/计算机协会杂志文章80余篇，谷歌学术引用近15000次。先后获得中国计算机学会青竹奖、德国亚历山大·冯·洪堡奖学金（Alexander von Humboldt Fellowship）、国际设计自动化会议40岁以下杰出创新者奖（DAC 2018 Under 40 Innovators Award）、中关村高聚工程高端领军人才奖、中国计算机协会科学技术奖技术发明一等奖等荣誉。曾获得ASP-DAC 19、FPGA17、NVMSA 17、ISVLSI 12最佳论文奖，以及12次国际会议最佳论文奖提名。任IEEE TCAD，IEEE TCSVT，IEEE ESL，ACM TODAES，ACM TECS等期刊的编委，ASP-DAC 2025等国际会议技术委员会主席（TPC Chair）。

Wang Yu is a professor, an IEEE fellow, and the Chair of the Department of Electronic Engineering and the Vice Dean of School of Information Science and Technology at Tsinghua University. He is also the Dean of Institute for Electronics and Information Technology in Tianjin. His research interests include the application-specific heterogeneous computing, processing-in-memory, intelligent multi-agent system, and power/reliability aware system design methodology. Yu Wang has published in more than 80 journals (56 IEEE/ACM journals) and 300 conference papers in the areas of EDA, FPGA, VLSI Design, and Embedded Systems, with Google Scholar citation of about 15000 times. He has received four best paper awards and 12 best paper nominations. Yu Wang has been an active volunteer in the design automation, VLSI, and FPGA conferences.

欧阳明高

中国科学院院士，清华大学车辆与运载学院教授，清华大学学术委员会副主任

OUYANG Minggao

Member of CAS; Professor of the School of Vehicle and Mobility, Deputy Director of Academic Committee of Tsinghua University

1993年获丹麦技术大学能源工程系博士学位，中国科学院院士，清华大学教授，国际交通电动化期刊国际交通电动化杂志创刊主编。长期从事新能源动力系统与交通电动化研究，2007—2021年任国家新能源汽车科技专项首席专家。先后在混合动力与电控系统、燃料电池与氢能系统、动力电池与储能系统、车网互动与智慧能源系统等方面取得一系列科研成果，推广应用经济效益超过百亿元。获国内外科技奖10项。孵化包括科创板上市公司在内的学生创业企业15家。SCI收录学术论文350余篇，他引20000余次，H因子78，5次入选科睿唯安全球高被引科学家。

Ouyang Minggao received a Ph.D. in Energy Engineering from the Technical University of Denmark in 1993. Currently, he is a Changjiang Distinguished Professor and the leader of New Energy Powertrain System team at Tsinghua University, where he is responsible for directing the research and development of Lithium-ion Battery Safety Design and Management, PEM Fuel Cell Powertrain and Hydrogen Systems, Engine Control and Hybrid Powertrains, Smart Battery and Smart Energy Systems. From 2007 to 2021, Ouyang Minggao had been the Chief Scientist of the China National Key R&D Program of New Energy Vehicles. He obtained many national and international awards. He is a member of the Chinese Academy of Sciences and Editor-in-chief of the international journal of *eTransportation*(IF13.66). He has published over 350 SCI papers, and was listed as a Highly Cited Chinese Researcher by Elsevier (2015–2020) and World Highly Cited Researcher by Clarivate Analytics (in 2017, 2019, 2020, 2021, and 2022).

新能源、新动力和新工科

欧阳明高

大家好，我是来自清华大学的欧阳明高。我分享的题目是《新能源、新动力和新工科》。我有三个观点与大家交流，第一个是问题导向的新动力研究型教学，这是我们20多年的研究历程。第一阶段即1994年开始的燃油汽车的动力研究，第二阶段也就是2001年开始的新能源汽车动力的研究，第三阶段即2017年后的新能源动力系统的研究，这三个发展阶段形成了三门研究型的教学课程。

现在我们的研究从安全研究逐步发展到安全电池的开发，包括：从本质安全的研究逐步发展到固态电池的研发，从被动安全的研究发展到安全系统的设计，从主动安全的研究发展到新一代的智能电池的开发。

基于对燃料电池和动力电池的研究，我们开设汽车动力系统学的课程，这是以系统为核心的学术体系，但更侧重动力装置的机理模型。

在第三个阶段，我们面对的问题是分布式电池储能的智能聚合科学问题，以及绿色氢能的秩序问题和固态电化学的前沿科学问题。我们从智能电池发展到智能充换电，再到智能滑板底盘和智慧能源重点，这是车网互动系统，所以仍然包含底层、中层、上层和高频、中频、低频，构成电池储能的智能聚合科学问题。

新能源革命的核心内容是什么呢？《第三次工业革命》的主要内容就是重大支柱。我把它概括为五大支柱、四大要素。五大支柱包括向可再生能源转型（光伏和风电）；集中与分布结合式的能源电力系统，使建筑变成微型发电厂；用氢气、电池等技术存储间歇式能源；发展能源（电能）互联网；电动汽车成为用能、储能回馈能源终端。四大要素就是硅能、储能、智能、氢能。所谓硅能，就是光伏与电力电子，也就是以硅为基础的光伏电池和功率电力电子器件。能量存储对于可再生能源革命来讲是至关重要的。智慧能源是分布式的，所以必须把它连起来，就是电能的互联网。

我们来定义一下能源技术科学是什么。它的上层就是系统科学与技术，具体看就是系统学，控制论，信息论，人工智能；底层是物质科学与技术，具体看就是固体物理，物理化学，材料科学。工程，就是工程科学与技术，那就是上层和底层的结合，也就是系统科学技术和物质科学与技术的结合，这就是我们的能源技术科学。为了实现三位一体的学科交叉，我们需要建立支撑平台，也就是多尺度集成计算与表证。

在此基础上，我们团队建立了电池储能、绿色氢能、智慧能源三位一体的学科交叉研究体系。在动力电池与电化学储能系统方面，我们有电池安全、智能电池、固态电池；在氢燃料电池与电解水制氢方面，我们有碳燃料电池和制氢，固体氧化物燃料电池和制氢，还有碱性电解舆情安全。

另外是智能动力与智慧能源系统，我们也有分布式的驱动系统、光储充换的互动能源系统、超级快充快换的耦合补电系统等，建立了各板块相应的研究中心和创业企业群。在电池层面，就是电池的装置层次，主要是过程科学，即热化学、热分析动力学、热物理与计算、流体力学、多场耦合与化学动力学进行液态电池热时空机理的设计。固态电池热时空机领域设计，主要处理能量流的问题。在上层我们更多是基于系统层次，主要是智能电池与充电控制、缺陷电池与安全监控、老化电池与智能管理，主要采用电化学与系统动力学、系统辨识与自由估计、大数据人工智能进行系统层面的研究，这就是我们的科学方法论。

我们的研究型教学和新能源科学的方法论，最终要服务于新工科，它是奠定新工科的基础，同时我们新工科的目标是培养创新创业的人才，这就是我要讲的第三个方面，即创新创业的新工科教育人才观。

第四次工业革命会催生先进的生产力，它需要先进的生产关系和先进的企业文化。所以我们的新工科建设也要与之相适应。我个人认为课程、论文、专利、转化、奖项，应当是研究型大学工科专业高水平研究的不同侧面，创新创业不会影响科研水平，反而会极大地提高创新效率和质量。因此，创新创业应当成为新工科发展的趋势和标志之一。在此基础上，我们的人才培养理念应当是创意、创新、创业、创优，回馈学校与社会，形成完整的链条，建立全生命周期的人才培养模式。

如何培养创新创业人才？一是进行哲学训练，抓主要矛盾、关键问题。二是进行数学训练，要学会升为提出问题，降为解决问题。三是进行科学训练，发现定义定位好问题，摒弃伪问题。四是进行素质训练，培养学生从多个角度看同一个问题。

创新创业人才的能力培养，一是批判性思维与创新能力。科学精神的核心是批判性思维，创新来自改变了意志而改变其问题意识。二是结构性思维与设计能力，我们能否有效地定义问题，有没有整体视野和分析框架，能否抓住重点，观点之间能否逻辑自洽，这些都是我们需要训练的。我们要基于结构化的思维才能产生架构设计，而架构设计对创新创业是无比重要的。三是工程师思维与动手能力。工程师思维就是所谓的工程意识，你要预判什么有价值、什么不靠谱。动手能力有先天的因素，但主要是从对技术和产品的快速试错和迭代中间训练出来的。四是艺术家思维与审美能力。审美产生热爱，热爱产生激情，激情是行为的内在驱动力，是内心燃烧的火。所以我们给干粮不如给猎枪，给猎枪不如激发其打猎的欲望，这就是能力培养。最后是培养目标。我们的目标是战略高度、学术深度、应用广度的三位一体。如果只有高度没有深度，那是空的；只有深度没有广度，那是虚的；只有广度没有高度，那又是俗的。

我们战略高度怎么做？要聚焦到点，学术深度沿着线，应用广度强调面。所谓聚焦到点，就是把全球热点、行业痛点、技术难点凝聚成前沿焦点和战略支点，点上突破，以点带面。所谓学术深度沿着线，就是顶层着眼，底层着手，由表及里，层层深入。所谓应用广度强调面就是要发挥学术影响力，培育创新生产力，把势能转变成动能。最后，高度要做到开创，深度要做到原创，广度要做到科创，这就是我们的三个维度，点、线、面结合和"三创"，这就是我们的培养目标。

巴特·范·阿雷姆

荷兰代尔夫特理工大学博士、事务副校长，交通建模领域教授

Bart van AREM

Pro Vice Rector Magnificus for Doctoral Affairs and Professor of Transport Modelling, Delft University of Technology, the Netherlands

代尔夫特理工大学副校长，土木工程与地球科学学院交通与规划系教授，IEEE开源期刊《智能交通系统》创刊主编。20世纪90年代末以来，在智能汽车分析及影响建模方面进行了开拓性研究，聚焦不同信息技术设施基础及区域空间设计的城市应用场景，在驾驶行为变化、网络交通流及交通模式变化等方面提出了创新见解。研究成果始终从产业应用出发，呈现出极强的建模能力和基于经验的模拟能力。

Bart van Arem is a professor of Transport Modelling at the department of Transport &Planning of the Faculty of Civil Engineering and Geosciences at TU Delft. Since the late 90s he has been conducting pioneering research on the analysis and modelling the implications of intelligent vehicles. Such implications may var from changes in driving and travel behaviour, traffic flows in networks and modal change, road and IT infrastructure and the spatial design of urban regions. His research has a strong modelling and simulation component based on empirics wherever possible and always with users of the research in mind. As the Pro Vice Rector Magnificus for Doctoral Affairs, he is responsible for the formal procedures and operation regarding all Ph.D. defenses at TU Delft.

迈向负责任的自动驾驶

巴特·范·阿雷姆

大家好,我是来自代尔夫特理工大学的巴特·范·阿雷姆。今天我想分享的是《迈向负责任的自动驾驶》,我们的研究和教育关注的车辆不仅仅是一种产品,它还应该成为一种交通服务,使人们能够移动并改善人们的生活,实现安全和可持续的交通。

我们和北京交通大学共同开设了一门交通运输工程的本科课程——交通规划,我负责高级课程的授课。交通规划这门课程旨在让学生理解交通运输如何解决社会问题,其影响是什么,它可以锻炼学生的概念思维、查找和分析文献、制订项目计划、团队合作,以及提出课题的能力。学生们需要在理论上研发一个概念模型,以了解实际是如何工作,以及这个项目可以解决哪些社会问题,并确定不确定性、风险和知识差距。他们需要大约两周的时间完成这一部分。我们将花费五年的时间实现这个目标。

现在,让我们转向关于负责任的自动驾驶部分。这是关于交通运输学课程的介绍。学生需要先学习很多技术性细节,比如交通模拟、交通理论、人类因素等。他们已经掌握了基础技术,现在需要找出所有这些知识是如何相互关联的。这门课程有不同元素的概念视野,学生需要分组完成,最后会得到成绩评定。完成分组任务后,学生需要独立完成一篇有关概念视野的文献综述。

关于概念视野的部分,需要将社会问题与相应的目标相结合。例如,关于可持续和宜居城市。这需要可持续的交通方式,并且需要运用一些技术手段,比如电气化和数字化,以推进特定的交通解决方案。所以你看见一条街道,实际上我认为这些街道来自鹿特丹或阿姆斯特丹,它也展示了如何重新设计这条街道。如果你有自动化车辆,你应该能够看到一个配送机器人。

但是有一个特定的条件,即自动化车辆能够安全且负责地运作。我们正在研究影响因素。有一种理论是有规划行为的理论可以用来观察道路使用者如何行动并与这辆车互动。这也是了解道路设计者和驾驶员或其他行人或骑车人行为意图的功能。这也与对自动驾驶车辆的期望和信任有关。这其中一个因素是评估实验对真实人员和车辆是不是安全的。

因此，我们通常使用虚拟现实技术。自动化班车和普通车的不同因素是它可以是一辆普通车辆，也可以是一辆自动化车辆。你还可以选择有斑马线或没有斑马线。我们在实验室里让人们使用 AVR 耳机。之后，我们回放这些场景，并快进人们的反应。我们还进行了进一步实验。总之，无论是常规车辆还是自动化车辆，最重要的因素是车辆与行人之间的速度和距离，这会影响行人的穿越决策。我们确实看到多用户交互提供了更多的真实感，但它增加了理论和技术上的复杂性，这是科学研究的巨大挑战。

我们一起研究了这个有意义的人类控制概念，它被用于军事和医疗领域，如果你有一个自动化系统，你想让它处于理智和有责任的人类控制下，应该同时满足两个条件，即跟踪与追踪条件和识别系统与之交互的流量条件。人类代理机构是有机构性的，他们都有自己的期望和理由。这可能是步行者在车辆设施区域行走，可能是系统制造商、运输经营者、道路经营者或乘客。所有这些角色都对系统有期望，系统应以可解释和可预测的方式行事，因此必须由这些人类代理机构协调行为。这是一个抽象条件，因此我们仍需要将其付诸实践，但它为实际开发正确的控制算法提供了方向。在整个自动化车辆的演员和操作链中，至少需要一个演员能够理解它，并对系统的操作负责。接下来，我们将更深入地讨论如何开始操作各种元素。

我们还开发了追踪分类法，其具有道德意识，可以识别参与控制和操作车辆的演员的角色，并将这些原则传递到法律和道德原则中。这是正在进行的工作。我们已经升级了这些理论，但仍存在一些问题。

这不仅是自身组件的行为，而且所有的传感器和通信设备也以相应的方式变化，以响应环境中的需要和原因，尤其是环境中的演员。我们要快速且更安全地从起点走到终点。希望它可以持续发展且有一定的公平水平，而这些推理可能不会同时进行。因此，需要一个指示器的机制。我们需要使用新的指标定义这是安全的良好指标。实施安全的实验也很重要。我们确实需要尽可能地进入现实世界。此外，我们还需要使用数字孪生技术。

首先，从教学方面入手。在我看来，技术非常重要。但后来也逐渐发现，还需要教育工程师，使他们也具有社会责任和社会影响力。因此，他们还需要在应用技术的上下文中表现出意识。接下来，我认为自动驾驶具有支持城市转型，使我们的城市更加可持续的潜力，并且在与气候变化有关的情况下，释放出现在由道路承担的空间。为此，我认为自动驾驶仍需要学习如何在保险空间内操作。因此，我们需要理解这一点。我们需要新的方法实施负责任的自动驾驶系列，我认为数字孪生、高级安全指标和虚拟验证场是前进的好方法。以上就是我发言的全部内容，谢谢大家。

胡·威廉姆斯
伯明翰大学工程学院汽车工程领域荣誉教授，英国皇家统计学会研究员
Huw WILLIAMS
Honorary Professor of Automotive Engineering of School of Engineering, University of Birmingham; Fellow of RSS

伯明翰大学工程学院汽车工程领域名誉教授，数学及应用研究所（曾任该机构副主席）研究员，英国皇家统计学会研究员，汽车工程领域独立顾问。汽车工程领域著名领导者，拥有广泛工业经验，在汽车新技术研究和开发方面做出了创新性探索。多年来，聚焦工程仿真模型的应用和工业相关课程教学，为世界多个知名公司提供广泛的项目管理服务。曾任捷豹、路虎产品开发团队高级工程专家、福特汽车集团全球十大质量工程技术研究员，对福特全球技术开发系统及"六西格玛设计计划"的成功应用做出了卓越贡献。

Huw Williams is an honorary professor in Automotive Engineering at the University of Birmingham. He is a very well-known leader in the field of automotive engineering with rich industrial experience and significant contribution to research and development of new vehicle technology. Huw is a Fellow and past Vice President of the Institute for Mathematics and its Applications and he is also a Fellow of the Royal Statistical Society.

Prior to leaving JLR to pursue a career as an independent consultant, Huw was one of only two people to hold the position of Senior Engineering Specialist (LL5 Senior Manager equivalent) in JLR's product development organisation. He has been involved in panel meetings of EPSRC and was a member of the peer review college. He has 32 publications and several invited speeches at national conferences. Huw was recognised by Ford Motor Company by being appointed as one of the ten worldwide members of the office for the Henry Ford Technical Fellow for Quality Engineering and contributed to Ford's Global Technology Development System and the development of Ford's Design for Six Sigma Programme. Pursuing a distinguished career in both management and technical specialist roles, Huw trained and practiced as a Six Sigma Black Belt, which led to his cefification as a Master Black Belt, where he achieved the best ever score in the qualifying exam: his projects saved millions of dollars and were praised by Ford's Vice President, Richard Parr-Jones CBE.

可持续车辆的最优系统

胡·威廉姆斯

大家好！我是来自伯明翰大学的胡·威廉姆斯。我想和大家谈论的是系统，我们如何教授系统，它们如何发展，为什么最优解是一个重要的概念，我们如何教授优化。最后，我将给出一些结论和建议。

系统工程非常重要，因为我认为这是工科学生知识上的差距所在。他们不太了解系统工程，这是由于他们的教育中缺少这方面的知识，因为大学往往是针对特定的系统进行专业化教学，但他们并不教授系统的概念。对我来说，系统的本质不仅是一组对象的集合，它还必须具有一定的目的或功能。

首先，如何教授系统呢？我们需要从解决方案开始，提出中立的问题陈述。车辆需要一个推进系统，如果我们只是说车辆的发动机将燃料和空气转化为机械能，学生们将永远不会有不同的想法。比如，车辆的推进系统实际上是通过喷气推进而不是车辆和地面之间的摩擦实现的。我们应该教授自上而下的功能驱动的失效模式与影响分析（FMEA），并使用边界图、系统状态流程图和功能树等工具。我们要教授系统分析，让工程师能够将系统分解为子系统和组件，并理解功能是如何分布在这些子系统和组件上的，这非常重要。

其次，系统的演化。我们知道马车的终结和车辆的兴起。这在英语中被称为"无马马车"。最初的名称是一种类似于有马马车，后是没有马的车辆，它遵循了一个曲线，逐渐演化成现代车辆。而这种车辆正在达到其极限。它已经达到了热效率和清洁排放的极限。我们也无法阻止二氧化碳的排放。所以现在我们正在进行一次进化跃迁，即转向电动车。从价值上说，电动车还存在一些问题，并不是所有方面都比汽油车更好。实际上它们行驶距离不够远。这就是为什么当新技术出现时，它通常比旧技术的价值稍低。

在新技术的早期阶段购买车辆有一个弊端，因为你要为改变技术而付出一定的代价。但是新系统也有它自己的S曲线，它会在时间上演变成什么样子。它需要退役了，因为它还有这条曲线要走。但也许我们可以预测这个演变，并且我们可以让这条曲线发展得更快。

电影《星际迷航》的传送装置中，当系统开始演变时，在新系统的早期阶段会存在不同系统概念之间的竞争。现在正在进行的一项竞争是，氢燃料电池和电池电动车之间的竞争。回想一下录像机时代，那时候家用录像系统（VHS）和 Beta Max 之间也存在竞争，但其中一个系统胜出了。现在在车辆领域，汽车最初被称为无马马车。早期的汽车也使用蒸汽动力或电力，但内燃机最终占据了主导地位。当阴极射线退役时，等离子屏幕技术与液晶显示屏技术之间也存在竞争。

现在我们知道液晶显示屏赢得了那场竞争，并且正在沿着 S 形曲线上升。最终，演化的飞跃是可能几乎没有任何系统。因此，留声机或唱片已被流媒体取代，而流媒体几乎没有任何系统。我们不再购买实体媒介，而是购买电子设备，可以将电子模式转化为声音。这些设备可以是手机或平板电脑，而不再需要买很多硬件。

我们看看汽车从最初的样子演化到现在。一开始发动机很糟糕，有大量的问题需要修复，直到今天我们拥有计算机控制的点火和燃油系统。汽车在演化过程中一次只有一个问题。现在工程师真正需要做的是走出这个过程，通过系统的演化并设计出理想的系统。关于最优化，这是人类制作的第一个轴之一。我们需要对技术应用系统进行优化，以便我们可以在不到十年的时间达到最优状态。

关于我参与的伯明翰的这个项目，我会帮助团队进行研究。这是一个多目标的优化问题，它正在研究自适应巡航控制和能量管理的协作。因此，这就是车辆在高速公路上相互协作以使用更少能量的方式。

伯明翰大学的研究团队正在将尖端的优化技术应用到汽车领域，他将这些想法引入伯明翰大学的本科课程。通过研究未来车辆概念的发展限制和探讨车辆系统合作带来更多最优解的方式。

我们如何教授优化技术？我们永远不能将系统只呈现为一个成品。在过去的传统工程课程中，我们会看到一个引擎，然后逐个分析每个子系统并理解其工作原理，但我们不应该把一切称为成品。工程中没有什么是完美的，这意味着我们需要妥协。我们应该设计问题，要求学生优化设计，而不是仅仅预测其性能。

最后，我的结论是：我们不能等待试错过程来交付最佳运行系统。最好的方法是将系统思维和优化融入现有的工程课程。谢谢大家！

管欣
吉林大学汽车研究院院长，中国汽车工程学会副理事长
GUAN Xin
Dean of Automotive Research Institute, Jilin University;
Vice President of the Society of Automotive Engineers of China

教育部长江学者特聘教授，现任吉林大学汽车研究院院长，兼任中国汽车工程学会副理事长。从事汽车专业大学教育近40年，成功主持研制了投资达2500万元的中国首台汽车性能模拟器，并成功应用到我国10多款自主品牌汽车的开发中。在国际上率先提出汽车方向与速度综合控制的驾驶员模型，实现了单一模型适用于绝大多数智能驾驶工况，实现了满足智能汽车L3以上等级的一种独特创新模型方案。

Guan Xin is the Dean of the Automotive Research Institute at Jilin University, a Distinguished Professor of Changjiang Scholars of the Ministry of Education, and the Vice President of the China Society of Automotive Engineers. He has been engaged in automobile professional university education for nearly 40 years. He had successfully developed the first full-scale automobile driving simulator and successfully applied it to the development of more than ten Chinese-brand cars and trucks. He had proposed a driver model for comprehensive control of vehicle direction and speed, a novel model solution that meets the level L3 above of intelligent vehicles, realizing a unique model that is suitable for most traffic driving conditions.

数字汽车时代产品开发学科高等教育的几点思考

管 欣

大家好！我是来自吉林大学的管欣，我分享的题目是《数字汽车时代产品开发学科高校教育的几点思考》。今天主要交流四个方面的内容。第一个是汽车的四个时代与专业知识范围。第二个是车辆学科到底是工程学还是技术学？第三个是汽车产品开发过程与专业能力。第四个是中国车辆工程专业相关内容简介。

第一，汽车的四个时代与专业知识范围。汽车工业实际上是伴随着汽车也就是整个世界工业的四个发展阶段的，从各个时代汽车的产品性能及手段的技术特征把汽车分成四个时代，分别是机械汽车时代1.0、机电一体化汽车时代2.0、电控汽车时代3.0和数字汽车时代4.0。下面逐一分析四个汽车时代的技术特征。

机械汽车时代1.0，采用纯机械结构实现性能，通过杠杆原理以及越来越复杂的结构实现性能的提升，如阿克曼转向机、麦克风悬架、多连杆、水动悬架等。汽车的运动实际上是人和机器相互作用，汽车驾驶性能就是要把汽车移走。比如说我们用眼睛耳朵来认知，那么大脑有意识的决策叫运动规划；通过小脑下意识来决策的，叫动作规划，其中也包括神经网络系统和生物电传输。机电一体化汽车时代2.0，我们增加了气动、液压、电动等机电一体化系统，进一步减小驾驶员的操作负担。我们实施了很多适应复杂工况的助力系统，提升了汽车的性能。电控汽车时代3.0，电控汽车主要作用是代替了人的小脑规划的决策系统，电控单元具有人脑的一部分功能，是嵌入式的控制，实现了自动化。我们现在的汽车还属于以电控汽车为主体，未来的发展重点是数字汽车（即数字汽车4.0时代），汽车加装了现今的传感器代替人的感官，同时也要进行大算力代替人的感知认知，包括这些大脑的决策活动，人类的驾驶行为绝大部分或者完全地交给机器系统。未来的汽车是以决策策略和规划策略为主导的，有生理学、心理学，包括与决策方法相结合。

第二，车辆学科到底是工程学还是技术学。车辆学科有科学技术、工程、市场经济和社会学几大门类，那么它的知识体系应该是技术学科，就是汽车学科里边的先进技术原理与方法。

第三，汽车产品开发过程与专业能力。我们原有的课程体系主要解决怎样把汽车设计出来，怎样把它加工出来。课程体系基本属于机电一体化汽车2.0时代的理论与技术。所以我们未来的汽车要实施转型，车辆工程应该重点研究如何配置方案，如何选择先进的总成和复杂系统，并把它集成起来，确保我们的产品设计功能和性能对客户来说是最好的。我们要做到高性价比，保证生产过程的集成，要保证下线生产的产品质量的一致性。所以车辆工程应该往这方面转型，这也就有了独特性。

未来的车辆工程学科教育定位，重点应该为整车汽车厂和系统总成的供应商，培养做系统集成、面向客户的这些工程师。这是教育定位。那么另外一个能力定位是什么？也就是说我们的能力定位先是我们能开发先进汽车整车产品，包括零部件供应商的一级供应商，我们应该能总成产品，这个就是集成研发。

另外一个汽车厂里面生产开发的实验装备，包括实验软件平台，研发生产制造过程的装备和软件平台，重点是车辆工程专业学习，因为它们合到一起都是为了保证汽车的性能和品质，同时保证汽车的生产一致性。若车辆工程如此定位，就有完整的独特性，也能涵盖与其他学科的交叉互动，实现独特存在的独立学科特征。

第四，中国车辆工程专业相关内容。车辆工程在中国包含道路车辆，也就是我们汽车产业，轨道车辆，还有铁道、地铁，再加上越野车辆，所以它们都是一致的。

重点研究车辆总体的设计开发理论，包括制造过程中的关键理论与方法，还要重点提升的是性能，品质低碳化、电动化、自动化、智能化、网联化和数字化等的性能水平。这些都是手段，最关键的是我们要提升产品的性能水平。

第二个研究重点是技术学方面的名词，既要让学生全面掌握，又要在总成系统上面能开发这些系统，而不是设计一个具体的机构，我们是要集成这些系统，要匹配这些系统。

最后，我们不同于其他学科的特点是什么呢？车辆工程学科是站在车辆产品角度和系统总成角度进行集成，也包括在生产制造过程中保证一致性，其他学科做的都是更专业的，像机械、电子、电器、通信、计算机，他们经过了四年的理论基础学习。我们什么都学肯定没有他们专业，所以这些总成系统级的开发和研究应该由其他学科去做。以上就是我分享的全部内容，谢谢大家。

埃米尔·卡捷普
加拿大滑铁卢大学机械与机电工程系教授，美国机械工程师协会研究员，加拿大机械工程学会研究员

Amir KHAJEPOUR
Professor of the Department of Mechanical and Electromechanical Engineering, University of Waterloo; CSME Fellow

  加拿大滑铁卢大学机械与机电工程系教授。在机电车辆系统领域担任加拿大一级研究主席，获得30余项专利，发表600余篇文章，实现多项技术转让，创办多家创业公司。加拿大安大略省专业工程奖章的获得者，加拿大工程学会、美国机械工程师学会和加拿大机械工程学会的研究员。

  Amir Khajepour is a professor of Mechanical and Mechatronics Engineering at the University of Waterloo. He achieved 30 patents, 600 publications, many technology transfers, and several start-up companies. He is a recipient of the Engineering Medal from the Professional Engineering Ontario, a fellow of the Engineering Institute of Canada, the American Society of Mechanical Engineering, and the Canadian Society of Mechanical Engineering.

体验式学习与工程专业的研究生教育

埃米尔·卡捷普

大家晚上好！我来自滑铁卢大学，我的实验室的名称是机电生态系统。在开始之前，我们讨论一下什么是实践学习，以及它意味着什么，可能会有帮助。总的来说，它表明您可以通过经验、测试和数据分析来学习。我要谈论的是，我们大学中的实践教育是什么，以及如何将这种类型的学习嵌入学生的普通课程。

关于我们开课的课程，所有这些活动都在沙利文工程思想下，思想诊所是它的一个想法，旨在改善滑铁卢大学的实践学习。

这种诊所的作用是研究如何在传统的工程课程中增加更多模块，以使学生成为更好的工程师。这些模块强调通过实验进行工程实践。他们开始的项目有通用课程，同时还有专业模块。其中一个独立的活动是他们需要将自行车进行分解、组装并从中学习。团队合作也是非常重要的，他们需要在核心课程之前完成这些活动。再次回到核心课程时，他们又需要完成其他模块，然后进入第二学年。第一学年的教育大约是 16 个月。第二学年他们需要完成更多的实践学习。这个思想诊所教授的就是团队合作、理解冲突管理、如何共同工作和互相沟通的技巧。

在工程设计日中，学生们被问到了一个开放性问题，他们需要作为一个团队一起设计、制造、测试并解决问题，每个周期有三次这样的活动，全程时间为 2 天，最终比赛结束。学生们需要运用他们的分析背景实现自己的目标，例如在机械工程中创建一个时钟，其中每个人使用的设备或零件都是相同的。在土木工程中，他们需要使用一样的材料建造一座水坝，并思考如何建造最好的水坝。这些活动可以帮助他们明白如何快速解决问题。

在大三的最后一个学期，他们有一个称为"工程峰会"的活动，聚集了所有的教师、校友、企业家和行业人士。这个活动让校友们更好地了解行业的运作方式。另一个模块被称为"分析竞赛"，主要是为了鼓励他们将所学的知识应用到他们的指数学习中。这适用于本科生课程，可以相对直接地把此类实践学习融入他们的课程。然而，对于研究生课程来说，就不是那么简单了，因为单一的课程并不适用于所有学生。他们在哪个教授的实验室里工作，取决于他们的教育或项目类型。这既可以是完全实验性的，也可以是分析性的。

为了将实践学习融入他们在实验室两年或四年的学习，我尝试建立由高年级和低年级学生，以及博士后技术人员组成的联合项目团队，他们将在3~6个月内进行工业驱动或探索性项目研究，以便教导他们如何一起工作、相互交流，以及如何进行实验和数据分析。这有助于他们将所学的分析背景理论应用于解决问题、设计实验或分析他们收集的数据。我还与所有的学生一起制订了带有非常强的分析、数值和实验组成部分的项目，这有助于他们使用在本科或大规模计划中学到的使用分析工具提出初步解决方案。

然后，他们需要使用或转化这些发现，并开始使用模拟工具尝试在更复杂的情境中使用这些解决方案。例如，在车辆系统中，我们可以提出方程式，比如自行车模型，这是了解技术和方法是否可行的好方法，但这还不够。因此，我们开始使用汽车仿真工具或其他仿真工具，以便在更复杂的场景中评估他们的解决方案。

在所有设计实验的项目中，他们还要与技术人员一起制造和完成完整的实验，并分析数据，找到解决方案，确定论文和项目的最终解决方案。

我认为他们教育成功的一点，是大型计划和大型研究活动可以将不同类型的知识或不同类型的专业知识融入团队活动。我们在母亲巴士或校园自主车辆巴士上开始了一个相对大规模的计划。在这个计划中，我们的学生对感知系统很有兴趣。

有很多项目，他们可以一起工作，提出新的活动和项目。我们有另一个大型方案。这是他们在过去多年设计的角落模块，拥有电动模型、悬挂、操纵、控制系统。主要的车辆组件都以某种方式内置于这个模块中。学生再次组成一个小组，在新的控制系统，即插即用控制器、自动驾驶，一起工作，并将其添加到此模块中。我们还将相同系统应用于自动农业、采矿、物料处理和其他应用中。另外，我们还有另一个非常大的车辆控制和智能交通领域的项目，许多学生组成小组在这些活动中工作。我们正在进行的一些工作包括通用车辆动态控制系统、基于代理的车辆系统、模型数据启发式控制系统、通用估计、健康监控等。

在过去几年中，我们已经开始研究如何将车辆级别和云级别的数据结合起来，以生成可用于车辆控制估算和其他方面的通用数据集。同时，我们还在探讨如何开发虚拟车辆设计和测试，以再次生成不需要制作原型的系统。测试环境可以提供尽可能接近现实的结果。此外，我们还有大型项目，特别是在超大空间和机器人应用方面。我们正在开展两个项目，其中一个是基于电缆的仓储机器人，可以在长度为20~30米，高度为10米的区域内移动。另一个是施工机器人，可以用于物料处理和建筑3D打印。学生们参与了电缆配置、冗余、分辨率拓扑、设计、控制等方面的工作。指数学习对学生的教育至关重要。我们的工程师需要处理许多不同的学科，这意味着他们必须合作，从不同的学科和不同的团队中得出解决方案。对于本科生来说，可以通过添加一些我们讨论的模块来补充传统的工程课程。

我们定义的研究项目具有三个主要组成部分：具体分析、分析和实验。这是另一种可以用来确保他们不仅学习理论和方程式，还可以通过实验进行学习的方法，因为现实、方程式和理论只是我们可以在适当的方程式和理论中捕捉到的现实的一部分。

短期项目是非常有效的，除了主要的硕士或博士课程，鼓励他们合作，鼓励他们通过实验和评估提出创新的解决方案，特别是与行业团队合作的联合项目，对学生来说有巨大的好处，因为当他们学习时，我们也可以教他们如何工作、工业问题是什么，以及无论是工业还是研究项目方面我们所面临的限制。

以上就是我发言的全部内容，谢谢大家。

左磊
密歇根大学讲席教授，美国机械工程师协会
ZUO Lei
Endowed Professor of University of Michigan; ASME Fellow

美国密歇根大学讲席教授，1997年清华大学汽车工程系校级优秀毕业生，2002年麻省理工学院机械工程和电子工程双硕士，2005年麻省理工学院机械工程博士。曾任教于弗吉尼亚理工大学和纽约州立大学石溪分校，是美国国家科学基金会产学合作研究中心（IUCRC）能量采集中心主任。主要研究方向是能量采集、蓝色海洋能、汽车动力学、振动控制、机电一体化设计和先进制造。已发表论文360余篇，其中15篇获最佳论文奖。曾获2017年度美国机械工程师学会达芬奇（Leonardo Da Vinci）奖、2015年美国机械工程师学会 Thar 能源设计奖、2011年和2015年年度100项最重要的技术创新奖（R&D100）、2014年度美国汽车工程师学会（SAE）Teetor 教育奖。

Zuo Lei completed his B.S. in Automotive Engineering in 1997 from Tsinghua University and his Ph.D. in 2005 in Mechanical Engineering from MIT. Zuo Lei joined the University of Michigan as an endowed professor in August 2022. He was previously the Robert E. Hord Jr. Professor of Mechanical Engineering at Virginia Tech, and the director of NSF Industry-University Cooperative Research Center (IUCRC) for Energy Hafesting Materials and Systems. His research interests include marine renewable energy, energy harvesting, automotive engineering, vibration and control, mechatronics design, and advanced manufacturing. Zuo Lei was the sole recipient of the 2017 ASME Leonardo da Vinci Award and the 2015 ASME Thar Energy Design Award. He also received R&D 100 Awards twice (2015 and 2011) and the 2014 SAE Ralph R. Teetor Educational Award.

能源采集：汽车节能和智能化的途径

左 磊

大家好，我是来自密歇根大学的左磊，很荣幸有机会参加专题讨论。我想谈一下有关车辆和交通能源的话题。

我看到一些话题涉及车辆，而我最近的焦点是能源方面。在过去的14年中，我在能源猎取方面积累了很多的经验，以车辆能源猎取及车辆的温度传感器为例，温度传感器是能源猎取的早期应用之一，通常每两分钟只需要一个数据即可。但是，当我们谈论智能轮胎时，需要更高的数据采样率，也可以对温度传感器或结果进行千倍的采样。

所以，我们能做的就是需要一个温度传感器，例如现在我们谈到的智能车辆，大多数人都依赖雷达和摄像头。我们最好在车尾上安装一些传感器，但这样做非常具有挑战性，需要大量的能量。

最好的稳定系统需要三个条件。为什么最好的稳定系统像一根梁？如果在重力下，只有水不会停留在中心。它会停留在左侧和右侧，所以，第一是双稳态；第二是随机性，这通常不需要噪声。如果噪声达到一定的水平，在第三个条件下，会有弱的周期性振动，振动变得更加强烈，这就是所谓的随机共振。在随机共振下，与不使用共振器相比，你可以轻松获得100倍以上的振动。

现在我们使用随机共振概念。提到之前的随机振动，更大的中心力还是随时间变化的转速。然后，我们使用大的中心力创建轮胎在旋转中的振动，它们的随机运动和重力提供弱的周期性运动。因此，我们可以在大频率范围内创建这种振动，这就是所谓的自我协调。基本上，车速变化时，可以获得不同的振动。因此，我们的测试可以获得一千万振动，这是传感器压力的一到三倍。第二个工作是能量减半的冲击。冲击已经被用于汽车中减少振动，我们不仅可以在舒适性和道路处理之间进行权衡，还可以提高功率效率。

现在我们可以使用一种制造技术来制造无缝横跨行材料。另一个假设是激光聚焦能量，结果是在非常局部的区域，我们可以获得非常高的冷却速率。这种冷却速率高达10^6度/秒。以这种方式，现代液体或金属可以在晶体生长之前非常快地变成固体。这创造了另一种结晶结构，传统的制造方式是金属消耗，以使它们具有高的冷却速率。因此，我们可以选择性使用激光烧结或熔化来实现高冷却速率淬火。我们可以形成无缝横跨行结构。

废气热能收集到哪里？基本上，我们使用相同的电材料从废气热能中收集能量，从废气中收集了驱动汽车所需的同样多的能量，因此，如果我们从废气中节省5%的能源，可以将燃油效率提高5%。

过去14年中，我的主要努力是推动大规模能源发展和交通工具发展。我们最近也关注海洋方面的问题。我目前的工作专注于三个方向。第一，推动海洋能源的收敛研究。第二，利用海洋能源为海洋中的所有事物提供动力，这是蓝色经济。第三，我们将研究拓展到离岸风能和潮流能。这是一个非常令人兴奋的主题。

虽然能源获取的难度相当大，1799年以来已经探索了250种以上的理念。但是目前还不存在研究的收敛点。因此，我们目前的工作是推动海洋能源的紧急研究。这涉及知识和技术的整合。我们使用多学科，包括海洋、能源、电力、电子、环境科学、水动力学、经济学、结构材料、制造业的知识，并建立三个技术平台，分别是海洋能量平台、海流能量平台和离岸风能平台。我们将其整合到蓝色经济系统中，最终创造一个天然的碳蓝色经济和社会。这是另一个图景。这里涉及真正的交通工具。我们以燃料电池汽车和纯电动汽车为例。我们从海洋中获取能量并将其用于海水开采，然后获得所需的电池材料。那么燃料电池呢？我们需要用氢气吗？我们可以从海洋中获得协同作用。我们可以利用淡化海水、水和电力将水分解成氢气。我们可以用它推动未来可再生能源交通工具，不仅是交通工具，还包括现代交通运输。无论如何，我的工作会持续下去，因此，我将我的实验室命名为"海洋可再生能源创新与教育"，简称"海冥"（Marine NAP）。

在我的教育中，我希望重点强调专业技能培训，培养学生进行研究。另外是课程学习，为学生打好基础。我希望能够把学生送到工业界学习获取研究经验，或者邀请工业研究员作为导师指导学生研究。

因此，我每月都与学生们共进午餐，召开月度会议。通过这种方式，学生们可以发展专业技能。我们还邀请一些校友与他们交流，以便他们为未来职业规划做好准备。因此，为实现海洋能源和蓝色经济的梦想，我们需要跨学科研究，不仅是机械工程或海洋工程，还需要工程和科学的结合。因此，我们需要为学生培养多维技能，特别是专业技能。

以上就是我发言的全部内容，谢谢大家。

IFEE 2022

第三届国际工程教育论坛
The 3rd International Forum On Engineering Education

分组论坛 B2
Panel B2

发展中国家可持续创新

Sustainable Innovation In Developing Countries

2022 年 12 月 9 日 20:00–23:00

承办单位简介

清华大学东南亚中心

2018年10月，清华大学东南亚中心奠基仪式在印度尼西亚巴厘岛举行，2022年11月，巴厘岛园区开园。作为清华大学推进全球化战略的重要组成部分，清华大学东南亚中心是清华大学以非学历教育和人文交流为主要职能的单位。中心将聚焦东南亚地区乃至全世界范围内的人才培养和人文交流，为印度尼西亚和东南亚国家在工业4.0时代的人力资源培训做出贡献，助力"一带一路"建设和联合国可持续发展目标的实现。

清华大学拉美中心

清华大学拉美中心于2018年12月6日在智利首都圣地亚哥成立，这是清华大学全球战略的重要举措，标志着全球战略海外布局基本确立。清华大学拉美中心是清华大学在拉美地区的联络和交流基地，服务于清华大学人才培养的中心任务，致力于打造中拉政府部门、学界、智库及企业界之间的一体化交流平台，发展清华大学与拉美国家的学术研究、人文交流和科技创新合作。

清华大学中国-非洲领导力发展中心

在联合国教科文组织的支持下，清华大学于2018年6月6日成立清华大学中国-非洲领导力发展中心（CALDI），中心致力于人文交流和教育与人力资源开发，培养中非领导人才，助力推进"一带一路"倡议的实施，为国家推进中非全面战略合作伙伴关系、实现联合国2030年可持续发展目标提供有力支撑。

About the Organizer

Tsinghua Southeast Asia Center

The groundbreaking ceremony for the Tsinghua Southeast Asia Center (Tsinghua SEA) was held in Bali, Indonesia in October 2018, and the Bali Campus was opened in November 2022. Being a key component of Tsinghua University's Global Strategy, Tsinghua SEA focuses on non-degree education and cultural communication. Tsinghua SEA is currently managed and operated by the School of Continuing Education of Tsinghua University, in conjunction with the Indonesian non-profit organization "United in Diversity", assisting the construction and operation of related facilities.

Tsinghua SEA aims at talent training and cultural exchanges in Southeast Asia and around the world, contributing to human resources training for Indonesia and other Southeast Asian countries in era of Industry 4.0. Activities and objectives of the Tsinghua SEA are in line with the Belt and Road Initiative (BRI) and the realization of the UN 2030 Agenda for Sustainable Development.

Tsinghua University Latin America Center

Tsinghua University Latin American Center was established in Santiago, capital of Chile, on December 6, 2018. It is an important move of Tsinghua University's Global Strategy and marks the establishment of its overseas layout. The Center serves as a base for Tsinghua's networking and exchanges in Latin America, and supports the university with its core task of cultivating talents. It is committed to building an integrated communication platform among Chinese and Latin American government agencies, academic, think-tanks and business communities, while endeavoring to expand cooperation in academic research, cultural exchanges and scientific and technological innovation between Tsinghua University and Latin American countries.

China-Africa Leadership Development Institute

With support from UNESCO, the "China-Africa Leadership Development Institute" (CALDI) was established by Tsinghua University on June 6, 2018, dedicating to cultural exchange and human resource development, to educate future Chinese and African leaderships for promoting the China-Africa comprehensive strategic and cooperative partnership, the Belt and Road initiative, Agenda 2063 as well as the UN Sustainable Development Goals.

分论坛主持

主持人 Chair

李越
清华大学继续教育学院教授、继续教育学院教学委员会主任委员
LI Yue
Professor and the Chair of Teaching Committee of the School of Continuing Education, Tsinghua University

清华大学继续教育学院教授、教学委员会主任委员，中国就业促进会副会长。曾任清华大学教育研究院副院长、党总支书记，清华大学党委办公室副主任，政策研究室副主任，清华大学高等教育学会秘书长，中国高等教育学会学习科学研究分会副理事长，清华大学亚洲研究中心主任，清华大学继续教育学院副院长等。主要研究领域为高等教育、教育管理、教育政策、一流大学建设和院校研究，以及大学生创业就业教育等。

Li Yue is a professor of the School of Continuing Education at Tsinghua University, the Chairman of the Teaching Committee, and the Vice President of China Association of Employment Promotion. He used to be the vice dean and secretary of Party General Branch of the Institute of Education at Tsinghua University, the deputy director of the Office of the Party Committee of Tsinghua University, the deputy director of the Policy Research Office of Tsinghua University, the secretary general of the Association of Higher Education of Tsinghua University, the vice president of the Learning Science Research Institute of the Chinese Association of Higher Education, the director of the Center for Asian Studies of Tsinghua University, and the vice dean of the School of Continuing Education of Tsinghua University. His research interests include higher education, education management, education policy, first-class university construction and university research, university entrepreneurship and employment education, etc.

主持人 Chair

宋健
清华大学电子工程系教授，ITU-R 中国专家组成员
SONG Jian
Professor of the Department of Electronic Engineering, Tsinghua University; Board Member of ITU-R

清华大学电子工程系教授，博士生导师。分别于1990年和1995年获得清华大学电子工程系学士与博士学位。1996年与1997年在香港中文大学和加拿大滑铁卢大学从事博士后研究。入选IEEE和IET研究员、中国电子学会和中国通信学会会士。国际电信联盟学术期刊《智能与融合网络》创刊主编、国际电信联盟无线电通信局6A工作组副主席、国家学术期刊《电气电子工程师协会广播汇刊》副主编、IEEE Access广播技术学会责任主编。发表学术论文超过300篇，出版多部学术专著，拥有2项美国专利和80多项中国专利。2016年获国家科学技术进步奖一等奖、2019年和2022年日内瓦国际发明展金奖等。

Song Jian is a professor and doctoral supervisor of the Electric Engineering Department of Tsinghua University. He received his B. Eng and Ph.D. degrees from Electronic Engineering Department of Tsinghua University in 1990 and 1995, respectively and worked there following his graduation. He then conducted Postdoctoral research work in the Chinese University of Hong Kong and University of Waterloo, Canada in 1996 and 1997, respectively. He is a Fellow of IEEE, IET, the Chinese Institute of Electronics and China Institute of Communications. He serves as the Founding Editor of *Intelligent and Converged Networks* the ITU Academic Journal, the Vice Chair of ITU Task Group 6A, an Associate Editor of *IEEE Transaction on Broadcasting*, a National Academic Journal, and the IEEE Access Managing Editor of China Radio Television Technology Association. He has published more than 300 academic papers and many academic monographs. He has two U.S. patents and more than 80 Chinese patents. He won the first Prize of China Science and Technology Progress in 2016 and the Geneva International Gold Medal for Invention in 2019 and 2022.

韩星
中国联通国际有限公司新加坡运营公司总经理
HAN Xing
General Manager of Singapore Operation Company of China Unicom International Co., LTD. (in charge of ASEAN region)

中国联通国际有限公司新加坡运营公司总经理，主管东盟大区，业务范围涵盖新加坡、印度尼西亚、缅甸、越南、泰国、菲律宾、马来西亚、澳大利亚、柬埔寨等国家。有25年工作经验，11年管理经验，熟悉东盟区域电信业务与数字经济发展状况，熟悉电信业、信息服务业和国际商务，熟悉网络通信工程、软件工程和数据科学，精通数据通信技术、电信通信技术和信息技术，对产业互联网和企业数字化转型等新兴数字应用领域有深入研究，善于领导团队和公司治理。

HAN Xing, General Manager, Singapore Operating Company, China Unicom Global Limited, is in charge of ASEAN region operations, including Singapore, Indonesia, Myanmar, Vietnam, Thailand, Philippines, Malaysia, Australia, Cambodia. He has 25 years of work experience and 11 years of management experience. He excels at ASEAN regional telecommunications business and the development of digital economy. He is familiar with telecommunications industry, information service industry and international business. Besides, he possesses network communication engineering, software engineering and data science and is proficient in data communication technology, telecommunications technology and information technology. He conducts in-depth research on emerging digital application fields such as industrial Internet and enterprise digital transformation, and is good at leading teams and corporate governance.

东盟区域数字经济——发展状况与产业互联网实践机会

韩　星

感谢主办方的邀请，让我能有这次机会与各位专家、学者交流。今天我分享的主题聚焦于东盟的数字经济，重点关注东盟区域，特别是发展中国家数字经济在整个东南亚区域的发展状况，以及在产业互联网方面的实践机会。

从行业角度来看，数字经济分为两个层面：第一个层面主要针对公共用户即一般消费者，我们叫作消费级互联网；第二个层面主要针对企业用户，我们把它称为产业互联网。数字化经济又包含四大板块，即数字化消费、数字化供应链、数字化生产、数字全球化。从消费级互联网来看，大家普遍认为美国、中国及欧洲各国已经进入了成熟期，对于企业市场来讲进入了快速发展期。在纯线上的业务（社交），国际巨头占据优势，在线上线下结合的业务（电商、支付、打车等）应用领域，还有很多机会。对于企业用户来说，美国、欧洲各国、中国目前已经进入快车道，正在进行快速的试验推广，率先挖掘价值。从整个产业情况来看，美欧中三个区域，以及其他国家构建数字主权体系，同时也争夺全球数字经济主导权，同时对数字税收、数据本地化、数据隐私、数字关贸协定等都有所界定，从工业革命的涟漪效应看，趋势一直从欧美传导到东南亚区域。总体来看，数字化有产业化的趋势，目前各个国家对于数据的重视程度越来越高。我们认为整个范式从实验科学到理论科学，再到计算科学，再到目前的数据科学的阶段，都是在不断的发展和演进过程中的。数字经济秉承着几个法则和规律，价值规律基于梅特卡夫定律，成本法则基于摩尔定律，竞争规则基于达维多夫定律。

从目前的情况来看，数字经济已经成为现在市场环境下世界各国推动经济复苏的关键动力和核心动能。2020—2022年，虽然各个国家的经济受影响比较大，但是数字经济仍然呈现出良好的发展态势和增长前景。以2020年的全球数字经济发展情况来看，数字经济的整体规模达到了32万多亿美元，从整体来看国内生产总值（GDP）的增速为负数，但是数字经济增长达到3.01%。从三大产业的占比来看，目前数字经济的比重也会进一步提高。进入2021年之后，全球数字经济的发展状况，比2020年的规模有更大的提高。数字经济整体规模从32万亿美元提高到38万亿美元，同比增长达15.8%，对于发展中国家来说，数字经济的增幅也达到了22.3%。从发展方向看，数字技术创新仍然是全球战略重点。全球数字化转型正由效率变革向价值变革发展，由企业内部向产业链、价值链拓展。全球范围内面向实体经济的工业、产业在互联网平台也在快速发展。从数据变量来看，目前各个国家达成的一个统一认识，就是释放数据要素价值，成为各个国家共同的探索方向。大家都在寻求可信数据空间，为数据要素市场和参与各方提供信任的技术契约，全球数据要素市场建设也进入一个多元的共建共创、企业竞争加速推进、定价策略多样探索的新阶段，在这个新阶段也就意味着更多的创新机会。

目前，新兴市场数字经济快速崛起，东南亚发展潜力巨大，消费互联网方兴未艾。刚刚提到数字经济的两个层面，一是消费互联网，二是产业互联网。首先分析消费互联网，它的基准是人口。从整个东南亚地区的人口来说，东南亚地区集中了6.55亿人口，年轻群体庞大，4亿互联网用户中有超过90%的人为移动互联网用户，为数字经济发展提供了良好的土壤。从各国人口来看，印度尼西亚、菲律宾、越南这三个国家的人口都已破亿，或将近1亿人。泰国和缅甸的人口基本集中在5000~7000万。从消费互联网角度来看，这些国家的各项应用还趋于起步阶段。根据预测，东盟区域互联网经济正以惊人的速度增长，到2025年将达到3000亿美元。目前，东南亚地区各个国家的数字主权正在陆续觉醒，区域合作也在逐步加强，产业互联网发展潜力巨大，《区域全面经济伙伴关系协定》《数字经济伙伴关系协定》的签订，都在推动亚洲数字贸易的发展，进一步助力经济数字化。同时，东盟区域各个国家签订了《东盟数字总体规划（2025）》与《东盟互联互通总体规划（2025）》，一方面维护了各个国家的数字主权，另一方面加强了各个国家的数字合作。这为整个数字基础设施的建设，以及数据创新都建立了统一的服务标准，并积极开发建设数字平台。此外，东南亚各个国家也在积极推动数字经济与智慧城市的建设，东盟领导人创立东盟智慧城市网络，涵盖10个成员国的26个城市，联手探索可复制的智慧城市解决方案，吸引了来自各地跨国企业的投资。

产业互联网数字化转型浪潮也方兴未艾，各个行业的数字化转型也在加速。未来5至10年，我们预判有两类企业会发展得很好，一类是数字化原生企业，另一类是数字化重生企业。这两类企业都会经历数字化转型的进展。从整体情况来看，企业也会经历信息化、流程化、业务数字化三个不同的阶段。中国联通在东南亚地区建立了中国联通集团的五大业务赛道，中国联通是数字信息基础设施运营服务的国家队，也是网络强国、数字中国、智慧社会建设的主力军，更是数字技术融合与创新的排头兵。在国际区域里，中国联通同时也做好了五大主业。一是做深大连接。主要是提高连接效率、增强连接黏性，做优连接应用，做厚连接价值。二是做强大计算。实现"连接＋感知＋计算＋智能"的算网一体化服务。三是做活大数据。激发数据要素倍增效应，发挥数字治理国家队作用，为数字经济打造"联通数据"第一服务。四是做优大应用。整合内外资源，重塑能力格局，面向千行百业做优大应用。五是做精大安全。构建从安全合规到安全服务、生态繁荣的"大安全"体系。

中国联通在东南亚国家联盟的8个国家成立了分公司，陆续构建可靠有序的信息通信基础设施，用于服务千行百业。主要体现在全球通信连接组网；为当地企业和人民提供全球互联网访问；联通云与数据中心服务；为企业提供信息与通信技术（ICT）解决方案与应用案例；全球物联网；全球移动网与语音。在中国联通千行百业数字化转型过程成功的案例里，在智慧矿产、智慧冶金、电子应用制造、节能电力、智慧交通、服装的敏捷制造、装备制造、计算机辅助制造、智慧港口、智慧旅游、智慧教育、应急救援、智慧法庭等领域都有相应的应用。

我向各位列举一个中国联通在东盟区域的产业互联网的应用案例。长城汽车在泰国最大的汽车制造园区里进行了数字化转型部署，项目内容包括制造业工业园区无线网络信号覆盖项目、旧有通信系统改造与新系统部署升级、办公网与工业生产网络系统部署与改造、制造园区智能监控、智慧生产现场辅助装备、厂区仓储智能物流供应链管理及自动导向车（AGV）小车协同、人工智能质量检测、机器视觉质检、预测性维护等方面，目前整体应用情况还是比较良好的。对于东盟区域来说，数字经济将是本区域可持续发展的重要支撑力量，我们也愿意为此付出很多的心力。

以上就是我的分享，感谢大家！

郭永新
新加坡国立大学电子与计算机工程系教授
GUO Yongxin
Professor of Department of Electronic and Computer Engineering, National University of Singapore

IEEE 院士和新加坡工程院院士。新加坡国立大学电子与计算机工程系教授，新加坡国立大学苏州研究院智慧医疗技术卓越研究中心主任，重庆研究院智能感知与人工智能研究中心副主任。撰写或参与撰写了 500 多篇国际期刊和会议论文及专业书刊中的四个章节；在中国、美国和新加坡拥有 50 多项专利。研究领域包括射频传感、天线和医学电磁；用于生物医学应用和物联网的无线电源；无线通信用宽带和小型天线；射频、微波电路和 MMIC 建模与设计。担任《IEEE 医学和生物学电磁、射频和微波杂志》主编（2020—2023 年）。IEEE 天线和传播学会的特聘讲师（2022—2024 年）。

Guo Yongxin is a full professor at the Department of Electrical and Computer Engineering of National University of Singapore (NUS). He is a fellow of IEEE and a fellow of Academy of Engineering, Singapore. Concurrently, He is the Director of the Center for Peak of Excellence on Smak Medical Technology at NUS Suzhou Research Institute and the Co-Director of the Center for Smart Sensing and Artificial Intelligence at National University of Singapore Chongqing Research Institute. He has authored or co-authored over 500 international journal and conference papers and 4 book chapters. He holds over 50 granted filed patents in USA, China and Singapore. His current research interests include RF sensing, antennas and electromagnetics in medicine; wireless power for biomedical applications and internet of things; wideband and small antennas for wireless communications; and RF and microwave circuits and MMIC modelling and design. He has graduated 19 Ph.D. students and hosted at NUS. He is serving as Editor-in-Chief of *IEEE Journal of Electromagnetics, RF and Microwave in Medicine and Biology* for the term of 2020–2023. He is a distinguished lecturer for IEEE Antennas and Propagation Society (2022–2024).

新加坡国立大学苏州研究院在人才培养、技术创新与交流方面的实践分享

郭永新

非常感谢大会组委会的邀请,有机会与大家进行新加坡国立大学在人才培养技术创新与合作交流方面的实践分享。在接下来的分享里,第一部分我会介绍新加坡国立大学与中国在人才培养、技术创新、合作交流方面的内容;第二部分我会分享新加坡国立大学借助民间力量开展科技交流方面的内容。

借此机会,先简单介绍一下新加坡国立大学和新加坡国立大学苏州研究院。世界权威学术排名机构(Quacquarelli Symonds,QS)发布了2022年世界大学排名,新加坡国立大学在全球排名第11,电子工程领域的成绩也是名列前茅。新加坡国立大学在人才培养、科学研究、创新创业方面具有卓越的领先优势。新加坡国立大学拥有17个具有本科和研究生学位的学院,2500多名教职人员,接近4000名专职科研人员。2010年11月15日,新加坡国立大学与苏州工业园区管委会签署协议建设新加坡国立大学苏州研究院。新加坡国立大学苏州研究院是新加坡国立大学在海外建立的第一家研究院,也是响应了中新两国政府层面合作的号召。另外,两国政府在重庆也成立了一家研究院,运作模式与苏州研究院差不多。

新加坡国立大学苏州研究院聚焦三个核心——教育、科研、产业化,通过校友联络办公室、产业联盟聚焦卓越研究中心,同时有财务、人事行政、院办、IT、市场与公共关系等部门的支撑。在科研方面,新加坡国立大学苏州研究院更加注重研究的创新性和原创性,引入新加坡国立大学的学科优势和科研资源,结合地方的产业升级科技需求,开展应用型的科技研究。目前,新加坡国立大学苏州研究院聚集了众多卓越研究中心,包括环境与能源纳米科技、智慧医疗技术、大健康生物与食品工程、人工智能创新及育成,以及生物医学等。在教育方面,一是电机与计算机工程系首次提出的"3+1+1"联合培养项目,本科三年在母校就读,第四学年到新加坡国立大学苏州

研究院学习，任课教师都是由新加坡国立大学委派，第五学年注册为新加坡国立大学正式具有硕士学位的研究生，继续硕士研究生阶段的学习，这种方式很好地解决了人才培养的问题；二是提出了"1+2+1"博士研究生培养计划，博士研究生到新加坡国立大学对应专业进行为期一年的基础学习，而后两三年攻读博士，到苏州研究院进行自己的课题研究；三是支持国际学生来华交流项目；四是行政管理培训项目。在产业化方面，新加坡国立大学苏州研究院致力于推动中新两国科技与产业的双向交流，协助以新加坡为主的国际科技成果实现有效转化，加快高科技初创企业落地发展，搭建全球顶尖科技产业交流的桥梁，推动国际技术创新，促进经济发展。

最后分享下 BLOCK71 Suzhou 品牌在技术交流方面的创新。BLOCK71是新加坡国立大学企业机构与知名企业、政府机构建立合作与战略伙伴关系的倡议。它通过提供项目和活动，作为技术生态系统的构建者与商业连接者，以催化、聚焦和发展创业社区的能力为目标，形成了一个与新加坡国立大学之间的创新和创业门户的全球网络。BLOCK71目前的布点有美国、日本的部分城市和印度尼西亚雅加达，及国内的苏州、重庆。目前新加坡国立大学苏州研究院已经孵化了80多家创新企业，总融资超27亿元。新加坡国立大学苏州研究院也举办了很多的创新创业活动，其中非常有名的就是中国—新加坡国际科技交流与创新大会，它由新加坡国立大学苏州研究院、BLOCK71 Suzhou及新加坡国立大学企业机构联合主办，旨在打造一个高层次国际科技创新交流平台，是非常有影响力的线下活动。

另外，简单介绍一下新加坡—中国科学技术交流促进协会（以下简称新中科促会）。新中科促会是经新加坡政府批准正式成立的非营利、非政治和非宗教的民间组织，主要是促进新中科技教育交流，推动两国经济共同发展，力争打造一个国际科技英才寻求发展、交流与合作的平台。新中科促会会员来自新加坡的世界级顶尖大学、国家研究院、理工学院、跨国科研机构以及高科技企业。会员全部拥有学士以上学位，75%以上的会员拥有博士学位。新中科促会自成立以来，接待了中国多个代表团的访问以及交流合作。另外，新中科促会也举办了有关人才、技术、资本的交流与对接活动。比如，2019年10月，举办了健康与人工智能的医疗技术主题创新论坛，邀请了新加坡的科技人员和中国的企业，还有部分投资人与政府园区。2022年9月，携手国创中心，组织专家沙龙，邀请投资人、技术人员进行技术交流和对接活动。新中科促会也协助举办博鳌亚洲论坛在新加坡的推介会，其间也邀请了新加坡通商中国总裁，以及中国驻新加坡大使馆科技参赞等嘉宾参加，推介会的反响非常好。新冠疫情期间，新中科促会也大力推动线上论坛，从2020年开始，举办了60多场线上论坛，涵盖工程技术、人工智能、遥感科技、生物医药、临床医学，以及中医、健康、考古和知识产权等各个领域，促进了新中两国科技人员的进一步交流，加深了新中两国的合作。我们协会也非常重视人才的培养，除了注重科研人员的培养，也在不断加强与博士后、博士研究生做进一步的联络交流，为此还成立了青年团，汇聚人才，壮大科研队伍。

德斯塔·梅布拉图
联合国环境规划署非洲司前副司长,南非斯泰伦博斯大学工程学教授
Desta MEBRATU
Former Deputy Director of the Africa Division, United Nations Environment Programme; Professor of Stellenbosch University, South Africa

工业环境经济学专业的化学工程师,斯泰伦博斯大学可持续发展转型中心特聘教授,亚的斯亚贝巴理工大学客座教授,非洲科学院(AAS)研究员。在企业、大学和国际组织有超过33年的工作经验。在联合国环境规划署(UNEP)工作超过13年,担任环境规划署工商项目负责人和非洲区副主任等职位。在专业期刊上发表了大量文章,并参与《可持续发展政策和行政手册》和《非洲发展福祉型经济的转型基础设施》的编辑工作。曾担任埃塞俄比亚化学工程师学会和埃塞俄比亚化学学会的主席。

Desta Mebratu, a professor at Centre for Sustainability Transition (CST) of Stellenbosch University, also teaches at Addis Ababa University Institute of Technology as a visiting professor. He is a chemical engineer by background with specialization in Industrial Environmental Economics. He has more than 33 years of experience working for industries, universities and international organizations. He worked for United Nations Environment Programme (UNEP) for more than 13 years holding different positions, including the Head of UNEP Business and Industry Program and Deputy Regional Director for Africa. He has widely published in peer-reviewed journals and co-edited the *Handbook on Sustainable Development Policy and Administration* and *Transformational Infrastructure for development of a Wellbeing Economy in Africa*. He served as President of the Ethiopian Society of Chemical Engineers and the Chemical Society of Ethiopia and is a Fellow of the African Academy of Sciences.

工程教育和非洲的优先事项

德斯塔·梅布拉图

大家好！非常荣幸可以参加本次分论坛。我分享的主题是《工程教育和非洲的优先事项》。首先，我会探讨非洲面临的挑战和优先事项，聚焦于一些影响创新体系的基本组成要素，如何实现可持续发展。其次，跟大家一起讨论21世纪的工程教育。当前也有一些主要的驱动因素，这些因素将会塑造非洲的未来。此外，也会谈一下非洲工程师以及结构转型。最后，做一个简要的总结。

首先，非洲面临的挑战和优先事项。非洲发展面临着很多挑战，一是粮食安全问题，到2030年，非洲每年粮食进口的费用，可能从500亿美元增加到1100亿美元；二是能源安全问题，这是我们面临的一个很严峻的挑战，目前在非洲有超过43%的地区没有足够的电力供应，这无疑给非洲的发展带来严重的阻碍，对社会、经济、环境等方面都会造成很深远的影响；三是制造业增加值问题，从世界银行2022年统计的数据可以看到，2021年撒哈拉以南的非洲的制造业增加值平均占GDP的12%左右，所以，对于非洲来说，工业化进程仍然任重而道远；四是基础设施差距问题，非洲的基础设施远远落后于其他发展中国家。这些也是我们目前发展的优先事项，预计每年需要投资1300~1700亿美元。总之，不管是交通、能源安全还是基础设施等，非洲和其他国家相比都是有很大差距的。虽然非洲面临着挑战，但也有很多的机遇：一是自然资源。众所周知，非洲自然资源十分丰富，比如土地、水、能源等，可以实现能源保障；二是战略资源。非洲拥有大量的战略资源，包括可再生能源和矿产能源，这对于全球的可持续性和气候复原力至关重要，与此同时，非洲也正在进行能源方面的转型，从而应对气候变化给人类带来的风险，这也是我们现在关注的重点；三是跨越式的发展机会。由于内在惯性最小，非洲在实现具有气候抵御力和资源效率等方面具有最大的跳跃机会；四是人口红利。非洲拥有大量的青年劳动力，他们正日益成为技术专家与创新者。目前非洲青年劳动力的数量还在迅速上升，青年人对于技术创新方面有非常浓厚的兴趣。

其次，介绍一下21世纪的工程教育。我们先要重新定义工程学的关键概念。经济系统是对能源、材料、信息的加工；可再生能源构成了21世纪能源系统的支柱；分布式制造、生产系统，最初由供应链效率驱动，现在更多地由可持续发展问题驱动；由数字化驱动的第四次工业革命（工业4.0），也将重新定义21世纪的全球经济结构。

再次，是非洲工程教育面临的挑战，其中有一个挑战是我们需要基于证据制定知识和与背景相关的解决方案，从而解决发展方面的挑战和优先事项，需要克服因工程师知识与国家专业技术需求之间不一致而产生的不协调问题。因为这个原因，我们在未来必须加强对工程师的培训，这是我们最为关注的一项优先事项，也是我们的一大挑战。另外，我们也需要发展创新的生态系统，创新生态系统本身也在不断地发展和演进。我们需要通过创新生态系统建立21世纪新的知识体系，挖掘创造力和创新精神。与此同时，我们也需要促进跨学科之间的交流和沟通，建立强大而有效的大学与产业之间的联系，从而有效地促进知识和技术转型、结构方面的转型。中国在这个方面树立了良好的典范，在产学研合作方面一直都是非常成功的。

接下来，是工程师和结构转型。我列出了五种结构转换类型：第一种是从不可持续的线性消费和生产模式，向资源高效、气候适应能力强的循环经济转型；第二种是从依赖自然资源的采掘型经济，向具有制造业增加值驱动的生产型经济转型；第三种是从分散的政策制定和规划过程向综合性转型；第四种是从孤立的政策干预向以结构转型为目的的变革性干预转型；第五种是从供应方驱动的增量跨越式发展，向改革性的跨越式发展转型。工程师在跨越式发展中发挥什么样的作用呢？在这里可以看到一些关键的特征。非洲必须实现跨越式的发展，正如我之前所说的一样，我们并不追求偶然式的跨越式发展，而是希望实现变革性的跨越式发展。要把相关的创新技术纳入变革过程，在这个过程中也有很多的驱动因素。在偶然式的跨越式发展中，绝大部分供给方面的驱动因素都是由外部因素驱动的，为了实现真正的变革性跨越式发展，就需要推动内部需求驱动。接下来看一下战略性的干预措施，它将骨干的基础设施与分布式电网发展结合起来，从而确保其包容性；通过区域合作促进动态专业化，促进区域价值链的发展，确保从各国的国家资源中获得最大的回报；促进大学与产业界的紧密合作，作为产业创新和技术发展的基础；开展"工业4.0准备评估"，以减小包括数字化在内的第四次工业革命的不利影响，并优化其收益；培养转型领导力，确保工业发展的主要参与者与利益攸关方之间的利益和战略方向保持一致。有了以上助力，我们可以确保整个变革在非洲大陆顺利展开。

最后是一些结论。实现非洲国家经济的可持续结构转型，不仅是非洲国家的需要，而且具有全球意义。因为非洲正处于发展的早期阶段，其惯性因素较低，因此在实现绿色工业化方面有着独特的跨越式发展机会。非洲的人口也在快速增长，如果到2050年非洲人口达到25亿人规模，我们必须实现可持续增长，包括在工程教育、研究、发展方面，这些都是开发与环境相关的创新解决方案的关键，从而满足非洲的需求和优先事项。非洲和中国大学之间的国际合作，对于提升非洲国家的教育水平和研究能力至关重要。与此同时，非洲的基础设施发展，不仅对非洲很重要，对全世界都是如此，我们也希望大家能够关注非洲大陆存在的机遇，包括在研究、教育、创新性方面的解决方案，还有人口红利等，所以我们必须加强合作，尤其是非洲和中国之间的合作，在教育和研究能力方面的合作，这也是非洲要实现变革性跨越式发展所不可或缺的因素。

萨特里奥·苏曼特里·布罗德乔内戈罗
印度尼西亚科学院院长
Satryo Soemantri BRODJONEGORO
President of Indonesian Academy of Sciences

　　印度尼西亚万隆理工学院机械工程系名誉教授，印度尼西亚科学院院长，有着长期而杰出的学术和公共服务生涯。1980年起，在万隆理工学院机械工程系任教超过30年，担任系主任（1992—1995年）和教务副院长（1995—1998年）等职务。主要研究领域为摩擦学、断裂力学、有限元分析、机械设计、高等教育发展与政策。

　　Satryo Soemantri Brodjonegoro is an Emeritus Professor in Mechanical Engineering at Bandung Institute of Technology, Indonesia as well as the President of the Indonesian Academy of Sciences. He has a long and distinguished academic and public service career: He had been a faculty member of the Mechanical Engineering Department at Bandung Institute of Technology for more than 30 years since 1980, serving as the Department Chairman (1992–1995), and Vice Dean of Academic Affairs (1995–1998). His research areas are tribology, fracture mechanics, finite element analysis, mechanical design, and higher education development and policy.

创新印度尼西亚

萨特里奥·苏曼特里·布罗德乔内戈罗

衷心感谢本次会议主办方的邀请。我想跟大家分享创新印度尼西亚的相关内容。

为了推动印度尼西亚（以下简称印尼）的创新，我们创建了一个叫作"创新印尼"的项目，这是一个国家基金和创新中心，旨在推动和支持印度尼西亚创新企业的发展，解决印度尼西亚对更多以创新为基础的企业和行业面临的根本问题。"创新印尼"是一项大胆的、充满想象力的长期倡议，聚焦当前企业转型，并且支持创新企业和行业的发展。为什么我们要推动创新呢？政府以及私营企业都已经形成了共识，那就是印尼的创新表现远远低于其潜力，在全球的创新排名中，印尼排第97名，在全球竞争当中不具备充分的竞争力，创新能力一直处于比较脆弱的位置。如果说印尼能够促进创新，加快向以知识为基础的经济过渡，就需要利用先进的技术和工艺，推动创新的发展和社会的发展，从而升级为领先的、具有竞争力的全球经济体。因此，"创新印尼"与其HUB和相关的融资合作伙伴一起，帮助发展和资助那些加速创新生产力和创新力的项目。

"创新印尼"包含几方面的内容：创新中心，协作，基金管理和融资，以及智力和影响力。第一项是创新中心。其目标是提供催化服务，与企业合作，促进创新的实现。创新中心将在帮助企业分拆和初创公司的过程中最大限度地推动其创新和增长，发挥领导作用。HUB将鼓励来自印度尼西亚各地的潜在投资者，开展相应的投资活动，它将为创新企业提供指导服务，促进一系列创新计划基地的建设。然后，我们也有相应的焦点范围，主要包括制造业、基础设施、建筑业、食品安全、粮食生产和使用、健康服务，还包括环境可持续性、旅游业等。此外，创新HUB项目中，有一些是在中心内进行的项目，也有一些在中心外进行的项目。HUB的一项主流服务就是与公司合作推进创新、提高生产力和增强竞争优势。同时它与现有的大大小小的公司，还有新成立的公司，共同开展创新工作。第二项是协作。"创新印尼"将特别鼓励涉及公共和私营部门伙伴关系的项目，使私营部门能够推动创新，并且帮助在私营部门、政府和学术界之间建立新的关系，使私营部门能够通过政府的扶持，在尖端研发的支持下推动创新发展。第三项是基金管理和融资。我们有不同级别的投资人，包括白金级投资人以及黄金投资人、银质投资人，还有普通投资人。与此同时，我们也有不同的融资渠道，并将基金导入创新HUB、创新中心中的一些项目。创新中心也有自己的管理机制，管理委员会下有审批委员会和审计委员会等。对于商业融资，我们也知道为技术和创新进行融资是一种特殊的金融领域，其成本高、时间长，所以"创新印尼"也是与商业融资伙伴进行合作。一些企业将通过捐赠基金进行融资，它将激励、促进和支持创新，而其他的一些企业则可以通过赞助方式进行融资，比如在城市创新竞赛中给予资助。然而，我们也将建立一个需要大量资金、用于发展和增长的企业通道。印度尼西亚创新协会将与一系列风险基金、商业天使基金和其他投资基金达成伙伴关系，对创新企业进行潜在的商业投资。印尼的创新也将通过承担部分开发和风险成本，刺激商业融资，也可以发展自己的商业基金，作为联合融资的启动器。

最后一项是智力和影响力。我们建议"创新印尼"应该建立在政府和私营部门之外，放在独立的印度尼西亚科学院内，在那里创新基金可以补充印度尼西亚的科学基金，也可以为相关的政府机构创造独特的新机会，以参与私营部门的创新。我们建议运营"创新印尼"的管理机构应该尽可能地保持精简。管理委员会由RPI及其主席设立，其提名会得到印度尼西亚共和国总统的认可。该委员会会确定自己的程序，并且负责基金的良好管理，确保其以一致、透明、公正、公平的方式运作。具体而言，该委员会将负责"创新印尼"的整体战略，包括中心及其计划、年度工作计划、招聘和人力资源等。资金审计委员会将是一个小型且管理严格的单位，成员来自管理委员会，每年至少召开一次会议，评估向其转移的资金申请，向管理委员会推荐可行的项目，供其最终决断。审计委员会将向管理委员会独立报告整个资助计划，以及支持的个别项目，包括资金回报率。审计委员会的监督活动将有助于确保基金按计划进行运作，将产生的任何盈余用于扩大和改善基金的服务供给，它还会对提出投资项目的过程进行审核。咨询委员会由来自印度尼西亚和国际上具有独立思想的创新专家组成，他们能够提供见解和相关的建议，从而保持发展基金对于印尼创新产业的影响。

那么应该如何衡量影响力呢？衡量该基金的经济和社会影响，这对其成功至关重要。我们用投资回报率（ROI）指标，监测创新印尼在增加就业机会、支持企业提高竞争力和其他社会效益方面的影响。与此同时，在包括新成立的和现有的企业中进行变革，不仅会影响这些企业，而且会在关键经济部门中产生连锁反应，使印尼的企业能够参与到未来的产业中。衡量影响力的关键指标包括新开办的企业数量、新增的工作岗位、营业额、利润率、销售额、出口和新市场、产品和服务的发展，以及持续创新的认证等。所有与基金有关的企业都需要详细说明它们目前在这些指标中的情况，并且同意开展年度跟踪调查，以便持续监测基金的影响力。通过在公共和私营部门建立创新和创业文化，"创新印尼"将帮助大学和科学院发展以创新为基础的研究，为下一代产品提供技术帮助，并培养未来的企业家。这里的影响相对容易跟踪，关键指标涉及研究导致的技术许可，或通过初创企业、衍生企业开发的数量。另外，在国家层面的衡量影响中，关键指标包括竞争力定位、国家创新排名、管理生产总值的影响，以及生产力等。

印度尼西亚面临的挑战是向高科技经济转型，以创新推动生产和经济增长。因此，基金必须鼓励并且创造机会，投资于促进这一变革和发展的活动，时间可能为20年。下一步，建议采取以下两个步骤：第一，成立指导委员会，指导完成筹资和设立阶段的工作；第二，编写招股说明书，提交给潜在的投资者。转型要在很长一段时间内持续进行，基金将通过支持那些在当前条件下可以实施的，而且有可能继续发展和扩大规模的倡议，从而为经济的长期发展作出贡献。

李晓潮
厦门大学电子科学与技术学院教授、委员会主任
LI Xiaochao
Professor and Director of Professor Committee of School of Electronic Science and Engineering, Xiamen University

厦门大学电子科学与技术学院教授委员会主任，IEEE高级会员，英国工程技术学会（IET）专业工程师，兼任厦门大学集成电路设计与测试分析福建省高校重点实验室主任，福建省集成电路设计工程技术研究中心副主任。主讲课程获得教育部国家精品在线和国家一流本科线上课程。福建省高层次人才，厦门"双百计划"人才，2017—2022年任厦门大学马来西亚校区电气与电子工程系主任。

LI Xiaochao is the Director of Professor Committee of School of Electronic Science and Engineering at Xiamen University. He is also an IEEE senior member, an IET Chakered Engineer, the Director of Fujian Key University Laboratory of Integrated Circuit Design and Measurement, and the Vice Director of Fujian IC R&D Engineering Center. Several of his online courses are awarded the National Best Massive Open Online Course and 1st-class Undergraduate Online Course. He is also awarded the talents of Xiamen and Fujian province. During 2017–2022, he was the Head of Department in Electrical and Electronics Engineering (Hons) of Xiamen University Malaysia.

全球化可持续性对厦门大学马来西亚分校电气和电子工程教育的影响

李晓潮

我本次分享的题目是《全球化可持续性对厦门大学马来西亚分校电气和电子工程教育的影响》。

首先，我简单介绍一下厦门大学与厦门大学电气工程学院的历史。厦门大学由著名爱国华侨领袖陈嘉庚先生于1921年创办，是中国近代教育史上第一所由华侨创办的大学，2021年是厦门大学建校100周年。今天的厦门大学早已跻身国家"双一流""211工程"以及"985工程"中国一流大学之列，达到了世界一流水平。电子工程是厦门大学最具有历史和潜力的工程学科之一。1924年，建立了物理系，1940年，成立机电工程系，1985年，创立电子工程系。2016年，成立电子科学与技术学院（微电子学院）。另外，厦门大学也是我国最早成立半导体学科的高校之一。2019年，教育部正式批复同意厦门大学承建国家集成电路产教融合创新平台。在"一带一路"倡议背景之下，中国工程教育也迎来了新的机遇，为实现全球繁荣和可持续发展助力，因此厦门大学在马来西亚建立了第一个海外校区——厦门大学马来西亚分校（Xiamen University Malaysia），成为第一个在马来西亚设立分校的中国高校。厦门大学的愿景是成为一所教学科研水平一流、文化多元、具有鲜明国际视野的大学。

如果希望工程教育走出去的话，就必须符合全球的标准，因为不同的国家具有不同的标准，这也是为什么我们必须要为工程教育找到共同标准。《华盛顿协议》是我们可以遵循的全球标准，是一项工程教育本科专业认证的国际互认协议，旨在建立共同认可的工程教育认证体系，实现各国工程教育水准的实质等效，为工程师资格国际互认奠定基础。厦门大学马来西亚分校成立了马来西亚工程师委员会（Board of Engineers Malaysia，BEM）。工程认证委员会（Engineering Accreditation Council，EAC）是由马来西亚工程师委员会（BEM）授权的工程学位课程认证机构。经过认证的课程涵盖各个学科领域，并且要达到适当的水平，比如电气工程，涵盖机器与机动、发电与高压工程、电力系统分析、电能利用、仪表与控制等领域；以及电子工程，涵盖电路与信号、数字与模拟电子技术、电力电子技术、通信系统等领域。为了能达到这些标准，需要把中国和马来西亚的项目融合起来，厦门大学电子科学与技术学院就是由电子工程系与机电工程系组成。我们通过项目融合推动马来西亚电子工程（EE）的发展，这也符合马来西亚在这个领域的巨大需求。东南亚国家联盟（东盟）是电子电气生产的重要枢纽，占东盟出口总额的最大份额（27%），而电子工程产业是马来西亚工业发展的重要驱动力。2020年，机电行业继续成为马来西亚出口收入的主要贡献者，占出口总额的39.4%。其中在半导体上，目前最大的12家半导体公司中有6家在马来西亚运营，而马来西亚也有非常强大的后台能力（即芯片封装和测试）；在发光二极管（Light Emitting Diode，LED）上，9家最大的LED公司中有3个在马来西亚开展业务；太阳能方面，马来西亚是全球第三大太阳能光伏组件和产品制造商，这些都是我们要在马来西亚开办校区，推动电子工程教育发展的原因所在。

厦门大学马来西亚分校的工程教育项目是四年制的电气与电子工程学士学位项目，这个项目共有161个学分，授课语言为英语，学生毕业后将获得脱产学习学位证书。该项目围绕一套核心课程设计，提供经典的电气工程基础，以及一些选修课程，让学生专攻感兴趣的领域，重点放在工程知识的应用上。主要课程分类共分为五个方面，即通识教育核心课程、通识教育选修课程、工程学核心课程、工程类选修课程、培训与项目研究。其中专注于工程的核心课程有工程学核心课程一和工程学核心课程二，主要是工程专业的学生所需要去学习的课程。工程学核心课程主要是基础的理科类课程，选修课包括电力、芯片设计等。此外，也会让学生参与一些项目，我们希望学生有更多的机会参加项目实践，因此在这个方面也有专门的行业学习和培训。针对培训，我们设置了4个学分，会让学生到相关行业的公司学习，学生就会有更多的行业知识。针对项目实践，我们设置了14个学分，占全部学分的8.7%。此外，我们也建立了目标导向型的教育，致力于持续不断地改善教学质量。为此，我们建立了一个XMUM EEE OBE模型，这个模型为每一门课程制定课程学习目标，也会给学生分配相应的教学内容，还会进行课程学习成果（course leaning outcomes，CLO）和专业学习成果（program learning outcomes，PLO）的匹配，12个课程都有相应的CLO和PLO。同时，也有相应的CQR行动，对于学生来说就可以评估学生的学习能力。在进行课程预期学习成果和专业预期学习成果的匹配之后，就可以去分析项目学习结果达成率，我们的目标是90%以上的学生都能够达到PLO要求。课程教育成果（program education outcomes，PEO）包括学生的专业性和个人的持续发展，以及社会的参与情况，这也就意味着毕业生或者学生会有助于社会的可持续发展，以及社会的福祉发展，可以推动可持续能源的设计、行业培训，以及其他的核心课程。此外，还有专门的学生俱乐部，学生有机会参加中国和马来西亚两国大学生创新创业比赛，并在2021—2023年获得相应的认证证书。除了四年制的电气与电子工程学士学位项目，厦门大学马来西亚分校还推出了硕士项目，这个硕士项目最少需要两年的时间。

以上是我分享的所有内容，谢谢！

罗威妮·西格玛
联合国教科文组织工程规划专家
Rovani SIGMONEY
UNESCO Engineering Planning Expert

南非化学及环境工程师，主要研究生物能源系统和生物燃料。曾作为自然科学部青年专业人员项目一员，2007年起在联合国教科文组织巴黎总部任职，在2011年国际化学年时主持了化学计划。此后，接管联合国教科文组织工程项目，与国际合作伙伴和项目专家合作，通过课程开发、实践培训和能力建设加强工程教育。工作重点是妇女和非洲问题，鼓励年轻人从事工程事业。作为哈拉雷教育团队的一员，从事高等教育、职业技术培训、减少灾害风险教育和儿童早期发展等方面工作，在《生命周期评估》《工程教育》和 Girls in STEM 等刊物发表文章。

Rovani Sigamoney is a chemical/environmental engineer from South Africa who staked in the platinum refinery/mining sector and then moved on to researching bioenergy systems and biofuels for Africa. She joined UNESCO HQ in Paris in 2007 as part of the Young Professionals Programme, in the Natural Sciences Sector and later ran the Chemistry programme and International Year of Chemistry 2011. She thereafter took over the UNESCO Engineering programme, working with international partners and program experts to strengthen engineering education through curricula development, hands-on training and capacity building. In line with UNESCO's global priorities on Africa and Gender Equality, it focuses on women and Africa. Rovani is passionate about women in engineering and encouraging more youth to pursue careers in engineering. Now, as part of the ED team in Harare, Rovani is excited to be continuing with girls in Science, Technology, Engineering and Mathematics (STEM) and also adding to her portfolio by working on Higher Education, TVET, Disaster Risk Reduction Education and Early Childhood Development. She has contributed to published articles on Life-cycle assessment, *Engineering Education and Girls in STEM*. Rovani coordinated the 2nd engineering report, one of UNESCO's flagship publications, entitled "Engineering for Sustainable Development", was published on World Engineering Day in 2021. Rovani previously worked in Brazil, USA and Ireland.

发展中国家的可持续创新

罗威妮·西格玛

衷心感谢本次会议主办方的邀请。我今天分享的主题是《发展中国家的可持续创新》。

人类的行动与2030年议程息息相关。联合国2030年议程正在逐步改变我们的思想。全球不平等正不断加剧，新技术的产生也增加了国家、人群与地区之间的差距，与此同时，人类活动也对地球产生了巨大影响，需要通过技术帮助我们解决一些问题，包括消除贫困等。第四次工业革命正如火如荼地进行着，它正在从根本上改变我们的生活方式，它通过提供强大的技术解决方案，鼓励消费者和企业做出对环境友好的决策，从而提高可持续性和生产力；它可以提供先进的技术解决方案，通过可持续产品和服务提高我们的生活水平。

我们知道，在实现可持续发展目标方面，工程学无疑处于核心的位置。在面临紧迫的地球危机和社会经济挑战的背景下，可持续和创新性的解决方案需要一个高效、透明、充满活力的工程界。此外，可持续发展目标中一个非常重要的目标就是消除贫困、减少不平等，包括性别的不平等。新冠疫情也给全球带来了健康危机和其他威胁，这就需要工程学推动社会的变革与转型，推动全球合作与信息共享，加强社会的相互关联性，让大家受益于创新成果，缩小技术知识和性别差异。新冠疫情让我们了解到工程师这样的职业在解决人类的基本需求，如消除贫困、推动安全和可持续发展，应对紧急情况、重构基础设施、缩短知识鸿沟，以及推动国际跨文化合作，都是非常重要的。不仅如此，工程也是社会经济可持续发展的主要驱动力，它能够促进创新和创造新产品及服务的能力。

我们看一下工程领域面临的全球挑战。比如，缺乏政策制定所需的工程数据；年轻人接受工程教育的比例较低，尤其是女性所占比例更低；许多国家，尤其是发展中国家的工程学科课程已过时；工程专业的年轻毕业生相对来说就业机会较少，导致年轻的工程师在这个行业的留存率较低；在商业和社会中对于女工程师角色的作用认识不足。基于以上种种挑战，我们必须重新看待工程学在新时代经济和社会中扮演的角色，我们需要更多全球的报告。联合国教科文组织于2021年3月4日世界工程日当天发布了第二部工程报告。该报告强调了工程在实现17项可持续发展目标的每一项目标中的关键作用。所有人拥有平等机会，是确保包容性和性别平等的职业关键，可以更好地应对实施可持续发展目标的工程师短缺问题。同时，它也提供了一个正在塑造我们世界的工程创新的概览，如大数据、人工智能等新兴技术。另外，它也分析了在第四次工业革命来临之际，工程教育和能力建设的转变，这将使工程师能够更好地应对未来的挑战。同时，它也强调了要解决特定区域差距所需要的全球努力，最后还总结了世界不同地区的工程发展趋势。这份报告涉及工程行业各个利益相关方：一是政策制定者，他们需要让青年工程师直接参与课程的学习和就业设计，为吸引青年工程师参与的项目提供资金，并为参与的组织提供奖励。二是行业领袖，与学生组织合作，直接交流当前的工程实践，缩小研究中所发现的差距；与服务于工程师的项目合作，运用技术和计划的解决方案，增加获得服务的机会。三是服务工作者，与合作者合作，更早地将年轻人引入工程领域（中学或之前）；设计在正式以及非正式场合，使用真实世界应用的课程，包括让学生体验真实的工程工作。

可以说，我们在用工程加速实现可持续发展的目标，工程学也在改变世界，使之变得更加美好。工程学本身也需要进行转型，变得更加创新、包容、合作和负责。工程创新对于实现可持续发展目标来说至关重要，尤其是对于发展中国家来说，我们需要用工程对抗新冠疫情和改善医疗保健，我们也需要促进可持续发展的水利工程、气候应急和减少灾害风险的工程、面向未来的可持续采矿技术，以及大数据、人工智能和智能城市。我们还需要与工程教育相关的能力建设，这些都是实现可持续发展目标的关键，这也是未来的工程师所必须具备的一些技能，同时我们也必须促进各地区工程的快速发展。通过实施可持续发展目标，我们需要建立面向未来的工程教育以及能力建设。

我们认为转型是关键，我们需要用工程实现整个社会的转型。其中就包含教育能力建设的多样化和包容性，利用大数据人工智能提升健康和卫生水平，建设智慧城市，拥有良好的清洁能源、水安全与气候变化。我认为，在教学和应用工程方面，需要跨学科合作，还需要给予学生更多选择和可能性的在线学习平台，这些目前已经变成了现实。我们应该鼓励儿童（特指5岁及以下），让他们在科学、技术工程和数学教育（Science, Technology, Engineering Mathematics, STEM）方面有更多的实践。我们需要把工程的重要性带给政策制定者，对于青年来说，必须让他们在很小的时候就培养起对科学和工程的兴趣，也为他们在大学期间更加顺利地完成工程学科学习奠定基础。2022年12月，《开普敦开放教育宣言》在南非开普敦发布，这对政策制定者会有非常大的影响，对于现在的年轻人成为未来的科学家和未来的工程师具有非常明显的政策助力作用。另外，我们也必须将知识传授给当地人，以对他们产生长期的影响力。

当我们面向未来，谈到第五次工业革命时，这次革命将是人类和机器在工作场所的结合，未来要实现这一点，工程才是关键。《可持续发展议程》是一份行动蓝图，工程师们正站在实现可持续发展目标的最前沿，利用他们的科学知识和经验，将创新理念转化为可持续性项目，造福所有人。技术正在快速发展，为未来提供了光明的前景，与此同时，我们也应当从伦理角度评估它们带来的新风险。工程专业必须被重新塑造，以解决当今的紧迫问题，并且为实现必要的创新提高全球责任感。目前大学已经对此有了非常深刻的认识，我们还必须提升政府和公民社会的相关意识，让大家都能认识到工程对于经济发展，对实现《可持续发展议程》的重要性。我们也必须提升对于未来工程师的教育与培训，这样才能让我们有更多的创新性解决方案解决全球的挑战，提高人们的生活质量。

世界需要更多的工程师、技术专家与人员，那么就从我们的工程教育开始吧，感谢大家！

弗朗西斯科·马丁内斯
智利大学工程学院院长
Francisco MARTINEZ
Dean of Faculty of Engineering, University of Chile

  英国利兹大学运输经济学博士，智利大学工程学院院长，智利大学土木工程系教授，复杂工程系统千年研究院高级研究员。主要研究领域包括城市经济学、交通与城市动力学、城市规模规律，并且关注经济均衡和数学模型。智利经济部资助的复杂系统工程研究千年项目主要研究人员，新加坡－麻省理工学院研究与技术联盟未来城市移动综合研究小组 SinMobility 项目合作伙伴。撰写或参与撰写了4部专业书刊、9个书刊章节和29篇国际期刊论文。

  Francisco Martinez, a Ph.D. in Transport Economics (1991, 1988) at the University of Leeds, UK, is the Dean of Faculty of Physical and Mathematical Sciences at the University of Chile. He was a Founder of the Land Use and Transport Laboratory (LABTUS) at the University of Chile. His current research interests include Urban Economics, Transport and Urban Dynamics, Urban Scale Laws and he focuses on economic equilibrium and mathematic models. He is a key research member of Millennium Institute for Complex Engineering Systems, granted by Ministry of Economics, Chile. He is also the Project Partner of SinMobility project, Singapore MIT Alliance for Research and Technology (SMART) Future Urban Mobility Integrated Research Group. He has authored or co-authored over 4 books, 9 book chapters and 29 international journal and papers.

更多样化、更好的工程技术实现可持续发展——来自南半球的创新

弗朗西斯科·马丁内斯

衷心感谢本次会议主办方的邀请。我分享的主题是《更多样化、更好的工程技术实现可持续发展——来自南半球的创新》。

在致力于控制气候变化方面，智利达成了强有力的社会共识。智利一直走在可持续发展的前列，在可再生能源生产、海洋保护和公共交通电气化等领域成长显著。目前，智利还在起草新的宪法，主要是讨论关于构建新的社会秩序和发展模式方面的前沿主题。我们坚定地支持并倡导社会和技术创新，社会的需求以及环境方面的挑战都会带来非常深远的影响。我们的目标是为所有人和生物打造更美好的家园。我们视自己为变革的引擎，为智利的社会、政治和技术变革提供支持。现在，我就向诸位介绍一下智利大学目前正在进行的一系列创新行动。我们致力于培养更多的女性工程师和科学家，也已经采取了一系列的平权行动，包括增加针对女性的奖学金和学术职位的数量；发起了多项研究和倡议（包括对一些主要建筑重新命名），以期深入变革男权文化；获得了联合国颁发的性别平等荣誉证书，以表彰我们不断推出领先政策的做法。

另外，我们也致力于追求社会的融合发展，推出了独特的"土著民族计划"。通过语言课程、论文、研讨会、学生辅导、实地调研、社区合作以及平权行动等方式，使我们的工程师培养方式去殖民化，所有的这些活动也得到了学生的大力支持和赞赏。我们也正在推动教学的创新，增加具有挑战性的研究生项目的数量，聚焦可持续发展，并从第一年开始贯穿专业学习全过程。与此同时，我们也推动机制的变革和创新，加速推动终身学习课程和项目，作为对工程公司和其他组织进行变革的工具。从支持学习的新技术，到线上信息，再到新知识，我们需要紧跟技术变革及其广泛影响的步伐。我们认识到，人工智能是一门新的语言，机器人也是推动技术变革和创新非

常重要的工具。所以，我们也在不断地加快人类社会各方面的创新，我们认为在教育模式上仍然面临着重大挑战，需要提高课程和项目的灵活性，以便服务于更加多元化的学生群体及其多样化的兴趣，并应对日益提高的信息获取门槛。

智利大学是一所设立于智利首都圣地亚哥的大学，成立于1843年。智利大学倡导终身学习的理念，它从基础科学到最终应用这一构建知识的线性模式得到了高度认可，但其不足也日益显露。这种模式首先是学习一些基本的知识，再逐渐应用起来，但是现在已经远远无法满足社会需求了。我们需要先进的教学方式，从而让学生在学习过程中更加投入，更好地参与和互动，这对许多学校而言是一项艰巨的挑战，我们正在设法解决这一难题，持续跟踪学生的进步情况，例如，我们开发了辍学预警系统，并设计了促进学生参与的策略，以维持他们的学习兴趣。我们也会推动学生社团组织的发展，以便在学生需要帮助时为他们提供支持。正如我刚才所说，我们致力于为所有人打造一个家园，这就意味着我们很重视多样性，也会继续致力于推动实现公平和多样性，坚定支持在智利和全球其他地区为人类和自然生物建造家园。我们认为大学需要扮演非常重要的角色，因为科学和工程可以作出至关重要的贡献，我们需要建立一个独立、智能、相互连接的、独特的、强大的网络，因此，我呼吁我们所有人共同努力，保障人类的生存权利，共促和谐发展。

我刚才提到学生的多样性，包括在社会经济、性别、遗传，以及文化之间的差异，因此智利大学在教学上也面临着很多挑战，与此同时，学生的需求也越来越大，主要体现在气候、可持续发展、女性主义、多元化团体的整合，以及不公平等领域的探讨中。在科技研究方面，我们看到人工智能、机器人、空间、能源、健康等领域，这些学生都很感兴趣，而且会积极参与的领域。为此，我们也做了一些教学方面的创新，包括开展一些灵活的项目，从而满足学生的多元化动机，以及丰富学生的个人简历；推动学生的积极主动性，加强他们在校园里的深度学习；开展一系列基于项目的研究，这些项目属于跨学科研究，通过跨学科教育将当前的研究发展趋势和研究成果纳入教学，并通过丰富的实践机会和其他计划促进学生的应用学习体验；虚拟校园的混合，目前智利大学正在学习技术方面的最新实践和最新趋势，包括刚才讲到的人工智能、数据分析，还有学术伦理等，还有多所支持卓越的研究中心，这些研究中心也一直在教学方面进行联合，在数据、实验室等方面进行共享，联合培养学生。

最后，再谈一下学校面临的挑战。一是任务研究，学校作为一所研究型大学，肩负着研究型大学的使命，需要积极应对或者解决国家和全球面临的挑战与难题，需要重视对社会技术发展的引领作用；二是学术成果发表，我们知道在学术发表方面成本非常高，这个渠道是有限的；三是获取数据的渠道问题；四是环境问题，呼吁大家积极采取行动。以上是我的个人发言。谢谢大家！

尹峰
国网浙江省电力有限公司电力科学研究院能源技术中心主任
YIN Feng
Director of Energy Technology Center of Zhejiang Electric Power Research Institute of State Grid Co., LTD.

国网浙江省电力有限公司电力科学研究院能源技术中心主任，教授级高级工程师，国家电网公司优秀工程技术专家，浙江省新世纪151工程人才。任全国电站过程监控及信息标准化技术委员会（SAC/TC376）副秘书长、中国自动化学会发电自动化专业委员会副秘书长、中国能源研究会智能发电专家委员会委员。曾获评2015年度中国自动化领域十大风云人物，中国自动化学会2018年度杰出自动化工程师。科研成果获省部级奖励15项，国家发明专利授权10余项；发表论文80余篇、专著3部；参编行业标准9部、国家标准2部、国际标准3部。

Yin Feng is the Director of Energy Technology Center of Zhejiang Electric Power Research Institute of State Grid Co., LTD., a professor-level senior engineer, a State Grid outstanding engineering and technical expert, and one of the Zhejiang New Century 151 engineering talents. He serves as the Deputy Secretary General of the National Power Station Process Monitoring and Information Standardization Technical Committee (SAC/TC376), the Deputy Secretary General of the Power Generation Automation Professional Committee of the Chinese Society of Automation（CAA）, and a member of the Intelligent Power Generation Special Committee of the Chinese Energy Research Association. He was rated as the Person of the Year in China's Automation Field in 2015 and the Outstanding Automation Engineer of Chinese Association of Automation in 2018.

自动化领域的国际合作与需求

尹 峰

我来自国网浙江省电力有限公司电力科学研究院能源技术中心，我分享的主题是《自动化领域的国际合作与需求》。

首先向大家介绍中国自动化学会在自动化领域里有关国际合作与交流开展的情况。中国自动化学会是我国最早成立的国家一级学术群众团体之一。钱学森被推选为中国自动化学会第一届理事会理事长。学会办事机构设在北京，挂靠在中国科学院自动化研究所。学会在全球范围内与自动化领域知名学术团体和权威学术机构开展了广泛深入的合作，特别是在自动控制、系统工程、模式识别、人工智能、社会物理信息系统（CPSS）等前沿领域合作密切，包括电气与电子工程师学会（IEEE）、国际自动控制联合会（IFAC）在内的老牌学术团体，以及国际模式识别协会（IAPR）、系统工程国际委员会（INCOSE）、国际先进人工智能协会（AAAI）等。

学会通过国际会议、高端论坛、交流互访、产品展销、国际工程合作等载体和形式与全球学术团体、各国政府和企业都开展了广泛合作。比如，第三届国际自动控制联合会网络物理与人类系统（Cyber-Physical & Human Systems，CPHS）研讨会，讨论了人—机—物融合的社会、信息和物理系统正被应用于工业、能源、交通等多个领域，由此带来的虚拟物理大融合将帮助人类社会解决很多目前物理系统难以高效解决的难题；与中国工程院联合举办的国际工程科技发展战略高端论坛，通过"线上＋线下"模式，共同探讨"面向CPS（信息物理融合系统）工程的建模与仿真技术"的未来发展之路；在第24届国际模式识别大会上，海内外知名专家会聚一堂，针对模式识别、机器学习、计算机视觉等相关领域，探讨最新成果和发展趋势；英国前卫生大臣保罗·伯斯托一行来访交流，分享了在原创平行智能理论体系及其在平行交通、平行医疗、平行农业、平行区块链、平行教育等领域取得的成绩。

学会现有近8万名会员，58个专业委员会分布在电力、冶金、化工、石油、交通、矿山、水利、轻纺、建筑、农业、国防等各行业系统与工程技术领域中，依托国际工程项目服务和产业推广开展深入合作。在工程领域主要合作的形式包括：为各工业领域提供自动化、智能化解决方案；开展国际标准化合作与应用推广；国际工程投资与项目合作；国际大型产品展销活动；人员职业培训和继续教育；前沿领域的学术交流。在工程教育领域，学会开展了自动化系统工程师（Automation System Engineer Accreditation，ASE）的资格认证工作，但国际合作方面开展较少。在教育资源方面，中国科学院自动化研究所2014年发起成立了青岛智能产业技术研究院，下属智慧教育研究所开展了很多关于教育领域的智能技术研究和产业化工作，研究平行系统、大数据、物联网等技术与教育的深度融合，面向智能时代的中小学人工智能教育体系、平行自适应智慧教育技术、产学研协同的智能产业技术开展教育培训。中国自动化学会发电自动化专业委员会利用会员单位与技术资源，成立智航教育基金会，联合青岛智能产业技术研究院开展了全国教育助学工作，正积极拓展相关自动化领域工程教育与培训工作。学会与"一带一路"沿线国家以及发展中国家开展的合作，主要是依托专委会会员单位开展的国际工程项目服务与产业推广进行。

接下来，再和大家分享一下学会在"一带一路"倡议下的工程合作与培训需求。中国自动化学会发电自动化专业委员会相关单位，在越南、印度尼西亚、巴基斯坦、白俄罗斯等"一带一路"沿线国家开展了一系列能源领域工程项目的合作建设工作，联合编制了一系列IEEE、国际电工委员会（IEC）国际标准，在工程项目实施中推广应用相关标准，提供合作支撑。我们参与建设的几个工程项目，在当地都是当时首个最高等级的发电项目，新技术、新标准、建设运维和管理方法的合作应用需求很大。

目前，国际工程合作中的人才培养主要面临以下几个方面的培训需求。第一，理念方法培训。思维理念的培养对工程合作或项目运营至关重要，但这点也是最难沟通交流和培养的，需要和谐的工作环境、人文环境、学习环境和情感环境。方法多种多样，如属在国人员的办公设备设施的优化配置、生活设备设施的配置、娱乐项目和日常激励等。第二，语言习惯培训。工作语言培训是工程项目正常推进的首要条件，不管是中国员工还是属在国员工，都需要双语交流和培训。例如中越项目，招聘越籍大学生的条件之一就是愿意接受中文强化培训（一般集中培训3个月），工作语言暂设定为中文，日常技术交流和现场作业都要求中文，技术资料均规定中英文，日常夜校进行中文培训、中文演讲、中文书写比赛等。中方人员主要是英语的撰写和交流培训，但中资企业这方面没有强制要求，基本都是自学。第三，专业技能培训。主要分两个方面——理论讲课和技能实操。理论授课实行企业内训师制度，公司聘任符合条件的中方技术能手和具备丰富经验的老师傅作为内训师，规定有培训任务、培训要求和考核奖励。符合条件的外籍员工可聘为初级内训师，负责辅导刚入门的学员。实操培训主要借助日常设备检修时间跟班学习，建立一定规模的实训基地（中心），利用修旧利废的设备和系统进行培训。第四，分析能力培训。主要是分析工程中发生的一些技术疑难杂症和异常事故事件。第五，人文环境营造。主要是双方文化、习俗和感情的交融，创造双方都能接受或认可的人文环境。

随着中国企业"走出去"的步伐加快，承揽的海外项目日益增多，需要更多中国技术和中国装备走向海外市场，需要更多中国工程技术人才走向世界舞台，需要更多的中国标准转化为国际标准，需要培养更多海外人才加入中国制造的技术体系。因此，要充分发挥国内外高校、制造与施工企业、社会团体与学术组织的国际化优势，不断消除技术服务贸易的壁垒，推动国际人才制度与职业资格接轨互认，在国际工程合作中培养各类技术型、复合型人才，结合交流合作开展合作地区本地化人才培养，加快推进国际标准化合作，促进"一带一路"建设高质量发展。

最后和大家分享几点国际工程人才合作与交流的建议。一是在属在国寻找可以合作的高校开展人员的联培联训，充分利用双方的需求和资源，形成框架协议，从语言、理论、技能和实习机会等方面开展深度合作。二是通过政府间的交流合作项目或企业间的关联开展互派学习交流。属在国中资企业可以与中国国内高校开展委托培养协议招收优秀的国际生进行专项培训。三是通过技术论坛、专业会议等形式开展跨国界、跨区域、跨专业线上活动，拓展专业视野和专业结构。四是工程上使用的设备及需要的系统的培训，最好的方式就是要求设备供应商专业技术人员开展远程培训，针对具体设备和系统进行全面细致的结构分析、原理讲解和问题解决。五是建立国际实质等效的工程能力评价体系，发挥社会组织在社会治理中的作用，探索推动工程技术人才资格国际互认。

以上就是我的分享，谢谢各位！

IFEE 2022

第三届国际工程教育论坛
The 3rd International Forum On Engineering Education

分组论坛 B3
Panel B3

青年学生可持续创新
The Sustainability Generation: Students Talk

2022 年 12 月 9 日 20:00–23:00

承办单位简介

清华大学苏世民书院

清华苏世民书院秉承"立足中国,面向世界"的原则,整合全球一流教育资源,依托清华大学综合实力,积极探索国际人才培养和人文交流新模式。苏世民书院位于清华园中心位置,建筑采用合院式布局,集古典传统与现代气息、东方神韵与西方风格于一体,已成为一道新的校园景观。

作为清华大学新百年发展的重点举措,该项目自2013年4月启动伊始即得到全球各界领导者的关注和支持。中国国家主席习近平和时任美国总统奥巴马分别两次发来贺信。苏世民书院每年在全球招收至多200名苏世民学者,并为每名学者提供综合奖学金。

该书院的目标是培养具有宽广国际视野、优秀综合素质和卓越领导能力,了解中国社会,理解中国文化,有志于为促进人类文明与进步、世界和平与发展贡献聪明才智的未来领袖。

About the Organizer

Schwarzman Scholars at Tsinghua University

Designed to inspire the next generation of global leaders, Schwarzman Scholars at Tsinghua University is the most significant program of its kind since the Rhodes Trust was founded in 1902. Adhering to the principle of "based in China, embracing the world", Schwarzman College is fundamental to responding to today's geopolitical landscape, integrating top educational resources from around the world and actively explores new ways to cultivate talent and mutual understanding. Located in the heart of Tsinghua's campus, the residential and academic building of Schwarzman College is designed to encourage a constant exchange of both ideas and cultures between students, faculty, and visiting leaders.

The Schwarzman Scholars Program was officially launched in April 2013 and Schwarzman

College was formally established in October 2015. Since its launch, the Schwarzman Scholars Program has received four congratulatory letters from Chinese President Xi Jinping and US former President Barack Obama. Each year, the program admits up to 200 scholars from around the world who will each receive a comprehensive scholarship.

The program aims to cultivate future leaders with a global perspective. With an understanding of Chinese society and its culture, they will be able to promote world peace and international development in innovative ways for the 21st century.

分论坛主持

主持人 Chair

康立新
苏世民学者
Konstantin TKACHUK
Schwarzman Scholar

俄罗斯年轻的领导者和企业家，致力于建筑和教育领域的尖端技术研究。在慕尼黑工业大学攻读土木工程硕士学位。领导建筑3D打印研究，旨在通过设计创造可持续建筑，并挑战在21世纪的建造方式。通过参与有关可持续发展目标主题的国际工作，力求促进青年平等获得教育和实现自我的机会。

Konstantin Tkachuk is a young leader and entrepreneur working in cutting-edge tech in the realms of construction and education from Russia. He graduated with honours from the Ural Federal University and is currently pursuing M. Sc in Civil Engineering at the Technical University of Munich. He leads research on construction 3D printing that aims to create sustainable buildings by design and challenges traditional construction manners of the 21st century. Through his engagement in international work on SDG topics, he seeks to foster equal access to education and self-realization opportunities for the youths.

主持人 Chair

陈兰
清华大学电子工程系本科生
CHEN Lana
Undergraduate Student of the Department of Electronics Engineering, Tsinghua University

清华大学电子工程系学生。高中期间，参与了多个可持续发展相关的学生组织，如担任缅甸学校项目的学生组织者，通过义卖、联系缅甸当地组织支教为缅甸的中小学筹款改善学校条件；参与北京德威国际学校的"Nightingale"项目，通过与北京外来打工子弟基金会合作，为京郊打工子弟学校提供每周一次的英语和音乐课，并通过慈善晚会等方式来筹集善款。在清华学习了更多的科技知识后，在非营利性行业组织实习，使用前沿的能源和IT技术帮助企业实现低碳减排。

Chen Lana is a undergraduate student majoring in Electronic and Information Engineering at Tsinghua University. During high school, she attended several student-lead SDG projects. She was one of the student leaders of the Myanmar School Project, which raises money to help improve the condition of schools in Myanmar, through organizing charity bazaars and contacting local charity groups. Lana also took part in Dulwich College Beijing's Project Nightingale, which cooperated with the Migrant Children Foundation (MCF) of Beijing, to give music and English classes to local migrant children's schools and to raise money for them. After learning more technical knowledge at Tsinghua, she interned at China Energy Storage Alliance, helping enterprises to achieve low-carbon and sustainable development using latest energy and IT technologies.

王婧怡
清华大学电子工程系博士生
WANG Jingyi
Ph.D. Student of the Department of Electronic Engineering, Tsinghua University

清华大学电子工程系博士，主要从事人机交互和社会计算等交叉学科研究。本科毕业于多伦多大学，心理学和分子遗传学与微生物学双专业学士，获得多伦多大学社会和人文科学优秀奖。随后，在哥伦比亚大学教育学院攻读了社会组织心理学的硕士学位。一直立志于创造一个包容和接纳的社区。曾在国际非营利组织国际野生生物保护学会（WCS）实习，负责培训协会人员，更好地为保护生物以及促进人与自然和谐共生的梦想做努力。

Wang Jingyi is a Ph.D. student studying Information and Communication Engineering under the Department of Electronic Engineering at Tsinghua University. She worked with associate professor Yong Li to conduct interdisciplinary research on human-computer interaction and social computing. She received her bachelor's degree from University of Toronto, double-majoring in Psychology and Molecular Genetics & Microbiology, and was given the 2018 UofT Excellence Award in Social Sciences and Humanities. She then pursued a master's degree in Social-Organizational Psychology at Teachers College, Columbia University. She has also interned at the Wildlife Conservation Society, an international non-governmental organization, to help protect biodiversity and inspire people to value nature.

校园垃圾管理

王婧怡

我想谈谈垃圾管理这个问题，分享一些关于统计数据以及我们的观察和对教职员工与学生的采访，同时提出我们发现的一些问题和解决方案。首先，在中国，每年会在垃圾分类产业上花费610亿元人民币。人们每年会产生超过235万吨的垃圾，造成超过500平方公里的大规模土地污染。我们注意到学校一般只提供有机或普通的垃圾桶，并没有很多便捷的回收站。对于很多大学来说，都普遍存在废物管理问题。例如，哈佛大学会把塑料瓶弯折，学生只允许使用自己的瓶子，大学也会举办回收可回收物相关活动，还有的学校将回收的瓶子用作艺术创作。在明日博物馆中，他们利用与垃圾相关的科学事实教育参观者。我们注意到许多大学的学校团体或其他组织在指导学生做垃圾分类，例如，清华大学学生绿色协会的志愿者们发起的"桶前值守一小时"活动。复旦大学有一个智能垃圾桶和回收箱，学生们可以把可回收的东西扔进去，同时可以获得积分和奖励，但垃圾桶有固定的工作时间，就不能随时随地扔东西，这给学生和工作人员带来了很多不便，而且他们又减少了其他垃圾箱的数量，使得垃圾桶的垃圾超载问题愈发严重。

我们由外部到内部看问题，首先是中国的社会环境。我们有很多外卖，产生了很多塑料杯、塑料碗和其他东西，这就产生了很多垃圾。与其他国家相比，很多人在推广和宣扬回收利用是一件非常好的事情，大家也鼓励他们的行为，这与社会规范有关，我们的制度和设置的规范影响了我们自己的行为和意识，以及我们对这种回收利用的态度。但是，垃圾回收的宣传力度还不够。

我们所要解决的目标问题是效率低下的垃圾分类和回收，人们对于垃圾回收的态度和认知，以及回收宣传不足。我们的目标是转变人们的垃圾回收态度和行为、得到清华大学的资源支持、提高自下而上的沟通效率，同时为其他学校树立榜样，形成大学垃圾管理联盟。

关于我们的解决方案，首先，在垃圾管理方面，我们可以尝试找到最合适的垃圾桶，设计一个可以展示废物管理生命周期的二维码，帮助学生们更好地理解垃圾回收的过程，而且学生们可以看到学校目前的回收状况以及自己对环境的影响。此外，我们将在每个垃圾桶附近提供可降解的袋子，为垃圾分类提供便利。其次，我们希望与组织合作、与学校和回收公司合作实施回收奖励制度，目的是教育和鼓励回收行为。所以我们所做的就是设计传感器和垃圾桶盖。比如在兼容原来的垃圾箱的基础上，设置新的传感器以清点回收物品，可以扫描二维码了解回收说明和好处，也可以收集你的奖励积分，用于学校公共事业或支持其他环境的事业。我们也愿意与不同的学生组织合作，以更好地推广他们的活动，实现更顺畅和透明的交叉沟通。同时为校园乃至世界的环境作出贡献，谢谢大家！

陆智泓
清华大学电子工程系硕士研究生
LU Zhihong
Master Student of the Department of Electronic Engineering, Tsinghua University

　　本科毕业于清华大学电子工程系电子信息科学与技术专业，随后在清华大学攻读通信及信息工程硕士研究生，主要研究方向为科学领域中的交叉学科发展模式。基于校园中存在的单车弃置问题，以第21届昆山杯创业大赛为契机，策划创业计划B-C-B二手单车交易平台——清清（Clean Queen）。该项目旨在为同学提供方便且快捷的二手单车出售服务，提高校园内单车的再用率并减少状态良好单车弃置的情况。该项目成功打入昆山杯创业大赛的复赛。

　　Lu Zhihong received his Bachelor's degree from Tsinghua University in 2022, majoring in Electronics Information Science and Technology. He continues his study at Tsinghua University with a Master's program in Information and Communication Engineering under the Department of Electronic Engineering. Currently, he works with associate professor Yong Li, focusing on the field of Science of Science, relating to the growth of interdisciplinary evolution and big data technologies. In the hope of encouraging the reuse and recycling of bicycles on the campus of Tsinghua, he and his schoolmates launched a startup program Clean Queen, a B-C-B second-hand bicycle trading platform, creating an efficient and convenient way for second-hand bicycle trading. Clean Queen has participated in the 21st Kun Shan Cup Entrepreneurship competition and reached the semi-finals.

智能碳足迹记录和共享平台

陆智泓

我要和大家分享的是我们的可持续发展目标项目——智能碳足迹记录和共享平台。首先，我简单介绍为什么要提出这个项目。其次，基于这个背景解释我们的解决方案是什么，并进行简要的市场分析，包括我们项目的需求、盈利能力和竞争对手。最后，我想具体谈谈我们如何实施计划。

首先，我们的项目背景。几十年来，碳排放一直是人们关注的焦点。将碳中和与达到二氧化碳排放峰值作为我国五年规划的目标之一。我们作为一个团队聚集在一起是想回应这一呼吁。我们的碳项目侧重于计算个人的交通碳足迹，但为什么是交通呢？根据《联合国气候变化框架公约》第26次缔约方大会的数据，碳排放的来源主要由工业、建筑和交通组成。作为个人，我们对减少碳排放有些无能为力，但我们可以通过关注交通碳排放缓解这种情况。

研究了市场之后，我们将我们的计划与竞争对手进行比较，发现高度自动化的碳足迹记录平台存在空缺，这个平台也有有趣的社交功能。为什么这两个属性非常重要？对于前一种属性，我们认为需要手动输入记录是一件麻烦的事情。这对继续参与这个平台的用户来说是一种阻碍。而后一个，我们认为社交属性是鼓励用户更加关注收集到的数据，这是我们最终的目标。

为了实现我们的设想，我们提出了碳（Carbon）作为解决方案。现在我介绍项目中提出的方法。碳项目主要包括三个模块。第一个模块是核心功能——碳排放计算。结合用户自定义的用户画像，计划实现准确的流量碳足迹以及时间线可视化，直观地显示用户的表现。第二个模块是本地为用户显示汇总报告，试图给用户带来成就感，比如将旅途中节省的碳排放量转换为可以种植的树木数量。第三个模块是社交分享模块，将社区属性引入平台，增加对使用用户的鼓励。

碳项目把提高人们的环保意识作为主要目标，而不是为了赚取利润。但为了让这个项目生存和发展，它需要盈利。我们分析了三种可能的方法。第一是广告，第二是与电商平台合作，兑换足迹节约奖励。第三是利用这个平台的社交属性，在呈现用户排名时引入皮肤或装饰，有些是免费的，有些是需要购买的。

其次，需求分析。我们的项目能满足谁的需求？我们总结了可以满足的三个条件。我们可以与企业合作，帮助彼此获得社会影响力。对客户来说，这是主要的目标持有人。我们采取了自动和鼓励的方式来记录、测量他们的交通碳足迹。我们的竞争对手呢？我们比较了现有的三个类似赛道的竞争对手。在我们看来，所有这些都存在不便之处，比如每次都需要手动编辑、跟踪和记录，以及不准确或缺乏社交互动。

总而言之，这个交通碳足迹记录仪有两个主要的目的，一是减少阻碍，二是引入社交功能。对于前一个目标，我们会尽量做到自动化，当然这个平台是免费使用的，每个有智能手机的人都可以使用。对于后一个目标，我们将引入社交功能，目前计划包括排名系统、迷你游戏和装饰系统。当然，方便是最关键的，所以我们尝试使这个平台尽可能地易于访问，最重要的是根据可视化数据，让用户知道在哪里生成报告很重要。

我所说的可访问性是指我们在哪里实现。目前，我们设想的平台是一个跨平台、跨设备的平台。最初我们想把它放在微信小程序上，因为用户不需要安装软件，它可以在不同的操作系统上使用，最大限度地提高了可访问性。但是，我们注意到微信应用程序编程接口（API）可能没有提供后台连续 GPS 跟踪等功能，因此，我们可以同时发布安卓版本和 IOS 版本的独立应用程序。对于管理记录，我们认为如果有一个基于网络的电脑终端提供全面的数据管理功能，用户体验将会大幅提升。

我的演讲就到这里，希望大家喜欢。

傅天予
清华大学电子工程系博士研究生
FU Tianyu
Ph.D. Student of the Department of Electronic Engineering, Tsinghua University

本科毕业于清华大学电子工程系，目前在清华大学继续攻读博士学位。主要关注高能效稀疏计算系统，广泛涵盖图计算、图神经网络等领域，曾在高性能计算研讨会（HPEC）、新加坡特许会计师协会（ISCA）等国际会议发表学术论文。稀疏计算是实现计算机认知智能的重要范式，希望借助算法和硬件的联合设计优化，使稀疏计算能更高效、精准、绿色，并惠及更多人。曾获国家奖学金、清华大学综合优秀奖学金、优良毕业生、优秀毕业论文、科技创新优秀奖学金、社会实践优秀奖学金、文艺优秀奖学金、电子之星等荣誉。

Fu Tianyu received his bachelor's degree from the Department of Electrical Engineering at Tsinghua University. He is currently pursuing his Ph.D. degree. His research interest lies in the energy-efficient sparse computing system, covering various areas, like graph computing and graph neural networks. Some of his works were published in international conferences such as HPEC and ISCA. Through software-hardware co-optimizations, he hopes to make sparse computing more efficient, accurate, green, and beneficial to more people. Fu Tianyu received several scholarships and awards, including the National Scholarship, as well as the Comprehensive Excellence Award, Outstanding Undergraduate Award, Outstanding Undergraduate Thesis Award, Excellent Science and Technology Innovation Award, Excellent Social Practice Award, Excellent Literature and Arts Award from Tsinghua University. In addition, he was once elected as the Star of the E.E. Department.

基于图神经网络的慈善资源匹配

傅天予

我想以一个例子开始今天的分享，那就是艾米的困境。艾米是一位42岁的单身妈妈。她有两个可爱的孩子，工作很努力，但她每天只能得到几美元的收入。就像所有的妈妈一样，艾米想给她的孩子最好的一切。她知道教育的重要作用，因此希望给她的孩子教育的机会。然而，艾米没有时间和知识去实现她的愿望。为了满足这些需求，联合国提出了可持续发展目标，呼吁采取行动，消除贫困，保护地球，改善世界各地每个人的生活和前景。

可持续发展目标项目在2020年提供了许多的实际资源，在教育方面取得了许多进展。2019—2030年，每年将提供1.3万亿美元的资金以实现与健康和教育相关的可持续发展目标。尽管做出了许多努力，但资源与需求之间的不匹配仍然是一个严重的问题。无数的机构针对各种不同的需求提供了无数的方案。然而，由于时间和知识的限制，很多像艾米这样的人无法获得最合适的资源。尽管有很大的需求，但许多资源并没有得到充分利用。在这种现象背后存在着数据难以获取和分析不善的问题。一方面，大多数数据以非结构化的方式提供。如果没有对底层信息的进一步说明，数据能提供的信息是有限的。大多数资源信息只是纯文本，例如冗长的文档、大量的电子邮件和繁杂的社交媒体文段，这样的信息很难进行比较和分析。因此，很难为有需要的人提供有用和及时的帮助。另一方面，这些信息很难获取。即使数据是结构化的，人们仍然需要依靠专业知识做出明智的决定。正如《可持续发展目标2022年报告》指出的那样，我们需要强大的统计基础，为有需要的人匹配最好的慈善资源。我们可以用蓝色圆圈代表不同的慈善组织，绿色圆圈代表组织的类型，比如城市机构和非营利组织。数量和圆圈大小表示它能提供的资源数量。在这种情况下，我们在这里要解决的匹配问题是选择一条匹配路线，为有需要的人提供最多的资源。

为了做到这一点，我们提出了资源流图数据结构，每个节点表示一个不同级别的实例，即特定组织显示为蓝色，组织类型显示为绿色，兴趣领域显示为橙色。每个边都意味着资源从上一级流向下一级。比如，从AHRCNYC组织到非营利组织，有1000的资源和200的资源，构成了非营利组织（NPO）可用的1200资源。基于资源流图，选择合适组织的问题就变成了选择连接有需要的人和具体组织的路线问题。例如，如果你想为教育领域选择最好的组织，我们可以选择从AHRCNYC到NPO再到儿童和教育领域的路线，然后计算该路径的资源流，以确定人们可以获得的资源。请注意，在这个例子中，匹配结果是通过始终选择资源最多的组织来获得的，这是具有基本数据分析能力的人的常见做法。由于AHRCNYC将其资源平均分配到儿童教育和健康医学两个领域，患者最终可以获得500个资源。资源流动图已经为用户提供了一个更高的视角，但经过进一步调查，我们注意到一个更有利的资源流动路径选择。我们现在不是简单地选择资源最大的路径，而是仔细研究每条路径以优化资源流。正如你所看到的，通过选择合适的组织，也就是儿童服务的管理机构，学生能获得的资源从500个增加到650个。

我们使用纽约市开放数据集来演示该系统，数据来自2019年度志愿者统计报告。这是纽约市对居民志愿服务和组织进行的最大规模的调查。这里用志愿者的数量来表示资源。我们将数据组织起来，构建资源流图，它包括495个组织，60种组织类型，10个兴趣领域。资源流图由2274条边组成，描绘了资源分布的概貌。我们在3D空间中绘制图形以提供对问题的直观和直接理解，组织、组织类型和兴趣领域注释分别从上到下排列。每个边的颜色和大小表明有多少资源流经其中。基于资源流动图的细致分析，我们现在能够提供对纽约市慈善工作的高水平洞察。比如以社区为基础的慈善组织提供了纽约市一半的志愿者资源，同时大部分志愿资源流向了残障群体和儿童。

有需要的人和组织都可以从这个系统中受益。对于有需要的人来说，他们将通过专业的慈善设施推荐得到最大的帮助；对于慈善组织来说，它们可以更好地实现慈善服务的社会效益最大化。借助资源流图，我们旨在解决慈善匹配问题。然而，我们不会止步于此，因为世界上有很多人都面临着和艾米一样的问题。因此，我们计划面向全世界所有的人提供这样的专业知识。

最近人工智能的发展使这样的愿景成为可能，图神经网络（GNN）已被广泛用于解决各种图学习问题，这也是我作为一名电子工程专业博士研究生的个人学术兴趣。由于今天时间有限，我不打算讲技术细节。不过我还是要展示一下，为什么图神经网络可以帮助我们解决这个问题。我先给大家介绍一下什么是图神经网络。图神经网络是一种特殊的网络，它可以学习到信息如何在整个图中流动，通过可学习的消息生成、聚合和更新影响这个过程。就像慈善资源的流动，只不过它配备了图神经网络强大的学习能力，所以只要有足够的训练数据，我们的图神经网络就可以学习到端到端的慈善资源流量分配应该如何优化。也可以用现在各种成熟的工具，将资源分配问题转化成图神经网络中标准的链接预测任务。有了这样神奇的工具，可以实现自动化分析，为有需要的人找到最好的资源类型。

回到艾米的困境，这位母亲如何为她的孩子找到最好的资源，希望在我们的帮助下，不用再绝望地搜索，不用再四处询问，只需要陈述需求，让系统完成其余的优化资源匹配。在这个系统的支持下，我们希望将慈善机构的营业额增加20%，这将带来超过1200万美元的市场扩张，同时仅在英国就有大约800万的潜在用户。我们将遵循社会商业模式，由政府支持项目的运转，不断缩小社会结构中的信息差距。

司锐雅
苏世民学者
Sreya VANGARA
Schwarzman Scholar

毕业于麻省理工学院（MIT），曾学习电气工程、机械工程和计算机科学，目前就读于清华大学苏世民书院。通过与马达加斯加和纳瓦霍族的全球清洁水合作，以及与普林斯顿大学合作的低成本核反应堆设计，改善了贫困社区的状况。通过基层教育计划支持可持续创新，在哈萨克斯坦、墨西哥和中国香港教授STEM课程。作为国家非营利性组织Synapse的联合主任，关注大学残疾人权益，并率先在麻省理工学院制定无障碍政策。通过苏世民学者项目，为农村社区开发使用廉价材料的小型核聚变装置。

Sreya Vangara studied electrical engineering, mechanical engineering, and computer science at MIT, and is currently a Schwarzman Scholar at Tsinghua University. Her research elevates underprivileged communities through global clean water collaborations with Madagascar and the Navajo Nation, as well as lower-cost nuclear reactor designs forged with Princeton University. Sreya also supports sustainable innovation through grassroots educational initiatives, and has taught STEM in Kazakhstan, Mexico, and Hong Kong, China. Sreya has advocated for collegiate disability rights as a co-director of the national non-profit Synapse, and spearheaded accessibility policy on MIT's campus. As a Ph.D. candidate at Stanford University, Sreya will design small-scale, accessible nuclear fusion devices to ensure an equitable path towards universal clean energy. Sreya is from the United States.

发展可持续的人道主义技术

司锐雅

我很高兴能与大家谈论发展可持续的人道主义技术，我的主要研究重点是核聚变，特别是小型、模块化、低成本聚变装置的反应堆设计，尤其是发展中国家负担得起的聚变装置。我还与各种非政府组织和非营利组织开发了清洁用水和无障碍诊断的公共卫生技术。

然而，我相信最有力的传播变革的途径是教育，我在世界很多地方做过志愿者，并在麻省理工学院的三个系担任助教。通过我的经历，我发现了改善人类状况的可持续和不可持续的技术。下面我们谈的这个项目技术是相当不可持续的。我制作了两个太阳能蒸馏器和一个太阳能脱盐器，它们利用太阳能蒸馏干净的水，使其远离杂质，从而生产饮用水。两者都是由我和团队在麻省理工学院环境工程实验室开发的，材料完全来自美国的材料和设备供应商麦克马斯特汽车公司。这些设备在实验室环境和马萨诸塞州波士顿的环境下都工作得非常好。然而，仅仅看这些设备，你能知道它们应该用在哪里吗？我猜不能。我与 Dig Deep 等非营利组织合作开发了这些蒸馏装置，以增加纳瓦霍族人的清洁水来源。

美国西南部的一个原住民保留地的地下水和河流被放射性物质污染。这些蒸馏器本应被补充到农村家庭的清洁用水需求。然而，当我们前往美国各地时，我们意识到在这些房子里安装的水管标准与我们的设备不兼容。此外，纳瓦霍族人有许多关于如何储存和处理水的规范，而我们并没有理解或遵守这些规范。因此，许多家庭对接受这些技术犹豫不决，这让我们非常沮丧。这就引出了一个问题，即我们如何开发可持续和适应性强的人道主义技术？我了解到这主要需要三个行动。第一，研发的竞赛和发展需要用户的参与。第二，材料和设备应在当地随时可用。第三，应该为用户提供基础教育，以实现长期维护和进一步创新。

接下来，介绍我与在马达加斯加南部运营的社会企业合作的项目。我是团队的首席工程师，带领团队为一个沿海村庄开发一种高效的太阳能海水淡化装置。我们发现岛屿的进口非常困难。通过观察道路旁的垃圾堆，确定可用的材料。大部分设备是使用联合国乳制品桶的剩余部分，这些桶通常在援助货物中被留在街上。任何特殊的设备都重新设计用3D技术打印。然后，我们与当地的一家自行车车间合作，很快就共同设计完成了一个最佳的制造流程。

最后，我们从欧洲国际合作机构和德国国际合作机构获得了一笔捐款，用于教授当地人基础工程知识，以及建立一个主要雇用女性的小工厂进行装配。一方面，像大多数农村家庭一样，妇女参与了部分水源需求的采购，延长了设备的寿命。另一方面，也通过刺激这些社区的经济实现收入流动。更重要的是实现女性在经济上的独立和赋权。

我们谈过延长技术寿命的问题，但关于促进欠发达地区的创新，我们该怎么做呢？这需要对所有孩子进行基本、普遍、技术性的教育。我曾有机会在中国香港以及墨西哥、哈萨克斯坦教授课程。我看到了孩子们惊人的创造力。在中国香港，我教学生基本的编程和微电子知识，然后让他们建造低空气密度、空气污染传感器，以了解工业对环境的影响。在哈萨克斯坦，学习乐高机器人搭建后，学生建造了一台演奏泰勒·斯威夫特歌曲的机器人。在墨西哥，我教网页设计和算法，接着学生创建了网站，以在互联网上永久保存家庭历史、文化和菜谱。年轻人是国家最宝贵的财富，通过工程教育激发他们的潜力，我们可以促进和支持国内人道主义技术的发展。

因此，这引出了一个我一直在思考的问题，即我们如何将高端技术应用于低端环境？例如，考虑核反应堆的复杂性和资源依赖性。它在全球的南部乡村实施是否可能？相比之下，太阳能是一种相对简单的技术，尽管效率低且生产效益不高，但仍被广泛应用。但我想问，我们是否真的能全面应对气候变化，实现人类公正？如果发展中国家无法利用高水平的技术发展国际市场，会发生什么？我在这方面有一些经验。我开发了一款微流控设备，它使用纳米制造和计算机视觉技术，准确测量饮用水中的微生物污染，这些微小的漂浮颗粒在图像中很容易被识别。该设备具有比目前的联合国系统标准更高的分辨率。

现在，尽管这种微流控技术是在狭窄的制造洁净室中开发的，但它只需要一个针头和一部智能手机就可以在户外使用。此外，我非常幸运地参与了一个项目，通过工程和合成手段，诱导临近的细菌分泌水泥，以自然和生物的方式制造砖和其他建筑材料。

在实验室中，我们使用其他高端技术设计这种细菌，但实施是在农村地区。细菌只需脂肪和营养补充剂就能自我繁殖和生长，就像给植物浇水一样。最后我留下一个问题，我们目前认为哪些技术是仅属于发达国家，但未来会出现在非洲南部的呢？最终我们能够在农村地区建造核聚变反应堆吗？我们如何从根本上改变工程产品设计过程以使其可行？您将扮演什么角色？我的分享就到这里，非常感谢！

德胜纳森
苏世民学者
Jonathan Peter-Oswin DASON
Schwarzman Scholar

从事可持续发展领域专业工作，专注于环境、社会和治理（ESG）。在马来西亚最大的电信公司工作期间，推进了业务转型并撰写了年度可持续发展报告。作为一名独立顾问，设计了马来西亚风险投资基金的 ESG 蓝图。合著了几本关于风险投资和初创企业的社会和治理出版物。在空闲时间，通过担任联合国马来西亚青年协会副主席在国家层面倡导可持续发展目标。期待通过技术的进步，帮助人类更加可持续地生活。

Jonathan has worked professionally in the field of Sustainability, focusing on Environmental, Social & Governance (ESG). He performed business transformation and wrote the annual sustainability report while working at one of Malaysia's largest telecommunications companies. Additionally, as an independent consultant, he designed the ESG blueprint of a Venture Capital (VC) fund in Malaysia. Furthermore, Jonathan has also been invited to be a Fellow at Penjana Kapital (a Malaysian government investment fund) where he co-authored several publications on ESG for VCs and Startups. In his free time, he advocated for the Sustainable Development Goals (SDGs) at the national level via his role as the Vice-President for the United Nations Association of Malaysia Youth. Jonathan hopes that through the progress of technology, humans will get to live more sustainably.

利用数字平台开展由青年领导的可持续发展目标运动

德胜纳森

非常感激能有这个机会分享我们团队在马来西亚开展的数字营销活动的经验,以促进联合国在马来西亚的可持续发展目标。

我们有两个关键的目标,一是为推动马来西亚青年发展生态系统作出贡献,二是一如既往地提高对联合国可持续发展目标的认识,重点在于教育。我们通过举办虚拟会议、在线活动实现这些目标。我们还在网上发布一系列的播客活动。我们还向公众发布了大量的信息图表,让公众了解联合国和联合国可持续发展目标。

在2020年和2021年,我们与超过50个组织合作,联合国驻马来西亚、新加坡和文莱的常驻协调员是我们董事会的成员。一些非政府组织、公民社会组织、青年组织和大学也参与了我们的活动。总的来说,我们吸引了成千上万的马来西亚青年。那么我们是如何做到的呢?我分享三个成功因素,然后谈一谈在线教育。首先,内容是吸引和激发人参与的关键。其次,我们认为合作是生态融合。最后,需要认识到的是,不是每个人都能够使用优秀的设备和高速互联网。

因此,问题变成了如何更好地吸引剩下那些人?内容是王道,一切都是虚拟的,而且你无法面对面。就像在本次会议上一样,我们现在被限制在二维和有边界的范围内,即矩形的屏幕,它们是小屏幕、手机或笔记本电脑。可能会有稍微大一些的屏幕,有些人甚至有曲面屏幕。在正常时期,特别是对于云南的青年来说,他们可以线下参加我们的活动,可以面对面,彼此交流,这实际上是一种社交活动。

那么,你如何在不面对面的情况下重现那种体验呢?如何使我们的活动脱颖而出?特别是将其与社交媒体上的信息洪流相比较时,人们的精神持续时间非常短。因此,对我们来说,制作非常好的内容是最重要的。我们通过数据驱动实现了这一点。我们充分利用数据,还会站在受众的立场上想象他们想看什么。因此,我们利用数据进行了大量的服务。我们定期进行这些服务并调研。

深度调研既可以是正式的，也可以是非正式的。我们会从社交媒体平台上追踪，分析收集的官方服务和社交媒体习惯数据。我们使用这些数据尝试确定年轻人喜欢哪些可持续发展话题，哪些平台最受欢迎。还有一些问题包括人们是更倾向于花费时间在科技论坛上，还是更喜欢花费在脸书（Facebook）上？他们在抖音上喜欢观看什么类型的内容？他们在脸书上更喜欢点击什么类型的内容？我们这样做是为了迎合目标受众，所以我们会测试如何调整信息表达方式来增加我们的注册数量。

在这里，我想分享 AB 测试的概念。首先，仅对 20% 的受众进行初始测试，其中的一半受众收到消息 A，另一半受众收到消息 B，这样就可以获得两个实验组。其次，基于 20% 的受众对消息 A 或消息 B 的响应，将响应更高的消息扩展到剩余 80% 的受众，这意味着 90% 的受众将接收到最有效的消息，从而提高参与度。我们还使用了同理心地图。这是一种实践，可以帮助我们将自己置身于受众的位置，有助于确定受众乐于学习和参与的内容与话题。

目前，我们已经举办了一系列关于国际事务的研讨会，探讨了一些关键主题，这些主题都来自数据以及用户的需求。在资源有限的情况下我们不主张垄断。我们的目标是完善马来西亚青年发展生态系统，那么逻辑上应该与其他组织合作，这样能够扩大受众和影响力。所以我们与各种组织合作，与他们一起做各种事情，从举办比赛到组织研讨会，再到在线宣传活动。

我们总在讨论如何在互联网世界吸引年轻人，但现实是，尽管马来西亚总人口中互联网普及率达到 95%，但往往忽视城市贫困者和农村地区的人。我们分析数据得知，接触互联网本身不是问题，真正的问题是互联网速度和服务质量。另一个挑战是设备类型。不是每个人都有台式机。我们在研究中发现，许多家庭只能共享一台智能手机设备。所以想象一下，如果一个家庭有三个孩子，他们不得不分享唯一的智能手机进行在线课程学习。他们可能在不同的教育阶段，有的可能是小学生，有的可能是高中生。这引起了我的反思。

我已经进行了大量在线教育活动，我在想还能做些什么解决这种难题，所以我联系了以前就读大学的教授。她正在做一些相关的研究，我们通过研究得到四个方面的结论。第一，我们应该采取限制自定义在线课程的方式。这意味着不要进行讲座或简单地一对一复制在线课程。相反，应该事先录制，并将课程时间用于讨论。因为当学生能够随时上网时，他们可以在自由的时间观看视频。第二，在学生所在的地方与他们见面。这是我们在青年群体中实践的做法。也就是说，如果学生喜欢抖音或其他平台，你就在那里上课。不要试图把他们转移到另一个平台，因为这将是非常困难的。第三，使用替代的评价方式。不要把重点放在手册、pdf 或文档形式的长篇文章或数学测试上，而是让他们制作视频，让他们在微信上录制语音。这样的效果很好。第四，"世界"通过互联网相连。我们不需要要求讲演者身在马来西亚，因为一切活动都是线上举行，我们可以在全球范围内找到最好的讲演者，并将其呈现在学生的屏幕上。

总的来说，我希望大家获得一些关于如何借助数字平台向公众宣传联合国可持续发展目标的实用经验。我们一起，为未来的建设做出贡献。谢谢！

袁斯陶
苏世民学者
Si Tou Un
Schwarzman Scholar

毕业于伦敦政治经济学院，主修政治与国际关系，是清华大学苏世民学者。为了在澳门推动实现可持续发展目标，参与创立并领导非政府组织"世望屋"的运营，曾在联合国大学澳门研究所发布了关于增强民间社会机构网路防卫的研究。

Christy (Si Tou) Un, graduated from the London School of Economics and Political Science majoring in Politics and International Relations, is a Schwarzman Scholar at Tsinghua University. To promote the Sustainable Development Goals in Macau, she co-founded and led the operation of the NGO Genervision House. She co-authored research publications on enhancing the cyber resilience of civil society organizations at the United Nations University Institute in Macao. She also had internship experiences at Zaatari refugee camp's UNHCR office in Jordan and the Chief Digital Office of the United Nations Development Programme. She was a guest speaker of 2021 TEDx Senado Square in Macau S.A.R.

为什么包容性数字化转型很重要？

袁斯陶

我想谈谈为什么包容性数字化转型对可持续发展和创新至关重要。它与四个具体的可持续发展目标息息相关，即优质教育，产业、创新与基建设施，可持续城市及社区，以及促进目标实现的伙伴关系。我将展示包容性数字化转型的重要性。这是我之前在联合国大学澳门研究所和联合国开发计划署首席数字办公室进行 ICT4D、网络安全和民间社会交叉领域研究工作中受到的启发。此外，我也将分享我在参与澳门非政府机构进行可持续发展倡导工作期间产生的一些见解。

全球现有的包容性差距是什么？以下是一些关键要点。尽管第四次工业革命带来了新的社会效益，但也带来了进一步的不平等。这种不平等加剧了以各种形式呈现的数字风险。例如，尽管低收入和中等收入国家只有不到一半的人能够接入基本的互联网，但其中90%的人仍然无法获得有意义的互联网连接。有意义的连接的特点是类似4G这样有更快的速度、适当的设备、无限的宽带的连接和日常使用。能够获得有意义连接的人获得工作、医疗保健服务或参加在线课程的可能性是仅拥有基本互联网连接的人的3倍。此外，这些不平等是互相交织的。这些是全球包容性差距的一部分，但不是全部。

如果我们采取包容性的全社会数字化转型方法，这些包容性差距就可以得到解决。根据联合国开发计划署（UNDP）采用的框架，数字包容性原则——可用性、可及性、采用性、意识和保护——应被纳入数字服务、产品、政策和基础设施中使用。包容性数字化转型还需要多方利益相关者协作，重点关注基础设施。政府、企业，法规，数据交换、数码身份和数字支付是可持续数字化解决方案的驱动因素。

在现代社会中，数字化不再是一种选择，数据对于推动社会进步变得越来越重要，例如将数字识别系统收集的数据与支付基础设施结合使用，以提供有针对性且平等的服务。世界银行的数字社会契约框架也值得强调，除了数据价值和信任，公平性对于充分利用数据也很重要。维护公平就是维护数字化包容性。以澳门为例，当我们与亚太地区的其他智慧城市进行比较时，澳门特别行政区距离成为智慧城市的目标还有一段漫长的路。澳门于2019年推出了特区政府数据开放平台，但目前该数据的使用价值较低，因为这些数据大多是不频繁更新的统计数据以及一些社会数据（例如人口普查数据和住房价格），并没有提供很多可以支持或记录智慧城市举措的资料。在公平方面，尽管澳门近年来努力提高数位素养，但市民的数位素养仍然相对较低，让他们无法充分利用数据。例如，《澳门居民互联网使用趋势报告（2020）》显示，24%的受访用户表示他们曾被侵害个人网络隐私，而33%的使用者表示他们在意识到自己的错误之前转发过假新闻。同时，澳门也缺乏一个充满信任的环境来维护用户的权益。例如，与2020年上半年相比，2021年上半年的网络犯罪率增加了400%。因此，可持续创新和发展必须考虑到数字包容性方面的公平性。

我想强调的一个方面是数字信任，因为所有有关信任的调查都显示，人们对科学和技术以及社会机构和关系的信任度正在惊人地下降。根据世界经济论坛最近发布的一份报告显示，数字信任的价值有三个目标结构，即安全和可靠性，问责和监督，以及包容、道德和责任的使用。同样，包容性是数字化转型的各个方面中不可或缺的一部分，而包容性也包含数字信任。

接下来，我谈谈网络安全。全球范围的民间社会组织越来越多地在"新常态"下发挥关键性的社会作用，帮助全社会提升应对不良事件的能力。这是通过提供服务、社会捐赠、传播有关大流行病的卫生措施等问题的信息，以及为处于社会边缘的群体发声实现的。

资源依赖理论是用于分析影响组织行为和结构的外部环境因素对组织的网络防卫的影响。该理论指出，组织行为、结构和成败取决于管理层的决策能力，而决策能力受到内部和外部代理人对关键资源的访问和控制的影响。这个理论有三个核心要素。首先，组织希望减少对外部因素的依赖，以降低环境的不确定性和约束。其次，组织内外存在权力分配。管理层承担起与外部利益相关者和组织内部参与者的桥梁和促进权力分配的作用。最后，组织内的决策和行动应该具有反馈效应，这会影响组织内资源的后续使用以及组织内权力的平衡。

就像世界各地的公民社会组织一样，调查结果显示，澳门的公民社会组织也缺乏财政资源、技术能力、风险意识，以及参与长期战略和应急网络防卫规划的能力。尽管71%的公民社会组织依赖信息与通信科技，但其中只有不到31%的公民社会组织认为它们的网络安全政策有效。更令人担忧的是，只有不到10%的公民社会组织对网络安全威胁进行了风险评估。在资源依赖理论框架的指导下，公民社会组织对从核心合作伙伴（如资助者）到临时服务提供商（如负责信息技术维护的服务提供商）的外部利益相关者的依赖，是组织不确定性的主要来源。值得注意的是，受新冠疫情的持续影响，作为公民社会组织的主要资助者——澳门社会工作局已采取措施来减少不同行业的开支，这意味着要减少公民社会组织的非核心开支，例如与网络安全有关的开支。此外，尽管组织管理层要处理与外部利益相关者的互动，以及实现网络防卫目标的内部资源和流程，但在管理内部资源和流程时，管理层在不同的资源依赖策略之间进行抉择时仍会面临困难。例如，51%的公民社会组织的管理层和董事会选择在短期内保持满负荷运营，而其中48%的人会选择削减运营以确保长期的持续性。尽管如此，公民社会组织的管理层在风险管理能力、网络安全风险意识和对当地网络安全格局的理解方面能力有限。这限制了他们减少组织的不确定性和增强组织网络防卫的能力。

总而言之，包容性数字化转型的途径是什么？首先，我们需要优先考虑和支持民间社会组织等边缘化群体，并将其作为创造包容性数字化转型的积极推动者。其次，在政策层面，我们需要将这些群体的需求纳入国家战略、计划和融资工具。最后，我们需要提供更多的能力建设和资源，以提高管理层的决策、谈判和利益相关者的参与能力。谢谢大家！

孟乐笛
苏世民学者
Melody KIRIMA
Schwarzman Scholar

孟乐笛，来自肯尼亚，毕业于北京交通大学车辆工程专业。2020年，在北京交通大学启动首个霍特奖校内项目。曾与创始人、投资者、教练和企业家合作，指导150多名学生进行社会企业家精神和创新精神的研习。对城市交通系统与经济发展的交叉学科感兴趣。作为苏世民学者，希望加深对中国治理、政策改革和公共交通创新的理解，更好地了解中国在消除贫困方面取得的成功，为领导交通系统转型以消除贫困的职业生涯做好准备。

Melody Kirima is a Vehicle Engineering graduated from Beijing Jiaotong University (BJTU), from Kenya. In 2020, she launched the first Hult Prize on-campus program at BJTU. She has worked with founders, investors, coaches, and entrepreneurs to mentor 150+ students on social entrepreneurship and innovation. Melody is interested in the intersection between urban transport systems and economic development. As a Schwarzman Scholar, she hopes to deepen her understanding of China's governance, policy reforms, and innovations in public transport and better understand China's success in poverty eradication in preparation for a career in leading the transformation of transport systems for poverty eradication.

可持续发展的汽车设计

孟乐笛

我非常热衷于可持续交通系统和汽车设计与可持续性的交叉研究。很高兴谈论关于可持续汽车设计的话题，并简要地介绍这个话题的重要性和必要性。

《联合国气候变化框架公约》第27次缔约方大会（COP 27）向我们展示了减少二氧化碳排放的必要性，即最大限度地保证全球气温每年上升不超过1.5℃，并减少生态系统的损失。2018年，绿色空间的一份研究显示，交通运输部门包括汽车制造业，其二氧化碳的排放量约占全球二氧化碳排放量的14%，其中9%来自汽车制造业。

目前，汽车制造业可持续性发展方向的主要关注点是发展新能源汽车，包括电动车和氢燃料电池车。然而，我认为在发展新能源汽车方面，仅关注其生产流程是不够的。目前，汽车产生的二氧化碳有10%来自其生产过程。在这10%中，有80%是由设计和制造过程决定的，包括材料选择、供应链等。因此，设计工程师在可持续性方面扮演着非常重要的角色，因为他们负责车辆设计的初始阶段。设计过程主要涉及三个明确阶段，即构思、设计和建造。我们可以在这三个过程中的任何一项中考虑和实现可持续性。

基于这一点，我想到一个概念，它不仅在汽车制造业中越来越普遍，而且在所有制造业中变得越来越普遍，那就是可持续性设计。可持续性设计包括设计物理对象和建造环境，以最大限度地利用资源，并确保其他因素的可持续性。

我的演讲将主要集中在这个广泛的概念中的三个主要概念上，即"可回收设计""环保设计"和"资源利用设计"。就像我之前提到的，我很关注设计与可持续性之间的交叉。

首先是"可回收设计"，它主要影响生命周期结束的车辆。我们如何使处理车辆的过程更加具有可持续性？可回收设计主要集中在汽车制造业中，主要涉及设计车辆和汽车零部件，它们可以被很容易地拆卸，然后用于处理、重新制造或再利用。近年来出现了一些趋势，即大多数汽车零部件也被设计成标准件，这使得它们在组装过程中更容易分类，并被用于同等或较低级别的用途。

设计可回收性的重要性在于它减少了对原材料的需求，这意味着我们无须生产新材料并增加碳排放。它也减少了最终进入垃圾填埋场的组件数量，这些组件会继续污染环境。这个过程在经济上也可行，因为它降低了生产新车辆的成本。因为如果你不生产新材料，那么建造新车辆、制造新车辆的财务限制就会降低。

其次是"环保设计"，当前的新兴趋势包括使用生物塑料代替石油基塑料。目前，在汽车工业中，石油基塑料仍然占主导地位。但是，已经出现了开发使用生物塑料的趋势，如聚乳酸，它主要来源于包括玉米淀粉在内的植物。这确保了如果这些材料被丢弃，大部分都可以在环境中被轻易地分解。它也涉及适合在空气动力学上运行的车辆，这减少了运行车辆所需的燃料量，从而减少了在车辆运行过程中进入环境的颗粒数量。

在燃油效率方面，通过使用较轻的材料，使车辆或者车辆的总质量更轻，减少了对燃油的需求，从而减少了由燃烧燃油引起的碳排放。最常见的例子就是在生产车辆底盘时用铝代替钢。因为铝更环保，也更易生产，因为它需要的水和能源较少。

最后是"资源利用设计"，主要包括使用可再生能源。在汽车工业中，可再生能源可以用于非吸引力的应用，如仓库的运行和生产过程。另一个我认为非常有趣的是使用三维制造，即专家所说的"加法制造"取代传统的"减法制造"的方法。在资源利用设计方面，3D打印吸引了众多专家的关注，因为它更加高效。不像整块材料切割，三维打印只需设计需要的东西，然后打印出来。它在减少排放方面也非常有效，因为供应商无须向制造商提供完成的部件，与其他的减法方法不同，三维制造不需要使用油和润滑剂或冷却液，这些最终会流入水体和土壤中。因此，对于寻求在生产过程中可行性最大化的制造商来说，这种方法越来越常见。

在设计可回收性方面，我提到有些部件在车辆制造商中的标准化程度正在逐渐提高，包括尾灯和挡风玻璃等。这些增加了材料被重新利用或制造的可能性。在使用基于生物的塑料或者在车辆制造中包含生物材料方面，我们看到一些消费后的塑料，如水瓶等，在经过处理后用来制造把手等。我选择这个主题，是因为当你提到可持续性时，就像我一开始说的，人们自动地想到电动汽车，但他们并不考虑整个生产过程。

随着汽车工业在实现可持续性目标方面的进步，我认为对于设计工程师来说，关注整个过程以确保生产价值链满足可持续性目标非常重要。设计工程师将继续扮演重要角色。此外，没有单一的指标可以用来表示可持续性，所有度量标准相互依存、相互作用，以确保可行性目标的实现。

吴舒遥
苏世民学者
Kelly WU
Schwarzman Scholar, United States of America

本科毕业于麻省理工学院化学工程专业，获得美国大学优等生荣誉学会（PBK）奖。她关心气候危机，并计划召集利益相关者，调整目标以实现能源系统转型。曾任麻省理工学院能源与气候俱乐部的主席。作为学生可持续发展领袖，帮助起草了大学的十年气候行动计划。她的研究和专业经验涉及化学工业规划、绿氢发展模型。

Kelly Wu graduated from MIT with a degree in Chemical Engineering and obtained the Phi Beta Kappa Award. She cares deeply about the climate crisis and hopes to convene stakeholders and align goals to enable energy system transitions. She was the president of the MIT Energy and Climate Club and helped draft the university's ten-year Climate Action Plan as a student sustainability leader. Her research and professional experiences involve mapping the chemical industry, modeling green hydrogen systems, and working for a Spanish renewables developer, oil major, and in energy investment.

理解能源、气候和可持续性领域的方法

吴舒遥

我分享的主题是《理解能源、气候和可持续性领域的方法》。首先，我是一个对能源转型、气候和可持续性问题非常感兴趣的人，希望将我的工作投入到解决这些问题中。这三个领域关联紧密，但也非常复杂，涵盖了整个经济社会。现在，我将重点讨论能源转型。

当我在高中做这项研究时，我才真正理解了能源系统是如何构建其他所有系统的，比如我们开的车，使用的电力，甚至种植的农产品。我本科在麻省理工学院化学工程专业学习了解决工程问题的技术。现在我正用它们来解决上述复杂问题。我将详细介绍可以帮助理解这个非常多样化的领域的具体方法。第一个是实践经验。我认为获得实践经验是绝对必要的，因为这是课堂上不会教的东西，这是你必须自己去寻找的。它确实可以告诉你很多你可能并不了解的关于能源空间的具体情况。我认为第二个非常重要的方法是用系统级的思维来理解能源、气候、可持续的空间。这种系统级的思维是考虑整个系统，而不仅仅是某一部分。即使你专注于一个非常具体的技术或者一个非常具体的领域，比如电动汽车或电网，也要明确你正在考虑的方面以及受到影响的人员和部门。

我通过化学工程中的控制体积概念来说明系统思考是一个非常有趣的例子。控制体积是指清楚地定义正在绘制系统的边界。例如，在这里，我们不考虑输入或输出，只关心反应器内部发生了什么。我们必须始终清楚地确定我们正在绘制的边界以及我们考虑和忽视的部分，以及当我们解决能源、气候和可持续发展领域的特定问题时，我们必须明确考虑哪些部分。因为我们忽略的部分可能需要由其他人在以后的过程中解决。

另一个我认为可以说明系统思维的例子是图网络。这是我实际构建的化学行业网络。它表明，当我们从系统水平思考时，我们可以理解其他方式无法看到的模式。在这里，构建这个图并对系统进行分析，可以帮助我们确定下一步研究的方向，以确定最具影响性的化合物，以便在将化学行业转变为更加可持续的行业时，将废物和能源方面的负面影响最小化。

我认为在学习能源、气候和标准领域的技术时，第三个重要的方法是伦理工程。它是一种工程方法，我们要知道创建低碳未来的创新利益相关者是谁，谁是创新的成果收获者和损失者。我认为伦理工程需要将这些技术真正地与问题联系起来，并确保我们创建的未来是公正的。

当我们考虑如何将私人汽车转换为公共交通以降低排放时，我们也必须考虑这些系统最终是为谁服务。这肯定会对那些离交通站更近、可以进入并到达这些站台的人有利。我们必须考虑未来的低碳系统对哪些人有益或不利，并考虑如何设计这些系统。美国威斯康星州的地图显示在这个州参与安装太阳能板系统的劳工分布，因此，决定在哪里建立太阳能农场的决策可能会对当地的就业和经济产生影响。

最后，我认为另一个帮助我探索这个领域的方法是参与社团活动。在麻省理工学院，我参与了许多能源和气候社团，这些社团真正起到了将来自多个不同领域的利益相关者聚集在一起的作用。你可以与学术界、政策制定者和学生们在同一空间和在公司一样讨论相同的问题。这是一个可以从所有不同的社会领域学习，挑战自己的想法，并提出最好解决方案的地方。通过了解你正在与之合作的社团，也可以设计出最好的方案。实际上我花了很多时间来研究我所在大学的学生们对可持续性的担忧和想法。一旦我有了这个理解，就能给出更多的原则性指导，帮助麻省理工学院为下个十年设计气候行动计划，这个计划关注大学做的研究，以及麻省理工学院将如何与气候空间的本地和全球利益相关者互动。因此，我认为在这个领域获得实践经验、使用系统级的思考、伦理工程、参与社团等方式，都是在解决你感兴趣的问题的同时，帮助你理解更大的图景，让你做出有影响力的决策。

IFEE 2022

第三届国际工程教育论坛
The 3rd International Forum On Engineering Education

分组论坛 B4
Panel B4

面向可持续发展与数字化转型的工程教育

Engineering education for sustainable development and digital transformation

2022年12月9日 20:00–22:00

分论坛介绍

国际工程联盟（IEA）于2021年6月正式批准了新修订的《毕业要求和职业胜任力》（GAPC）框架，纳入联合国可持续发展目标，目的是使未来的工程专业人员能够推动可持续发展目标。在工程教育认证中如何落实可持续发展的理念和方法？在工程教育中，如何考虑技术、环境、社会、文化、经济、金融和全球责任的影响？同时，在数据指数级增长和信息技术迅速迭代的时代，数字化、人工智能正在赋能工业革命，这对工科学生的计算思维、数据分析能力提出了更高的要求，如何培养有数字胜任力的工程创新人才？

为积极推动工程教育可持续发展，本次研讨会聚焦工程教育专业认证与教育数字化转型，邀请了来自联合国教科文组织二类中心、国际工程联盟、中国工程教育专业认证协会、中外大学专家学者、研究机构负责人，共同探讨可持续发展与数字化转型背景下工程教育的新机遇、新挑战、新发展。

Panel Introduction

The International Engineering Alliance (IEA) officially approved a newly revised Graduation Attributes and Professional Competencies (GAPC) framework in June 2021 to incorporate the UN SDGs, aiming to enable future engineering professionals to advance the SDGs. How can the concept and approach to sustainable development be implemented in engineering education accreditation? How can the impact of technical, environmental, social, cultural, economic, financial and global responsibility be considered in engineering education? Meanwhile, in the era of exponential growth of big data and rapid iterations of information technology, digitalization and artificial intelligence are empowering the industrial revolution, which puts higher demands on the computational thinking and data analysis ability of engineering students and engineers, and how to cultivate digitally competent engineering innovators?

In order to actively promote the SDGs, this sub-forum focuses on the accreditation and digital transformation of engineering education, invites experts and scholars from UNESCO center, International Engineering Alliance (IEA), China Engineering Education Accreditation Association (CEEAA), universities deans, faculties, and heads of research institutions to discuss new opportunities, new challenges, and new developments of engineering education.

承办单位简介

联合国教科文组织国际工程教育中心

联合国教科文组织国际工程教育中心（ICEE）由中国工程院和清华大学联合申请，经2015年11月联合国教科文组织第38届成员国大会批准设立。2016年6月，国际工程教育中心签约暨揭牌仪式在北京举行，时任中国工程院院长周济和联合国教科文组织总干事博科娃分别代表中国政府和联合国教科文组织签署协议。清华大学校长邱勇为中心理事长，教育部原副部长吴启迪为中心副理事长及主任。

愿景

致力于构建以平等、包容、发展、共赢为基础的全球工程教育共同体，支撑经济社会的可持续发展，推动人类共同文明和进步。

使命

围绕世界各国特别是发展中国家的工程教育质量与公平重大议题，坚持创新驱动和产学合作，将中心建设成为智库型研究咨询中心、高水平人才培养基地和国际化交流平台。

About the Organizer

The International Center for Engineering Education

As a Category II center of UNESCO, the International Center for Engineering Education under the Auspices of UNESCO (ICEE) was unveiled in Beijing on June 6, 2016. ICEE was proposed jointly by Chinese Academy of Engineering (CAE), a national consulting organization in engineering science and technology in China, and Tsinghua University, a top university well known in engineering science education. Zhou Ji, the former President of the Chinese Academy of Engineering, and Irina Bokova, the former Director-General of UNESCO signed the agreement on behalf of the Chinese government and UNESCO respectively. Qiu Yong, President of Tsinghua University is Chairperson of the Governing Board of ICEE, Wu Qili, former vice minister of Education in China is vice Chairperson of the Governing Board and director of ICEE.

VISION

ICEE is committed to building itself into an equal, inclusive, developmental and win-win engineering education community for the promotion of quality and equity in engineering education amongst countries in the world.

MISSION

ICEE aims to be a think-tank for policy research, an incubator for high-caliber personnel, and an exchange and cooperation platform in global engineering education.

分论坛主持

主持人 Chair

吴启迪
国际工程教育中心副理事长、主任，教育部原副部长
WU Qidi
Director and Vice Chairperson of Governing Board of ICEE,
Former Vice Minister of Education, China

联合国教科文组织国际工程教育中心主任，国家教育部原副部长，同济大学前校长，中国工程教育专业认证协会前任理事长。长期从事控制理论、控制工程和管理工程领域的教学、科研和管理工作。曾获颁联邦德国大十字勋章。清华大学通信技术专业本科毕业。获清华大学自动控制专业硕士学位、瑞士联邦苏黎世理工学院电子工程博士学位。

Wu Qidi is the Director of ICEE under the Auspices of UNESCO. She served as Vice Minister of Education and the Former President of Tongji University, and the Chair of Governing Board of China Engineering Education Accreditation Association. Qidi Wu has long been engaged in teaching, research and management in the fields of control theory, control engineering and management engineering. She was awarded the Grand Cross of the Order of Merit of the Federal Republic of Germany. She graduated from Tsinghua University with an undergraduate degree in communication technology. She received her master's degree in automatic control from Tsinghua University and her Ph.D. in electrical engineering from the Swiss Federal Institute of Technology Zurich.

主持人 Chair

杨华中
清华大学电子工程系学位委员会主任、教授
YANG Huazhong
Professor and Chair of Academic Degrees Committee,
Department of Electronic Engineering, Tsinghua University

清华大学电子工程系长聘教授。IEEE 研究员，EDAA 北京分会主席，*International Journal of Electronics* 等国际期刊编委，IEEE ASP-DAC2020 大会联席主席。先后承担了"九五"科技攻关、国家重点基础研究发展计划（"973"计划）、国家自然科学基金重大研究计划、"863"计划、国家重大专项、国家重点研发计划等 10 余个国家项目，研究成果孵化了多个高新技术企业。曾获教育部技术发明一等奖、纽伦堡国家发明展金奖、中国公路学会科学技术奖一等奖、教育部长江学者特聘教授、北京市优秀教师、"973"计划先进个人、国家杰出青年基金等奖项。

Yang Huazhong is a tenured full professor of Department of Electronic Engineering at Tsinghua University, an IEEE Fellow, and an Associate Editor of *International Journal of Electronics*. He gained a bachelor's degree in semiconductor devices and physics from Tsinghua University in 1989, and a master's degree and a doctor's degree in circuits and systems from Tsinghua University in 1991 and 1998, respectively. He is the general co-chair of IEEE ASP-DAC2020 Conference. He has successively undertaken more than 10 national projects, including the "973" Program, the major research project from NSFC, the "863" program, the national major special projects, and the national key research and development program. His research has incubated several high-tech start-ups. He was a recipient the Godmedal of Nuremberg Invention Exhibition from iENA, the Distinguished Young Researcher Award from NSFC, and the First-Class Prize of Technical Invention and the Cheung Kong Scholar Award from the Ministry of Education of China.

伊丽莎白·泰勒
国际工程联盟《华盛顿协议》主席
Elizabeth TAYLOR
Executive Committee Chair of Washington Accord, International Engineering Alliance

国际工程联盟《华盛顿协议》主席。在从事设计和施工工程师职业生涯后进入学术界。一直从事各种公益工作。目前任澳大利亚柬埔寨儿童信托基金会主席。最近从人道主义援助机构澳大利亚RedR主席的职位上退休，并继续担任RedR国际主席。曾因对工程的贡献获得澳大利亚勋章。澳大利亚工程师协会荣誉院士、澳大利亚公司董事协会院士、技术科学与工程院院士，被认为是澳大利亚100位最具影响力的工程师之一。

Elizabeth Taylor is the Chair of the Washington Accord, International Engineering Alliance. Following her career as a design and construction engineer, Elizabeth entered the academe. Since 2013 she has run her own consultancy. Elizabeth has always engaged in diverse pro-bono work. Currently, she is the Chair of the Cambodian Children's Trust Australia. She recently retired as the Chair of RedR Australia, a humanitarian response agency, and continues as the Chair of RedR International. Elizabeth is an Officer of the Order of Australia, being recognized for her contributions to engineering. She is an honorary fellow of Engineers Australia, a fellow of the Australian Institute of Company Directors, as well as fellow of Academy of Technological Sciences and Engineering, and she is considered one of Australia's 100 most influential engineers.

可持续发展的工程教育认证

伊丽莎白·泰勒

我分享的内容是可持续发展的工程教育认证，希望能够帮助大家探索工程教育及实现可持续发展目标。

我作为国际工程联盟《华盛顿协议》主席，工作中经常涉及工程教育内容。我们通过项目认证去学习，与不同文化、不同背景以及不同部门合作，找到更好的方式分享思想，将可持续发展理念贯穿工程教育认证工作中。

联合国可持续发展目标是所有人实现美好的可持续发展的蓝图，能够解决人类面临的诸如贫穷、不平等、气候变化、环境变化、和平以及正义等重要问题。工程师在其中发挥了巨大的作用。

希望通过此次分享，让大家对《毕业要求和职业胜任力》标准能够掌握得更好，并考虑通过协作的方式，在世界范围内推进工程教育和工程实践的执行，加强与可持续发展的联系。2021年6月，IEA协议成员表决通过了修正后的新标准，并在2022年3月向WFEO大会提交。这项工作得到了联合国教科文组织国际工程教育中心的支持，国际工程教育中心将该标准翻译成联合国教科文组织的五种官方语言。目前，《毕业要求和职业胜任力》标准已经在网站上公布，可以帮助IEA成员实现工程认证，获得IEA的标准服务。所有签署方（成员）一致同意，截至2024年制订在其管辖范围内可实施的路线图，并缩短实施时间。这只是将可持续发展理念融入工程教育开端，必须在实施适合的认证系统之前完成。因为，实现可持续发展需要不同以往的工程能力，包括工程思维的蜕变、工程实践的转变、教育模式的创新及强大的认证模式。

探讨工程教育的蜕变时，不能仅仅重复做过的事情，而需要以不同的思维方式考虑未来的变化和不确定性。作为工程师需要对工作承担个人责任，并具有系统化思维，对未来设想保持开放态度。很多年前，我和学生共同制作过一张图，帮助我们思考在学习过程中，尤其是在举办工程方面的活动时遇到的问题。

在可持续发展转变的过程中，我们要用不同的方式去审视做事的方式：需要改变对未来的看法，用循环性的观点看待人文学科的努力，并提出一些让人痛苦的问题，比如工程师到底是灭绝还是繁荣的工具？需要确保在提出这些问题的时候，我们已经想到了合作和推动可持续发展的方法，而不仅仅是专注发展。我们还需要问一些其他令人痛苦的问题，比如我们能否意识到在更大的系统中人类是可以被牺牲的？这些问题的提出不是增加负面信息，而是为了思考如何实现一个更具可知性的未来而对人类重新定位。

实际上，在学习转变的过程中，对于真理要时刻保持批判和质疑的能力，才能开展有意义的创新性工程教育模式。发展路线中还包括很多其他元素，例如我们如何创建可持续性的未来？依此建立的工程教育基础框架具有一个非常强大的机制——基于成果的教育或者是标准空间。这些要与可持续发展及联合国可持续发展目标保持一致。

如果要求每个通过教育的学生都能实现一些目标，就需要工程教育实现巨大转变，包括教师要根据不同情况转变为培训师、教员、促进者或者导师、指导者等。这意味着，工程教育需要进行一些工作阐述，要转向更加正式的验证过程，比如需要具备验证的模型。可以通过获取学习当中的元素，记录其实现方法，来满足对未来目标的需求，并与可持续发展及可持续发展目标保持一致。展望未来，如何能有将上述内容整合在一起的工程认证模式，将工程思维、工程教育和工程实践作为可持续发展的系统去转变，而不是仅仅专注于发展。这就是我们目前从事的工作，实际上是将专业知识和课程整合到系统表达和建模的工程过程当中。

澳大利亚是如何尝试进行工程教育的？工程课程如何进行？如何在这一地区进行验证？如何在这个范围内进行认证？在国际环境下推行和应用协定与协议，每个部分都需要开展合作，利用多样性的创新能力来应对复杂变化。转向可持续发展的未来，就需要应对复杂性、颠覆性和变革，这样才能真正实现可持续发展。研究结果表明，当系统被一种文化和世界观所捕获，像过去的百年工程学历史一样，或者当一种知识重申一种指标，他们智力的灵活性和敏感度就会大大降低。所以，所有人的积极参与将会带来更加丰硕的成果，这需要成为合作和认证发展的基础。

如何真正面向可持续发展的未来，IEA 有效地应对新冠疫情带来的影响已经成为一个范例。新冠疫情爆发后，IEA 所有成员开始通过座谈会、会议、讨论、小组、研讨会等协作方式分享如何应对这种特殊性的经验。同时，在不影响教育质量的情况下，也可以开展在线教学和学习。这些都是没有办法独立完成的，需要进行共同努力创造一个共同的美好未来。所以，我们可以通过平衡多样性使理念和方法得以应用而实现在工程教育和认证中实施可持续发展的理念和方法。

周爱军
中国工程教育专业认证协会常务理事、秘书长
ZHOU Aijun
Executive Director and Secretary-General of China Engineering Education Accreditation Association

世界工程组织联合会（WFEO）第一届中国委员会委员。哈尔滨工业大学毕业，工学硕士。长期从事工程教育认证、高等教育评估、高等教育信息化的研究与实践工作，致力于中国工程教育改革和国际化进程，推动高等学校建立"产出导向"的教育教学体系和"持续改进"的质量文化。推动中国工程教育认证加入《华盛顿协议》，推动中国工程教育落实联合国可持续发展目标（SDGs）和毕业要求以及职业胜任力（GAPC）。

Zhou Aijun is currently the Executive Director and Secretary-General of China Engineering Education Accreditation Association (CEEAA), and a member of the first Chinese committee of the World Federation of Engineering Organizations (WFEO). After graduating from Harbin Institute of Technology with a Master Degree in Engineering, Zhou has long been engaged in the research and practice of engineering education accreditation, higher education evaluation and higher education informatization. He is committed to the reform and internationalization of engineering education in China, and works hard to promote the establishment of an output-oriented education and teaching system and a continuous quality improvement culture in colleges and universities. He has made contributions to China's accession to the Washington Accord in engineering education accreditation and to the implementation of SDGs and GAPC in China's engineering education.

可持续发展与数字化转型下的
中国工程教育质量保障

周爱军

可持续发展和数字化转型是推动工程教育改革的重要动力。基于这个主题，我分享三个观点：第一是关于工程教育数字化转型的内涵、核心和要求；第二是关于工程教育和可持续发展目标的关系问题；第三是适应数字化转型和可持续发展目标以及中国工程教育专业认证协会对于认证标准的修订情况。

第一，工程教育数字化转型。习近平总书记在2014年的国际工程科技大会上指出，信息技术成为率先渗透到经济社会生活各领域的先导性技术，将促进以物质生产、物质服务为主的经济发展模式向以信息生产、信息服务为主的经济发展模式转变。随着大数据、云计算、5G、人工智能技术的飞速发展，人类社会已经进入数字化时代。生产生活和数字化密切相关，教育领域实现了信息技术与教育教学的深度融合，工程教育也正在经历全面数字化转型。

我们可以从显性现象、隐性内在逻辑和核心能力这三个方面分析。工程教育的数字化转型表现为教育的全要素、全流程的数字化转型，工程教育的各种要素、教学的内容，教学的资源数字化较早也最丰富。目前互联网已经建成了海量的慕课资源，其他慕课、微课等各种形式的课程资源也正在被广泛使用。丰富的教学资源和泛在的高速网络，也为时时可学、处处可学提供了条件，并改变了传统的教学模式。网络和数字技术进步也改变了千百年来形成的教学形式，全新的教学环境和场景不断被设计出来，使其能够更好地适应千禧一代互联网原住民的思维和学习方式。数字化转型更加深远的影响是对传统教育价值观的冲击。数字化不是对传统教育的补充，而是一种根本性的变革。一方面，数字化教育、数字化时代使得数字化思维、数字化素养成为必需；另一方面，教育标准更加多样化，个性化教育成为必然趋势。工程教育数字化转型的核心要求是数字能力，这包括学生的教学、数学素质能力的培养和教师素质能力的建设。以数字能力为核心的新型学生能力培养，需要构建面向未来的新型能力培养目标的结构。我们要更新教师的观念，提高其数字化教学能力，创新教学模式。

第二，工程教育可持续发展目标。2021年联合国教科文组织发布《工程——支持可持续发展》报告。WFEO主席龚克教授在报告中指出："当今世界所面临的首要问题是维持人类发展和保护地球。在这种背景之下，工程在实现可持续发展方面发挥着核心作用。"工程和工程师对17项可持续发展目标都不可或缺。工程教育在培养未来的工程师，是工程能力建设的重要力量。

为适应可持续发展目标，工程教育要在技术和价值两个维度进行变革。首先，技术维度要实现可持续发展目标。比如目标6为所有人提供清洁水和卫生设施，目标7经济适用的清洁能源，目标9建造具备抵御灾害能力的基础设施，目标11建设宜居城市等。工程教育培养的工程师，需要创造性学习和思考的能力、解决复杂问题的能力，以及跨学科和国际合作的能力。其次，价值维度要实现可持续发展目标。在工程设计和制造过程中节约自然资源，减少废物排放，注重对生态环境的保护，推动技术进步，实现经济发展和生态环境保护之间的平衡，关注工程和社会的关系，通过工程能力提升解决诸如性别平等、贫困等社会问题，注重工程伦理教育，关注工程师的个体发展。重视工程师的伦理素养对于推进可持续发展进程具有非常重要的意义。

第三，适应可持续发展和工程教育的数字化转型。在适应可持续发展和工程教育的数字化转型方面，中国工程教育专业认证协会在标准的修订方面做了一些前期工作。2021年，国际工程联盟发布的新版《毕业要求和职业胜任力》主要是落实联合国教科文组织17个可持续发展目标的有关要求，增加了计算思维、可持续发展、全生命周期、零净碳排放目标、多样性和包容性的内容。

中国工程教育专业认证协会（以下简称协会）为了建立中国特色国际实质等效的认证标准，开展了标准的修订工作。在落实可持续发展目标方面，协会在2021年组织了工程教育国际研讨会，以"可持续发展"为主题开展了基于可持续发展目标和新版GAPC的认证政策标准、程序修订的广泛研讨，还组织众多的大学校长、行业组织、系主任等开展对毕业要求问卷和调查的专题研究。

中国工程教育专业认证协会在2024年开始使用新版的认证标准。谢谢大家。

达米恩·欧文斯
国际工程联盟《国际职业工程师协议》主席
Damien OWENS
Chair of International Professional Engineers Agreement, International Engineering Alliance

  国际工程联盟《国际职业工程师协议》主席，爱尔兰工程师协会总干事，电子工程师，2010年加入爱尔兰工程师协会，担任注册官和首席风险官。2019—2022年欧洲工程教育认证网络（ENAEE）主席和2019—2022年国际工程联盟主席。中国香港工程师学会前认证委员会成员，欧洲工程教育学会董事会成员和爱尔兰国家研究办公室伦理委员会医疗器械委员会成员。爱尔兰特许工程师和工程师协会会员。

  Damien Owens is the Director General of Engineers Ireland. As an electronic engineer, Damien joined Engineers Ireland in 2010, serving as its Registrar and Chief Risk Officer. Damien was elected president of the European Network for Accreditation of Engineering Education (ENAEE) for the 2019–2022 terms and chair of the International Engineering Alliance for 2019–2022. He is a former member of the Accreditation Board of the Hong Kong Institution of Engineers, a board member of the European Society for Engineering Education and a member of the Medical Devices Committee of Ireland's National Office for Research Ethics Committees. He is a Chartered Engineer and Fellow of Engineers Ireland.

将可持续性纳入认证和能力标准

达米恩·欧文斯

非常荣幸能够和大家分享演讲内容,也非常感谢国际工程教育中心及各位老师对我的邀请!我是电信行业的特许工程师,也是爱尔兰工程师协会总干事。我根据在爱尔兰工程师协会的工作经验,针对"将可持续性纳入认证和能力标准"分享个人观点。

爱尔兰工程师协会(以下简称协会)的认证标准5~6年审查一次,2014年首次审定标准,2021年开始更新新的标准。协会在工程教育可持续发展方面也做出了努力,认证评审委员会包括五名学术成员和两名行业成员,可以为高等教育机构提供一些机会,获取更多反馈。整个认证过程需要由爱尔兰工程师协会认证委员会、执行委员会和理事会批准。认证审查工作包括对志愿者、学者和行业雇主展开调查,以便认证能够采取更具有可持续性的认证方法,组织关于"工程教育:未来技能、标准和流动性"方面专门的认证审查工作坊,确保符合国际工程联盟和欧洲工程教育认证网络等国际标准,与利莫瑞克大学、都柏林理工大学、爱尔兰国立高威大学等爱尔兰高校开展研究合作,与各种利益相关者合作,并成立评审委员会认证委员会的认证经验和审议情况。

目前,很多大学进入第五个认证周期,协会认为有必要了解认证当中的核心内容,包括数学、理工科等方面,同时也非常关注团队合作等关键因素。我们在高校及行业成员组织中开展调查,来确保工程师在可持续发展的未来拥有相匹配的技能。通过调查分析未来工程师最需要的关键技能,我们发现,知识理解、可持续性设计工程以及灵活性等关键词已经凸显出来。

协会希望从学术核心出发确定相关标准,包括如何合作、如何高效工作,同时希望工业界以及学术界提出所需工科毕业生的重要能力,并由此分析出学者以及雇主之间的认知差异,比如雇主更关注沟通能力、团队合作能力,而不是学术能力。在学术教育方面,基本的工程知识将会作为重要关注点,当然也会存在一些更加复杂的问题。这个调查强调在不同领域未来工程师所需能力的差异。

2014年,协会出台了相应标准。我们在现有标准的基础上进行了调查,基于收集的信息对标准进行优化。方案成果相关性的调查数据显示,"毕业生应对支撑其工程分支的数学、科学、工程科学和技术具有先进性的知识和理解"选项中,选择强相关的比例为73%。协会拟采用基础性、综合性、独立性的方法,在数据科学、人工智能、互联网等方面做出更多努力,将工程教育作为非常重要的发展方向。其中,协会很多项目需要根据国际工程联盟的标准进行设计,融入可持续发展目标,希望获得雇主的反馈。工程师在实现可持续发展目标中发挥着至关重要的作用。同时,协会将在工程师对社会以及全球责任、工作团队沟通协调、社会交流等方面提供一系列解决方案,以便高校能够培养出具有可持续发展理念、具备社交技能的未来工程师。协会在可持续性、领导力、可持续发展目标以及实现目标的核心能力相关标准方面,增加了关于人类以及环境责任方面的专业知识。

爱尔兰工程师协会提供在工程管理方面的项目,包括引入工程管理原则、财务决策、数据科学分析和技术等,同时非常关注社会责任以及伦理道德方面的事务。这些内容在标准中也得以体现,包括项目设计结果以及结构方面的八大关键领域、知识理解和设计调查等。作为工程教育方面的标准,这些是协会所期待的未来具有资质的工程师应该具备的特征。例如,在工程管理方面,希望未来工程师能够更好地适应社会,为可持续发展作出贡献,让社会从中受益。

协会也强调关于项目成果方面的内容,包括不同项目、不同成果,例如在创新创意、可持续性、实际技能等方面的提升。协会非常关注沟通技能,需要相应的认证评审,还非常关注团队合作能力、可持续性发展。在项目管理方面,协会通过关注工程师项目的灵活性、质量保障等方面,以不断提高解决复杂问题的能力。这些是工程教育比较关键的组成部分,在设计领域的工程师必须具有能够应对复杂工程设计问题并提供解决方案的能力。协会需要将可持续发展纳入解决复杂问题的过程,时刻谨记使用可持续的方法,把这一点作为解决问题的重要环节,以便能够更好地关注、理解、承诺在工程实践过程中对全人类和环境的专业和道德责任。

协会为学生专门引入可持续性的理念,比如净零排放等。学生需要了解联合国可持续发展目标,并对现有系统进行研究,还应该培养实现可持续发展目标的能力,包括批判性思维、思考的方式等。能力建设可以分为几个维度,包括在课程设置过程中,对可持续发展目标框架的考虑;在设计未来的发展愿景方面,采用系统性思维方式,全面考虑问题。例如,在设计层面,若设计生态系统,需要动员哪些方面的资源和力量,怎么建立合作伙伴关系,如何进行团队协作沟通。工程师并不是孤岛,需要和他人进行合作,共同实现最终目标,这些都需要在决策的过程中有所反映。谢谢大家。

安妮特·科莫斯
丹麦奥尔堡大学工程科学与可持续发展问题基础学习中心（UCPBL）主任
Anette KOLMOS
Director of Aalborg Centre for Problem Based Learning in Engineering Science &Sustainability, Aalborg University

工程教育和问题导向式学习（PBL）教授，联合国教科文组织奥尔堡工程科学与可持续发展问题基础学习中心主任。曾任联合国教科文组织丹麦奥尔堡大学工程教育PBL主席（2007—2014），欧洲工程教育学会（SEFI）主席（2009—2011），SEFI工程教育研究工作组创始主席。2013年荣获国际工程教育学会联盟（IFEES）全球卓越工程教育奖，2015年成为欧洲工程教育学会研究员。主要研究领域包括性别和技术、问题导向式教学、员工发展等。现任《欧洲工程教育杂志》副主编，曾任《工程教育杂志》（*ASEE*）副主编。

Anette Kolmos is a professor in Engineering Education and Problem Based Learning (PBL) and the Director for the UNESCO Aalborg Centre for Problem Based Learning in Engineering Science and Sustainability. She was the Chair for UNESCO in Problem Based Learning in Engineering Education, Aalborg University, Denmark (2007–2014), the President of SEFI (European Society for Engineering Education) (2009–2011), as well as the Founding Chair of the SEFI-working group on Engineering Education Research. She was awarded with the IFEES Global Award for Excellence in Engineering Education in 2013 and the SEFI fellowship in 2015. Dr. Kolmos' research areas include gender and technology, project based and problem-based curriculum (PBL), change from traditional to project organized and problem-based curriculum, development of transferable skills in PBL and project work, and methods for staff development. She is an Associate Editor for the *European Journal of Engineering Education* and was an Associate Editor for *Journal of Engineering Education* (*ASEE*).

面向可持续工程教育转型

安妮特·科莫斯

非常感谢大会对我的邀请。我分享的是工程教育可持续发展方面的内容。

新冠疫情期间，学校普遍采用在线教育方式，很多大学开始向使命驱动型大学转变。使命驱动型大学的教育内容是什么，也是现在讨论较多的。它不像可持续发展目标那么简单，不仅包括教育也包括科研内容，更像是教研。

大学有非常传统的学术方向以及理论教学，理论课程也很多。在过去的30年中，工程教育已经开始向产学结合转移，但还需更进一步地转变为更具混合性的学习模式，使其能够采用综合方式进行教育，使学生拥有自己的价值观，并且能够实现以学生为中心的教育，这成为大学教育的核心。但是这并不意味着不关注高等教育的学术性，而是需要更多的产业界人士参与其中。因此，我们需要重新思考可持续性和教学之间的关系。

我们需要新型的教育，需要新能力强调系统性思维，包括创新性的合作能力、批判性思维、自我意识、协作规范、战略性综合问题解决方案等。这些能力是可持续性发展方面的关键能力，也是传统教学中会关注的能力，但并不是全部。在学习工程相关课程中，我们需要从系统角度思考，也要从民众角度思考，在教学中强调问题和任务，在不同项目和工程中要考虑不同学科之间的互动，进行跨学科的教学，包括个人和团队合作等。

什么是真正的课程设计？它包括知识、技能和能力，这是英国的巴奈特教授课程设计的方法。艺术、文科与理工科的课程设计稍有区别。知识和行动在理工科中占比较高，我们需要让行动再扩大一些。

2020年9月至2021年1月，我们采集相关数据进行分析，建立了15个焦点小组，每组包括60位参与者。参与者不仅有老师还有学生，访谈内容涉及学到的知识或者总结的经验。调查结果显示，新冠疫情期间教学系统有所调整。最初，系统缺乏人与人之间的互动，教学以教师为中心，成为对学生的单向输出。在这种模式下学生上课不习惯问问题，也不主动发言。很多学生反馈他们必须更加积极主动地利用学习资源和方法参与翻转课堂的学习。例如，学生要在课前预习课程视频，上课的时候采用数字化方式参与和交流。分组时候的讨论异常热烈，这体现出数字体系的优势。

在使用 PBL 模型时我们得到哪些经验和教训？PBL 模型在协作、内容和方法上是具有高度适应性的模式；数字学习空间是对实体空间的补充，要关注现场教学的价值，特别是师生之间的互动和交流；项目监管变得更加灵活和高效，但邮件等新型交流方式的加入让督导的追踪工作更难以进行。

我们用了两个学期探索 PBL，发现学习过程中的状态很重要。老师的工作时间不断增加，在电脑前工作的时间较长。学生的心理状态也成为非常大的问题，很多学生表示比较抑郁。近几年，新入学的学生通过线上方式进行学习，缺乏过去的社交环境和社交网络，存在较大的隐患。

我们通过研究了解到，PBL 模式未来的发展方向可以是混合式的。学生非常喜欢数字化课程，却不喜欢数字化项目。他们希望能够在闲暇时间聚集，面对面展开项目讨论。过去这几年，远程教学的方式出现了很多问题。当谈及变化的时候，我们需要考虑如何适应数字化带来的变化。学生需要执行新的发展战略，将数字课程和线下学习结合起来，强调人与人之间交流的重要性。这是学生未来需要具备的非常重要的能力。有些大学的学生仍然在家学习，这种教学模式确实比较困难。将来我们希望采用混合教学模式，利用实体空间促进学生紧密地沟通与合作，接受老师的更多辅导。

谈到转型过程中的不易，我引用两位科学家的名言，达尔文说过"物竞天择，适者生存"，爱因斯坦说过"生活就像骑自行车，你要保持平衡，就要不断前进"。同样的道理，从大学的角度出发，我们也应该改变教学模式，模式设计不仅要从学术角度，还要从学生学习角度进行考虑。未来，我们还要沿着这个方向不断发展，采用更多的混合式学习模式，参与其中并延续相关任务。

黄翊东
清华大学学术委员会副主任，电子工程系原主任
HUANG Yidong
Deputy Director of Academic Committee, Tsinghua University;
Former Dean of Department of Electronic Engineering, Tsinghua University

长江学者，新世纪百千万人才工程国家级人选。长期从事光电子器件领域的科学研究及人才培养工作，曾任清华大学电子工程系系主任，清华大学天津电子信息研究院院长，是清华大学电子信息大类课程体系的主要创建人之一。发明"八分之一波长位移分布反馈"的新结构，开发出光通信抗反射DFB激光器，两次获得NEC研究功绩奖；近20年来聚焦微纳结构光电子器件，承担过国家自然科学基金重点项目、"973计划"项目以及多项国际合作项目，带领课题组研制出世界首创具有自由电子辐射、实时光谱成像、动态轨道角动量辐射、量子态产生及操控等功能的集成光电子芯片；发表论文350余篇，被引用数千次；拥有140项专利。

Huang Yidong received the B.S. and Ph.D. degrees in optoelectronics from Tsinghua University in 1988 and 1994, respectively. From 1991 to 1993, she was with Arai Laboratories, Tokyo Institute of Technology, Japan, on leave from the Tsinghua University. In 1994, she joined the Photonic and Wireless Devices Research Laboratories, NEC Corporation, where she was engaged in the research on semiconductor laser diodes for optical-fiber communication and became an assistant manager in 1998. She received the Merit Award and Contribution Award from NEC Corporation in 1997 and 2003, respectively. She joined the Department of Electronics Engineering at Tsinghua University in 2003, as a professor, and was appointed by the Changjiang Distinguished Professor and the National Talents Engineering in 2005 and 2007, respectively. She was the Vice Chair (2007–2012) and Chair (2013–2019) of the Department of Electronics Engineering. Now she is Vice Chair of Academic Committee of Tsinghua University. Professor Huang is currently engaged in research on nano-structure optoelectronics. She authored/co-authored more than 350 journal and conference papers and holds more than 140 patents.

面向可持续创新人才培养的电子信息课程体系

黄翊东

非常高兴有机会和大家分享清华电子系关于课程体系的思考和实践。

如何在电子信息课程体系层次上实现可持续创新人才的培养？可持续创新人才需要哪些素质？基础科学和专业基础面宽，不仅专业知识要专，还需要具备超越专业的能力，如认知能力、实践能力，以及具备人文社科知识、充分的工程实践训练，与科学发展同步，了解学科发展的历史脉络，提高彼此协作、与社会互动的能力。我们要教什么？电子系有两个一级学科，还有若干个二级学科，覆盖了电子信息领域众多的核心概念，其中包括实际应用。

科学与工程是不断发展的，要教的内容越来越多，知识量不断增长。特别是在电子信息领域，在原来的信息与通信工程、电子科学与技术两个学科之后，还会有新知识、新学科出现，例如集成电路的交叉学科。除了基础科学知识，还要教授人文知识，增加学生的实践经验，安排一定的课外活动，提高工程科学能力，培养其综合素质。基本矛盾在于膨胀的知识量与有限的学制。我们知道学生应该具备这样的素质，却没有足够的时间把这些知识都教给他们。

如何从课程体系的层面解决基本矛盾？清华大学电子系的课程体系发展历程如下：20世纪50年代开始建立了最初的课程体系；20世纪80年代，改进了课程和教材，引入课程改革方面的经验；从20世纪90年代到现在，建立宽口径、厚基础的新课程体系。

2007年开始，时任电子系主任、现任清华大学校长的王希勤老师主导发起新一轮课程体系改革。此轮课程体系改革的目标是：打破两个一级学科的壁垒，培养出"信息+电子"专业的人才；更新课程内容，加入课程发展历史，培养学生创新思维；加强实验教学、课外学习等环节，培养学生综合素质。

在课程改革过程中，我们的认识在不断进步和发展，通识教育并不是简单地把众多知识塞给学生，而是要让学生掌握知识体系的发展脉络，全面提高综合能力。通识实际上是将很多知识一起教授，但并不是大而全的教学，这会让学生完全丧失选择权，缺少选择的机会。时间不足而所教知识过多，因此重要的课程被压缩学时，造成科普式教学。其实很多系统是同构的，把几个主要系统深入了解就可以举一反三，继而实现真正的"专业打通"。

我们认识到应该增加学生选择的自由度，而不是要求每个学生选修所有课程。每个学生选择的课程可以不同，培养模式也可以不同，但是要在一定的边界条件下完成自由组合。就像吃自助餐，在营养配比合理的情况下，可以根据口味选择菜品。电子系是清华大学最大的院系，学生人数众多。每年有两三百个学生是在"专业打通"的课程体系下培养出来的。"专业打通"是指课程体系，而不是培养被专业打通了的同一模式的两三百个学生。

在课程体系的改革中，我们对于通识和专业打通的认识是在不断演化的。怎样理解之前提及的基本矛盾，教师要教授很多知识，包括"专业打通"，可以通过"营养配餐"即必修课进行解决。同时，我们还需要根据学生的兴趣提供丰富的显性课。回归到基本矛盾，我们要教授的知识量很多，但是时间有限，就需要借助现代学习理论。现代学习理论是非常具有启发性的，学生带着已有的知识来到教室，我们要了解学生已经知道了什么，并在这些知识的基础上有差别地教学，这样学生既容易接受又节省时间，提高了学习效率。

另一个概念是非常重要的"核心概念"。知识体系中有很多知识，但是都是有架构的。繁多的知识之间是相互衔接成体系的。知识体系建立在为数不多的"核心概念"基础之上，很多知识内容不过是"核心概念"在某种具体条件下的实例。换言之，"核心概念"要在各个具体的实例中得以体现，学生通过这些实例的学习加深对"核心概念"的理解和掌握。

正如图1所示，知识体系的概念是有限的，更多的知识内容来源于一些实例，怎样能够把知识体系的构架显性化、搭建起来？在一个概念构架背景下，可以帮助学生理解和记忆一个事实与观念。

怎样把知识架构梳理出来，提升教学效率？知识在不停膨胀，使用组合的方式时间肯定不够用。能不能用化合的方式，把所有知识背后的相互关系梳理出来，把内在联系显性化，如此就有可能在更少的时间里教给学生更多的知识。由于相互关系能够梳理清楚，学生对这些知识的理解可以更深入，掌握得更牢固。这不是因为教了很多，而是每门课课时都在减少，最终成为科普课程，因为教得少了，更加凸显出知识体系和核心概念，从而获得更好的教学效果。

图1 知识体系的核心概念和实例

专业知识构架还没有梳理出来，如图2所示，两个一级学科还有众多二级学科的知识点都不尽相同，如何将这些概念统一起来？其实就是信息的载体和系统之间的相互作用，不同的是信息载体的形式和相互作用的系统。电子系所有知识内容都可以统一在这样一个开放的知识体系构架之下。学生学完后，可以去发明新的信息载体，发明新的信息系统，发现新的相互作用规律。我们把电子信息科学技术知识载体梳理出来后，还开设了一门课程——电子信息科学与技术知识体系导引，希望学生一入学就能够了解知识构架，并在"地图"引导下学习所有的课程，并激发学生学习专业知识的兴趣。

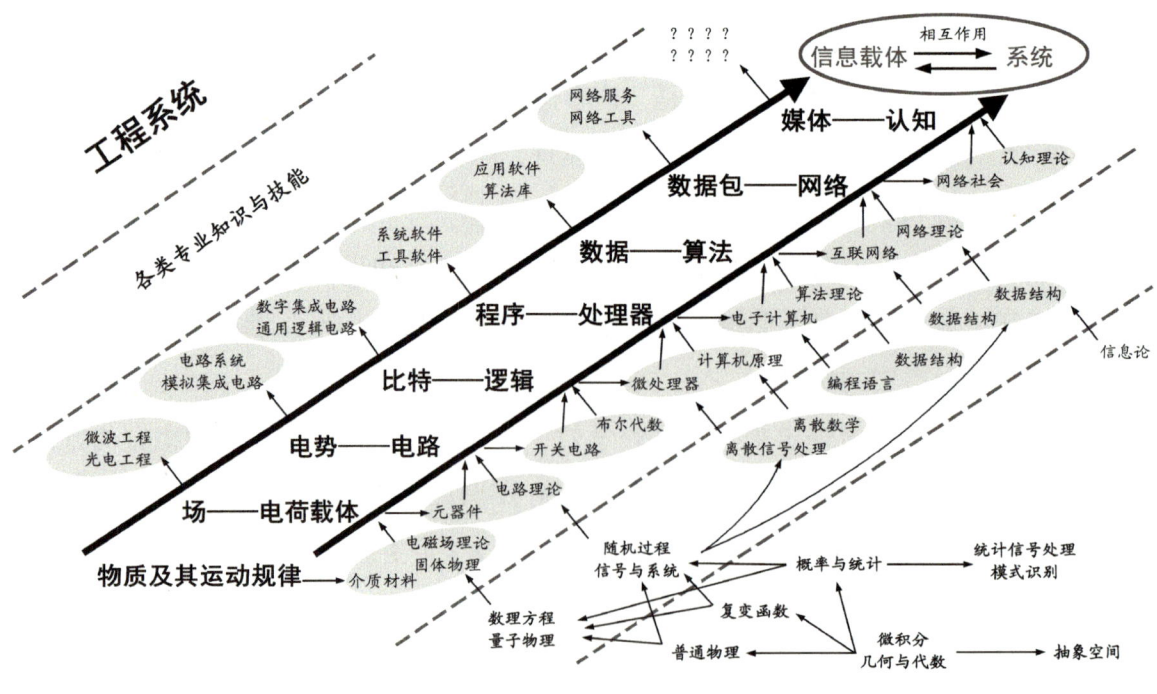

图2 电子信息科学与技术知识体系

在这个知识体系构架之下，我们构建了10门核心专业课，覆盖了两个一级学科的核心概念，也包括学生需要的数学和物理等基础课程。学完这些核心课程之后，其余的20多个学分给学生自主选择课程。学生根据兴趣和职业发展规划选择本系专业课、兄弟院系专业课等，构建了覆盖两个一级学科的全新课程体系。学生学习核心课程之后，就基本掌握了电子信息领域的核心概念。目前，核心课程的教材也在陆续出版中。

为了提升学生的综合素质，我们还设置了贯穿本科生和研究生体系的40门实验课供其选择。2008年，实验教学中心成立，占地1500平方米，拥有设备1200余件，每年可接纳2000名学生选修实验课程。特色实验课程包括光电课程，还有通信电磁场等，同时建立了人工智能大数据平台。

2018年，电子系迎来第二次学科国际评估，邀请麻省理工学院副校长，斯坦福大学、伯克利大学等知名大学的电子工程系主任，为课程体系做评估。专家对课程体系给予了很高的评价，认为核心课程的构架在电子和信息两个学科之间构架起了一座桥梁，真正打通了专业。

我们非常欢迎兄弟院校一起参与课程体系的改革，探讨如何能在有限的学制下应对可持续发展人才的培养，把更多的知识、更强的能力传授给他们。因此，我们举办了两期师资培训班介绍课程，希望有更多教师参与进来。同时，我们也在推动教学国际化进程，建立了清华大学海外学生项目，与伯克利大学等一些学校签订课程共建的协议。国外院校的学生到清华大学电子系上课，回校后可以认定学分。我们的课程质量可以满足他们对人才培养的需求。

以上是我分享的内容，谢谢大家！

李曼丽
清华大学教育研究院教授
LI Manli
Professor of Institute of Education, Tsinghua University

北京大学教育学博士。现任清华大学教育研究院长聘教授、博士研究生导师。兼任教育部高等学校教学指导委员会秘书长、中国教育发展战略学会高等教育专业委员会副理事长、中国高等教育学会教师教育分会副理事长等。2008年入选北京市社科优秀人才"百人计划",2013年入选教育部新世纪优秀人才支持计划,2012年、2019年分别获得清华大学年度先进工作者荣誉,2022年获"北京市优秀教师"称号。多次获全国和北京市人文社会科学研究优秀成果奖、全国和北京市教育科学研究优秀成果奖。

LI Manli is a Ph.D. in Education at Peking University. Currently, she is a tenured professor at the Institute of Education at Tsinghua University, and also the Secretary General of the Undergraduate Teaching Steering Committee for Education, Ministry of Education, the Vice President of the Higher Education Committee, Chinese Society of Educational Development Strategy, as well as the Vice President of the Teacher Education Branch of China Association of Higher Education, etc. She was selected as one of the Excellent Talents in Social Sciences in 2008 Beijing "100-Talent Plan", and in the Support Program for New Century Excellent Talents in University, Ministry of Education in 2013. She was awarded as an Outstanding Worker of the Year, Tsinghua University in both 2012 and 2019, and as an Excellent Teacher of Beijing in 2022. She won the Award for Outstanding Achievements in Humanities and Social Sciences Research and the Award for Outstanding Achievements in Educational Scientific Research in China and Beijing for multiple times.

面向创造的学习：数智时代的工程教育

李曼丽

感谢校内外、海内外工程教育同行，很荣幸参加本次论坛。我的分享是关于近十年我们在教育信息化背景下从中观和宏观层面做出的努力。

第一，数智时代工程教育面临的机遇和挑战。近十年来，教育信息化发展的步伐不断加快，数字化是教育发展的战略机遇，高水平教育信息化可能带来高水平的教育现代化，人工智能大数据等科学技术的迅速发展，必将塑造高等教育教学理念和教学模式的新形态。

数字化存储传播技术的突破，将使很多个体学习者从重复机械的记忆学习向应用知识创造价值和创新应用等方向转变，这是正在发生的理念转向。如果高校还停留在原来单纯的知识讲解，这样的授课模式必将落后于时代的发展。

数字技术和人工智能技术改变了一些人的工作环境，并对人才素养提出了新的要求，主要体现在以下四个方面。一是易变性，技术迭代的速度比以往任何时候都快，要求个体具备快速和终身学习的能力。二是不确定性，快速发展的技术加大了不确定性，使得现实生活中充斥着大量的结构不良问题，要求学生发展思维创新和迁移能力，从传统的知识接收者变为主动的问题解决者。三是复杂性，随着社会分工的不断细化，在一个大系统下的子系统越来越分化，细致的分工会使技术的复杂性不断递进。人类工业文明的大趋势就是让人可以简单地理解和驾驭更大的系统，所以要关注学生思维能力的培养。四是模糊性，现在生活有很多的美好，也有更多的冲突，美好和冲突经常不期而遇。中国作家老舍说："生活是种律动，须有光有影，有左有右，有晴有雨。"这种滋味在当代社会里体现得更充分。高等教育面临着教学理念的转型，如何利用更先进的方法形成工科人才的主动探索能力、创新创造能力和构建能力，这是工程教育要思考的一个本质性问题。

第二，卓越工程师教育的中国经验及案例。2010年前后，中国已经建成世界最大规模的工程教育体系，高等工程教育在高等教育中的比例位居世界第一，工程教育在校生规模在高等教育中占比始终保持在1/3以上。但是，在工程教育的培养过程中存在突出的问题，例如，工程型人才培养和工程实际结合不紧密，工程教育科学化的倾向比较严重，对学生的工程意识和工程素质培养不足，实际解决复杂工程问题的能力和创新创造能力培养的力度不够。

因此，2010年中国教育部启动了"卓越工程师计划"1.0。这个计划分为三个方面。第一，加大行业和企业的深度培养参与力度；第二，督促学校按通用标准和行业标准培养工程人才；第三，强化培养学生的工程能力和创新能力。在教学改革的同时，增加完善了一系列中国工程师的职务聘任制度、考核制度，包括工程教育的认证制度。

2018年10月，由于新一轮世界科技变革和产业变革孕育的兴起，中国工程教育界达成了一些集体性的共识，认为人工智能和数字化的技术将为人类社会带来难以估量的作用和影响，它将引发重塑、颠覆、重构，以及改变现代的很多业态分工和组织方式。所以，要重构人类的生活学习和思维方式，乃至改变任何世界的关系，这对高等工程教育将产生实质性的影响。

如何在这一大变革时期携手共创美好未来？工程教育变革创新是全世界高度关注的一个共同话题，中国教育部适时提出了新工科建设问题，新工科及时发布了"卓越工程师计划"2.0，提出以"大科学观""大工程观"的社会需求为导向，以"人本内涵"为主线，在工程教育"融合创新"范式引领下进行工程教育改革。

21世纪以来，全球科技创新空前活跃，新一轮科技革命和产业变革正在重构，为全球的创新版图，全球的经济结构，信息生命制造、能源空间、海洋等领域的原创突破，前沿技术颠覆性的技术提供了更多的创新源泉。工程师不仅要具备纵观全局的能力，还要与不同学科的人并肩合作，提出创新性的解决方案。然而中国的本科教育存在一些共同的问题：必修课负担很重、评价的标准不合理、工程教育学术界缺乏主动鼓励创新的生态。在这种情况下中国工程教育如何突破困境？

和大家分享一个本科教育改革的案例，它是清华大学电子系之外的另一个改革，也是中国数百个工程项目改革中比较具有代表性的一个。清华大学教授、中国科学院院士郑泉水先生从2009年开始负责工程教育的试点改革班——"清华学堂人才培养计划"钱学森力学班（以下简称清华钱班）。这是一个人才培养的新的改革模式。郑先生提出必须让学生飞起来，所以在引领改革10年中形成了独特的培养模式，在中国高等教育界影响甚广。

对清华钱班项目两年多的田野研究发现，郑院士在工程教育中特别关注本科阶段构建创新人才培养的生态系统。他反复强调"杰出的人才培养不是揠苗助长，而是要让人才自己冒尖"。为此，他主要做了三件事：第一，大幅度缩减学分，从170个学分降到140个学分；第二，增加了本科三阶段的进阶式研究性学习计划，以真实项目驱动本科生的科研研究；第三，重新设计本科通识教育课程，重点关注学生宽厚的人文素养积淀。清华钱班改革的灵魂是始终寻求破解"钱学森之问"，目的是培养"敢于研究别人没有研究过的科学前沿问题"的创新人才。经过改革，清华钱班计划尝试为拔尖创新人才积累宽厚的知识和能力基础，同时让学生能够享受教育的创新成长环境。

为了让大家更容易理解创新生态视角下的学生学习模式，我分享一个案例。这个案例是全班众多本科生案例中的一个，我们长期追踪了这名学生的学习过程。案例的主人公是清华大学的一名男生，他看起来和清华大学其他男生并无不同，经常穿着一件黑色外套，骑着蓝色电动车，飞驰在校园的宿舍和实验室之间，每周安排一两个晚上在跳舞队和朋友练舞。同时他也是一名中学物理奥林匹克竞赛金牌获得者。他是清华大学普通男生的一个缩影，唯一的不同就是他在解决超滑微发电机问题的时候，眼睛里总是闪烁着光彩。这名男生就是黄宇轩，本科一年级开始参与主导研究性学习项目，这也是他持续至今研究的一个方向。在全班的传统培养体系中，没有让学生直接介入真实的问题，只是找问题的痛点，同时让学生提出一个变革性的解决方案。在这个过程中，黄宇轩同学进行了一个颠覆性技术的开发，其间他不断提出问题，并开展自主学习。学习这个项目需要的课程，例如数值计算、程序设计、电工电子技术、电路设计等，他会在不同阶段自主选择不同的课程模块，开展高度的个性化精深学习。全班特别鼓励学生能够进行低成本的尝试，哪怕是试错，也值得付出时间和机会成本。所以，黄宇轩同学从本科一年级开始，通过多层次的理解，参加到这个重大科技前沿的真实、挑战性问题中，逐步提升进阶的研究，从传统的被动学习中解脱出来，在导师帮助下开展主动学习，挑战研究性学习，成功地研发出了超滑微发电机，最终获得《中国科学》评选的颠覆性技术大奖的最高奖。可贵的是，该案例对于工程教育的理论和实践是一个非常值得展开的话题。

第三，面向数智时代工科大学生学习研究。清华大学的工程教育一直备受国际社会的关注，随着工程系统的复杂性、不确定性、跨学科性等特点的不断增强，工程教育必须适应快速变化的工程需求，中国的新型工业化道路关键就是要培养一大批工程技术人才。信息技术突飞猛进，技术发展也在不断地尝试改变人类大脑的认知结构，比如脑机接口。世界经济论坛发布的《2020年未来就业报告》指出，2025年人类和机器分工的变化将导致8500万个工作岗位被取代，9700万个数字化相关的新岗位将会产生。

工程教育在未来面向一个新的目标，即怎样去培养学生的创新能力，尤其是高阶思维？新时代充满了不确定性、复杂性的问题，对人类高阶思维能力提出了更高的要求。高阶思维能力包括创造分析、综合关系建立和元认知等更高的要求。以往的创造力理论，经典的理论解释可能是有限的，需要重新研究工程师的创造创新能力，需要新的工具，所以清华大学组织了一支由工程学、教育学、心理学、计算机科学等学科专家组成的交叉研究团队，试图探求高等工程教育发展的理论与应用问题，将相关的学科内容聚焦到拔尖工科学生培养这一问题。利用相关的领域研究开发工程教育，形成具有学术意义的、有价值的、创造性的关于工科学生学习规律的研究成果。

我们的任务是聚焦数智时代工科生、创造性学习的核心、高阶思维能力，基于跨学科整合的视角，以及工程教育的真实学习情境与学堂在线平台产生的海量学习行为数据，深入研究数智时代学习情境的特点，工科学生的学习行为特点，以及高阶思维能力和学习成效之间的互相联系和内在机理，提炼工科学生高阶思维的关键学习行为中的关键要素。我们近期在准备开发的工具，依据真实数据针对学生开发《数智时代工科大学生高阶思维能力量表》《数智时代面向高阶思维的学习情境感知量表》。希望这些研究为数字技术背景下，高等工程教育创新心态以及拔尖创新人才培养提供新的追踪测评和认知工具。

我们将依托清华大学的卓越工程教育试验田，继续探索卓越工程人才培养的深层次规律，也希望和国际工程教育学术界继续共同交流，共同进步。

闭幕式
Closing Ceremony

IFEE 2022
第三届国际工程教育论坛
The 3rd International Forum On Engineering Education

闭幕式主持

主持人 Chair

罗毅
中国工程院院士，清华大学电子工程系教授
LUO Yi
Member of CAE; Professor, Department of Electronic Engineering, Tsinghua University University

　　1995年获国家杰出青年科学基金资助，1999年获聘教育部"长江学者奖励计划"特聘教授。1997—2012年担任集成光电子学国家重点联合实验室主任，现任北京信息科学与技术国家研究中心副主任，国务院学位委员会电子科学与技术学科评议组召集人。主要研究化合物半导体光电子器件及其集成应用技术，包括激光器、LED、光调制器、光探测器，以及其在光纤通信、宽带信息感知、半导体照明等领域的应用。发表学术论文367篇，授权发明专利34项。获得国家技术发明奖二等奖3项，国家科技进步奖二等奖1项。

Luo Yi is a professor of the Department of Electronic Engineering at Tsinghua University, an academician of the Chinese Academy of Engineering, and the Deputy Director of Beijing National Research Center for Information Science and Technology. He received his B.S. degree from Tsinghua University in 1983, and his M.S. and Ph.D. degrees from the University of Tokyo, Japan, in 1987 and 1990, respectively. He has been a professor in the Department of Electronic Engineering at Tsinghua University since 1992. His research focuses on compound semiconductor optoelectronic devices and their integrated application technologies, including DFB lasers, LEDs, light modulators, and photodetectors, and their applications in optical fiber communication, broadband information sensing, and semiconductor lighting.

袁驷
国际工程教育中心执行主任，清华大学校务委员会副主任
YUAN Si
Executive Director of ICEE; Vice Director of the Council of Tsinghua University

清华大学原副校长、教务长，"长江学者奖励计划"特聘教授，国家级教学名师。历任清华大学土木工程系主任、土木水利学院院长、教务长、副校长，2014年至今任清华大学校务委员会副主任。第十三届全国人大常委、全国人大环境与资源保护委员会副主任委员，中国土木工程学会监事长，教育工作委员会主任，中国力学学会结构工程专业委员会名誉主任，中国教育国际交流协会副会长，《土木工程学报》主编、《现代教育技术》编委会主任委员、《建筑结构学报》编委会副主任委员，教育部工科基础课程教学指导委员会主任委员、教育部力学基础课程教学指导委员会主任委员，教育部在线教育研究中心主任，联合国教科文国际工程教育中心（ICEE）执行主任等。

Yuan Si is the Former Vice President and Provost of Tsinghua University, a distinguished professor of Changjiang Scholars and a national-level master teacher. Yuan served as the Director of Department of Civil Engineering, the Dean of School of Civil Engineering, and the Vice President and Provost of Tsinghua University, and he has been the Vice Chair of Tsinghua University Council since 2014. He is currently a member of the Standing Committee of the 13th National People's Congress, the Vice Chair of Environmental Protection and Resources Conservation Committee of the 13th National People's Congress, the Chair of China Civil Engineering Society (CCES), the Director of Education Working Committee of CCES, the Honorary Director of Structural Engineering Committee, Chinese Society of Theoretical and Applied Mechanics (CSTAM), the Vice President of China Education Association for International Exchange (CEAIE), the Editor-in-Chief of *Civil Engineering Journal*, the Chair of the Editorial Board of *Modern Educational Technology*, the Vice Chair of the Editorial Board of *Journal of Building Structures,* the Chair of the Teaching Steering Committee of Engineering Basic Courses of the Ministry of Education, the Chair of the Teaching Steering Committee of Mechanics Basic Courses of the Ministry of Education, the Director of MOE Research Center for Online Education (RCOE), and the Executive Director of International Centre for Engineering Education under the auspices of UNESCO (ICEE).

第三届国际工程教育论坛总结和闭幕词

袁 驷

第三届国际工程教育论坛成功落下帷幕。这次论坛以"电子信息技术与可持续创新"为主题，由清华大学、中国工程院、联合国教科文组织共同主办，16位院士、89位专家共享了智慧，共有超过2000人参加了在线会议，展开了异彩纷呈、见解深刻、充满活力的全球性对话。

开幕式上，中国工程院院长李晓红院士、UNESCO驻华代表处夏泽翰主任、中国UNESCO全国委员会秦昌威秘书长分别致欢迎词，呼吁建立更加紧密的全球伙伴关系。清华大学校长王希勤教授、日本东京工业大学校长益一哉教授做主旨报告，他们从经济社会发展需求、工程学科演化、大学教育教学创新的角度，分享了对未来工程教育变革的深刻思考。特邀报告人龚克教授、王晓云女士，分享了他们对可持续发展和数字化转型背景下的工程教育转型的深刻见解。

"电子信息使能技术"分论坛紧扣云计算、大数据、人工智能、智慧医疗等新兴技术发展前沿，来自柏林工业大学、清华大学、芝加哥大学、普渡大学、纽伦堡大学、北京航空航天大学、微软亚洲研究院的8位专家分享了对信息技术未来发展的深入见解、本领域工程教育的典型实践、从绿色通信发展与智慧赋能可持续发展的可能路径和互补人工智能促进技术进步的生动愿景。

"城市韧性"分论坛邀请了清华大学建筑学院、英国伦敦大学学院、日本金泽大学、深圳建筑科学研究院的6位院士和专家。他们从智慧建筑和智慧城市、零碳建筑和可持续发展社区、建筑设计创新研究、城市规划设计、绿色建筑以及建筑学科和工程学学科相结合等不同视角，探讨了全球建筑领域发展现状与未来趋势，特别是讨论了产业、科研及人才培养的紧密互动关系。

"数字医疗"分论坛聚焦于数字化与医疗健康产业的未来增长动力，邀请了7位数字医疗领域的知名学者及产业领军人物，分别从医疗大数据、医疗智能设备、数字医疗的发展趋势以及产业发展潮流等角度，共同探讨了人才培养、产业发展和科学研究的未来方向。圆桌讨论环节，报告人和5位与谈人就"数字医疗是过度炒作还是未来可期"展开了热烈的讨论。

"新型电力系统"分论坛邀请了来自美国弗吉尼亚理工大学、英国帝国理工大学、埃克塞特大学、清华大学、天津大学、西安交通大学、华北电力大学、哈尔滨工业大学、太原理工大学、长沙理工大学等国内外高校的教授、校长出席。6位报告人就储能领域的工程教育与人才培养、面向新型电力系统的"电气+"人才培养、服务"双碳"战略的地方高校工程人才培养、电气工程与数据科学结合培养工程人才等话题做了专题发言，四位嘉宾以圆桌会议形式，深入讨论了学科布局、课程改革、产教融合的重点难点问题。

"智能新能源汽车"分论坛重点研讨了智能新能源汽车发展中的关键技术产业应用和人才培养问题。6位来自中国、荷兰、英国、加拿大、美国等国的著名学者及工程科技领域的杰出领袖，探讨了各国在新一轮产业变革背景下的工程人才需求、培养模式，结合新能源汽车、自动驾驶、数字汽车时代的产品开发、有效节能途径等热点话题，研判了汽车工业发展趋势、聚合行业高端资源、搭建全球人才培养交流创新平台方面的新趋势和新思路。

"发展中国家可持续创新"分论坛特别关注了发展中国家在电子信息技术领域的发展情况、经验以及思考。8位国内外专家分享了全球和区域的继续工程教育在可持续发展中发挥的特殊作用和重要意义，对未来加强跨区域合作提出了很有价值的建议。

"青年学生可持续创新"分论坛是专门设置的。我们开展工程教育，要听听学生的声音。来自清华电子系的同学分享了他们在参与哈佛联合课程的学习中，如何运用电子信息技术解决SDGs问题的项目设计方案。来自清华大学苏世民书院的同学分享了可持续发展及数字化转型背景下的项目实践、思考和建议。同学们还针对如何在数字化时代平衡数据利用与个人隐私保护，如何进行可持续效果评估如碳足迹追踪，如何将可持续发展理念融入课程，青年如何为实现SDGs作贡献等问题，展开了热烈研讨。

"面向可持续发展与数字化转型的工程教育"分论坛，聚焦于可持续发展和数字化双重转型下的工程教育认证标准与评价实践、课程体系与高阶思维培养等议题，来自国际工程联盟，丹麦UCPBL，中国工程教育专业认证协会，清华大学电子系、教育研究院的6位专家分享了他们的前瞻性思考。

第三届国际工程教育论坛是一届多学科交流、跨文化互鉴、多机构协作的盛会，也是一届共享发展成果、共商未来合作的盛会，取得了丰硕的成果。中国工程院、UNESCO驻华代表处、中国UNESCO全国委员会为论坛举办给予了大力支持，清华大学电子系、发展规划处、国际工程教育中心共同筹划组织，清华大学建筑学院、医学院、电机系、车辆学院、苏世民书院、东南亚中心、中非领导力中心、拉美中心、UNESCO继续工程教育教席的同事们承办了分论坛。他们都做了卓有成效的工作。在此，我谨代表清华大学和国际工程教育中心，向所有分享智慧的专家、支持和组织会议的机构和个人致以衷心的感谢。

女士们、先生们，工程是人类赖以生存、发展、进步的创造性和推动性力量。工程科技、工程教育和工程人才，是解决可持续发展和数字化转型中一系列重大挑战的战略性支撑。虽然论坛即将落幕，但我们的对话、合作和友谊仍将继续。让我们携起手来，为工程教育的发展绘就更美好的明天。

祝各位健康，谢谢！

附录：英文演讲稿（节选）

Engineering Education and Sustainable Innovation

Li Xiaohong

Member of Chinese Academy of Engineering;
President of Chinese Academy of Engineering

Distinguished guests, friends,
Ladies and gentlemen,

On behalf of the Chinese Academy of Engineering, I extend a warm welcome to all participants of the 3rd International Forum on Engineering Education. Thanks to digital technology, we can come together virtually from different parts of the world despite time and space constraints. This reflects the charm of engineering and aligns with the theme of our conference-electronic information technology and sustainable innovation.

President Xi Jinping once said that "Science and technology are primary productive forces, talent is the first resource, and innovation is the first driving force." Thus, high-quality development of engineering science and technology, engineering education, and engineering talent becomes more important than ever before. Here are three suggestions on this topic:

Firstly, electronic information technology drives sustainable innovation, and engineering talent is the key. The new round of technological revolution is accelerating, and digitization and digital industrialization continue to progress. As a result, this places new demands on the knowledge structure and abilities of engineering talents. They should possess innovative capabilities, the ability to solve complex engineering problems, computational thinking and data analysis abilities, lifelong learning skills, ethical responsibility, and more.

Secondly, engineering science and technology and engineering education are critical in addressing major challenges faced by global sustainable development. Global issues such as the COVID-19 pandemic, climate change, and energy crisis are interwoven and overlapping. UNESCO's second engineering report, *Engineering for Sustainable Development*, explains the essential role of engineering and engineers in achieving the United Nations' 17 sustainable development goals and puts forth a series of important recommendations. In recent years, international practices have also shown that engineering science and technology and engineering education are vital to achieving economic, social, and environmental sustainability.

Thirdly, high-quality development of engineering education and international exchanges and mutually interactive learning are crucial. The industrialization process and engineering education systems vary between countries, and traditional and modern models have their own characteristics, and local challenges are different. Speakers at this forum come from all walks of life in the international community, including education experts, corporate experts, university professors, and young students. We look forward to everyone's valuable insights and ideas, and hearing people sharing successful experiences, discussing development plans, and building global partnerships.

In conclusion, engineering contributes to the well-being of all mankind. Through joint efforts, engineering science and technology, engineering education, and engineering talent will make greater contributions to a more sustainable and better world. Thank you for your attention!

Electronic Information Technology and Sustainable Innovation

Shahbaz KHAN

Director of UNESCO Beijing Office

I am honored to have been invited to participate in this important conference. Engineers play a crucial role in meeting basic human needs, promoting safety and sustainable development, addressing emergencies, rebuilding infrastructure, bridging the knowledge gap, and promoting cross-cultural collaboration. Today's forum provides us with a valuable opportunity to understand the critical role that engineering plays in social and economic sustainable development and to exchange insights on engineering education.

We are at a unique turning point in human history where crises and opportunities intertwine. The Fourth Industrial Revolution is overshadowed by global challenges such as COVID-19, climate change, inequality, violence and insecurity, and disruptive emerging technologies. In this context, engineering innovation is becoming a key element that influences and changes the pattern of social development, placing higher demands on future engineers and engineering education practitioners and researchers.

Through this platform, we can promote interdisciplinary collaboration, research, innovation, and sustainable talent development towards our sustainable development goals. Let us work together to promote sustainable innovation and achieve greater success for learning-oriented careers, therefore providing solutions for sustainable development goals. Thank you for participating in this forum, and I look forward to discussing more topics on engineering innovation and sustainable development in the future.

Reform of Engineering Education

QIN Changwei

Secretary-General of the Chinese National Commission for UNESCO

I greet the attendees of the 3rd International Engineering Education Forum and express gratitude to the organizers and experts in engineering education. President Xi Jinping points out that engineering technology is an important force in changing the world and that breakthroughs in engineering technology can drive profound changes in social productivity and promote human civilization. I highlight the importance of accelerating the training of engineering talents in electronic information technology for sustainable innovation. The United Nations held a Global Education Reform Summit in September, calling for a fundamental re-examination of the purpose and curriculum of education. I emphasize the need for accelerated reform in engineering education and the importance of this forum. UNESCO attaches great importance to engineering education and advocates sharing scientific and educational resources through cooperation. The International Engineering Education Center has done a lot of work to promote international exchange and cooperation in engineering education. I hope that this forum will explore effective ways to solve major problems in engineering education, to share best practices, to propose strategies for promoting reforms, and to make new contributions to global education reforms and the development of world engineering education.

Plenary Speech

Fostering Innovators for a Sustainable Future

Kazuya Masu

President of Tokyo Institute of Technology

Thank you for the introduction. I'm honored to be here today at the third International Forum on Engineering Education organized by Tsinghua University and the Engineering Education community. As the president of Tokyo Institute of Technology, I would like to share our approach to engineering education and cultivating innovative leaders needed by society in the future.

We recognize that innovation is imperative for achieving carbon neutrality and sustainable development goals, and we believe that engineering education should go beyond specialized skills to foster individuals with broad perspectives who can apply their expertise to society. We have two initiatives to support this approach: Liberal Arts Education and the Laboratory for Design of Social Innovation in Global Networks (DLab).

Our wedge-shaped education combines liberal arts education and specialized education to promote an upward spiral of knowledge and ability. DLab aims to foster inclusive and interactive dialogue between Tokyo Tech and the public to envision a "future we all want". We take into account current issues and emerging science and technology to create future scenarios that consider the expected role of universities.

At Tokyo Institute of Technology, we strive to succeed as an educational institution that nurtures innovators in various engineering fields. By encouraging individuals with broad perspectives who can apply their expertise to society, we hope to contribute to a better, more sustainable future. Thank you for the opportunity to share our approach today, and I look forward to exploring additional topics related to engineering education and innovation.

Engineering Education: Promoting Sustainable Development and Digital Intelligent Transformation

Wang Xiqin

President of Tsinghua University

Ladies and gentlemen, welcome to the third International Engineering Education Forum. I am honored to represent Tsinghua University and express our warm welcome to all participants. The forum is jointly initiated and hosted by Tsinghua University, Chinese Academy of Engineering and UNESCO. It is held every two years to bring together renowned scholars and outstanding leaders in the field of engineering education, engineering science and engineering management from around the world to discuss innovative development in engineering education, to promote global engineering science and social progress, and to address major global challenges.

This year's forum will last for three days, focusing on "Electronic Information Technology and Sustainable Innovation". Sustainable innovation is a technological innovation model based on sustainable development concepts and perspectives. In the current global situation and era, engineering education will play an irreplaceable role in promoting sustainable development and digital transformation.

The speech goes on to describe how engineering education is changing with new trends such as interdisciplinary talent cultivation, integration of knowledge from natural sciences and humanities, and closer ties between universities and economic development.

Invited Guest Speeches

Transformation of Engineering Education: Adapting to the Dual Demands of Sustainable Development and Digital Transformation

Gong Ke

Professor of Nankai University

I believe that engineering education needs to reform to cultivate responsible engineers who possess innovative skills to serve the world's sustainable development. In this era of digital transformation and the urgent need for sustainability, it is essential to incorporate green, low-carbon, efficient, and safe technologies in curricula and teaching methods. Industry-academia-research collaborations and international cooperation can broaden our perspectives and improve our competence. Engineers play a crucial role in achieving sustainable development goals, and they must balance human welfare with natural costs.

The Fourth Industrial Revolution requires talent cultivation from various aspects, and electronic information education must transform into a sustainable development enabler. To achieve sustainable development, engineers must acquire both cognitive and practical skills. The transformation of engineering education is necessary to meet the demands of the Fourth Industrial Revolution and sustainable development goals. China faces a significant challenge of transitioning from its coal-based energy structure to a renewable-energy one, where engineering technology innovation plays a vital role in controlling fossil fuel consumption and building a new energy system.

To meet the requirements of sustainable development and the Fourth Industrial Revolution, engineering education must break down disciplinary boundaries and foster collaboration across industries and cultures to increase professional competence. Universities and enterprises need to collaborate to develop effective mechanisms for joint training of engineering students, focusing on reforming engineering education curricula while increasing support for engineering education. As a result, engineering education has a crucial responsibility in nurturing excellent engineers who can drive our social progress sustainably, making greater contributions to our society's development.

Green data communication: Intelligent Physics and Engineering Will Contribute to a Sustainable Society

Dieter BIMBERG

Member of GAS, Member of NAE, Member of RAS,
Professor of Technical University of Berlin

With the development of the Internet, energy consumption has become a serious issue that needs particular attention. Many new applications such as Blockchain, Streaming, and Internet of Vehicles, require heavy data exchanges, which result in great energy consumption. It is reported that the energy consumption of Blockchain has reached 70.3TWH, resulting in approximately 34Mtons of carbon dioxide emissions. Big data-related electricity consumption has already reached 10% of global usage. Future Internet not only needs a higher data rate but also a lower energy-to-data rate ratio (EDR), i.e., 100–400Gbit/s data rate and 100fj/bit EDR.

To achieve green communication, the research team of the reporter has made great efforts. This report introduces their recent advancements on this issue. The first is the structure of the optical cable. Through optimizing the power reflection, 75% of power consumption was reduced in the data transmission. The second is the structure of the VCSEL. The aperture distribution was optimized to reduce the heat radiation impacts on the cable. The third is the energy consumption of CMOS and the optical interconnection. With the combination of these improvements, the research team of the reporter has successfully achieved 500fJ/bit EDR on the condition of 60Gbit/s data rate in the experiment. In the end, the reporter calls for more attention to green communication, which is of great importance for the future Internet.

High Speed Optoelectronic Devices are Enabling Technologies for Information Technology

Luo Yi

Member of CAE: Professor of the Department of Electronic Engineering, Tsinghua, University

Today's topic is high-speed photonic devices. At present, optical communication has brought us many conveniences. In China, optical fiber has been deployed everywhere even in remote rural areas. There are over 1 billion mobile users using 5G and WiFi every day. Improving the data rate is the most important thing that researchers are constantly exploring. One of the key tasks is to develop high-speed photonic devices such as lasers, modulators, monolithic integrated light sources, and high-speed detectors.

This report shows the recent advancements of the research team of Prof. Luo. They have developed the laser modulator that supports a 28Gbit/s data rate. This modulator can support error-free transmissions for 22 kilometers. By collaborating with MIT, they also proposed the thin film lithium niobate modulator, which enables improvements on optical constraints and velocity matching by integrating electrons and optics. The experiment shows that this modulator has very low half-wave voltage and high performance of the RF power. All of these work promote the development of high-speed photonic devices and bring us closer to ultra-wideband communication.

Complementary Artificial Intelligence Can Augment Human Technology Advancement

James A. Evans

Director of the Knowledge Lab in the Department of Sociology and the institute for Computer Science, University of Chicago

This report talks about complementary artificial intelligence (AI). The concept of AI was proposed by Alan Turing in 1945. But at that time, the idea was still very preliminary and used in a computer game named imitation game. Today, AI is more about simulating the human brain. But with the prosperity of AI, some ethical issues have emerged. Thereby, a new technology named Alien intelligence was proposed, which is complementary to AI. Alien intelligence promotes a better understanding of the essence of science and also enhances the complementary relationship between nature and science. It is used to test the reliability and correctness of published scientific conclusions, and also to associate and classify existing scientific research. With these two functions, the report shows that the conclusions in centralized communities have lower reproducibility compared with decentralized communities. Other common methods such as inference, induction, and deduction are also introduced in this report.

The second part introduces the basic process to turn this assumption into reality. The report shows that the cycle of hypothesis, validation, and enhancement is the basic way to improve a model. This process needs cooperation and designs. The report also emphasizes the importance to adapt the basic model to different situations, finding the key factor in the model building.

Educating the Next Generation Engineers

Weng Cho CHEW

Professor of Purdue Universit; Member of NAE, US

At present, the issue of cultivating the next generation of engineers has received more and more attention. The growth of knowledge is like the growth of the tree. When the knowledge reaches the top of the tree, many branches will be separated, all of which are then developed to specific technological applications in the real world.

This report first talks about how to cultivate excellent engineers for our society. Our society are now facing many problems including global warming, climate changes, increasingly frequent wars and inequality. So, the first thing of the engineer cultivation is to let engineers know their social responsibilities. The second is the interdisciplinarity. Knowledge does not grow on just one tree, but grows together on many large trees. Through communication and interaction, the knowledge could be spread more widely.

This report secondly talks about what can educators do. It emphases the importance of the knowledge simplification. Many examples were given to show how to teach the students the essence. On this basis, the concept of STEM education was introduced in detail. The STEM is the abbreviation of four disciplines: Science, Technology, Engineering, and Mathematics. Finally, the reporter appeals that educators and engineers unite together to shoulder their social responsibilities. The society will definitely become greener, more united, and more fair driven by technologies.

Synthetic Molecular Communication: Fundamentals, Results, and Challenges

Robert SCHOBER

Professor of University of Erlangen-Nuremberg,
Canadian Academy of Engineering Fellow

This report shares a new kind of communication named molecular communication. Different from traditional communication system that works in the meter scale, the molecular communication is applied to the nanoscale communication system. Its typical application is in the fields of medicine, biology, and nanotechnology.

To achieve the communication objectives, the main strategy of molecular is diffusion. The transmitter cell sends signals to the environment. These signals spread in the environment through Brownian motion until the receptor cells receive them. If the binary modulation is used, the receptor would count the amount of received signals and evaluate whether it is exceed a certain threshold. If it exceeds, it is judged as 1, otherwise it is judged as 0.

The applications of molecular communication can be divided into two types: micro applications and macro applications. Micro applications mainly include targeted dug delivery, health monitoring, biological nano Internet of Things, and some applications in the environmental field such as monitoring and degrading some pollutants. Macro applications include the detection of oil, natural gas pipelines and explosive gases, the communication between aircraft turbines, and control of chemical process.

To promote molecular communication, three aspects of effort are required. The first is to develop efficient theoretical models. The second is to design all the functions required for the communication system, including modulation, encoding, detection, channel estimation, and interference suppression. The last is to develop an experimental platform for verification. Finally, reporter emphases the importance of interdisciplinary approaches for further developing molecular communication.

Exploration on Engineering Education in the AI Era

Ma Xin

Outreach Director of Microsoft Research Asia

The topic of this report revolves around the exploration of enterprises in engineering education. Prof. Ma comes from Microsoft Research (MSR), which was established in 1998. The reason why MSR has become a very successful research institution in China is closely related to its excellent talent cultivation system, which constantly iterates and innovates. Thereby, Ma started from the perspective of the enterprise to show their efforts on engineering education.

The first thing reporter shared is to promote computational thinking. The main idea of computational thinking is to allow students to develop an interest in learning other subjects through computational science. From 2014 to 2017, they united teachers interested in computing teaching, collected first-hand teaching materials, and made multiple revisions and iterations to the courses. As a result, they uploaded 126 courses on computational thinking on MOOC, helping the infiltration of basic computer courses from universities into primary and secondary education.

In addition to computational thinking, the reporter also shares their experience in collaboration with universities to offer many interesting courses. One is the software practical technology course cooperated with Peking University. Another is the Advanced Machine Learning course cooperated with Tsinghua University.

On this basis, Prof. Ma introduced their recent project named AI Edu on GitHub. They upload many AI-related courses and also share real, open-source projects. Students can practice on it and give feedback on the community platform. Through this process, this community can be constantly enriched.

Prof. Ma believes that schools, students, and enterprises will work together as a tripartite force. As an enterprise, they will closely cooperate with universities and students and take on responsibilities in engineering education.

Swarm Intelligence Control Technology for Human Habitations

JIANG Yi

Professor of the School of Architecture, Tsinghua University; Member of CAE

The focus of smart buildings and cities should be on infrastructure management, which plays a crucial role in the healthy operation of buildings and cities. However, there are still issues with decentralized and independent operation, and the incompatibility between terminal intelligence and system intelligence. To overcome these difficulties, a swarm of intelligence control technology characterized by centerlessness, flattening, and distribution has been proposed, similar to the control system within the human body. A new system architecture for buildings and cities is constructed by combining a limited number of basic units into various buildings and cities, or using this model to adapt and describe various forms of cities and buildings while maintaining the maximum basic unit unchanged. Additionally, using CPN to undertake distributed computing, each terminal and module has its own computing function, and each node is equivalent. Each system collaborates and calculates with each other, and finally, the software for automatic configuration, automatic recognition, automatic modeling, automatic organization, and plug and play needs to be developed to promote true intelligence in buildings and cities. This path requires a large number of talents to join the development team, and a swarm of intelligence attempts to establish a new ecological environment, to mobilize people from relevant industries, and to jointly complete this undertaking. So, there is still a need to cultivate a new generation and promote this technology.

Research on Innovation of Architectural Design Oriented by Scientifc Methodology

ZHUANG Weimin

Professor of the School of Architecture, Tsinghua University; Member of CAE; National Engineering-Survey-and-Design Master

Architecture is a complex system, and relying solely on the human brain for creative research can lead to many problems. Therefore, it is necessary to use intelligent technology to supplement the shortcomings of the human brain and to make design decisions more scientifically.

With the rapid development of machine learning, the transition from image recognition to relationship mining is a good solution for architectural design decision-making. Transforming the calculation of relationships between multivariate data and complex variables into graph theory calculations through graph representation learning makes it easier to be accepted for the public.

Due to the lack of a scientific decision-making process in traditional infrastructure processes, we need to develop a set of full life pre strategy-post evaluation techniques to achieve intelligent management and control of large-scale and complex projects throughout the entire process.

To achieve this, there are four objectives: First, to propose an intelligent planning complex decision model, to propose graph topology intelligent generation logic and fuzzy evaluation algorithm, and to develop an intelligent recommendation tool that can quantify decisions; Second, to develop non-sensor human perception technology in large-scale building environments, based on mobile robot environmental field perception technology, to extract ubiquitous human perception data, coupling perception space and information; Third, to develop multi professional intelligent design methods and technologies aiming at improving quality and performance throughout the entire lifespan, and to develop optimization algorithms and application platforms; Fourth, to solve the mapping relationship between the multidimensional quantitative indicator system of pre planning and the feedback of post use evaluation indicators, and to deduce the cycle of pre planning-post evaluation. The technical roadmap of these four targets needs to integrate interdisciplinary research.

Summary: Taking basic research as the most basic core, achieving theoretical construction. Then, after several key technologies are developed, and corresponding products are obtained, they could then be ultimately implemented in demonstration projects.

Prediction and Demonstration of Spatial Experience Based on Human Factors Analysis Technology

Li ZHANG

Professor and Dean of the School of Architecture, Tsinghua University;
National Engineering-Survey-and-Design Master

The built space experience of public buildings comes from people's subjective feelings. However, due to inaccurate predictions during the design and decision-making stages, the outcome is not always as expected, and it even causes significant resource waste. Nowadays, due to the increasingly mature technology of immersive environments and the development of human factor measurement technology, it can provide more reliable and multi-dimensional objective technologies, greatly improving the prediction performance and guiding design iterations.

By analyzing the four activities of senses-nerves, body, time and space-objective data is obtained and linked to four spatial experience tasks to determine subjective spatial feelings, forming new spatial experience predictions. These four spatial experience tasks include recognition, roaming, sharing, and body sensation, corresponding to different spatial scales. Applying this technological path to design practice could add human factor analysis beyond the traditional design process and therefore to improve the public experience.

The application of human factor analysis technology in the design of the Winter Olympics diving platform has brought significant benefits to the design work through objective experimental information, which has also been verified in feedbacks during and after the competition. Greatly improving the accuracy of spatial experience prediction from the human side and breaking through the bottleneck of traditional subjective judgment is a new opportunity empowering the ancient architectures in this era.

Planning Support System of Regional Metropolis in Japan

SHEN Zhenjiang

Professor of Kanazawa University; Foreign Fellow of EAJ

The traction of urban regulations and policies is a powerful means of sustainable urban development. It is important to utilize professional technology in planning and design to reproduce the form of sustainable construction. Our research focuses on urban environment, urban disasters, and urban resource utilization, exploring sustainable urban policies, and visualizing them through computer technology simulations.

Urban planning and land division within cities in Japan are constrained by policies and regulations, and then we look at how to develop the economy and production within these boundaries. Before implementing these policies and regulations, it is necessary to simulate their effectiveness and future impact. Taking Kanazawa City as an example, due to the outflow of young people, the land vacancy in the central area is severe, and the ecological problems in the suburbs are becoming increasingly serious. How to carry out urban regeneration and apply policies of compact cities is very important. So the government introduced a housing promotion policy in the central area, hoping to promote the return of young people to the central area. We simulated the effectiveness of this policy and the results showed that elderly people are more willing to move back to the central area.

We also simulated the disaster prevention capacity of Kanazawa City, and the results showed that the earthquake prevention capacity of Kanazawa City is insufficient, especially that many shelters need to expand to increase the number of people they can accommodate.

In addition to policy research, sustainable urban design is also important. We have done some work to enable more people to participate in urban design. Finally, we have also done some work in building energy conservation, hoping to contribute to urban resilience.

Review the Origin, Create the Future

YE Qing

Chairman of Shenzhen Building Research Institute Co., LTD.

We have found in practice that the lifespan of current buildings is very short. People constantly build and develop, but they disrupt the balance of nature and bring about high carbon emissions. The first step in green transformation is to change our thinking concepts. The logic of industrial civilization is always ineffective, but we need to use the thinking of ecological civilization to return to our roots and coexist with nature.

The development of green buildings has shifted from a focus on "objects" to a focus on "people". We need to turn buildings into the green mountains of the city, and the impact of architecture on human health cannot be ignored. Improving human life efficiency and our happiness index will become the core value of green buildings.

Elaborate on the practical results of integrating green technology and building technology through the headquarters building with a history of 20 years and the newly built green building this year.

By rationally utilizing ventilation, lighting, rainwater, and green plants, not only energy conservation and consumption reduction have been achieved, but also the symbiosis between human and nature has been achieved. In addition, by comprehensively utilizing the internal space of the building, it has transformed from a simple office building to a shared office mall. In addition to the office area, there are also kindergartens, canteens, apartments, and so on. In this year's green building construction process, the public was involved in the design. After completion, many laboratories were introduced to jointly build this building, achieving comprehensive sharing of space and rules, resources and time, people and time, and between people.

Collision of ideas and technological progress all aim at achieving a happier life in the future and contributing our efforts to a better society.

AI with Life Science

Zhang Yaqin

Foreign Member of CAE; Dean of the Institute for AI Industry, Tsinghua University

Artificial intelligence has become an important engine for both industry and societal change. In the field of life sciences, we are rapidly entering the era of Digitalization 3.0. Gene sequencing, high-throughput biological experiments, and brain-machine interfaces are making our brains, bodily organs, cells, and proteins digitally accessible. This produces astronomical amounts of data that, combined with new AI algorithms and powerful computing, are forming a new intelligent scientific computing paradigm known as the Fourth Paradigm.

The Fourth Paradigm is accelerating the development of life science, biomedicine, genetic engineering, personal health, and other fields towards faster, more accurate, safer, more economical, and more inclusive directions. AI research in protein and structural prediction, gene editing, antibody TCR, and personalized vaccine development, precision medicine, drug design, and others have become cutting-edge research topics globally.

In summary, the academic and industrial sectors must work together to promote the development of life sciences, biomedical research, genetic engineering, personal health, and other fields from isolated open systems to closed, collaborative ones. This will result in faster, more accurate, safer, more affordable, and more widely available innovative models in life sciences and biomedicine. Thank you all!

Intersection of Medicine and Engineering in Beihang University

Fang Jiancheng

Member of CAS; Former Executive Vice President of Beihang University

I would like to report our exploration in the field of medical engineering cross-discipline, with a focus on "Intersection of Medicine and Engineering in Beihang University". My report will cover two aspects: firstly, my views and understanding of medical engineering cross-discipline; secondly, the new technological directions taken by my research team.

Medical engineering cross-discipline is the only way to develop high-end medical equipment. China has embarked on the road to prosperity and places great emphasis on human health. As engineers, we need to play our role and work with medical experts to make contributions to medical equipment technology based on problem-solving. This is why my team has been devoted to the development of medical engineering cross-discipline in recent years.

Currently, high-end medical equipment such as X-ray, CT, B-ultrasound, and structural MRI are used for structural imaging of the human body in cases of structural diseases. However, there is another type of disease called functional disease, which is not effectively diagnosed by imaging with currently available functional MRI technologies. New methods for measuring or imaging human functional information are needed. For example, cells contain very weak electrical signals that were previously difficult to measure. We know that our bodies have mitochondria, which generate electric potential and voltage differences. Now, with the development of extremely weak magnetic field technology, even the weakest electric current can produce a magnetic field. By using this signal, we can capture a wide range of functional information about the human body. My team has achieved excellent results in the diagnosis of functional diseases by researching extremely weak magnetic field technology. We can now detect early warning signs of heart disease, diagnose brain disorders, conduct research on traditional Chinese medicine treatment mechanisms, and diagnose cancer.

In conclusion, scientific and technological innovation requires a dual-wheel drive of talent cultivation and practical innovation. By training top talents in medical engineering cross-discipline through practical innovation, I hope that medical and engineering experts can work together to make the necessary contributions to the development of public health through medical engineering cross-discipline. Thank you.

Paradigm and Technical System of Accurate Hepatobiliary Surgery

Dong Jiahong

Member of CAE; Dean of the Clinical School of Medicine; Tsinghua University

I am very glad to share "Paradigm and Technical System of Accurate Hepatobiliary Surgery" with you today. I will report in four aspects.

First, the source and iteration of the precision surgery concept. Since the 21st century, the great progress in biomedical sciences and the gradual rise of evidence-based medicine, the penetration and integration of modern technologies centering on information technology have significantly enhanced the determinism of surgical practice, enabling a paradigm shift towards precision surgery based on determinism.

Second, the core technologies of precision liver surgery. According to the new concept of precision liver surgery core technologies, the three categories of core technologies, namely visualization, quantification, and controllability, promote the systematic exploration and practice of precision liver surgery core technologies, becoming the cornerstone of supporting determinism surgical practice.

Third, the dominant surgical procedures for precision liver surgery. For different clinical characteristics of hepatobiliary diseases, we apply the concept and core technologies of precision liver surgery to form a series of dominant surgical procedures for precision liver surgery. Precision surgical procedures include localization resection, quantitative resection, and configuration resection. Among them, localization resection is a liver resection based on lesion localization and precise resection.

Finally, the paradigm of precision liver surgery. An academic paradigm refers to the theoretical foundation and practical norms on which conventional science relies. It is the worldview and behavior of a group of scholars engaged in a particular science. The ideas and principles of precision liver surgery and the innovative technology systems that support it have been tested in years of extensive clinical practices.

In summary, the construction and practice of the precision liver surgery paradigm, this modern surgical technology and knowledge system, integrates my team's innovative ideas and technical elements, and also brings together the knowledge, experience and wisdom of many experts both home and abroad in this field. This paradigm solves a series of technical difficulties in the field of hepatobiliary surgery, improves the effect of surgical treatment of complex hepatobiliary diseases, and leads the innovation and transformation of modern hepatobiliary surgery concepts and paradigms. Thank you all.

New Era of Healthcare Driven by AI

Huang Guangbin

Mind PointEye Pte Ltd Founder, Professor of Nanyang Technological University

Artificial intelligence (AI) is the beginning of a data-driven smart revolution, and its development will lead the third industrial revolution. As a result, it will affect various industries, including healthcare, creating significant opportunities for the sector.

The question of whether AI or human brains are stronger is difficult to answer since they are two different functions with varying applications. Therefore, there may be instances where humans outperform machines, and vice versa. However, in many applications, we can make the most of AI's characteristics to assist us in accomplishing tasks that are beyond our abilities.

When we consider healthcare as a particular application or system, it raises an important question of how to use AI's advantage to overcome the limitations that doctors face. As doctors have limited energy and time, similar to drivers who get fatigued, if a physician sees 20 patients a day, it amounts to only about 300,000 patients over their lifetime. In contrast, AI could see billions of patients in a matter of hours while analyzing data from thousands of years. Hence, AI could create a super-doctor that surpasses human capacity.

The primary advantage that AI has over doctors is the abundance of data, including data from previous centuries and the real-time data shared globally. On top of that, other hardware such as sensors, devices, and technologies can be integrated with AI. Therefore, when discussing AI, we must consider it in conjunction with various technologies rather than solely relying on data.

In conclusion, AI is the beginning of a data-driven smart revolution that will impact various industries, including healthcare. While there may be instances where humans outperform machines, AI's primary benefit over human doctors is its abundance of data. The trend for AI development involves increasingly robust capabilities, lower power consumption, and faster speeds. The importance of network technology, such as 5G and 6G, will rise in data sharing and analysis. If the entire healthcare industry becomes AI-driven, it will truly transform the sector.

Digital and Intelligence Health Industry

Zhang Dalei

Founder of Airdoc

I would like to share my perspective on the digital healthcare industry and its potential applications.

Airdoc was founded with the aim of addressing the unmet needs for early detection and long-term management of chronic diseases. We envisioned leveraging medical artificial intelligence to extend disease diagnosis from traditional tertiary hospitals to primary care facilities. However, this is not a problem that can be solved solely by an AI algorithm. From an algorithmic perspective, we can classify and interpret ocular fundus retinal vessels and nerves to identify differences between healthy individuals and those with diabetes, glaucoma, cataracts, or other ischemic diseases. However, even if we excel at the classification and interpretation processes, in real-world scenarios, most applications may still be impractical. Traditional retinal cameras require a relatively dark environment and professional operators, which inevitably leads to high unit economic costs and affordability issues for users. Therefore, we need to find a way to establish a device that users can self-examine and operate without relying on surrounding operating environments and personal financial capabilities, so as to popularize chronic disease detection.

So how can we solve these problems? Artificial intelligence and machine learning can assist by performing some auxiliary work. For example, we can construct an AI-based decision-making model through image recognition and natural language processing, and build a real expert network through AI. Throughout the process, we only assign part of the work to doctors, while the other part is completed by machines and algorithms, in order to reduce unit economic costs and serve more patients. In addition to testing, we can also see a significant demand for myopia treatment, as well as safety issues with various treatment plans available in the market. Therefore, we have developed a platform where doctors can program remote control commands to ensure the safety of the treatment process. By providing continuous and comprehensive diagnosis of patients throughout the treatment process, we hope to provide continuously adjusted treatment plans to achieve the best treatment results.

Overall, we can see that there is still a lot of work to be done in the digital healthcare field. Airdoc is also conducting extensive research in areas such as health, myopia, cardiovascular and cerebrovascular diseases, and neurological diseases. We hope to continue to grow and develop with colleagues from various industries, and bring the best products to everyone in the future. Thank you.

AI in Healthcare: Challenges and Opportunities

LIU Nan

Associate Professor at the Centre for Quantitative Medicine and Programme in Health Services and Systems Research, Duke-NUS Medicine School

Hello everyone, I will share the application of AI in healthcare from a medical perspective.

Whenever we talk about artificial intelligence, we always ask such a question: Why should artificial intelligence be used in the medical field? Due to the increased data storage capacity and stronger data analysis and classification capabilities, real-world data, such as disease levels, electronic health records management, medical claims databases, wearable devices, etc., can be easily obtained and analyzed. Analyzing real-world data is related to analyzing the potential risks and benefits behind the data.

However, if the scale of data becomes extremely large and the data is collected without control and optimization, our current data processing capabilities would not allow to analyze a large amount of heterogeneous data. Artificial intelligence and machine learning have further explored the boundaries of algorithms. Through computer science branches, artificial intelligence and machine learning can be associated with data analysis and data optimization to provide predictive analysis and predictive models. Overall, artificial intelligence can be used to analyze some conceptual data. We can use artificial intelligence and machine learning to select different variables to further understand different dimensions. In addition, artificial intelligence is essential for information fusion. Because the data comes not only from one data source, we hope to analyze medical data from different sources to analyze the integrity and fusion of the entire data. This is why artificial intelligence and machine learning are critical in digital medicine, medical IoT, and large-scale data analysis.

Of course, artificial intelligence also faces some challenges. So far, the challenges of artificial intelligence and the medical field are the ambiguity of data. The data quality itself has some problems, and the uniqueness of the data may lead to data imbalance in the field of artificial intelligence. In addition, privacy and monitoring are also a hot issue in artificial intelligence. The basis of data sharing is privacy protection and regulatory approval.

In general, opportunities and crises always coexist. With the patient as the center, our patients can wear many wearable devices or sensors to collect data and realize telemedicine. Undoubtedly, the world is entering a global data network shared from an independent data supervisor. Cloud computing and cloud services can realize the interconnection of all things and transmit such medical services through international networks. Thank you.

Role of Engineering in Advancing Medicine & Health

Chwee Teck LIM

NUS Society Chair Professor of Biomedical Engineering;
Director of the Institute for Health Innovation and Technology

Today I will share the "Role of Engineering in Advancing Medicine & Health".

Data and research show that we are now in a rapidly aging world. While aging, there will be a series of chronic diseases, such as hypertension, arthritis, heart disease, diabetes, depression, dementia or cancer. To solve major health challenges, the first step is disease prevention, and the second is early detection and early treatment. Solving health and medical problems requires multidisciplinary and interdisciplinary efforts, including cooperation between scientists, engineers and patients.

It's admitted that applying artificial intelligence to healthcare is of great significance. I would like to add that there is no technology without data in the world. Artificial intelligence requires data to operate effectively. Therefore, we need technology to collect high-quality data. To obtain patient-generated health data, we can use some wearable devices. Wearable devices are a hot topic of study. In fact, many people wear watches to continuously collect data from our bodies. If we use wearable devices, the collected data will not only be accurate and reliable but also be complete and real-time, which can help us meet the high-quality and high-standard data requirements. At the same time, we can use wearable devices to further accurately monitor personal health, to influence the decision-making process of different populations, and to let users believe that their decisions can be influenced, thereby helping us prevent and detect diseases, and leading us to the path of precise diagnosis and treatment.

Finally, I would like to summarize that for some real-time data like ours now, if we want artificial intelligence to work, health and patient data must be accurate, complete, and real-time. I believe wearable devices can ensure the quality of these data. By collecting some data every day, artificial intelligence can establish a baseline. At the same time, if patients deviate from their daily routine, they can also remind patients as early as possible to see a doctor immediately.

In general, I believe that medical wearable devices can help us explore a better medical and health management system. When we consider designing engineering for medical and health care, we must consider that our ultimate goal is not only to further improve clinical outcomes and to reduce medical and health costs, but also to further increase our life expectancy.

Thoughts on Several Issues of Smart Power Distribution System

WANG Chengshan

Member of CAE, Professor of Tianjin University

With the development of new electric power system, Tianjin University focuses on the demand analysis of energy storage industry, puts forward the training strategy of excellent engineers, and discusses the engineering education and talent training of energy storage specialty. We integrate superior resources through the approved national energy storage production-education innovation platform to achieve crossover integration. In order to improve the quality of education, the university focuses on the selection, training, evaluation and support of outstanding engineers and scientists with national spirits, global vision, forward-looking judgment and interdisciplinary understanding.

The energy storage specialty plans to enroll 60 new students this year. In the course system construction, we emphasize basic knowledge, cross-integration and project-oriented curriculum system oriented by practical ability. The school improves students' practical ability by means of school-enterprise dual tutorial system and enterprise internship. In addition, the university also sets up training bases with enterprises and research institutes to share experimental equipment and data, so as to achieve a close combination of talent training and enterprise needs. In the process of talent training, the school attaches great importance to the cultivation of practical ability and the mode of integrating production and education, and strives to improve the comprehensive quality of students. We emphasize that with the combination of multiple degrees and the export of diverse talents, graduates can be engaged in energy storage battery manufacturing or fuel cells. Students are encouraged to pursue further studies and are divided according to their interests and development needs during the senior year. In the basic course of energy storage design, in order to ensure the course effectiveness, teachers of different disciplines are organized into topic groups to jointly design. The school also carries out high-end training programs, such as training programs for high-level energy storage talents with non-academic degrees, and encourages the community to take optional courses in order to transfer more outstanding energy storage professionals.

Engineering Education and Research in the Age of Smart Grid and the Evolving Power System

Saifur RAHMAN

Professor at Virginia Tech; IEEE President-Elect

My talk will focus on engineering education, smart grids, and the evolving power system. A smart grid is made up of multiple components, such as thermal power plants, nuclear power plants, hydropower stations, solar photovoltaic power plants, electric vehicles, factories and smart buildings, etc., which work together to achieve more efficient power transmission. The goal of the smart grid is to improve the reliability, safety and cost effectiveness of the grid. To achieve this goal, we need to adopt advanced sensors, communication technologies and distributed computing technologies. The emergence of smart power grid increases the degree of intelligence of power grid and improves the operation efficiency and cost effectiveness of power grid.

In addition to transmitting power, smart grids can also be monitored, controlled and dispatched in real time. It allows us not only to improve the convenience of power transmission, but also to achieve more functions, such as improving the operating efficiency of smart grids through voltage control, volume optimization and conversion between different voltage levels. However, the emergence of the smart grid has also changed the traditional grid, and the communication technology of the grid has gradually become an important part of the integration of information flow and current, which means that we also need communication technology to achieve end-to-end transmission. The popularization and development of this technology will have a profound impact on the future energy industry, contributing to the global energy transition and reducing carbon emissions.

In smart grid research, we need to consider the instability of distributed generation and renewables, as well as changes on the demand side. We need to discuss how to adapt to changes in distributed generation, the intermittency of solar and wind power, and whether supply and demand match during different seasons and periods of peak demand. What's more, the emergence of a smart grid will require a diverse group of professionals, including not just power engineers, but also computer engineers and sensor engineers.

Data Sciences and their Influence on Smart Grid Education

WANG Zhongdong

Vice President and Professor of University of Exeter

This report focuses on the impact of international engineering education, specifically in the areas of data science and smart grid education. The report first provides a brief introduction to the University of Exeter, a research and education institution committed to energy and power studies. It then discusses power engineering education and the use of data science in the energy industry. To prepare the next generation of electrical engineers to meet future demand, they emphasize the development of a course on smart grids and sustainable energy systems offered at the University of Exeter.

The report also explores the key role of data science in achieving near-zero emission goals and how to apply it in the energy industry alongside artificial intelligence. They believe that empowering consumers to be both producers and consumers, relying more on data and technology, and considering network security to resist cyberattacks is crucial. Additionally, the report highlights the need for different types of power systems, including smart grids, to meet current socio-economic needs. To achieve near-zero goals, the UK needs to stop emitting carbon stored underground. This implies to switch to green energy sources such as wind, solar, tidal, biomass, and hydropower. However, they have intermittent issues. Therefore, smart grids will be crucial in the future to ensure real-time information exchange between producers and consumers. In smart grids, supply-demand balance is crucial to no longer relying on fossil fuels.

To educate the next generation of electrical engineers to meet the future demand, we emphasize the development of a course on smart grids and sustainable energy systems offered at the University of Exeter. The course provides a platform to understand the application of data science in smart grids, enabling engineers to master the latest technology. This elevates the future electrical engineer's intelligence level in power system management through digital twinning and electrical system equipment projects. We can also improve the power system's resilience through AI, big data, IoT, and cloud computing technologies. To ensure the education system is adaptable to future needs, data science and AI applications should be incorporated into the course design.

Exploration of "EE +" Talent Cultivation Facing New Type Power System

BIE Zhaohong

Vice President and Professor of Xi'an Jiaotong University

This report mainly discusses the exploration of electric + talent training under the background of two-carbon strategy and new power system construction. Under this background, the electrical discipline of Xi'an Jiaotong University has carried out a series of reforms. It mainly involves four aspects: interdisciplinary, integration of industry and education, integration of science and education and global convergence.

In response to the new requirements, Xi'an Jiaotong University has established the electric + teaching system, which mainly includes three sections: subject basis, frontier crossing and practical teaching. The integration of industry and education is also very important in cultivating outstanding engineers for the construction of new power system. Through introducing enterprises into the campus and building school-enterprise collaborative elite classes, the integration of industry and education is carried out in an all-round way.

In terms of the integration of science and education, Xi'an Jiaotong University has fed back its advantages in scientific research into talent training. It has built six new platforms in the Innovation Port and cultivated students' innovativity through the platform of national facilities. So far, the platform has nurtured more than 130 graduates.

In addition, Xi'an Jiaotong University gathers high-quality resources from all over the world to cultivate high-level talents with international competitiveness. Its approach includes the reciprocal exchange and joint class training program with Polytechnic University of Milan and France Higher School of Electric Power, which has been well received by all parties since 2012.

Xi'an Jiaotong University hires 32 overseas academicians and professors to set up an English curriculum system, founded upon the national intelligence base. We join the

European TIME Alliance to share global curriculum resources. We participate in international cooperation projects and send more than 40 students every year. As the leading unit of Foreign aid degree program of Ministry of Commerce, it admits 40–50 international students every year. We also operate a Ph.D. school, invite professors to teach, and enhance students' global competence.

Innovation and Practice of Energy and Power Engineering Talent Training in Regional Colleges Supporting the "Dual-carbon" Strategy

ZENG Xiangjun

Vice President and Professor of Changsha University of Science and Technology

This report discusses how local colleges and universities can cultivate relevant talents in the field of energy and power in order to achieve the two-carbon goal. The discussion will be mainly from three aspects of elaboration and explanation.

Firstly, this report introduces the current situation of talent training in electric power and the importance of realizing two-carbon goal, emphasizes the important role of electric power in reducing carbon, and lists the relevant policies and plans.

Secondly, it introduces the requirements of dual-carbon talent training, including solid foundation, industrial consciousness, interdisciplinary and international vision, and mentions the training program of carbon-neutral talents formulated by the education department.

Then, the report describes the challenges faced by local colleges and universities in the field of energy and electric power talent training. Taking Changsha University of Science & Technology as an example, it expounds the specific measures to solve the dilemma, and focuses on the innovation and practical measures taken by the university to cultivate outstanding talents with practical application ability in the field of two-carbon energy. These include interdisciplinary specialty setting, double degree class setting and integration of industry and education, establishing education and teaching centers in collaboration with schools and enterprises, attaching importance to practical ability training, proposing five-stage progressive innovation and entrepreneurship talent training mode, promoting international cooperation and training practical engineering talents. We have achieved remarkable results in cultivating a large number of high-quality talents in the field of two-carbon energy, and our promotion experience has been recognized by local colleges and universities in Hunan Province.

New Energy and New Engineering Education

OUYANG Minggao

Member of CAS; Professor of the School of Vehicle and Mobility, Deputy Director of Academic Committee of Tsinghua University

The core content of the new energy revolution can be summarized into five pillars, four elements, and three bottlenecks. The five pillars include transitioning to renewable energy, combining centralized and distributed photovoltaic and wind power, turning buildings into satellite power plants, storing intermittent energy with hydrogen fuel cells, and developing an energy internet. The four elements are silicon power, energy storage, intelligent energy, and hydrogen energy. The three bottlenecks are system integration, technological innovation, and policy support.

The speaker also discusses the interdisciplinary nature of energy technology science, which combines material science, engineering, and system science. The research team has established a cross-disciplinary research system in battery, energy storage, green hydrogen, and intelligent energy. The team also focuses on the process science, system science, and interdisciplinary research to serve the goal of the new engineering.

Towards Responsible Automated Driving

Bart van AREM

Pro Vice Rector Magnificus for Doctoral Affairs and Professor of Transpof Modelling,

Delft University of Technology, the Netherlands

Bart van Arem from Delft University of Technology gave a speech about responsible autonomous driving and their transportation engineering courses, which focus on making vehicles not only products but also traffic services for improving people's lives sustainably and safely. One of the courses requires students to develop a concept model, to propose a project plan, and to conduct a literature review to understand how transportation can solve social issues, incorporating technology such as electrification and digitalization. Another course covers technical details of traffic simulation, traffic theory, and human factors, and teaches how to relate and apply them to real-world problems. Van Arem's team also uses virtual reality technology to evaluate the safety of autonomous vehicles' interaction with pedestrians and vehicles by testing factors like speed and distance.

Optimal Systems for Sustainable Vehicles

Huw WILLIAMS

Honorary Professor of Automotive Engineering of School of Engineering,
University of Birmingham; RSS Fellow

Huw Williams from the University of Birmingham would like to discuss the topic of systems, their education and evolution, the importance of optimal solutions, and how optimization can be taught. Systems engineering plays a critical role in bridging the knowledge gap for engineering students. It is not commonly taught in universities in a comprehensive manner, and its value cannot be overstated. A system is more than a mere collection of objects; it must have a distinct function or purpose. Teaching systems engineering requires starting with an unbiased problem statement and employing techniques like boundary diagrams, system state flowcharts, and functional trees. Understanding how systems evolve and how to anticipate those changes is also critical. Finally, we may optimize the system to improve its functionality.

Some Thinking about the University Education for Automotive Industry of Cyber Vehicle Era

GUAN Xin

Dean of Automotive Research Institute, Jilin University;
Vice President of the Society of Automotive Engineers of China

The speaker, Guan Xin from Jilin University, gives a speech about the development of networked automotive products. He talks from three main aspects: the four eras of automobiles and their professional knowledge scope, whether metrology is an engineering or a technical discipline and the emphasis on engineering and technical aspects in this discipline, and the process of developing automotive products and the necessary professional abilities. Guan Xin analyzes the technical features of the four eras of automobiles: mechanical automobiles, mechatronics automobiles, electric control automobiles, and digital automobiles. He also explains the human and machine interactions involved in driving performance. Finally, he discusses the knowledge system of metrology and its importance in automotive engineering.

Tech-enhanced Engineering Education Sparks Explosive Development of EdTech

WANG Shuaiguo

President, XuetangX.com

Founded by Tsinghua University in 2013, Xuetangx.com became the first international partner of International Centre for Engineering Education (ICEE). Backed by ICEE, the platform has provided quality services for more than 67 million learners of all kinds. In recent years, online education has seen the explosive development of educational technology. Serving over three million people per second, Rain Classroom supported online teaching in more than 900 colleges and universities nationwide during the COVID-19 pandemic and provided quality services for more than 62 million learners. An increasing number of teachers are willing to apply online education technology to physical classrooms, resulting in an increasingly blurred border between face-to-face education and online education. We hope that this technology can narrow the gap between offline engineering education classrooms and remote engineering education classrooms. We will also continue to update product applications and technology research and development.

Experiential Learning and Engineering Graduate Education

Amir KHAJEPOUR

Professor of the Department of Mechanical and Electromechanical Engineering, University of Waterloo; ASME/CSME Fellow

Amir KHAJEPOUR from the University of Waterloo will discuss practical education and its integration into regular coursework. Mechatronic Systems Engineering laboratory employs the Sullivan Engineering Ideas Clinic to enhance practical learning. Modules emphasize engineering practice through teamwork, communication, and collaboration. Activities include Engineering Design Day and Engineering Peak. For graduate courses, practical learning is integrated into research projects with a joint project team consisting of senior and junior students and postdoctoral staff. This approach facilitates practical skill development and problem-solving ability by collaborating with industry professionals on real-world problems.

Energy Harvesting for Sustainable and Intelligent Vehicles

Lei ZUO

Endowed Professor, University of Michigan; ASME Fellow

Lei Zuo, a skilled energy harvester, spoke on vehicle and traffic energy topics at the conference. Lei's recent focus has been on energy. He explained that for intelligent vehicles, sensors are necessary to collect data, but they require significant energy. Lei described the best stable system as having three conditions: a stable equilibrium, low noise levels, and weak periodic vibration. He then discussed the concept of random resonance, which is used to create continuous resonance and self-tuning vibration. Lei then talked about using energy harvesting for intelligent traffic systems, which can be achieved through energy parking to enable active infrastructure. Lei's vision is to implement a car-to-infrastructure network to enhance road safety and conditions.

Digital Economy in ASEAN: Development Status and Practice Opportunities of Industrial Internet

HAN Xing

General Manager of Singapore Operation Company of China Unicom International Co., LTD. (in charge of ASEAN region)

Digital economy has become a key momentum and core growth driver for countries around the world to promote economic recovery under the impact of COVID-19. From 2020 to 2022, despite being greatly affected by the pandemic, various countries still enjoyed sound momentum of development and bright growth prospects in digital economy. In terms of development direction, digital technology innovation is still a global strategic focus.

Today, the digital economy is developing rapidly in emerging markets. Southeast Asia boasts great development potential, and the consumer internet is flourishing. Southeast Asia has a large young population, and mobile internet users account for more than 90% of the 400 million internet users, laying a favorable foundation for the development of digital economy. The digital sovereignty of Southeast Asian countries is gradually awakening, and the regional cooperation is being gradually strengthened, which actively promotes the development of digital trade in Asia and further contributes to economic digitalization. Moreover, the countries in Southeast Asia are also making active efforts to develop digital economy and smart cities. ASEAN leaders have established the ASEAN Smart Cities Network (ASCN), which covers 26 cities in 10 member countries and aims to jointly explore replicable smart city solutions. It has attracted investment from multinational companies from all over the world.

NUSRI's Practice Sharing in Talent Training, Technological Innovation and Exchange

GUO Yongxin

Professor of Department of Electronic and Computer Engineering, National University of Singapore

On November 15, 2010, witnessed by the Vice President of China Xi Jinping and the Singapore Prime Minister Lee Hsien Loong, National University of Singapore (NUS) and Suzhou Industrial Park Administrative Committee signed an agreement to found the NUS (Suzhou) Research Institute (NUSRI). NUSRI focuses on three cores, namely education, scientific research and industrialization. In terms of scientific research, NUSRI attaches importance to the innovation and originality of research, and gives play to discipline advantages and scientific research resources of NUS to carry out applied scientific and technological research combining scientific and technological needs of local industrial upgrading. In terms of industrialization, NUSRI is committed to promoting the bilateral exchange of science & technology and industries between China and Singapore, contributing to the effective transformation of international scientific and technological achievements with Singapore as the mainstay, accelerating the establishment and development of high-tech start-ups, building a bridge for the exchange among top scientific and technological industries in the world, and promoting international technological innovation and economic development.

BLOCK71 Suzhou is an initiative by NUS Enterprise in collaborative and strategic partnerships with established corporates and government agencies. By providing projects and activities, the initiative, as the builder and business connector of the technological ecosystem, aims at catalyzing, highlighting and developing the ability of the start-up community and forming a global network of innovation and entrepreneurship portals connecting with NUS. BLOCK71 enjoys a global presence in the United States, Japan, Jakarta in Indonesia, as well as Suzhou and Chongqing in China.

Engineering education and Africa's priorities

Desta MEBRATU

Former Deputy Director of the Africa Division, United Nations Environment Programme;
Professor of Stellenbosch University, South Africa

The realization of sustainable structural transformation of African economies is not only the need of African countries, but also of global significance. Africa is in the early stage of development with low inertia, indicating a unique leap-forward development opportunity to realize green industrialization. It is also facing a rapidly growing population. If the population reaches 2.5 billion by 2050, we must achieve sustainable growth in engineering education, research, development, etc., which are the keys to develop innovative solutions related to environment, so as to meet Africa's needs and priorities. International cooperation between universities in Africa and China is crucial to building educational and research capabilities of African countries. Moreover, the infrastructure development of Africa is important not only for Africa, but also for the whole world. We should pay more attention to the opportunities on the African continent in research, education, innovative solutions, demographic dividends and other aspects, so it is necessary to strengthen cooperation, particularly the cooperation in education and research capacity between Africa and China, which is also essential for Africa to achieve transformative and leap-forward development.

Innovative Indonesia

Satryo Soemantri BRODJONEGORO

President of Indonesian Academy of Sciences

Innovative Indonesia, a national fund and innovation center, aims at promoting and supporting the development of innovative enterprises in Indonesia. It was established to satisfy the fundamental demand for more innovation-based enterprises and industries in Indonesia. It is a progressive and imaginative long-term initiative that focuses on transforming existing enterprises and supporting the development of innovative enterprises and industries.

At present, Indonesia's innovative performance is far below its potential. It ranks 97 in the global innovation ranking, indicating that it is not fully competitive, and innovation has always been in a relatively vulnerable position in global competition. If Indonesia demands to promote innovation and transition to a more knowledge-based economy, we need to use advanced technology to promote the development of innovation and society, so as to upgrade to a leading and competitive global economy. Therefore, Innovative Indonesia will work together with its HUB and relevant financing partners to identify, support and fund the projects that accelerate innovative productivity and creativity.

Globalization and Sustainability on Electrical and Electronic Engineering Education in Xiamen University Malaysia

LI Xiaochao

Professor and Director of Professor Committee of School of Electronic Science and Engineering in Xiamen University

Founded in 1921, Xiamen University is the first university founded by overseas Chinese in China's modern education history. Electronic engineering is one of the engineering disciplines in Xiamen University that boasts the longest history and most potential. The Department of Physics was established in 1924, the Department of Mechanical and Electrical Engineering in 1940 and the Department of Electronic Engineering in 1985. In 2016, the School of Electronic Science and Engineering (Microelectronics College) was established. In addition, Xiamen University is also one of the earliest universities in China to establish a semiconductor discipline. In 2019, the Ministry of Education approved Xiamen University's construction of a National Integrated Circuit Industry-Education Integration Innovation Platform. In the context of the Belt and Road Initiative, China's engineering education also encounters new opportunities to help achieve global prosperity and sustainable development. Therefore, Xiamen University established Xiamen University Malaysia, its first overseas campus, becoming the first Chinese university to set up a branch in Malaysia.

Electronic and electrical products account for the largest share (27%) of the total exports of the Association of Southeast Asian Nations (ASEAN), an important hub of electronic and electrical production. And the electronic engineering sector is an important driving force for Malaysia's industrial development. Xiamen University Malaysia has launched a four-year bachelor's degree program and a master's degree program in electrical and electronic engineering. In addition, it has also established a goal-oriented education mode, aiming to continuously improve its whole teaching quality.

Sustainable Innovation in Developing Countries

Rovani SIGMONEY

UNESCO Engineering Planning Expert

In achieving the goal of sustainable development, engineering is undoubtedly at the core. In the face of pressing challenges from the Earth and social economy, engineering is the knowledge and practice to solve problems. Engineers are crucial in meeting basic human needs, eliminating poverty, advancing security and sustainable development, coping with emergencies, reconstructing infrastructure, shortening the knowledge gap, and promoting international cross-cultural cooperation. Moreover, as the main driving force for the sustainable development of social economy, engineering can improve the ability to create new products and services and provide solutions.

On March 4th, 2021, the World Engineering Day, UNESCO released its Engineering Report II, which emphasizes the key role of engineering in achieving each of the 17 Sustainable Development Goals. This report, involving all stakeholders in the engineering industry, advocates a worldwide engineering partnership, and calls on all stakeholders, such as governments, policy makers, academia, educators, industrial circle, foundations and civil societies, to participate in it. In addition to the importance of global partnership of the engineering community, this report also emphasizes the necessity to strengthen capacity building in developing countries.

To Achieve Sustainable Development with More Diversified and Better Engineering Technologies: Innovation from the Southern Hemisphere

Francisco MARTINEZ

Dean of Faculty of Engineering, University of Chile

Chile has reached a strong social consensus in its efforts to control climate change. Always being at the forefront of sustainable development, Chile has seen a remarkable growth in renewable energy production, marine protection and electrification of public transport, etc. Chile is committed to training more female engineers and scientists, and has also taken a series of affirmative actions, including increasing the numbers of scholarships and academic positions for women. A number of studies and initiatives have been launched with a view to deeply transforming the patriarchal culture. Chile has won an honorary certificate of gender equality issued by the United Nations in recognition of its continuous introduction of leading policies in this regard.

Universidad de Chile is a member of the Association of Pacific Rim Universities, the International Forum of Public Universities, Universitas 21 and other famous university alliances. It advocates the concept of lifelong learning, and is supportive of students' diversity, including differences in socioeconomic status, gender, heredity and culture. It is committed to promoting students' initiative and strengthening their in-depth study on campus. It carries out a series of interdisciplinary research, bringing the current research and development trend and research results into teaching through interdisciplinary education. It also enriches students' applied learning experience through rich practice opportunities and other programs.

International Cooperation and Demand in Automation

YIN Feng

Director of Energy Technology Center of Zhejiang Electric Power Research Institute of State Grid Co., LTD

Established on November 27th, 1961, the Chinese Association of Automation (CAA) has its office in Beijing and is affiliated to the Institute of Automation, Chinese Academy of Sciences. CAA has nearly 80,000 members, and 58 professional committees from various industrial systems and engineering technology fields, such as electric power, metallurgy, chemical engineering, petroleum, transportation, mining, water conservancy, textile, architecture, agriculture, and national defense. It has carried out in-depth cooperation based on international engineering project services and industrial promotion.

With their accelerated pace of "going global", Chinese enterprises are undertaking an increasing number of overseas projects. There is a growing demand for Chinese technology and equipment to enter overseas markets, for Chinese engineers and technicians to get on the world stage, for Chinese standards to be transformed into international ones, and for overseas talents to join the Chinese technological system. Therefore, relevant units of the Power Generation Committee of Experts of CAA have carried out a number of cooperative construction projects in the energy field in BRI countries such as Viet Nam, Indonesia, Pakistan and Belarus. They have also jointly compiled a series of IEEE and IEC international standards, translated some national standards and industrial standards, and popularized the application of relevant standards in implementing engineering projects, so as to facilitate global cooperation.

School Waste Management

WANG Jingyi

Ph.D. Student of the Department of Electronic Engineering, Tsinghua University; Canada

Waste management is a problem that many schools encounter, where only organic or ordinary garbage cans are provided on campus, with an absence of convenient recycling stations. The problems we are aiming to address are inefficient waste sorting and recycling, people's attitudes and awareness of waste recycling, and inadequate recycling promotion. Our goal is to encourage a change in attitudes and behavior towards waste recycling, to support the university's resources, to improve bottom-up communication, and to set an example for other schools to form a University waste management alliance.

An Intelligent Carbon Footprint Recording and Sharing Platform

LU Zhihong

Master Student of the Deparment of Electronic Engineering, Tsinghua University; Hong Kong S.A.R., China

Carbon emissions have been in the spotlight for decades. Our government has made carbon neutrality and peaking carbon dioxide emissions one of its goals in its most recent five-year plan. Our Carbon project focuses on calculating an individual's transport carbon footprint and consists of three modules: carbon emissions calculation, summary report display for users, and social sharing module. The carbon footprint recording and sharing platform has two main purposes, one is to reduce barriers and the other is to introduce incentives. Finally, we can build the system into a cross-platform, cross-device, accessible platform.

Charity Resource Matching with Graph Neural Network

Fu Tianyu

Ph. D Student of the Department of Electronic Engineering, Tsinghua University; China

The mismatch between resources and needs in education is a serious problem, in which data are difficult to collect and poorly analyzed. In order to solve this problem, we propose the resource flow graph data structure, so that people and organizations in need can benefit from this system and solve the charity matching problem. The implementation plan is to learn how to optimize end-to-end charity resource flow allocation with the help of graph neural networks, and to convert resource allocation problems into standard link prediction tasks in graph neural networks with various mature tools. We will follow a social business model in which the government supports the operation of projects that can continuously narrow the information gap in the social fabric.

Developing Sustainable Humanitarian Technologies

Sreya VANGARA

Schwarzman Scholar, United States of America

The development of sustainable and adaptable humanitarian technologies requires three actions. First of all, the competition and development of R&D require the participation of users. Second, materials and equipments should be readily available locally. Third, users should be provided with basic education to achieve long-term maintenance and further innovation. To promote innovation in less developed areas and to extend technological life, basic, universal, and technical education is needed for all children.

Leveraging Digital Platforms for Youth-led SDG Campaigns

Jonathan Peter-Oswin DASON

Schwarzman Scholar, Malaysia

The United Nations Youth Association Malaysia has two key objectives. One is to contribute to the development of the Malaysian youth ecosystem. The other is, as always, to raise awareness of the United Nations Sustainable Development Goals (UNSDGs), with an emphasis on education. We do this by hosting virtual conferences and online events. We also run a series of podcasts and publish them online. We have also released a large number of infographics to inform the public about the UN and the UN Sustainable Development Goals (SDGs). Two factors make a project successful. One is that the content is engaging and the key to engagement. Second, cooperation is ecological integration rather than reinventing the wheel.

Why Inclusive Digital Transformation Matters?

Si Tou UN

Schwarzman Scholar; Macau S.A.R., China

Inclusive digital transformation is important for sustainable innovation and development. In particular, it holds relevance to the four specific SDGs to the right, namely quality education; industry, innovation, and infrastructure; sustainable cities and communities; and partnerships for the goals. What are the pathways to inclusive digital transformation, including the dimension of cybersecurity? First, we need to prioritize and support marginalized communities, like civil society organizations, as active agents in creating inclusive digital transformations. Second, at the policy level, we need to mainstream the needs of these communities in national strategies, programs, and funding instruments. More efforts in South-South and triangular digital cooperation are also vital to equip countries in the Global South with best practices from their neighbors. Third, we need to provide more capacity-building and resourcing to improve the decision-making, negotiation, and stakeholder-engagement capabilities of the management.

Automative design for sustainability

Melody Kirima

Schwarzman Scholar; Kenya

Sustainable design involves designing physical objects and building environments to maximize the use of resources and ensure the sustainability of other factors. The first is "recyclable design", which mainly affects vehicles at the end of their life cycle by disassembling, processing, remanufacturing, and reusing scrap car parts. The second is "green design", where emerging trends include the use of bioplastics instead of petroleum-based plastics. The third is "resource use design", where renewable energy can be used for non-attractive applications.

Methods for making sense of the energy, climate, and sustainability space

Kelly Wu

Schwarzman Scholar, United States of America

The three areas of energy transition, climate, and sustainability space are very interconnected, but also very complex, encompassing the whole economy and the whole society. We need to use systems-level thinking to understand energy, climate, and sustainable space. This system-level thinking is about the whole system, instead of just part of it. When we address specific issues in the field of energy, climate, and sustainable development, we must be clear about which components to consider. Ethical engineering is also an important way to learn about relevant technologies, and getting involved in community activities is also a way to help explore this area.

Engineering Education Accreditation for Suntainable Development

Elizabeth TAYLOR

Executive Committee Chair, Washington Accord, International Engineering Alliance

The United Nations Sustainable Development Goals (SDGs) are a blueprint to achieve a beautiful and sustainable development for all. They address important challenges we face, such as poverty, inequality, climate change, environmental change, peace and justice. Engineers play a great role in it.

In June, 2021, members of the IEA accord voted to adopt the revised new criteria, which was submitted at the WFEO conference in March, 2022. This work was supported by the International Centre for Engineering Education under the auspices of UNESCO (ICEE). The Graduate Attributes and Professional Competencies (GAPC) was translated into the five official languages of UNESCO and published on the internet. It aims to help IEA members achieve engineering accreditation and grant them access to IEA criterion services. By unanimous consent of all signatories/members, the road map that can be implemented within its jurisdiction will be formulated by 2024, and the implementation duration will be shortened.

The transformation of engineering education not only repeats what have been done, but also requires us to consider the future changes and uncertainties in different ways of thinking. Engineers should take personal responsibility for their work, have systematic thinking and be open to the future. Many years ago, I worked with engineering students to create a schema that can help us think about the problems we encounter in the learning process, especially in engineering activities. In the process of sustainable development transition, we should take a new look at our ways of doing things in different ways and maintain the ability to criticize and question the truth at all times, so we can implement the meaningful and innovative engineering education modes.

Quality Assurance of Chinese Engineering Education in the Context of Sustainable Development and Digital Transformation

ZHOU Aijun

Executive Director and Secretary-General of China Engineering Education Accreditation Association, CEEAA

Sustainable development and digital transformation are important driving forces for engineering education reform. Therefore, I share some information and opinions about connotations, cores and requirements about the digital transformation of engineering education, the relationship between engineering education and sustainable development goals, and the revision of accreditation criteria by China Engineering Education Accreditation Association (CEEAA) in the adaptation to digital transformation and sustainable development goals.

President Xi Jinping pointed out at the International Conference on Engineering Science and Technology in 2014 that information technology has become the first leading technology to penetrate into all fields of economic and social life, and will promote the transformation from the economic development model based on material production and material service to a new economic development model based on information production and information service. With the rapid development of technologies like big data, cloud computing, 5G and artificial intelligence, human society has entered a digital era. Production and life are closely related to digitalization. The deep integration of information technology and education and teaching has been realized in education sector, and engineering education, without exception, is undergoing a comprehensive digital transformation.

In 2021, UNESCO released the report *Engineering for the Sustainable Development*. In the report, Professor GONG Ke, President of WFEO, pointed out, "The primary problem faced by the world today is to maintain human development and protect the earth. In this context, engineering plays a pivotal role in sustainable development." Engineering and engineers are indispensable to the 17 sustainable development goals. Engineering education is training future engineers, representing an important force in engineering capacity building.

In terms of the adaptation to sustainable development and the digital transformation of engineering education, China Engineering Education Accreditation Association (CEEAA) carried out some preliminary work in the revision of criteria. In 2021, the International Engineering Alliance (IEA) issued a new edition of Graduate Attributes and Professional Competencies (GAPC). In order to implement relevant requirements of the 17 UN sustainable development goals, the contents of computational thinking, sustainable development, whole life cycle, net-zero carbon emission goals, diversity and inclusiveness were added. CEEAA also carried out the revision work to establish accreditation criteria with international substantial equivalence and Chinese characteristics.

Incorporating Sustainability into Accreditation Criteria

Damien OWENS

Chair of International Professional Engineers Agreement, International Engineering Alliance

Engineers Ireland is a founding member and signatory of the International Engineering Alliance (IEA) accords and agreements. In the past seven years, it has maintained consistency with the IEA Accreditation Criteria. Whenthe review of *Graduate Attributes and Professional Competencies* (GAPC) coincided with the review of Irish Engineer Accreditation Standard, the latter was seen as fully compliant with the former. Sustainable development is an important theme across all sectors in Ireland. This results from our experience in combining accreditation criteria with the emerging demand of sustainable and circular economy.

Engineers Ireland provides various accreditations according to criteria of IEA and other institutions. It integrates sustainable development work with member organizations and universities, and employs many frameworks (such as the professional competence framework) as its key measures for a series of accreditations. The accreditation criteria of Engineers Ireland are reviewed every five to six years. The criteria were first approved in 2014, and the new criteria will be updated in 2021.

Engineers Ireland implements projects in engineering management, including the introduction of engineering management principles, financial decision-making, data scientific analysis and technology. It is also very concerned about affairs related to social responsibility and ethics. These contents are manifested in their criteria, including project design results, eight key areas of structure, knowledge understanding and design investigation, etc. Meanwhile, the institution emphasizes the content of project achievements, including different projects and different achievements, such as the improvement of innovation, creativity, sustainability and practical skills.

Transformation to a Sustainable Engineering Education

Anette KOLMOS

Director of Aalborg Centre for Problem Based Learning in Engineering Science & Sustainability, Aalborg University

As a result of the COVID-19 pandemic, online education has been widely used for young students, which has always been the most critical part of the academic issue. The next generation of academic experts and scholars will be part of the solution to this issue, so we need to embed sustainability into education. What have we done in Europe? At present, many universities are beginning to transform into mission-driven universities. There are a lot of discussions about the teaching content of mission-driven universities. This is not as simple as the sustainable development goals. It is a method of the same type, but more extensive to some extent, including not only education but also scientific research content. It is more like teaching and researching.

From September 2020 to January 2021, we collected and analyzed relevant data, and set up 15 focus groups, each with 60 participants. These participants consisted of not only teachers but also students, and the interview content involved the knowledge they have learned or the experience they have gained. The findings show that the teaching system has been adjusted during the pandemic. At the beginning of the pandemic, the system lacked the interaction between people, and the teaching was teacher-centered and served a one-way output to students. This mode aroused our concern, because students are not used to asking questions or taking the initiative to speak in class. We have also summed up positive experiences, including the flipped classroom mode. The feedback from many students reveals that they must actively use learning resources and methods to participate in the study of flipped classroom. For example, students should preview the course video before class, and participate and communicate in a digital way in class. Group discussions were extremely lively, which manifests the advantages of the digital system.

From the viewpoint of universities, we should also change the teaching mode, and the mode should be designed from not only an academic perspective but also a perspective of student learning. In the future, we will continue our efforts in this direction. More blended learning modes will be adopted, and we will participate in them and continue relevant tasks.

Curriculum System of Electronic Information for Training Sustainable Innovative Talents

HUANG Yidong

Deputy Director of Academic Committee, Tsinghua University; Former Dean of Department of Electronic Engineering, Tsinghua University

In the field of electronic information, how to cultivate sustainable innovative talents at the level of curriculum system? What qualities do sustainable innovative talents need? They should have a broad basic scientific and professional foundation. In addition to being specialized in professional knowledge, they should also have the ability to go beyond their majors, such as cognitive ability and practical ability, knowledge of humanities and social sciences, sufficient engineering practice training to keep pace with scientific development, an understanding of the historical context of discipline development, and the ability to cooperate with each other and interact with society. What should we teach? The basic scientific knowledge must be both in-depth and extensive.

Since 2007, WANG Xiqin, the Director of the Department of Electronic Engineering and now the President of Tsinghua University, has initiated a new round of curriculum system reform. The goal of this reform is to break through the barriers of the two first-level disciplines and cultivate talents majoring in "information + electronics". The reform updated the course contents, introduced the development history of courses, cultivated students' innovative thinking, and strengthened experimental teaching, extracurricular learning and other links to cultivate students' comprehensive quality.

"Core concept" is a very important concept. In knowledge system, the knowledge is numerous but structured and interconnected into a system. The knowledge system is constructed on the basis of a few "core concept", and many knowledge contents are just examples of "core concepts" under certain specific conditions.

Going on Learning for Innovation: Engineering Education in the Digital Age

LI Manli

Professor of Institute of Education, Tsinghua University

In the past decade, the development of educational informatization has been accelerating. Digitalization is a strategic opportunity for educational development, and high-level educational informatization may lead to high-level educational modernization. The rapid development of science and technology such as artificial intelligence and big data will certainly shape new forms of teaching ideas and teaching models in higher education. Digital technology and artificial intelligence technology have changed the working environment of some people, which put forward new requirements for talent literacy, mainly manifesting in four aspects, namely variability, uncertainty, complexity and ambiguity.

Around 2010, China completed the largest engineering education system in the world. However, there were several prominent problems in the training process of engineering education, namely, the lack of close combination of engineering talents training and engineering practice, the excessive scientization of engineering education, and insufficient training of students' engineering consciousness and quality, practical ability to solve complex engineering problems and ability of innovation and creativity. Therefore, in 2010, the Ministry of Education of China launched the Plan for Educating and Training Outstanding Engineers (PETOE) 1.0.

In October 2018, with the emergence and rise of a new round of world scientific and technological revolution and industrial changes, Chinese engineering education community reached some consensuses that artificial intelligence and digital technology will bring inestimable effects and influences to human society. They will reshape, overturn and reconstruct the world, and many modern business divisions and organizational methods will be changed. The Ministry of Education of China put forward new engineering disciplines construction and released PETOE 2.0 in time.

Since the beginning of the 21st century, global scientific and technological innovation has been unprecedentedly active, and a new round of scientific and technological revolution and industrial changes is being reconstructed, which provides more sources of innovations for global innovation map, global economic structure, original breakthroughs in information, life, manufacturing, energy, space and maritime sectors, and cutting-edge and disruptive technology. Engineers should not only be able to see the big picture, but also cooperate with people from different disciplines and work out innovative solutions.

Tsinghua University established an interdisciplinary research team consisting of experts in engineering, pedagogy, psychology and computer science, aiming to explore the theory and application of the development of higher engineering education and to focus relevant discipline contents on the training of top-notch engineering students. Research in related fields will be used to develop engineering education to form valuable and creative research results with academic significance on the learning pattern of engineering students.

后　记

国际工程教育论坛是经中国教育部批准，由清华大学、中国工程院、联合国教科文组织共同主办的系列国际性学术会议，每两年举办一次。第一届、第二届分别于2018年9月、2020年12月在清华大学召开。第三届论坛由清华大学电子系、发展规划处、国际工程教育中心共同筹划组织，清华大学建筑学院、医学院、电机系、车辆学院、苏世民书院、东南亚中心、中非领导力中心、拉美中心、UNESCO继续工程教育教席等承办了分论坛。

2022年12月，清华大学、中国工程院、联合国教科文组织共同主办的第三届国际工程教育论坛，会议以"电子信息技术与可持续创新"为主题，汇集了全球18个国家和地区的全球工程教育、工程科技和工程管理领域的知名学者和杰出领袖及青年学生等2000余人，共同探讨工程教育的创新发展，促进世界工程科技和社会的进步，应对全球性重大挑战。

2015年，联合国通过17项可持续发展目标，为全球各国可持续发展指明了方向。科技创新是落实联合国2030年可持续发展议程的重要手段，对推动全球可持续发展具有重要意义，其价值和作用正日益凸显。第三届论坛以联合国可持续发展目标为指导框架，通过以电子信息技术的渗透性学科特点突破学科壁垒，与其他相关学科紧密合作，围绕八个不同议题展开研讨，促进以可持续发展为导向的科学交流，开展联合创新研究，培养具备深厚人文情怀、国际化视野和创新潜能的复合型工程人才。

工程是人类赖以生存、发展、进步的创造性和推动性力量。工程科技、工程教育和工程人才，是解决社会可持续发展和数字化转型中一系列重大挑战的战略性支撑。面对诸多全球性挑战，工程促进可持续发展应该有更大的作为，工程师应该有更大的作为。本书将第三届论坛诸位专家学者的演讲报告整理汇编并正式出版，汇聚了来自演讲者对于技术交流与人才培养有价值、有意义的理论研究、实践探索和经验总结。希望本书能够为工程师、工程教育者以及研究者提供有益参考。希望全世界的工程科技界同行们携起手来，共同推动工程教育在世界范围的全面均衡发展。

受新冠肺炎影响，本届论坛以线上和线下相结合的形式召开。在此，向参与会议筹备与服务工作的所有师生们致以诚挚的谢意！向参与本书编辑的徐立辉、李晶晶、朱盼、李懋坤、乔伟峰、黄蓓、罗菲、方欣然、郝富霖、王雪琪、甘之正、沈一帆、黄铮、陈伟翔等老师和同学表示衷心的感谢！中央编译出版社为本书的出版做了大量工作，在此一并感谢！

由于时间仓促，书中难免有不当之处，恳请广大读者提出宝贵的意见和建议。

联合国教科文组织国际工程教育中心（ICEE）

2023年11月